Wakefield Press

One and All
Labor and the Radical Tradition in South Australia

Philip Payton is Professor of History at Flinders University, as well as Adjunct Professor in the National Centre for Australian Studies at Monash University and Emeritus Professor of Cornish & Australian Studies at the University of Exeter (where he was Director of the Institute of Cornish Studies from 1991 to 2013). He completed his first doctorate at the University of Adelaide in 1978, and is an Hon. Fellow of the Australian Academy of the Humanities. Recent books include *The Maritime History of Cornwall* (edited with Alston Kennerley and Helen Doe) and *Australia in the Great War*. This volume, *One and All: Labor and the Radical Tradition in South Australia*, was commissioned by the Don Dunstan Foundation and assisted by the Office of the Premier of South Australia.

One and All

Labor and the Radical Tradition in South Australia

Philip Payton

Wakefield
Press

Wakefield Press
16 Rose Street
Mile End
South Australia 5031
www.wakefieldpress.com.au

First published 2016

Edited by Julia Beaven, Wakefield Press
Designed and typeset by Wakefield Press
Printed in Australia by Griffin Digital, Adelaide

National Library of Australia Cataloguing-in-Publication entry

Creator: Payton, Philip J., 1953–   , author.
Title: One and all: Labor and the radical tradition in
                South Australia / Philip Payton.
ISBN: 978 1 74305 430 7 (paperback).
Notes: Includes index.
Subjects: Australian Labor Party. South Australian Branch.
                Cornish – Australia – History.
                South Australia – Politics and government.
Dewey Number: 324.29407

CORIOLE

McLAREN VALE

Contents

'One and All:

This motto, the watch word and battle cry of the Cornish,

is of great antiquity.'

Mining Journal, 1859

Foreword

The election, in May 1891, of Richard 'Dicky' Hooper – a Cornish miner from Moonta – as the first Labor MP in State Parliament might have represented a shock to the political establishment of South Australia. But his historic victory, in fact, resulted from the inception and steady growth of a determined and well-organised local labor movement – one that owed much of its origins to the zeal of Cornish copper miners who settled in the Mid North and on Yorke Peninsula during the early decades of the colony.

As Philip Payton explains in this meticulously researched and superbly told story, among the many cultural traditions the Cornish brought with them was a belief in education and self-improvement, a deep devotion to the Methodist faith and an oftentimes fiery attachment to radical politics. In their adopted home of South Australia, these traits helped create an embryonic trade union movement and, in turn, led to the formation of the forerunner of today's Labor Party.

The work of the early labor activists was carried out on fertile political ground. Unlike neighbouring colonies, South Australia was conceived and founded as an 'experiment' – a new society predicated, in the eyes of radicals and Nonconformists, on religious and civic freedom and economic and social mobility.

The practical implementation of such principles led to a series of social and political milestones, establishing South Australia's early democratic credentials. These included the introduction of universal male suffrage and the secret ballot, the granting to women of the right to vote and stand for Parliament, and, in 1910, the formation, under John Verran (another Cornish miner), of the first majority Labor government in the world.

'One and All': Labor and the Radical Tradition in South Australia outlines not just the early successes of the Cornish Methodists, but also their long-term and profound influence on the South Australian Labor Party and, in particular, the great latter-day reformist, Don Dunstan – who was, like me, of Cornish descent.

The circumstances of the ALP's formation and development in South Australia were quite different from those of the party in the eastern States and nationally. But, as we learn from this vivid account, such differences did not prevent the local organisation from also undergoing flux, ferment and damaging splits – such as during the conscription debate of World War I and in relation to the Premiers' Plan to combat the effects of the 1930s Depression.

Life in modern Australia is a world away from the experiences of the working folk of the 1800s, and the Labor Party has naturally evolved and adapted to our changing society.

This volume vividly retells the story, however, of the early struggles, and of how a passionate and hardworking group of miners, with a unique mixture of religious and political motivations, translated ideals in action and laid a rock-solid foundation for equality and social justice. The Cornish miners of the Mid North and Yorke Peninsula made an overwhelmingly positive and disproportionately large contribution to our civic and political culture, and we South Australians – and especially the ALP of the post-War period – remain in their debt.

I thank and commend Philip Payton, the Don Dunstan Foundation and Wakefield Press for reminding us, through *'One and All': Labor and the Radical Tradition in South Australia*, of our political heritage and the remarkable way in which everyday workers have advanced the common good and made our State a better place to live.

Jay Weatherill
Premier of South Australia

Labor or Labour?

It is difficult to be precise or definitive in dealing with the terms *Labor* and *Labour* (not only competing spellings, but questions of upper and lower case), so throughout this book I have attempted to adhere to the following convention. When dealing with the several political parties in Australia (for example, United Labor Party; Australian Labor Party) I have adopted the spelling Labor, as per common usage. Likewise, I refer to the Labour Party in the United Kingdom. However, usage in both primary and secondary sources is far more diverse and often inconsistent, and when quoting directly from original documents, newspapers, articles and books, I have allowed the author's preference (capitalisation as well as spelling) to stand. Additionally, and perhaps somewhat controversially, I have adopted *Labor* as a generic term, referring, for example, to the wider 'Labor movement' (trade unions and other associations) and identifying an embryonic 'Labor movement' in early pre-union collective action and organisations. Indeed, this usage is implicit in the title of this book, *'One and All': Labor and the Radical Tradition in South Australia.*

Philip Payton

Preface

In November 2009, as part of the activities associated with the launch of the bid to acquire National Listing (and ultimately UNESCO World Heritage Site status) for the Cornish copper-mining landscapes of South Australia, I gave an after-dinner address at Ayers House in Adelaide, hosted by Jay Weatherill, then Minister for Environment and Conservation in the South Australian government. Although the bid was, of course, strictly apolitical, I recognised that the early days of the Labor movement in South Australia's mining towns would be of particular interest to the Minister, not least as he was himself of Cornish descent, and I dealt with these in my talk.

Subsequently, Jay Weatherill suggested that the topic should be written up in detail, providing as it did an alternative and distinctive narrative of the Labor movement in South Australia, especially when compared to the eastern States, shedding new light on the origins of the Labor Party here in this State. Later, towards the end 2012, Jay Weatherill, now Premier, renewed the suggestion, and in May 2013 the project leading to this volume *'One and All': Labor and the Radical Tradition in South Australia* was born.

The book falls neatly into four parts. The first, entitled 'Radical Traditions', begins by examining South Australia's radical credentials (not least through the eyes of former Premier, Don Dunstan), and shows how the Province's foundation in the midst of the so-called Reforming Thirties in Britain paralleled an upsurge in political radicalism in Cornwall, the source of many of South

Australia's early migrants. Part Two, 'Copper and Organised Labor', traces the impact of the predominantly Methodist Cornish settlers, first at the Burra (and the strike of 1848) and then at Moonta, Wallaroo and Kadina on northern Yorke Peninsula, where an embryonic trade union movement first appeared. Part Three, 'Rise and Fall', explores the parallel efforts in the Labor movement on Yorke Peninsula and in metropolitan Adelaide to secure representation in the South Australian Parliament, which was at last achieved in 1891. Tom Price emerged as South Australia's first Labor Premier in 1905, and John Verran as Premier led the State's – and the world's – very first majority Labor government in 1910–12. Yet Labor's fortunes were mixed. The conservative Legislative Council proved a constant thorn in the party's side, while fierce controversies over conscription during the First World War and later over the Premiers' Plan split the party down the middle. However, as Part Four, 'The Natural Party of Government?', demonstrates, despite these and other vicissitudes, Labor re-emerged strongly after the Second World War, leading to the incomparable Dunstan Decade of the late 1960s and 1970s. This was a prelude to South Australia's more recent contemporary political history which, although outside the principal scope of this book, is sketched briefly in the concluding chapter of Part Four, indicating the continuance of the State's radical tradition in the Labor Party up to and into the twenty-first century.

Commissioned by and conducted under the aegis of the Don Dunstan Foundation, this project was funded with the assistance of the Office of the Premier of South Australia. Led by its Executive Director, Donna Harden, the Don Dunstan Foundation is a charitable trust that works with the University of Adelaide and Flinders University to gain a deeper understanding of social justice issues and to share these understandings with the greater community to influence change. It has been a great privilege and a huge pleasure to work with the Don Dunstan Foundation, especially Donna Harden, with her infectious enthusiasm and tireless dedication to the Foundation's cause, and I am deeply grateful to her and her team, particularly Sharna Pearce, Olivia Power and Ben Waters. Likewise, I am extremely grateful to the project's Steering Committee, chaired by John Williams and including Don Hopgood, David Pearson, Angas Story, Chris Sumner and Ben Waters, together with

Donna Harden, which has provided invaluable advice and feedback at every stage of this book's development.

I am similarly indebted to academic colleagues and students in the School of History and International Relations at Flinders University, notably Lance Brennan, Darryl Burrowes, Brian Dickey, Matthew Fitzpatrick, Prudence Flowers, Carol Fort, Lauren Gobbett, Bronte Gould, Stephanie James, Catherine Kevin, Margrette Kleinig, David Lockwood, Peter Monteath, Tony Nugent, Melanie Oppenheimer, Eric Richards, Ella Stewart-Peters and Andrekos Varnava, not least for their searching questions and critical comments at seminars presented on work in progress. Thanks too to the staff of Flinders University Library, especially the Special Collections team –Mary Addyman, Gillian Dooley, Kylie Jarrett, Adele Lenz, Tom Snook – for arranging access to the Don Dunstan and John Bannon Collections. Over many years I have also benefitted from the expert assistance of the staffs of the State Library of South Australia and the Barr Smith Library at the University of Adelaide, and again I offer my thanks. I also acknowledge the National Trust of South Australia, Moonta Branch, for allowing access to its archival and newspaper collections. Thanks too to the members of the Cornish Association of South Australia and the South Australian Mining History Group for their interest and assistance, and especially to Michael Bollen and Wakefield Press, South Australia's premier scholarly imprint, for agreeing so readily and with such enthusiasm to publish this book. The Wakefield team, not least Julia Beaven and Michael Deves, have been enormously helpful as they have smoothed the way towards publication.

At the Institute of Cornish Studies, University of Exeter, I owe an immense debt of gratitude to my erstwhile colleagues, Bernard Deacon and Garry Tregidga, and I am likewise indebted to the History staff at Exeter's Penryn campus in Cornwall, especially Tim Cooper, Bryony Onciul, Catriona Pennell and Nicola Whyte. More generally, I am indebted to those many chroniclers of Australia whose works I have consulted, especially those who have written on Labor history, politics and biography, notably Neal Blewett, Frank Bongiorno, Brian Dickey, Nick Dyrenfurth, Dino Hodge, Don Hopgood, John Hirst, Dean Jaensch, Stephanie McCarthy, Ross McMullin, Jim Moss, Andrew Parkin,

Allan Patience and Malcom Saunders. Additionally, I have been helped in very many ways by a great number of other people, principally in Australia, and I should like especially to record my gratitude to Hamish Angas, Lynn Arnold, Angela Bannon, the late John Bannon, Peter Bell, Geoffrey Blainey, Carl Bridge, Noel Carthew, Liz Coole, Paul Coole, Ann Curthoys, Mel Davies, Vesna Drapac, Lynn Drew, Greg Drew, Paul Eggert, Erik Eklund, Charles Fahey, Rob Foster, Rae Frances, Bill Gammage, David Gill, Kay Gill, Melissa Hay, Elizabeth Harris, Neville Harris, Ian Henderson, Brian Hill, Nola Hill, Carol Howard, Ed Jaggard, Keith Johns, Bill Jones, Catherine Kevin, Christopher Kleinig, Jan Lokan, Keith Lokan, Clem McIntyre, Alan Mayne, Susan Pearl, David Pearson, Anne Pender, Wilfrid Prest, Bruce Scates, Beth Scott, Pam Sharpe, Jason Shute, Ros Shute, Simon Sleight, Evan Smith, Matthew Spriggs, Phyllis Tharenou, Kathryn Thomas and Paul Thomas. My apologies to anyone I have inadvertently missed!

Finally, I should add a very special 'thank you' to my wife Dee. We have shared many adventures in Cornwall and Australia, and Dee has eagerly embraced all the excitements and opportunities – some daunting! – that life has thrown at us, not least completion of the index for this book (for which I am hugely grateful).

Philip Payton
School of History and International Relations
Flinders University, Adelaide
26 January 2016, Australia Day

PART ONE
RADICAL TRADITIONS

Chapter 1

Radical Traditions – South Australia

'On the face of it, South Australia might have seemed an unlikely and unrewarding area for the experiment'.[1] As he penned his political memoirs, published in 1981 after his retirement from active politics (he was Premier from 1967 to 1968, and again from 1970 to 1979), Don Dunstan mused on the chain of events that had led him to high office in South Australia. Born in Fiji of Australian parentage in 1926, Dunstan had been educated in his parent's home State, first at St Peter's College and then at the University of Adelaide, where he obtained a law degree. Returning to Fiji shortly after his mother's untimely death, Dunstan began work as a litigation lawyer. He enjoyed the challenge, although he devoted more hours than was good for his health. Eventually, too, he began to worry about the long-term relevance of his work. As he explained in his memoirs, he doubted whether he was really 'contributing to the sum of human good by what I was doing'. Lawyers, Dunstan complained, merely patched up 'messes and mistakes in human behaviour', sorting out the difficulties that people had made for themselves.[2] He yearned instead, he said, for something of greater and more fundamental social value.

Don Dunstan's 'experiment'
'I believed then, as now', Dunstan wrote in 1981, 'that it is possible to build a society in which individual citizens have security of food, shelter, work and

services', a society 'which will celebrate their worth as individuals ... their differences [and] their strengths', and 'where all citizens have an equal and effective say in their own governance and an opportunity to participate in and to influence the decisions affecting their lives. It is possible', Dunstan insisted, 'to build [such] a social democracy – a dynamic society in which there would be equal opportunity to act creatively in a social context'. This could not be achieved everywhere in his lifetime, he conceded, but he was certain that he could at least 'build a model'. This was his 'experiment', and South Australia was to be the laboratory in which the social democratic 'model' was developed.[3] As we shall see (in Chapter 9), Dunstan proved spectacularly successful in building his model. He entered the South Australian Parliament as Labor member for the Adelaide suburb of Norwood in 1953, and as Premier ushered in what became known nationally and internationally as the Dunstan Decade when, as Allan Patience has argued, he 'helped to restore and rejuvenate the social democratic tradition in the Australian Labor Party'.[4] But, as Dunstan had admitted, at first glance South Australia had seemed an unlikely place in which to perform his experiment and construct his social democratic model. Why?

As Don Dunstan himself explained, by the time he entered South Australian politics in the early 1950s, the State had long since acquired its reputation as socially and politically staid. It was, perhaps, the most conservative of all Australian States, he said, where every institution – 'even the trade unions' – was slow to change, and everywhere there was a demand for conformity and a suspicion of novelty.[5] Moreover, he continued, since 1933 the conservative Liberal and Country League had been in government in South Australia, the Labor Party seemingly condemned to perpetual Opposition. Adelaide was dubbed 'the city of churches' by both admirers and detractors, a label that had acquired negative as well as positive connotations, with its supposed intimations of 'wowserism' and 'kill-joy' opposition to frivolity, drinking and gambling. Indeed, Dunstan added, the churches in South Australia were overwhelmingly 'puritan' in flavour, as he put it – Methodists, Lutherans, Baptists, and so on – reflecting the relative weakness of both Anglicanism and Roman Catholicism (the latter in marked contrast to the Eastern States),

Don Dunstan. [Courtesy News Limited and Flinders University Library]

and attesting to the State's distinctive religious history. This 'puritanism' was part of South Australia's conservative culture, Dunstan suggested. 'On Sunday everything closed', he recalled: 'The whole State appeared shrouded in Calvinist gloom. There was no organised sport, no entertainment, and it was considered improper to appear to enjoy oneself.'[6] Yet, as Dunstan also recognised, religious distinctiveness was but one component of a wider 'sense of difference' that had often distinguished South Australia from other parts of the continent, and which gave the State its separate identity. Moreover, as Dunstan was keen to acknowledge, this 'puritanism' was deeply paradoxical, for behind the conservative façade was an ingrained if sometimes latent radicalism, in the churches themselves and in the wider society they sought to influence. As he observed, 'there had always been an element of radicalism in South Australia', and, significantly, among the first European settlers in the early colony (or 'Province') of South Australia were Chartist radicals (see Chapter 3), many of them religious 'puritans', who had arrived 'with the black book of the Charter in their pockets', as Dunstan put it dramatically.[7]

Chartists, Methodists and Radicalism

The Chartist movement had emerged in Britain in 1838 (just two years after the foundation of South Australia) in the heady atmosphere of the Reforming Thirties, taking its name from the so-called 'People's Charter'. Drawn up in May of that year by reformist agitators, including the Cornishman William Lovett, the Charter demanded universal male suffrage, secret ballots, abolition of property qualifications for Members of Parliament, payments for MPs, equal electoral districts (to ensure one-man, one-vote, one-value), and annual elections. John Wesley, the founder of the Methodist movement, had preached a politically conservative acceptance of one's lot in life, with due reward given later in Heaven. His followers, however, were apt to be as concerned with this life as the next, and Methodism swiftly developed a moral code that taught compassion, concern for the needy, and the equality of men (and women) before God. Not surprisingly, many of Wesley's adherents turned to Chartism.

Likewise, in South Australia, according to Dunstan, Methodists and other 'dissenters' (or 'puritans', as he liked to call them) were 'unable to contain the lively sense of injustice which inequality . . . inevitably aroused amongst their largely working-class supporters'.[8] Chartism appealed instinctively to such people, Dunstan added, and later in the nineteenth century the emergent Labor Party in South Australia would draw 'many members and supporters from the ranks of Methodists', attracted by its moral code. Indeed, he continued, 'numbered amongst its leaders were men who were labelled "speakers in the pulpit style"'. Skilful orators, and given to Biblical allusion, such speakers were often Methodist lay (or 'local') preachers, regular and powerful performers in the many Nonconformist churches scattered across the colony. As Dunstan remarked, they tended to be 'conservative about matters which related to family, sex, drink or gambling', giving South Australia its staid reputation, but were 'radical about rights to political expression and concern for fairness and equality of opportunity'.[9] Moreover, they were highly influential.

'The most potent religious movement in nineteenth century South Australia was Methodism', agreed David Hilliard and Arnold D. Hunt, and by the mid-1870s Methodism rivalled the Church of England as the largest denomination in the colony.[10] Indeed, by 1870 Methodism's constituent

6

groups – principally the Wesleyans, Bible Christians and Primitive Methodists – were already dominant in several respects. In that year the Wesleyans sported 148 churches throughout the colony, the Bible Christians eighty-one, and the Primitive Methodists ninety-nine. The Church of England, by contrast, could muster only sixty-four. Likewise, the Wesleyans could boast thirty-one clergy, the Bible Christians twenty, the Primitive Methodists twenty-two, and the Church of England just thirty-eight. The disparity was even more pronounced in the numbers of lay preachers – 259 Wesleyans, ninety-eight Bible Christians, 191 Primitive Methodists, and fifty-four Church of England. So too in the number of Sunday-school scholars – 11,429 Wesleyans, 3,492 Bible Christians and 4,312 Primitive Methodists, compared to 4,198 Church of England.[11]

On 1 January 1901 the Wesleyans, Bible Christians and Primitive Methodists in South Australia joined together to form a united Methodist church, comprising almost 25% of the State's religious adherents. Although there were areas of concentration, notably the copper-mining district of northern Yorke Peninsula, where in the 1891 census an astonishing 80% of the local population was returned as Methodist, Methodist influence permeated South Australia, town as well as country, its appeal evident in Adelaide as well in the rural areas.[12] Although usually conservative on moral issues, as Dunstan averred, the Methodists were not always as dour as he had imagined. Not all were offended by the pejorative term 'wowser'. Instead, many South Australians eagerly embraced the term, proudly (if ironically) claiming it as an acronym of 'We Only Want Social Evils Remedied', a slogan supposedly displayed on banners at rallies demanding restrictions on the sale of alcohol or a clamp-down on prostitution.[13] Such objectives were morally conservative. Yet banners, slogans and demonstrations evidenced passionate devotion to the right to political expression, together with a belief in the ability of political action to achieve social change and societal improvement. Both were fundamental components of political radicalism, as Dunstan appreciated, essential elements of his imagined social democracy.

Moreover, as P.A. Howell has noted in his study of South Australia at the turn of the twentieth century, Methodists were not as socially staid as their detractors sometimes suspected. They may have avoided public houses, dance halls and theatres but often enjoyed a vibrant social and cultural life, conducted through the medium of the Methodist church – everything from concerts and picnics to outings and visits to the seaside – as well as frequenting temperance hotels and being active in Freemasonry and friendly societies. They may have eschewed horse-racing but enthusiastically embraced football, cricket and athletics.[14] By no means as narrow-minded or introvert as their critics suggested, South Australia's Methodists were thus actively engaged in the community of which they were so conspicuously a part. For many, their concern for social justice and societal improvement had led seamlessly to political radicalism of the type detected by Dunstan, producing *and* explaining the conservative-radical paradox he had identified so deftly.

Perhaps, Dunstan mused, South Australia was after all not such an odd choice for his 'experiment' in social democracy. Maybe, even, South Australia lent itself to the development of the innovative political 'model' he had sketched for himself. Certainly, many of the objectives sought by the early Chartists had been achieved in South Australia long before other parts of the Anglophone world, and, as he reviewed the State's history, Don Dunstan appreciated afresh the strength of its radical tradition and its impressive record of progressive legislation. As he put it, South Australia 'had been the first place in the world to get manhood suffrage and the secret ballot'. It was also the first 'to establish a children's court, [and] to establish a system of simple land registration (Torrens Title) which swept the common-law countries of the world'. Above all, he acknowledged, South Australia was the very first place in the world 'to elect a majority Labor government', and was 'only the second in the world to grant votes for women' (the first was New Zealand).[15]

As Dunstan had observed, it was hardly surprising that the Methodists had been so intimately involved in the rise of the early Labor Party in South Australia. Many, he added, were of Cornish birth or descent, for 'the Cornish were overwhelmingly Wesleyan in religious persuasion'. As he explained, the discovery of copper in the 1840s, 'particularly at Kapunda and at Burra and later [in 1859–61] at Wallaroo and Moonta brought a flood of Cornish miners to South Australia'. This meant, he continued, 'that South

Australia's labour force, unlike that in most of the rest of Australia, was Cornish rather than Irish'.[16] Dunstan was overstating the case, of course. Despite the ethno-occupational visibility of the Cornish in South Australia, there were immigrant working people – skilled as well as unskilled – from a variety of other backgrounds, most obviously the English and Scots, together with a large contingent of Germans. Likewise, the Irish, though numerous, were but one component of a heterogeneous workforce in other parts of Australia, even in neighbouring Victoria where they were especially strong. Nonetheless, Dunstan's comparison was well-made, even if exaggerated, and nowhere was it more pertinent than in the contrast between the predominantly Methodist flavour of the Labor Party as it emerged in South Australia and the Irish-Catholic complexion of its counterparts elsewhere, especially in the eastern States.

Methodists, Catholics and Labor in Victoria

Yet the Cornish-Methodist influence *had* also been important elsewhere in Australia – in the silver-lead-zinc mining district of Broken Hill, for example, just across the border from South Australia in New South Wales (see Chapter 5), and on the Victorian goldfields. In Victoria, as Frank Bongiorno makes plain, religious dissent, 'especially Methodism', was a 'powerful influence' in the mining districts in the nineteenth century, not least in the Amalgamated Miners Association (AMA), a trade union which – as Bongiorno notes – exhibited a working-class liberal radicalism which helped lay the foundations for the State's Labor Party.[17] The Bendigo Miners' Association, for example, a constituent of the AMA, sported Cornishmen, no doubt predominantly Methodist, in all its leading executive positions in the early 1880s, the roll call of Association presidents peppered with tell-tale Cornish surnames until at least the Great War, among them Dunstan, Grigg, Laity, Rowe, Treleavan and Trewartha. In 1883 the *Bendigo Advertiser* published the Association's rallying cry, a doggerel verse sporting the tell-tale Cornish motto, 'One and All':

> United may we stand,
> Guarding throughout the land,

Right against Wrong,
Justice we seek for all,
Ready at duty's call,
Our motto 'One and All',
We shall be strong.[18]

Methodist influence in Victoria's mining districts sought to make miners model citizens, 'transforming the "mob" into citizenry', according to Bongiorno, the Amalgamated Miners Association advocating mutual improvement activities and lending support to numerous goldfields institutions.[19] It gave financial assistance to local brass bands, lending libraries, hospitals and benevolent organisations, and was involved in friendly societies, sports clubs, local councils, and school and mining boards. Such activity won popular approval across the community, and some local businessmen were even made honorary members of the AMA, such was the breadth of consensus achieved in this emergent civic culture.

William Trenwith, the son of a Cornish cobbler and a leading activist in the Victorian Operative Bootmakers' Union, argued that in Australian colonial society, with its inherent egalitarianism and commitment to liberal and democratic values, social radicalism could exist alongside capitalism in felicitous equilibrium. As he put it, writing in 1886, 'employers and employed stand on absolutely equal terms – the one wishing to buy labor, and the other having it to sell'.[20] James Nankervis, AMA President, another Methodist of Cornish descent, agreed, insisting in the Melbourne *Age* in 1904 that it was the duty of government to arbitrate between capital and labor, and to perform 'the role of the father in the parable in the Old Book to reconcile the two sons, if he might so call them', should they find themselves in dispute.[21] Such opinion helps to explain the otherwise puzzling partnership that sometimes existed between Labor and Liberal politicians in the Victorian Parliament in this period. William Trenwith himself, despite being a vocal advocate of independent Labor representation, nonetheless entered the Victorian Parliament in 1889 under the National Liberal League banner. In 1892 he established a separate Labor caucus, yet by 1894 was leading a United Labour and Liberal Party, the two strands – sometimes complementary, sometimes conflicting – having merged once more. Only in May 1896 did this finally metamorphose into a truly independent United Labor Party.

Partly a result of this long gestation, aided by the built-in rural bias of the electoral system, Labor did not find itself in government in Victoria in its own right until as late as 1952, although it had formed minority administrations in 1913, 1924, 1927–28, 1929–32, 1943 and 1945–47, with a grand total of barely six years in office. Additionally, Labor had supported the Country Party government of Albert Dunstan (no relation, apparently) from 1935 to 1942. Again, this appears an unlikely alliance but, as Geoffrey Blainey has explained, in Victoria the Country Party had long sported a radical wing, especially in the north-western wheat belt, where many goldfields workers had gone to try their luck farming.[22] Albert Dunstan's father was among them, a Cornish Methodist-miner who, like many of his countrymen, had at length abandoned the gold mines to take up land on what was then Victoria's outback frontier. Dunstan junior joined the Country Party, and led the foundation of a breakaway group, the Progressive Country Party, which within weeks had formed more than 100 branches, mainly in the north-western wheat belt, where his father and other former gold-miners had settled. Albert Dunstan managed to gain – and hold – the balance of power in the Victorian Parliament, keeping Labor in power in 1927–28 and 1929–32. He also managed to negotiate the reunification of the Country Party, largely on his terms, and, after the defeat of the Labor Party, joined a coalition administration in Victoria led by the Liberals. In 1935, now leader of the Country Party, Dunstan shifted his coalition allegiance to the Labor Party, and in doing so became Premier of Victoria, a position he would hold for a decade.[23]

As Blainey has observed, Albert Dunstan's eventual defeat in 1945 evidenced the final waning of what he termed the 'nonconformist Protestant lobby in Victoria'. As Blainey explained, Methodists and other Nonconformists had long been powerful in Victorian politics. But, he said, this Protestant lobby 'was vulnerable because its political influence lay essentially in the Liberal and Country parties and not in Labor where Catholics were strong'.[24] The Methodist-Nonconformist estrangement from Labor in Victoria had begun by the end of the nineteenth century, and after Federation in 1901 there was an increasing identification of Roman Catholicism with the Labor Party. As the Labor Party had forged its own separate identity, appealing unambiguously to the working-class, so it was natural that the many workers of Irish-Catholic origin in Victoria would be drawn to its ranks. Moreover, the Labor Party was formally opposed to religious sectarianism, a principle which many Catholics found attractive at a time when they felt disadvantaged within the community, not least by what they saw as an encroaching 'Protestantised' secular State education system. As Frank Bongiorno has argued, in Victoria many 'Catholics believed that Labor was the party most likely to give Catholics a fair deal'.[25] Catholics flocked to join, to the dismay of many Methodists and other Nonconformists who began to detect a malign 'alliance' between the Labor Party and the Catholic church in Victoria, a fear exacerbated by Catholic attitudes during the Boer War, which Protestants interpreted as being less than supportive of the British Empire's cause. Sectarian suspicion would reach new heights during the First World War, where in the conscription crisis of 1916–17 Victoria's Catholic population proved resolutely 'anti-conscriptionist' – much to the chagrin of Protestant 'pro-conscriptionists' – and redoubled Catholic support for Labor. As Bongiorno concluded, by then 'Labor's reputation as the Catholic party was, for good or ill, now secure'.[26] And if this was true for Victoria, it was also apparent across much of Australia. As Dean Jaensch has observed, 'most of the Protestant influence resigned' in the Federal Labor Party in the aftermath of the conscription crisis, 'leaving the Irish Catholic component with a controlling vote. The party moved to the Left in rhetoric, ideology and policy'.[27]

Privileging the Cornish

In South Australia, by contrast, despite the antagonism between institutional Methodism and Labor during the conscription controversy, Methodism remained a crucial strand of Labor Party identity after the First World War. Unlike neighbouring Victoria, there were relatively few Catholics likely to challenge the relationship between Methodism and Labor, and the intimacy survived the upheaval of the war years. Don Dunstan, tracing the early fortunes of the Labor Party in South Australia, privileged the Cornish role in this enduring relationship. As he readily admitted, he was himself of Cornish descent, and proud of it. His forebears, he explained, had come to South Australia from Cornwall in the early days, settling at Monarto, 'an arid, shallow valley with little vegetation except low mallee scrub', where they wrested a living from the unpromising soil.[28]

It was a heritage that Dunstan remembered (as a boy, 'I was taken there for church reunions',[29] he recalled), and when, as Premier of South Australia, he was approached by the business community of Moonta, Wallaroo and Kadina – the former copper-mining towns of northern Yorke Peninsula – for support to encourage economic regeneration, he suggested that they develop a cultural tourism strategy based on their Cornish past. 'When I proposed the establishment of a Cornish Festival, in Australia's "Little Cornwall", people of Cornish descent came flocking', he wrote: 'The staid citizens of the three towns were soon dancing the Furry Dance in the streets of Wallaroo.'[30] In fact, Dunstan had already undertaken a study tour of Cornwall itself, seeking to discover how the distinctive Cornish identity had been deployed there to promote tourism. He returned to South Australia brimming with enthusiasm, exclaiming: 'I think that, if properly developed, that unique triangle of towns [on Yorke Peninsula] can draw and display its Cornish heritage in such a way that there is a continuing and expanding tourism industry that will, quite literally, revitalise them.'[31]

In privileging the Cornish and emphasising the role of Methodism, as well as sketching the strands of radical continuity, as he saw them, from Labor's early days to his own premiership, Don Dunstan drew particular attention to John Verran. It was Verran who had become the first majority Labor Premier of South Australia in 1910, heading what was hailed at the time as the very first Labor government 'in the history of the world'.[32] Born in 1856 at Cusgarne in the parish of Gwennap, deep in the old copper-mining district of west Cornwall, Verran emigrated to South Australia with his parents as a child, settling first at Kapunda (where he was employed as a pickey-boy at the mine, sorting ore) before moving to Moonta where he worked underground as a miner. Although only a youngster when he left Cornwall, John Verran remained overtly Cornish in outlook and manner, his ethno-occupational and ethno-religious identity fostered by his lifetime immersion in the community life of Moonta, Wallaroo and Kadina. 'He was known as "Honest John" ', wrote C.C. James in his history of Gwennap, published in 1947, and in his native parish was honoured as 'a strong Trade Unionist and a fluent speaker ... a very strong Temperance Reformer and Methodist Local Preacher' who 'owed his advancement to his adherence to principle and sheer hard work'.[33]

John Verran's reputation in Cornwall was matched in South Australia, as Dunstan noted. He was a 'Methodist lay preacher', wrote Dunstan, 'folksy, flamboyant and nearly illiterate', cast almost stereotypically in the 'pulpit style', and 'legends about him, too, are legion'.[34] There was the time, Dunstan explained, when Verran 'mounted the pulpit and informed his congregation of fellow-Cornishmen in Moonta that he was going to preach on the greatest little three-lettered word in the Bible "L-U-V" '. This was not, as Dunstan supposed, a measure of Verran's alleged near-illiteracy but reflected instead his self-effacing Cornish wit. On another occasion, Dunstan added, Verran was questioned by 'a portly matron' who demanded more details about Labor Party policy. 'Give us figures Jan, gives us figures', she insisted. As Dunstan tells it, Verran 'came to the edge of the platform, caressed his own considerable *embonpoint* and said, "Mither, the less thee and me talks about figures the better" '. Neither dour nor staid, the saucy response was indicative of the impish Cornish humour that fed the Verran 'legend', and was a revealing insight into the lighter side of popular Methodist culture that observers – especially critics – were inclined to miss. Dunstan provided a further, perhaps even more surprising, example. Speaking at a temperance meeting at Moonta, Verran 'stood brandishing a bottle of whisky in his right hand while his left hand was holding back his frock-coat and resting in his trouser pocket in his customary stance. "My friends", he cried, "what I hold in my hand has been the ruin of many a widow and orphan child!" A voice from the crowd said, "Which hand, Jan?" '.[35]

Dunstan also appreciated that such wry anecdotes were often illustrative of the links between popular culture, Methodism and politics. Like William 'Billy' Hughes, Prime Minister of Australia for much of the First World War, Verran left the Labor Party over the conscription issue and joined the

National Labor camp. Nonetheless, Billy Hughes and John Verran had their political differences, and were keen to air them. On one occasion, so the story goes, Hughes had out-manoeuvred Verran in a public debate. Returning to Moonta, Verran observed the headline 'Hughes trounces Verran' as a paperboy delivered the local Sunday newspaper. 'Mr Verran, what do you think of Mr Hughes?' asked the bold but cheeky paperboy. Verran looked the lad in the eye. 'My boy, I never speak ill of a man', he replied, 'especially on the Lord's day. But coom down t'chapel 'night and I'll tell thee what the good Lord thinks of the dirty little rat!'.[36] As the Adelaide *Advertiser* observed in its obituary of John Verran in June 1932, he 'was noted for his plain speaking and repartee, and some of the replies attributed to him have become almost legendary'.[37]

Don Dunstan was not alone in privileging the Cornish and the Methodists in explaining the distinctive history of South Australia's Labor Party. Robert Hetherington and Bob Reid, writing as long ago as 1962, acknowledged the significance of the Labor-Methodist nexus.[38] It was a recognition that would become *de rigueur* thereafter for those commenting on the State's distinctive politics. Malcolm Saunders, for example, writing as recently as 2003, was careful to note that in 'South Australia the Labor Party itself had almost always been dominated by Nonconformists rather than Catholics'.[39] As he explained: 'Traditionally, Catholics have tended to dominate most state branches whereas Methodists, in particular, have been conspicuous among the leaders and members of the South Australian branch.'[40] As if to reinforce the point, Saunders added in a further article (in 2005) that, for much of its history, 'the leadership of the state branch had been dominated by Cornish Methodists'.[41] The enduring quality of this Cornish-Methodist prominence struck historian John Lonie as especially telling. As he remarked in his analysis of South Australian politics during the inter-war period, the Cornish-Methodist influence had continued to remain strong, despite the major structural changes that had overtaken the South Australian economy since 1918 – not least the closure of the Moonta and Wallaroo copper mines in 1923. As he put it, by '1930 the ALP [Australian Labor Party] itself did not mirror, in its hierarchy, the changes that had taken place in the composition of the work force since the time of the party's inception, and especially since the end of World War I'. Instead, Lonie argued, 'its composition and ideology reflected the social situation of the 1890s. Of note was the still very strong Methodist flavour which derived in the first place from the mine workers of Burra and Wallaroo who were of Cornish stock'.[42] More colloquially, Don Hopgood noted in his study of the inter-war years that, well into the 1920s and 1930s, the cartoonist's stock stereotype of the South Australian Labor politician was a corpulent Cousin Jack (Cornish miner), complete with Moonta billy-goat beard of the type John Verran had sported.[43]

Dean Jaensch, in his survey of *The Government of South Australia*, published in 1977, emphasised the corollary of the Labor-Methodist nexus. 'Nor has there been a prominent Catholic element in Labor party affairs', he agreed, 'the founders and early members were overwhelmingly Methodists, and "good-living" ones at that'.[44] Again, it was a sectarian distinction that was politically significant well into the inter-war period, and even beyond. In 1927, for example, the Labor Party endorsed Frank Coulson, a Roman Catholic, to fight the safe Labor seat of Port Adelaide. He was defeated in the subsequent election by an unofficial 'Protestant Labor' candidate, Tom Thompson, such was the level of hostility to Coulson's religious affiliation and its supposed political implications, not least a 'soft' line on the sale of liquor.[45] Indeed, the Labor Party in South Australia did not acquire a Catholic leader until as late as 1949 (on the resignation of R.S. Richards, another Cornish Methodist), when Mick O'Halloran was elected to the position.

It was a situation summed-up by John Bannon, Labor Premier in the 1980s. A distinguished historian in his own right, Bannon affirmed the distinctive nature of the Labor Party in South Australia. As he observed in 1991: 'The major difference between the background of the S.A. Leaders and their counterparts in other States is the fact that only three have been Catholics – reflecting the Methodist/protestant tradition of the S.A. working class which produced a unique mix of social policy – and the "conscience vote".'[46] Bannon's successor as Labor Premier was Lynn Arnold, another politician with scholarly leanings. Writing in 1994, Arnold added his own historical perspective. He too pointed to the 'significant cultural input' of the Cornish, and emphasised that 'Cornish "low church" views on society have left more impact on South

Australia than just the State's largest Primitive Methodist chapel [on Yorke Peninsula]'. These views 'were to result in a perception of "wowserism" that characterised the state, in the eyes of other Australians, up until the nineteen sixties'. But far more importantly, he added, they were expressed 'by Cornishmen in the State parliament', contributing to the distinctive quality of South Australian politics. As Arnold concluded, the 'Labor Party in South Australia ... has through this difference of history been somewhat different in its *modus operandi*, from, for instance, the Labor Party in Victoria, which had a much stronger Catholic influence in its history'.[47]

More recent scholarship has offered similar conclusions, David Hilliard noting in 2015 in his chapter 'Methodism in South Australia, 1855–1902' that 'Methodist chapels in the mining areas played an important role in fostering working-class organisation and action'. As Hilliard has explained, these chapels were 'self-governing institutions', and 'they encouraged their (male) members to acquire skills in public speaking, the formulation of ideas, administration, financial management and the arbitration of disputes'. Moreover, he continued, they 'also supplied a moral framework: a language of social justice derived from the Bible and the teachings of Jesus'. In this way, 'Methodists, many of them local preachers, were prominent in the early labour movement ... of the labour members elected to the South Australian Parliament during the 1890s at least five were Methodists, more than from any other denomination'.[48]

'Paradise of Dissent'

However, as even Don Dunstan acknowledged, the Methodist-Nonconformist influence in South Australian Labor was by no means exclusively Cornish. In 1905 Tom Price, Labor leader, became Premier in a Labor-Liberal coalition government which lasted until his death in 1909. According to Dunstan, Tom Price was 'respectable', a 'stonemason, a Methodist lay preacher, and a Rechabite'. He 'typified an element which remained strong in the Labor Party until the 1960s'.[49] However, although Dunstan did not say so, Price was a Welshman, born at Bymbo, near Wrexham, Denbighshire, in industrial North Wales in 1852. He arrived in South Australia in 1883, working as a stonemason and becoming clerk of the works for the erection of Islington Railway Workshops, north of Adelaide. He was appointed secretary of the Operative Masons and Bricklayers Society in 1891, and was later both secretary and president of the Stonecutters Union. He became chairman of the United Labor Party in 1900.[50] 'Price was not a forceful figure',[51] according to Dunstan, a rather hasty assessment for which Stephanie McCarthy's recent biography offers a splendid corrective.[52] Dunstan admitted that Price 'managed to obtain a first reform of the property suffrage of the Legislative Council', but was quick to point out (not quite correctly) that it 'was only a reduction of the value of the required rental, as the Independent Liberals [Price's coalition partners] were not prepared to support adult suffrage'.[53]

From Dunstan's perspective, Tom Price was overshadowed by John Verran, the ebullient Premier in South Australia's (and the world's) first majority Labor government. Yet Price represented an important strand in the Labor Party's tradition. As Bill Jones has expressed it, his 'example reflects the acknowledged Welsh prominence in the Australian Labor movement'.[54] Crawford Vaughan, who became Labor Premier in 1915, was reputedly of Welsh descent, and both his grandfathers had been Chartists in Britain.[55] More particularly, Welsh settlers in South Australia contributed to its Nonconformist character – Methodists, Baptists, Congregationalists – many arriving from the Swansea area to assist in the development of the colony's copper-smelting industry. There were early concentrations at Burra and Kapunda but the Welsh – including their language – were most visible (and audible) on northern Yorke Peninsula. As Bill Jones has remarked, the Welsh had much in common with the Cornish, the predominant group on the Peninsula. They both had 'Celtic origins' and 'many shared characteristics'.[56] Both groups claimed to be 'Ancient Britons', more 'British' than the English, and both Welsh and Cornish developed strong ethno-occupational identities centred on the mining industry – in Britain and in transnational communities overseas, including South Australia.[57] Religious Nonconformity gave them a shared outlook on life, with a tendency towards political radicalism and common cultural and social patterns. In 1930 one Welshman remembered fondly the 'happy association of the Cornish and Welsh at Wallaroo, Moonta and Kadina in musical, social and public gatherings'.[58] In South Australia, the Welsh and Cornish were complementary; in politics as in much else.

Of course, there were a great many Nonconformists in South Australia – Methodists and others – who hailed from neither Wales nor Cornwall. Methodism had also flourished in the Midlands and the North of England, where Anglicanism was relatively week. Among early well-known Wesleyans in the colony, for example, were Jacob Abbott, a farm labourer from Northamptonshire who became a prominent full-time preacher, and John Ridley (famous as manufacturer of the 'stripper' harvester) who emigrated from County Durham in 1839. As South Australia developed its own institutions, such men emphasised the importance of the 'Nonconformist conscience' in moulding their social and political imperatives, explaining that it was the duty of 'conscience' to remind politicians that they should pass Christian laws designed to promote the public good.[59] Methodists also insisted that only men of impeccable character should be raised to political power. Such men, it was believed, could be expected to support reformist agendas and, as Arnold D. Hunt put it, they were considered 'more likely to have in mind the welfare of the community as a whole'.[60]

As Dunstan acknowledged in his memoirs, very similar attitudes had also been apparent in the principles that underpinned the foundation of South Australia in 1836. To that extent, South Australia was a child of the Reforming Thirties. In Britain, Edward Gibbon Wakefield, a devotee of the Utilitarian thinker Jeremy Bentham, had proposed the creation of a free (non-convict) settlement, to be colonised according to 'systematic' lines where migration would be funded by land sales, and controlled accordingly. It was, said Dunstan, a theory which 'appealed to a group of radical members of [the British] Parliament and dissenting churchmen'.[61] There would be free emigration, free trade, freedom of religion and free institutions, a Utopian dream of undiluted 'liberal superiority', as Eric Richards has described it.[62] The laboratory for these radical ideas would be South Australia, and the principles of 'systematic colonisation' were enshrined in the *South Australian Act* of 1834, forging the only British colony whose foundation rested upon the sanction of a parliamentary statute.[63]

Religious freedom was an important component of the mix. After the 1832 *Reform Act*, Nonconformist dissenters could be elected to the British parliament. But various disabilities remained, not least the compulsory payment of tithes to the established church, the Church of England. Some began to contemplate the separation of church and state, and others looked overseas for opportunities to create a society where such separation existed as a founding principle. This was the atmosphere in which the *South Australian Act* had been passed in 1834. The South Australian Association, and its attendant Board of Colonisation Commissioners, was not dominated numerically by dissenters, as some have assumed. But the Nonconformists were a powerful and vociferous component of those organisations planning the new colony. Together with liberal-minded Anglicans sympathetic to their views and aims, they worked tirelessly to mould the characteristics of the embryonic Province of South Australia. Prominent among the dissenters were George Fife Angas (Baptist), Robert Gouger (Congregationalist), and Rowland Hill (Unitarian), who ensured that Nonconformist voices were heard and acted upon. As Angas declared, his aim was to 'provide a place of refuge for pious Dissenters of Great Britain, who could in their new home discharge their consciences before God in civil and religious duties without any disabilities'.[64] Many individuals of dissenting persuasion were thus attracted to early South Australia, seeking religious and civic freedom and social and economic mobility. Such was their success that, strictly speaking, the terms 'dissenter' and 'Nonconformist' were made redundant, for there was no established church from which to dissent or to which to refuse to conform. This was the paradoxical 'Paradise of Dissent', as Douglas Pike dubbed it in his ground-breaking history *Paradise of Dissent: South Australia 1829–1857*, first published in 1957.[65]

An illuminating insight into this early period in South Australia's political history is presented in Reg Hamilton's recent book *Colony: Strange Origins of One of the Earliest Modern Democracies*. In this penetrating case study, Hamilton asks how it was that by 1856, on the eve of the granting of responsible self-government, South Australia had achieved the secret ballot, universal male suffrage, and the separation of church and state. He answers his question by looking at the experiences of his own forebears in Dover, Kent, who became emigrants to South Australia (Richard Hamilton arrived in 1837), seeking to escape the disabilities from which they suffered at home.[66] They, and people like them, as Hamilton demonstrates, consciously shaped the character of the South Australia they had helped to settle. In October 1840, for example, there was an election in which ratepayers voted to elect the Corporation of Adelaide, possibly the first formal democratic election to be held anywhere in Australia. Likewise, although women in South Australia did not formally gain the vote until 1894, they could vote in local government elections from as early as 1861. Meanwhile, Aboriginal men in the colony were always assumed to have the vote, an indication of the desire to achieve the equality of indigenous and settler communities before the (admittedly British) law.[67] As Geoffrey Blainey has observed, 'in Adelaide, already a town of churches, a sympathy towards Aborigines seems to have been widespread'.[68] Such was the nature of early South Australian radicalism. To admiring observers, South Australia appeared 'A Model Colony', as Henry Cornish dubbed it in 1880.[69]

Like Douglas Pike in *Paradise of Dissent*, Reg Hamilton in his more recent study has emphasised the ideological influence of Britain's Reforming Thirties in steering the South Australian project. Yet Pike, having admitted his 'warm admiration for the founding colonists' (as Eric Richards has described it), appeared somewhat disappointed in South Australia's subsequent progress.[70] 'After its lusty youth', Pike wrote disapprovingly, 'Adelaide became sedate, gentle and unenterprising. No new ideas disturbed the calm and orthodoxy as generation succeeded generation'.[71] It was a stark assessment that appeared to anticipate Don Dunstan's own analysis, which would stress the seemingly uninspiring and 'conservative outlook' of South Australian society apparent in much of the nineteenth and especially twentieth centuries, the long Playford era before and after the Second World War. The early radical impulse had been somehow nipped in the bud, it seemed, or at least had been put on perpetual hold. Why was this?

Notwithstanding the democratic innovations emphasised by Hamilton, Dunstan had detected the seeds of conservative inertia, as he imagined it, in the early institutional development of the colony. First of all, he explained, the original intentions of the Wakefieldian settlement scheme were subverted when 'special surveys', far larger than the standard allocation of land to would-be settlers, were permitted. According to Dunstan, these 'special surveys ... allowed wealthy investors to lock up large areas of land and appropriate the best of those areas for themselves'. These acquisitions, Dunstan continued, 'were the foundation on which was built a privileged class of well-off land-owners who were able to exert a consistent conservative influence for the whole of the history of South Australia'.[72] Secondly, the Legislative Council set up in 1851 was surprisingly conservative in concept, given the colony's founding principles, but reflected the interests of the newly created class of landowners. It consisted of eight non-elected members (local 'worthies' nominated by the Crown) and sixteen members from electoral districts across the colony. To be able to vote in elections to the Legislative Council, a man had to be in possession of freehold estate to the value of £100, or be a householder occupying a house with an annual value of £10, or have a leasehold estate worth £10 per annum. Under this provision, less than a third of adults in the colony were entitled to vote. As Dunstan observed, acidly, 'this was not a democratic measure'.[73]

When, in 1856, South Australia acquired responsible self-government on the basis of universal male suffrage for its Lower House, democracy appeared to have triumphed. According to Dunstan, 'many South Australians in the 1850s were imbued with the democratic spirit and so demanded manhood suffrage, the secret ballot, and electorates containing equal numbers of voters'. However, Dunstan explained, 'there was no way ... that the landed minority ... would relinquish their power to a popular majority'.[74] They insisted upon, and got, an Upper House – the Legislative Council in a new guise – elected as before on a property qualification. This Upper House, Dunstan claimed, was more powerful than the House of Lords in Britain. It had the right to veto any legislation, including money bills, and consistently frustrated the attempts by reformist governments, made in the Lower House (the House of Assembly) according to the convention and practice of the Westminster system, to push through their legislative programs. Indeed, it was not until more than 120 years later, in 1975, that Dunstan himself finally achieved root and branch reform of the Legislative Council. It then gave South Australia, according to Dean Jaensch, 'the fairest electoral systems in mainland Australia'.[75] But long before that, as Dunstan was acutely aware, radical governments had quivered or crumbled in the face of the Legislative Council. He had been dismissive of Tom Price's supposedly tentative attempt at reform, and knew that John Verran's Labor government of 1910–12 had effectively been undone by the Legislative Council.

However, Dunstan argued, this conservative veneer had failed to extinguish the radical spark in South Australia. He noted that 'the very same group' of landowners who had benefited from the 'special surveys', had also 'established proprietorship over rich deposits of copper in the 1840s', mines which produced 'Australia's main early mineral exports'.[76] But he also knew that the development of these deposits had precipitated the large-scale immigration of Cornish miners and their families, to whom he attributed the perpetuation of the colony's radical tradition, not least what was to become the enduring Cornish-Methodist impact in the Labor Party. Moreover, Dunstan insisted that the conservative influence in South Australia had been consistently resisted by radical politicians. Even more than his regard for John Verran, was Dunstan's admiration for charismatic and controversial Charles Cameron Kingston, radical liberal Premier of South Australia from 1893 until 1899. His was a lengthy premiership, at the time a record in the colony, and it was also extremely productive. As Dunstan admitted, 'Kingston was no socialist'. But 'Charlie' Kingston 'supported the emergent trade unions' and promoted the establishment of the Trades Hall in Adelaide, important developments in campaigning for the eight-hour day and securing proper apprenticeship laws.[77] 'Kingston's great energy was manifested in democratic directions', according to Gordon Combe in his *Responsible Government in South Australia*, first published in 1957.[78] He secured votes for women, established a State bank, introduced new factory regulations, enacted a progressive system of land and income tax, and was responsible for the very first conciliation and arbitration legislation in Australia, designed to settle industrial disputes. Kingston tried unsuccessfully to reform the Legislative Council (which had watered down his arbitration law). But he earned distinction as a founding father of the Australian Federal Constitution, and was one of the first South Australian Members of the new Federal Parliament when it met in 1901.

This was not exactly the sleepy indolence into which Douglas Pike had imagined South Australia to have slipped. Maybe Pike was too close to his subject. Or perhaps, writing in the early 1950s, still in the midst of the lengthy Playford era, and without the benefit of Dunstan's later hindsight, he was not yet equipped to take the longer view. A fairer assessment, possibly, was that offered by Geoffrey Blainey in 1980. 'South Australia in a quiet way retained many of its early characteristics', he insisted: 'It held the smallest proportion of people of Scottish or Irish descent but to compensate for the Celtic deficit it had the largest Cornish communities. With Queensland it also held the largest settlement of Germans'.[79] Moreover, he added:

> In religion it was also the main deviant, being exceptionally strong in the nonconformist churches. In the 1880s it had a higher proportion of Methodists than any other colony and also a higher proportion of Baptists, Congregationalists, Lutherans, Unitarians, and members of the Church of Christ and Salvation Army than any other colony. Adelaide was often likened to Christchurch in New Zealand, for both cities had been founded loosely on the Wakefield principle of planned colonization and were essentially English, but Christchurch was Anglican whereas the real cathedrals in Adelaide were chapels [Nonconformist churches] in which the candle and cross were taboo.[80]

This was the social and religious reality which underpinned the perpetuation of South Australia's radical tradition, as Don Dunstan readily understood. It was this legacy, no doubt, that gave Dunstan the confidence to believe that in South Australia, despite initial appearances to the contrary, it remained 'possible by democratic action to change the political, social, and cultural life of a whole community markedly for the better'.[81]

Chapter 2

Radical Traditions – The Cornish at Home and Abroad

South Australia was founded in 1836, at the height of the Reforming Thirties, as the decade was known, when the spirit of reform swept Britain. In one sense, as we have seen already, the establishment of the new Province of South Australia was a direct result of this reformist mood. And nowhere was the mood stronger than in Cornwall, from where many of South Australia's early colonists were recruited, and where the period 1790 to 1885 saw the 'transformation of Cornwall from a Tory into a Liberal stronghold', as Australian historian Edwin Jaggard has put it.[1] As Jaggard has also observed, there was in early nineteenth-century Cornwall 'an almost Antipodean egalitarianism', an 'inherent self reliance encouraged by Methodism ... the traditional Cornish independence of mind producing farmers [and others] willing to freely voice their opinions'.[2] It was an attitude noted by the contemporary travel writer William White, who in 1851 observed that 'a strong spirit of distinct nationality is still cherished in Cornwall', and that the Cornish had 'a habit of thinking for themselves, as you will find by their shrewd remarks'.[3]

The absence of a powerful aristocracy in Cornwall ensured a society less deferential than elsewhere, and the organisation of mining, agriculture and fishing routinely drew together men of different socio-economic classes through their common speculative interests. Moreover, as Jaggard has added, despite Wesley's expectation that his followers would eschew politics ('a naïve hope'), by 'the 1830s Methodism and Liberalism were becoming identified with each other, producing a nexus in Cornwall electoral politics throughout most of the nineteenth century'.[4] Springing from the radical wing of the old Whig party, the Liberals emerged as the radical opponents of the Tories, a position they held until usurped by Labour in many parts of Britain (but not Cornwall) in the early twentieth century. In Cornwall, the consolidating Methodist-Liberal nexus survived the rise of Labour, and the Liberals continued to be viewed as the radical 'Cornish party' until the Second World War and even beyond, developing an anti-metropolitanism that anticipated the rise of Cornish nationalism.[5]

The Friends of Parliamentary Reform

In 1809, in the first attempt in Cornwall to mobilise this emerging radicalism, the Friends of Parliamentary Reform was founded by Sir John Colman Rashleigh, a member of the minor gentry who had been much influenced by the French Revolution. Although, he insisted, he was 'never at any time a Republican', he nonetheless admitted to political opinions that 'certainly were more democratic in their leanings than even the most liberal of the Whigs'.[6] Before the Friends' intervention, politics in Cornwall had been remarkably stable, controlled by a small number of inter-related 'county' families whose cosy collusion was supported by the notorious 'rotten' and 'pocket' boroughs, where corruption was rife and the franchise severely restricted. However, in a series of public meetings across Cornwall, Rashleigh and his 'Friends' initiated a demand for parliamentary reform that would continue unabated until the *Great Reform Act* of 1832. These meetings came to a head in 1831, when well-attended public gatherings in January, March and October attracted enthusiastic miners, fishermen and agricultural workers, as well as the usual minority of 'freeholders' who actually had the vote. There were demands for the abolition of 'rotten' boroughs, an extension of male suffrage, and shorter parliaments.

When the 1832 Act was at last passed, there was great celebration in Cornwall. At Falmouth, for example, the jubilant town was 'decorated with Flags and Laurel', as Barclay Fox the prominent Quaker noted in his journal.[7] At Redruth blazing tar barrels were placed atop the chimney stack of Pednandrea mine, a local landmark, and at nearby Chacewater tar barrels were burned in the streets and fireworks let off, while a grand procession marched through the town, led by a band. Further east, at Roche, the festivities included a symbolic drama, marking the demise of 'Borough Mongering', and a feast for the poor comprising two bullocks and five sheep.[8] Moreover, with the widening of the franchise attendant upon the new Act, the reformist spirit now apparent across Cornwall ensured that the Liberals would become the dominant voice in Cornish politics and in Cornwall's representation in the newly constituted Parliament. Although there had been agitation for reform throughout Britain, the Friends of Parliamentary Reform in Cornwall, according to historian Brian Elvins, was 'a group without many parallels in other parts of the country'.[9] At any rate, according to Elvins, Rashleigh and his Friends 'broke the existing mould of politics in Cornwall, laying the foundation for Liberal supremacy, and establishing a [radical] tradition which lasted into the twentieth century' and beyond.[10]

In capturing the attention of the Cornish populace, Rashleigh and Friends had been aided by the radical *West Briton* newspaper, which was 'virulently anti-Tory' in its editorial policy, as Edwin Jaggard has observed.[11] Established in 1810, by 1831 the *West Briton* had achieved a substantial circulation lead over its rival, the Tory *Royal Cornwall Gazette*, and had done much to articulate and mobilise radical opinion in Cornwall in the run up to the 1832 Act. Its first editor was Edward Budd, a schoolmaster and Wesleyan local preacher at Liskeard in east Cornwall, who had been encouraged by the Friends of Parliamentary Reform to accept the position. The choice of *West Briton* as the paper's title was intended, no doubt, to echo the radical *North Briton*, John Wilkes' famous eighteenth-century broadsheet. It also reflected Cornish insistence that they were West Britons, descendants of the original Ancient Britons, a people apart from the Anglo-Saxons on the eastern side of the Tamar border, and independent and forthright in their views. Indeed, the 'Independence of Cornwall' – meaning Cornwall's insistence upon its right to formulate and express its own political opinions – was to emerge as a popular editorial theme in the *West Briton*.[12] As Budd made clear in the first issue of

27

the *West Briton*, published on 20 July 1810, the newspaper's purpose was 'to give the calumniated advocates of a temperate and constitutional reform an opportunity of explaining their real sentiments', for 'Reform of some kind is not only expedient but absolutely necessary'.[13] He chose his words carefully. But this did not prevent political opponents from denouncing him as a 'Satellite' of Richard Cobbett, the radical agitator, and from insinuating that he favoured the subjugation of Britain to 'the power of France', that he advocated rampant 'democracy', and that he expressed dangerous opinions that 'would produce a commotion that shall terminate in a turbulent republic or a military despotism'.[14]

The *West Briton* busied itself in the election years of 1812, 1818, 1820 and 1826 with its vigorous pursuit of parliamentary reform, drawing particular attention to the illegal activities of the 'Borough Mongers' in Cornwall. But it did not neglect other issues deserving of radical support. At the end of 1821, for example, the newspaper gave its backing to Nonconformist resistance to the payment of tithes to the Anglican Church. Specifically, it lent its support to a farmer, Anthony Geake of Trecarrel, who, despite having won a civil action against the local rector, was nonetheless imprisoned by an ecclesiastical court at the rector's request.[15] More generally, the *West Briton* supported the agricultural community in its opposition to tithes, high rents and high taxes, and did much to highlight the rural distress then widespread across Cornwall. After 1832, the newspaper continued to press for further reform in a variety of areas. As Budd put it: 'Unless the abuses of the corrupt system which have so long cursed this country be rectified, the privilege granted by the Reform Act will be worthless.'[16] Abolition of slavery, reform of the Church of Ireland, poor law reform, and the admission of Nonconformists to universities were among the prominent causes championed by the *West Briton*.[17] As the *Royal Cornwall Gazette* complained in 1841: 'The *West Briton* has committed itself to those who glory in the name of Radical.'[18]

Isaac Latimer and South Australia

The *West Briton* was also a 'Dissenting Newspaper', according to its critics, reflecting the overwhelmingly Methodist-Nonconformist affiliation of its subscribers.[19] In particular, as Brian Elvins has observed, 'the *West Briton* emerged as a supporter of emigration', not least 'for those Cornish desirous of leaving for economic, political or religious reasons'. Like its Methodist readership, the *West Briton* embraced emigration as a radical 'improving' cause, Elvins explained, and 'when it referred to "the rage for emigration", as it frequently did, it did so in sympathetic terms'.[20] This was especially so after Isaac Latimer joined the staff of the newspaper as chief reporter in 1837. An accomplished journalist, Latimer had worked previously in the Midlands and in London for the *Morning Chronicle*, 'the leading Liberal newspaper' in England, according to Claire Tomalin, (where among his colleagues was Charles Dickens), a 'reforming newspaper [which] set out to rival *The Times*'.[21] Imbued with this Liberal spirit, Latimer arrived in Cornwall in the midst of the Reforming Thirties. He moved into Rosewin Row, a fashionable street in Truro, the *de facto* capital of Cornwall where the *West Briton* was published, and immediately turned his attention to the cause of emigration.

For many, the Great Reform Act of 1832, welcome as it was, left too many key issues unaddressed or unresolved. Some, fearing that further reform at home was unlikely or even impossible, decided that emigration was the only alternative. After 1815, Cornish miners had been attracted to the developing copper and silver mines of Latin America, and by the 1820s and 1830s Bible Christians from north Cornwall were already finding their way to Prince Edward Island and other parts of maritime Canada, as well as to the United States. Likewise, some Cornish families had been attracted by the offer of assisted passages to Cape Colony in the 1820s, and there were similar attempts to entice would-be 'free' emigrants (as opposed to convicts) to New South Wales and Van Diemen's Land. Latimer swiftly immersed himself in this emergent 'emigration culture', carefully examining the motives and aspirations of those who chose to move overseas. Typical of the grievances that sped many abroad were those articulated by Samuel James, a Methodist yeoman farmer on the Lizard peninsula of west Cornwall. He had decided upon emigration, he explained: 'To escape the heavy charges of supporting certain useless institutions.' There was also the desire to 'escape from supporting a State religion' and to 'live under free and useful institutions'. He wished to avoid, he said, 'supporting the abominable oppression of the Poor Law Bastilles [the workhouses]', and wished to 'go where the light of heaven, the vital air, the fish of the sea and the produce of the earth, necessary for the sustenance of man, are free for all as intended by their Great Creator'.[22] Eventually, Samuel James went to America. But he might as easily have decided upon South Australia.

Isaac Latimer, meanwhile, had been drawn to the prospects of the new colony. He had studied Wakefield's scheme of systematic colonisation, and had observed the deliberations of the South Australian Commissioners. He arrived in Cornwall immediately after the foundation of South Australia, and was duly impressed by the enthusiasm that the new province had excited, especially (as he reported in the *West Briton*) when John Marshall, South Australia's Emigration Agent in London, visited St Austell 'at the request of numerous applicants in this part of Cornwall [to] hold a meeting ... for the purpose of affording information as to the terms and conditions on which free passage may be obtained'.[23] Marshall was followed shortly by Rowland Hill, Secretary to the South Australian Commissioners, who held a similar public meeting at Falmouth intended to recruit a 'number of persons of the labouring classes' for the new colony.[24] A few months later, in March 1839, Isaac Latimer announced, once again through the pages of the *West Briton*, that he himself had now been appointed Special Agent for Truro and neighbourhood by the South Australian Commissioners.[25]

In explaining his role to the newspaper's readers, Latimer emphasised that the 'many evils necessarily generated under the old system of Colonial misgovernment will be avoided by the wise and judicious plans pursued by the promoters of the Colonization of South Australia'. Not putting too fine a point on it, he added that 'emigrants to South Australia will not come in contact with the mass of iniquity that prevails in the other Australian Colonies, as no convicts are permitted to be sent to this part of Her Majesty's dominions'.[26] Indeed, he insisted, 'NO CONVICT SHALL EVER BE TRANSPORTED THITHER ... the vice and demoralization of Australia has reference only to New South Wales, Van Diemen's Land, and Norfolk Island ... the morality of South Australia is secured in every way that can be thought of'.[27] Turning to the other advantages of the colony, Latimer explained that there were free passages available for workers from a wide variety of occupations – shepherds, wheelwrights, farriers, brickmakers, and a host of others – as well as their families. As he put it: 'Every kind of laborer [sic] and artisan may, if married, of good character, and within the age prescribed by the Commissioners, obtain a free passage to this flourishing colony.'[28] There was also land to be bought in the colony, and he was 'ready to negotiate sales . . . at a uniform price of £1 per acre, in sections of 80 acres each'.[29]

An experienced lecturer accustomed to speaking on 'improving' subjects – such as his talk on the art of printing at the St Austell Useful Knowledge Society in December 1839 – Latimer held a series of public meetings up and down Cornwall to advocate emigration to South Australia. He spoke at Bodmin, at the King's Head in Chacewater, and at the Market House in St Austell. The latter, it was reported, 'was extremely crowded, by persons from a great distance', and many 'letters of the most pleasing nature were read, which had been received from Cornish emigrants, who all spoke in most flattering terms of the province'.[30] In publicising South Australia, Latimer was assisted by John Stephens' recently published volume, *The Land of Promise*. Stephens was a Methodist of Cornish descent – his father was born at St Dennis, near St Austell – and his brother Joseph Rayner Stephens was a leading Chartist as well as Wesleyan minister. John Stephens would later emigrate to South Australia, arriving in January 1843, and under his editorship the *South Australian Register* became the leading radical voice in the colony, the province's equivalent of the *West Briton*.

In the pages of *The Land of Promise* Stephens explained the principles of the Wakefieldian system. 'Land, capital, and labour, are the three grand elements of wealth', he wrote: 'the art of colonization consists of transferring capital and labour from countries where they are in excessive proportion to the quantity of fertile land, to countries where there is plenty of fertile land, but neither capital nor labour'.[31] If all this sounded rather hypothetical, then he was keen to emphasise that:

The superiority of South Australia, not only over the British colonies in North America, and Africa, and Asia, but also over New South Wales,

Swan River, King George's Sound, and Van Diemen's Land, themselves, appears to be established on testimony that cannot be disputed. Persons who have had experience of all the other colonies in question agree in awarding the palm of decided excellence to the new settlement.[32]

EMIGRATION

TO

South Australia.

Mr. I. Latimer,

(AGENT FOR SOUTH AUSTRALIA)

Having been requested to explain the principles of C O L O N I Z A T I O N adopted by the SOUTH AUSTRALIAN COMMISSIONERS with regard to this Colony. begs to announce that he will deliver

A FREE

LECTURE

ON TUESDAY EVENING NEXT, AUGUST 27, 1839,

At the King's Head Inn, Chacewater.

As the Lecture is particularly intended for the instruction and benefit of the WORKING CLASSES, it is hoped that all those who feel interested in the subject will give their attendance punctually.

The Lecture will commence at Seven o'clock *precisely*, and at the conclusion the Lecturer will be happy to answer any questions relative to the Colony. Mr. Latimer will be in attendance at the KING'S HEAD previously, to give information to any Laborer, Mechanic, or Artisan, who may be desirous of obtaining a FREE PASSAGE to the Colony.

Truro, August 19, 1839.

E. HEARD, PRINTER, &c., BOSCAWEN-STREET, TRURO,

Emigration to South Australia, a free lecture by Isaac Latimer.
[Courtesy Royal Institution of Cornwall]

Some 10% of all applications in the United Kingdom for free passage to South Australia in the period 1836–1840 were lodged in Cornwall, such was the success of Latimer's efforts and Stephens' purple prose. Those enthusiastic letters written back by early Cornish settlers found their way into the *South Australian News* and the *South Australian Record*, published in London by the Commissioners to promote emigration to the colony. No doubt suitably edited before publication, they spoke eloquently of the advantages of the new colony. Political and religious freedom were frequent themes. 'We have a [Methodist] chapel as large as Budock Chapel', wrote Samuel Bray from Falmouth, with 'about one hundred in society'. Thomas Sleep, also from Falmouth, added that 'none of us desire to return to the bondage which holds our fellow countrymen', while John Holman insisted that 'I am freer than when I was in England . . . we would not be back to South Petherwin for £500'. John Oats agreed, writing pointedly from Adelaide to his relations in Cornwall: 'if you mind to bind yourself in the chains of slavery all the days of your life, you had better stay where you are'.[33]

Hungry Forties and 'Lawless Tinners'

The Reforming Thirties were followed in Cornwall by the Hungry Forties, when the potato blight struck, just as it had in Ireland and the Highlands and Islands of Scotland. The potato was an important staple in working peoples' diets in Cornwall, especially in the mining districts, and the crop's failure in 1845 and again in 1846 was a serious matter. Fortuitously, the 'emigration culture' and 'emigration trade' that had emerged in the years after 1815 had established lasting conduits which sped many of those who might otherwise have starved to, by now, familiar destinations overseas. To this was added the discovery of rich copper deposits in South Australia, first at Kapunda and then at Burra Burra (see Chapter 3), which attracted thousands of Cornish miners and their families during the 1840s, as did the development of equally spectacular copper discoveries in the Keweenaw Peninsula of Upper Michigan in the United States.[34] As one Cornish emigrant, from Launceston, wrote home in 1845, extolling the virtues of South Australia, the 'colony is getting on in a very prosperous state – there is no cry in our streets for bread'.[35]

For those who did not emigrate, at least immediately, a more desperate remedy in the Hungry Forties was that of riot. Notwithstanding the ameliorating effects of Methodism, Cornwall in the mid-nineteenth century was still 'West Barbary' in most popular imaginings of the region, a remote and forbidding land of wreckers and smugglers. As John Stevenson has observed, Cornish 'tinners' (as the miners were known) 'were regarded as virtually beyond the pale of civilization'.[36] Cornwall had an unenviable reputation as one of the principal centres of food rioting in Britain, and the tinners turned routinely to riot as a means of securing fair prices for corn and other staples in times of dearth. These 'lawless (or riotous) tinners',[37] as they were commonly labelled, had risen in 1709, 1727–29, 1748, 1757, 1766, 1769–99, 1810–13, and 1831, and now in the 1840s would do so again, protesting against shortages and high prices, and demanding fair prices for bread as well as attempting to prevent the export of wheat and barley from Cornish ports.[38] In the hard winter of 1846–47, bands of angry and starving miners laid siege to Cornish towns such as Callington, Launceston, Wadebridge, St Austell, Redruth, Helston and Penzance.[39] In May 1847 a small army of quarrymen, copper miners, tin-streamers and china clay workers from all over mid-Cornwall converged on the port of Wadebridge, on the Camel estuary. As the *West Briton* newspaper reported, providing a revealing insight into the conduct of Cornish food riots in the 1840s:

> the owners of the corn in the cellars proceeded to ship it on board a vessel . . . when information was received that a large body of men from the [nearby] Delabole quarries was approaching . . . and soon after about four hundred men entered the town, and proceeded at once to the quay . . . [as] a great proportion of the men were really in want of food, the magistrates and others purchased all the bread procurable in the town, and distributed it amongst them, each receiving half a part of a loaf on his passing over the bridge on his way home.[40]

Having already placated a seething mob only twenty-four hours earlier, the magistrates were relieved that they had averted another dangerous confrontation. However, the *West Briton* continued, as the retreating Delabole quarrymen crossed the bridge:

a rumour was spread that the party of the preceding day were again at hand. This rumour was soon realised, and between three and four hundred men entered the town, each armed with a bludgeon, and marched on the Quay, cheering as they proceeded. The quarrymen, or most of them, then returned, and mixed with others (streamers, china clay men, and tinners from Roche, Luxulyan, St Austell &c.), and when assembled together they presented a most formidable appearance, and created great consternation.[41]

Thomas Oliver, a Cornish miner who later emigrated to Australia, recalled a similar riot in Helston in the 1840s, when 'Coinage Hall Street was thronged with miners from the bottom to the Market House on the top of the street, all armed with shovel handles and pick handles'. The Riot Act was read, Oliver remembered, but when the soldiers present were ordered to fire a volley in the air, over the miners' heads, they refused, fearing for their lives. 'If they had fired', Oliver opined, 'every man of them would have been killed or disarmed'. Eventually, the miners were persuaded to disperse but not before, as at Wadebridge, the magistrates had handed out food to the needy. 'I saw a great quantity of bread distributed among the hungry crowd', Oliver recorded.[42]

Critics of Cornish behaviour saw such rioting as typical of the worst excesses of 'West Barbary'. The Cornish were 'very strange kinds of beings, half savages at best', wrote one visitor in 1775: 'They are as rough as bears, selfish as swine, obstinate as mules, and hard as the native iron.'[43] However, not all observers disapproved. There were those were impressed by the apparent restraint of the rioters, and the means by which they sought to achieve their ends. The threat of violence, rather than violence itself, was often persuasion enough to ensure fair prices. At Callington in 1847, for example, the miners had seized all the stored grain in the locality, selling it at 'their own price' to the hungry, and then returning the proceeds to the owners.[44] This was a fine illustration of what might be achieved by direct action, some thought. Chartists, for example, detected in Cornish food riots a radical impulse of which they readily approved. The *Northern Star* newspaper, commenting favourably on a Chartist deputation to Cornwall in 1839, described one such situation:

The men of Cornwall, seeing the people dying with want, and at the same time seeing shiploads of corn in the port to be exported, what did they do? Did they petition for the corn to remain to feed their starving countrymen? No, Sir, but with arms in their hands, seized the vessel, sold the corn at market price, and gave the money to the captain. This is a noble example for the whole country to imitate.[45]

Indeed, it was thought by the same newspaper that 'Cornwall would, 'ere long, become one of the strongholds of democracy'.[46]

John Rule, in his discussion of nineteenth-century Cornwall, saw riots as essentially apolitical, and the growing influence of Methodism as fundamentally conservative. He also argued that the influence of Chartism in Cornwall was limited. Repeated as recently as 2006 in his *Cornish Cases*, this 'quietist' interpretation was long accepted as the conventional wisdom, an echo of Eric Hobsbawm's authoritative opinion that 'Methodism in Cornwall produced an atmosphere of resignation and acceptance which worked against militancy'.[47] However, recent work by Jaggard and others has comprehensively altered our view, as has Bernard Deacon's critical review of *Cornish Cases*, where he has noted an accumulation of 'evidence [that] serves to chip away at the quietist thesis'.[48] Rule himself had acknowledged the existence of small-town radicalism in Cornwall, citing the case of John Spurr, the Truro cabinet-maker and Chartist who in the 1830s repeatedly opposed the local conservative elite before moving to London in 1839 and emigrating to Australia in 1850.[49] Deacon has also pointed to widespread Chartist activity in the 1840s in the towns of west and mid-Cornwall and has suggested that the high membership of friendly societies in the early nineteenth century, especially in the mining areas, was evidence of growing mutual association, the forerunner of artisan trade unionism across Britain.[50]

Penzance and Truro emerged as the principal and most consistent centres of Chartist sympathy in the period 1839–1850. Camborne, Falmouth, Hayle and Redruth were also prominent until the mid-1840s, while in the early 1840s Chartist activity was evidenced across mid- and west Cornwall, from St Ives and Helston in the far west to St Austell, St Columb, Padstow and Wadebridge further east. As Deacon has concluded: 'Far from being exceptionally rare [as Rule suggested], Chartism in Cornwall remained present throughout the 1840s.'[51] Thereafter, Chartism in Cornwall appears to have declined earlier than elsewhere. But this may have been a result of rising emigration in the late 1840s to South Australia and Michigan and in response to the gold rushes in California and Victoria, with many Cornish Chartist supporters leaving for overseas destinations.

As Bernard Deacon has also pointed out, 'Cornish involvement at the very heart of the Chartist movement was provided by William Lovett, now recognised as the author of the People's Charter'.[52] Born in Newlyn, near Penzance, in 1800, Lovett was the principal draughtsman of the People's Charter, with its famous six democratic demands – universal suffrage, annual parliaments, equal electoral districts, the secret ballot, payment of MPs, no property qualification for MPs – and was an advocate of free universal education, press freedom, and temperance reform, as well as a supporter of women's rights.[53] He moved to London when he was twenty-one and became involved in radical politics shortly after. When he and John Spurr, the erstwhile Truro cabinet-maker (now also in London), were among the 500 leading Chartists arrested in the aftermath of the Newport Riots in South Wales in November 1839, there was outrage in Cornwall. This mirrored consternation across Britain at the death sentences handed down to the three leaders of the Newport insurrection. In Birmingham, for example, 30,000 signatures demanding a pardon for the condemned men were collected in a matter of days. In Cornwall, 1,100 signatures on a similar petition were collected in Hayle in only two days at the end of January 1840.[54] In the face of such popular discontent, the insurrectionists' sentences were commuted to transportation for life to the Australian penal colonies. Coincidentally, the ship carrying the three men to Australia was forced to put into Hayle by stormy weather and heavy seas. As soon as the news broke, local people congregated at the quayside, where they discussed plans for rescuing the 'martyrs to the cause of liberty'. According to one report, even 'those hitherto opposed to the Chartist movement put forth their plans as freely as any'. Tellingly, it was agreed that 'the only thing wanting was to circulate the plan among the Cornish miners in order that it might be carried into effect'.[55]

A further petition demanding Lovett's release from prison was circulated in Redruth in March 1840, and donations for the prisoners' families were received from well-wishers in Hayle, Truro and Redruth.[56] By the late 1840s Chartist enthusiasm had begun to fade in Cornwall, although as late as May 1848 a meeting of 1,500 reformists at the Market House in St Austell declared in favour of the People's Charter.[57] Revealingly, this upsurge in Chartist support had been prompted by an attempt to levy a church rate, indicating the common ground that Chartism and Nonconformity often enjoyed. Indeed, as early as April 1839 some 15,000 people were alleged to have attended a Chartist meeting at Gwennap Pit, that 'cathedral' of Cornish Methodism where John Wesley himself had once preached to similarly large crowds.[58] Likewise, as Bernard Deacon has observed, at a more individual level Methodist rhetoric was detectable in the letters of Caroline Maria Williams from Camborne, addressed to 'Chartist sisters everywhere', which appeared in the *Northern Star* in July 1842. 'I and you are slaves, white slaves', she exclaimed, evoking Methodist abhorrence of slavery, warning (with further religious allusion) that 'Talk of freedom, whilst the land is reeking with oppression, might make a devil blush'.[59] The rhetoric of Cornish patriotism also informed Chartism in Cornwall, with frequent recourse to 'the Cornish motto "One and All"', and reference to the Cornish folk-hero 'Trelawny'. Likewise, 'Cornish boys' were told to do 'their duty', and at Helston local Chartists insisted that those who did not embrace their cause 'deserve not the name of Cornishmen'.[60]

Recently, Daniel Simpson has added further to the debate, arguing (among other things) that the entwined influences of radicalism, Chartism and Methodism can be detected in the conduct of the mid-nineteenth-century food riots in Cornwall. By the 1840s, he suggests, these protests were increasingly politicised, and reflected the prevailing radical mood in Cornwall. Although Methodism traditionally abhorred violence and lawlessness (*vide* its opposition to smuggling and wrecking, and its frequent concern that Chartist protest might lead to disorder), Simpson infers that radical Methodists in Cornwall were increasingly implicated in food riots. Methodist intervention in food riots may have been intended to exert a restraining influence on the behaviour of the miners in their demand for fair prices. But such moderation was hardly conservative in effect, for it handed the rioters the moral high ground, as well as giving clear direction and purpose to their protests. As Simpson suggests, Cornish Methodism by the 1840s had acquired a militant radical dimension, which both borrowed from the wider Chartist movement (sharing its Christian moral code) and informed existing forms of traditional protest. It was, as we shall see (in Chapter 3), a potent mix which would guide the actions of strikers at the Burra Burra mine in South Australia only a few years later in 1848. As Simpson insists, repudiating the 'quietist' thesis and acknowledging the pervasive impact of political radicalism: 'Wesleyan Methodists in Cornwall were motivated to improve the world as it existed in the present, rather than to fatalistically expect salvation in death.'[61] This mood of Methodist radicalism was not confined to Cornwall – as Geoffrey Blainey reminds us, the leader of the six agricultural labourers transported from Tolpuddle in Dorset to Van Diemens Land in 1834 for forming a trade union was a 'Wesleyan preacher named George Loveless'.[62] But, as Simpson indicates, Cornwall was by now a major centre of radical action. As he concludes, 'Wesleyan Methodists in Cornwall ... sowed the seeds for the enthusiastic reception of Chartist missionaries in the 1840s and 1850s, and later for the cementation of Cornwall as a bastion of liberal politics throughout the twentieth century'.[63]

'Tribute' and 'tutwork'

Integral to John Rule's quietist thesis was the view that the emergence of trade unionism – and a wider political Labour movement – was retarded in Cornwall by the 'tribute' and 'tutwork' system of employment and remuneration that existed in almost all Cornish mines.[64] Here the miners performed part of the entrepreneurial function themselves, in contracts that related to the value of ore won or the amount of ground excavated. The former was known as 'tributing'. Individual sections of the mine ('pitches') were contracted out to individual miners or – more usually – small groups of miners ('pares') as a result of open bidding on 'survey day'. Prior to this bidding, each pitch was inspected by an experienced mine agent ('captain') who would estimate the value of the ore that it contained. Each pitch would then be offered at 'captain's prices'. For a rich section of ground the captain's price might be as low as a few shillings in the pound, so that for each pounds-worth of ore raised the individual tributer or pare received only a couple of shillings. For lower-grade pitches, however, the captain's price might be considerably higher, an incentive for a tributer or pare to work indifferent ground. It was unusual, in fact, for tribute pitches to be let at captain's prices. More often, there was considerable competitive downward-bidding between rival tributers or pares, especially for attractive sections of ground. A pitch was awarded to the lowest bidder, often at a figure well below captain's prices, and the tributers – being in a sense self-employed – were required to provide their own tools, candles, blasting powder, timber and other equipment. In the larger mines, they were also expected to contribute to the club and doctor fund, from which they could draw in times of illness or injury.

Tributing was something of a gamble. An apparently rich section of ground might suddenly fail, leaving the tributer with little remuneration for his toil. But equally, indifferent ground might suddenly yield pockets of high-grade ore ('sturts', in Cornish parlance), affording a tributer substantial earnings during that particular 'take' or contract period. Tutworking operated in similar fashion, although here contracts were concerned with the amount of ground mined rather than the value of ore won, and were let at so much a fathom. Such contracts were normally reserved for the sinking of shafts or the driving of levels, which involved the removal of 'dead' ground with no intrinsic value. There remained an element of risk, however, for apparently soft ground might lead unexpectedly to much harder rock, with the result that tutworkmen were unable to sink or drive as fast as they had anticipated, with their remuneration cut short accordingly.

From Rule's perspective, the tribute and tutwork system exhibited numerous deleterious features, with miners sometimes forced to steal ore from one another in order to make any money during a particular 'take', and others left with little or no remuneration to feed their families after an apparently promising piece of ground had failed to live up to initial expectations.[65] Moreover, the tribute and tutwork system, because it effectively set one group of miners against the next as they competed for contracts, militated against collective action and retarded any sense of workers' solidarity. This,

40

more than anything, Rule argued, obstructed the growth of trade unionism and an attendant Labour movement in Cornwall. He was not alone in this opinion. A.K. Hamilton Jenkin, doyen of Cornish mining historians, wrote in his classic *The Cornish Miner*, first published in 1927: 'Foremost of all . . . among the reasons for the peaceableness of the Cornish miner was the peculiar system of wages under which he habitually worked.'[66]

Forgetting for a moment the venerable tradition of riot that stretched back into the eighteenth century, Jenkin took as his cue the latter decades of the nineteenth century, which may indeed have seemed 'quiet' compared to what had gone before. Writing in 1891, L.L. Price, commenting on the tribute and tutwork system, remarked upon 'the contrast between strikes and rumours of strikes in other parts of the country and the peaceful condition of Cornwall', a situation that would prompt even 'the dullest observer' to conclude that 'Strikes are unknown'. Price attributed this apparent state of affairs to the beneficial effects, as he saw them, of the method of employment and remuneration that prevailed in Cornish mines: 'This advantage may be admitted without hesitation to belong to the system, whether it take the form of tribute or tutwork'.[67] Unlike Rule, writing a century later, Price in the 1890s saw the competitive spirit between pares of tributers as essentially positive; not only did it make strikes unlikely but it also allowed the miners to share directly in the creation and distribution of wealth.

However, whatever the advantages and disadvantages of the system, it did not make for the universally pliant and passive workforce that Price desired and Rule regretted. Even Jenkin conceded that Cornish miners were routinely 'frank and independent in their ways and speech', unafraid to express their opinions or to take their superiors to task.[68] Tributers and tutworkmen had been ringleaders in the periodic food riots that swept nineteenth-century Cornwall, and their avowed 'individualism' and 'independence' were tailor-made for the spirit of Cornish radicalism as it spread. Indeed, as D. Bradford Barton commented as long ago as 1965 in his seminal *A History of Tin Mining and Smelting in Cornwall*, strikes 'were by no means as uncommon as some writers would have us believe'.[69] As early as February 1831 there had been a brief strike at Fowey Consols and Lanescot copper mines, near St Blazey, when the miners combined to try to force a rise in tribute rates. The strike was broken swiftly, however, its leaders incarcerated in Bodmin Gaol, the other tributers persuaded to return to work by the deployment of armed troops in the vicinity.[70] Similarly, there was a brief strike at Consolidated Mines in Gwennap in 1842 over working hours and conditions of employment, when the men talked fleetingly of forming an association and marched to Carn Brea Mines to urge the tributers there to set up a 'working miners' union'.[71]

During the 1840s Mining Association delegates from the North of England visited Cornwall to encourage solidarity with striking Durham miners and to discourage potential Cornish blacklegs from travelling north. In 1853 there was a serious strike at Bosweddan mine, near St Just-in-Penwith, over the victimisation of a pare of tributers whose leader had been implicated in a food riot six years earlier. The strike led to disturbances at other mines in the locality – Levant, Spearn Consols, Spearn Moor, Boscean, Botallack, Balleswidden, and Wheal Owles – and some 2,000 miners attended a mass meeting in a field near St Just, where they demanded better tribute rates (to which most of the mines readily agreed) and threatened that any local storekeeper refusing them credit 'should never, at any future time, receive the support of the miners'.[72] There were further short and inconclusive strikes at Balleswidden in 1856, 1857 and 1859, the latter over tutwork rates.[73]

Strikes

The first really determined attempt at organised trade unionism occurred in early 1866, at the east Cornwall and Tamar Valley copper mines which had by now eclipsed their western counterparts in terms of their richness and economic importance. Dissatisfaction with various conditions of employment had been voiced in these eastern mines during 1865. In January 1866 disgruntled miners went on strike at Wheal Trelawney lead mine (near Menheniot, in that locality), and the trouble spread swiftly to neighbouring workings. Miners throughout the district held meetings at Liskeard, Gunnislake, Callington, and across the Devon border at Tavistock. Hundreds were reported joining a new mining association, whose leaders – significantly – were Methodist local preachers. This organisation was launched in February 1866 as the Miners' Mutual Benefit Association. Its constitution was decidedly radical, with rules such as those which proposed the setting up of workers' committees to determine whether the captain's prices set for tribute and tutwork contracts were sufficient, and what action was to be taken if they were not.[74]

Bernard Deacon has suggested several reasons for this sudden upsurge in collectivist sentiment in the district, pointing to the influence of the discussion that attended Lord Kinnaird's Parliamentary Bill to improve conditions in British metal mines.[75] The competitive spirit in negotiating tribute and tutwork contracts was also less noticeable in east Cornwall, according to Deacon, compared to the more 'traditional' areas of west Cornwall, with many men at the eastern mines unwilling to engage in downward bidding to secure contracts. The copper mines in the area were also benefitting from the price rises (albeit temporary) of late 1865, the miners insisting that increased profit should be reflected in increased remuneration. Contact with visiting representatives of striking coal miners in Newcastle heightened local interest in trade unionism. There was also an atmosphere of flexibility and change, men who had come from the old western mines to work in the newer mines of east Cornwall having experienced the effects of geographical uprooting and distancing from the traditional methods of the west.[76]

Certainly, the mine owners perceived what was for them a new and dangerous phenomenon, and acted quickly and in concert to meet the threat. At Drakewalls and other mines in the Tamar Valley, the employers took pre-emptive action, 'locking-out' Association members. At Devon Great Consols (over the border, near Tavistock) there were fears of a mass invasion from across the Tamar. The lawless tinner was still fresh in memory, and nearly 300 soldiers and special constables were hurried from Plymouth to protect the mine if necessary. In the Caradon area of east Cornwall, however, it was the Association which took the initiative. Strikes were declared at several local mines over insufficient tribute and tutwork contracts, and a massive open-air meeting – reputedly attracting some four to five thousand miners – was held on the bare moorland of Caradon Hill to articulate the workers' grievances. Characteristically, the meeting began with a hymn and prayers.

By now a clearly defined, embryonic union was forming, its ringleaders two Methodist local preachers from the nearby village of St Cleer, Arthur Bray and Henry Clift.

The Caradon action received a swift riposte from the employers, however, who made it clear that the more radical claims of the Association would never be accepted. Playing for time as they planned their counter measures, and attempting to wrong-foot the miners, the employers also proposed the formation of an alternative Association, in which both employers and employees were represented. The Caradon strikes continued into March 1866 but in the Tamar Valley mines the 'lock-out' had already been successful in forcing the miners back to work under existing conditions. This signalled the general collapse of industrial action and of the short-lived Association itself. A little over three weeks since the initial Drakewalls 'lock-out', the strike was over. Many had threatened that they would emigrate rather than bow to the employers, and many did just that – taking with them their new experiences of trade unionism and industrial action to destinations as diverse as the Isle of Man, the North of England and, especially, South Australia.[77]

Emigration, already a prominent feature of Cornish life, was set to become yet more important in the aftermath of the strike. Following the Assocation's demise, the copper industry itself collapsed, the 'great crash' of Cornish copper in 1866 a result of declining copper prices and the financial crisis precipitated by the collapse of the Overend-Guerney Bank.[78] Richer, shallower and less costly overseas mines – such as the recently discovered Wallaroo and Moonta workings in South Australia – were able to survive the ensuing period of low copper prices, as well as benefitting from the surge of Cornish emigrants attendant upon the collapse of Cornish copper.[79] But in Cornwall the mines were abandoned one by one. Many famous names – Fowey Consols, St Day United – faded from the scene, and by 1871 every one of the celebrated Gwennap copper mines was closed. Some east Cornwall mines struggled on towards the close of the century, but to all intents and purposes the once great Cornish copper mining industry was already at an end. As the *West Briton* put it in January 1867, reviewing the extraordinary events of the preceding year:

The year now ended is one of the most disastrous for the mining interests of Cornwall during the present century. Certain indirect prejudicial influences have tended to paralyse nearly all our industrial resources, such as the failure of banks and public companies, leading to panic, distrust, an absence of speculation ... all the miseries and privations have fallen upon us which await crushed speculators, a partially-employed working class, and a general languor and depression in trade.[80]

The strength of the Cornish transnational identity that had by now emerged was reflected in the reaction of overseas emigrant communities to the widespread distress in Cornwall. In 1868, for example, Cornish folk on the Oven River diggings in Victoria sent home £71 to support unemployed miners.[81] A decade later, and the emigrants' concern for their countrymen and women had not diminished. At Kapunda in South Australia, a public meeting was held to discuss alarming correspondence describing conditions in Cornwall. The Mayor, J. Rowett (originally from St Austell), read extracts from letters received from contacts in Marazion, Penzance, Helston, Redruth and Truro. Rowett thanked 'God his father brought him from Cornwall when he was young', and Henry Wheare – who had emigrated from Marazion in 1847 – felt that 'South Australians should support the Cornish miners in their distress, for to the energy of some of them in opening up the mines, the colony owed its prosperity'. There were those who objected that they 'should be sorry to see it [the relief effort] made altogether a Cornish question', and others insisted that it 'must not be considered a Methodist movement'.[82] But such voices remained a minority, and when the 'English Mail' sailed from Port Adelaide in June 1879 it carried contributions for Cornwall from South Australia to the tune of £4,000 – £300 of which had been raised in Kapunda.[83] Here was a reciprocity that reflected the continuing close contacts between Cornwall and South Australia, an intimacy that was refreshed by the continued arrival of Cornish emigrants. It was a close relationship which involved the two-way transfer of information, opinion and ideas as well as funds and goodwill. In this way, Cornwall was kept abreast of developments in South Australia, not least news of industrial relations in the colony's copper mines, while South Australians in turn were made aware of the first faltering steps towards trade unionism in the Cornish mines.[84]

In the disastrous year of 1866, many Cornish tin mines had also been abandoned. However, while Cornish copper did not survive the trauma of 1866, tin mining appeared to rally. Not only did some of the old copper mines fortuitously strike tin at depth but a rise in tin prices prompted a boom in tin mining in Cornwall in the early 1870s. The early 1870s were a time of economic expansion in Britain as a whole, ushering in a period of renewed optimism and increased expectations which was reflected, among other things, in a spate of strike action for better pay and conditions in industries throughout the United Kingdom. Cornwall shared in this new mood, and grievances in the tin mines centred around two main issues, the low levels of remuneration and the infrequent payment of wages. Captain's prices for tribute and tutwork contracts were alleged to be artificially low, with the result that miners frequently had to draw 'subsist' – an advance of wages – to get them through the month. But employers were increasingly reluctant to grant subsist, and their determined adherence to calendar months in determining pay periods was an increasing source of discontent. In longer 'five week months', the miners complained, their remuneration was no greater than in a shorter, 'normal' month.

In December 1871 several hundred miners attended a meeting at St Blazey to protest against the 'five week month', their example followed shortly by gatherings in the Caradon and St Just districts. Meanwhile, in the Camborne-Redruth area two large mines – Tincroft and Carn Brea – suddenly announced the abolition of the five-week month, to be followed in February and March 1872 by similar announcements from almost every other mine in Cornwall. The employers could afford to be generous. Tin prices were high, and strikes were to be avoided if at all possible. Besides, there were other ways of controlling wages, not least through manipulation of captain's prices. However, the tin boom evaporated almost as swiftly as it had arisen. The discovery of vast new tin deposits at Mount Bischoff in Tasmania plunged Cornwall into renewed gloom. Even in 1873 prices were beginning to fall, but 1874 was far worse.

Scores of tin mines were abandoned in 1874, 1875 and 1876, and by 1896 the Cornish tin mining industry was facing oblivion with only nine mines still in production. In these conditions several mines attempted to re-introduce the five-week month, provoking strikes in large mines across Cornwall such as Wheal Jane, Wheal Basset and South Condurrow. Realising now their tactical error, the employers swiftly abandoned the re-introduction. The miners interpreted this as another triumph, and at Camborne in March 1874 announced the formation of a miners' trade union. But the timing could not have been worse. The Camborne union came to nothing, a victim of short-term organisational problems but also strangled by the longer-term crisis of the Cornish mining industry. Like the striking copper miners of 1866, the militant tin miners of the early 1870s saw their industry crumble before their eyes. As the *Mining Journal* put it: 'What Chili has done for Cornish copper mining, Australia bids fair to do for its tin mining.'[85] Again, many of these leaders of men would take their newly formed ideas and experiences to the mining frontiers of Australia, America and elsewhere.[86]

As Gillian Burke observed, the 'diminution of the Cornish industry during these years was most certainly one important factor in the delayed Trade Union organisation on any scale in Cornwall'.[87] And, as Bernard Deacon has added, if one compares the relative experiences of Welsh coal miners and Cornish metal miners in this period, it is not until after 1866-74 that their trajectories begin to diverge. Until then both the Welsh and Cornish had moved forward hesitantly, sometimes naively, as they struggled with the notion of collective action and tried to organise themselves accordingly. In Cornwall, as we have seen, this came to little, as the copper and then tin industries entered their catastrophic decline, resulting in widespread unemployment and mass emigration. In Wales, however, the coal industry went from strength to strength, and in this atmosphere of continual expansion the powerful and influential South Wales Miners Federation – the 'Fed' – rose to be a mighty trade union.[88] In Wales, too, the consolidation of trade unionism proved to be the prelude to the rise of the Labour Party, and the coal mining districts of South Wales soon acquired their lasting reputation as a Labour heartland.

The 'Great Emigration'

In Cornwall, by contrast, the conditions in which the Labour Party might have thrived had been largely removed. Yet the excitement caused by the industrial unrest of the 1870s had had a radicalising effect, albeit temporary, most notably in the Camborne constituency where in the general election of 1885 (the first in Britain in which a majority of men were able to vote) the official Liberal candidate was defeated by the Radical Liberal C.A.V. Conybeare, who had successfully mobilised the 'new' votes. As Henry Pelling observed in his study of British elections, Camborne constituency in the 1880s 'was very Radical'.[89] The *West Briton*, describing Conybeare's victory, observed that 'the creed of the overwhelming majority . . . is neatly, precisely Democratic . . . It is as Cornish as the Cornish pilchard and Cornish humour . . . These men are so downright democratic even in their religion'.[90] Conybeare's shopping list was impressive: anti-landlordism, abolition of the House of Lords, disestablishment of the Church of England, votes for women, the local option (for public houses to be closed on Sundays), graduated income tax, and Home Rule All Round (including for Cornwall). It was a moment when, according to Charles Angwin (later a prominent Labor politician in Western Australia), Cornwall demonstrated its reputation as 'that home of sturdy pioneers and still sturdier democracy'.[91]

John Rowe adds a telling insight when he remarks that an important contribution towards the Conybeare victory was the encouragement and moral support of Cornish miners in America.[92] It was an influence that would endure, and a growing indication that the radical impulse had to a considerable extent already moved abroad, part of the baggage that Cornish emigrants took with them to their new homes overseas. In other circumstances Conybeare's victory might have heralded a general shift to the left. But he lost his seat in 1895, for the reasons summarised by Pelling: 'the acute depression in the tin and copper industries in the middle of the 1890s demoralised the miners. Many of them lost the vote owing to dependence on poor relief; others emigrated.'[93] Conybeare was replaced as MP for Camborne by a Liberal Unionist, A. Strauss, one of those who had broken away from the Liberal Party over Irish Home Rule. But Strauss was defeated in turn in 1900 by the Radical Liberal and 'pro-Boer' W.S. Caine. Like Conybeare before him, Cain claimed the support of the Cornish overseas, the *Cornish Post* newspaper reporting that 'out of 700 Cornish miners home from South Africa, at least 650 had voted for him'.[94]

Thereafter, the shift to the left stalled. A Social Democratic Front candidate achieved a derisory 1.5% of the vote in Camborne in 1906 (when the Liberals won every seat in Cornwall). In the 1918 election, as the First World War drew to a close, Labour Party candidates in Camborne and St Ives achieved very respectable shares of the vote – 48 and 38.4% respectively – but in 1923 Labour was swept aside as the Liberals once more won every Cornish seat, as they did again in 1929. Cornwall, in the aftermath of deindustrialisation and emigration, had failed to participate in the new 'age of alignment' in British politics, when the principal national contest became Labour versus Conservative, and remained locked instead in its Liberal-Methodist nexus. It was not until 1945 that Labour won its first seat in Cornwall.[95]

To observe the full flowering of the Cornish radical tradition, then, we should follow the Cornish emigrants overseas where, as Catherine Mills has observed, 'Cornish miners played a progressively more active role in industrial unrest abroad'.[96] On the mining frontier of America, according to Richard E. Lingenfelter, the Cornish were 'the leaders of the mining labor movement of the West'.[97] In the gold mines of Grass Valley, in California, for example, where the tribute system survived into the 1950s, the Cornish were a significant element of the community, in May 1869 forming the Miners' Union of Grass Valley.[98] Union members were promptly 'locked-out' at the North Star mine, and at the neighbouring Empire their colleagues came out on strike in sympathy. Various grievances were aired, from the introduction of (allegedly too dangerous) dynamite to the proposed replacing of 'double-jacking' (two-man mining teams) with 'single-jacking'. But the strike was resolved amiably enough, the miners prepared to compromise in return for union recognition. In the 1870s there was further unrest at Grass Valley but by then many of the Cornish had moved on to the silver mines of Virginia City and the Comstock lode in neighbouring Nevada. As early as December 1866, the year that industrial unrest had erupted in Cornwall, the Cornish had established the Miners' Union of Gold Hill, a predominantly Cornish settlement near Virginia City, which was successful in securing union recognition as well as winning a minimum wage of $4 a day at mines throughout the Comstock region.

From there, the Cornish influence spread rapidly across the American west. In 1873 they formed the Central City Miners Union in Colorado, although the union's perceived ethno-occupational and ethno-religious exclusivity alarmed many co-workers, prompting 'hostility toward the Cornish by Irish and American miners and the community at large'.[99] Likewise, in the Butte copper mines in Montana, the Cornish wrestled with the Irish for control of the miners' union: 'bad blood between the Irish and Cornish miners . . . would slowly grow to a dispute of grotesque proportions.'[100] Yet the Cornish and Irish could on occasion claim common cause, as in their strike for the eight-hour day at the large Calumet and Hecla copper mine on the Upper Peninsula of Michigan in 1872. Further east, on Rhode Island and in Maine, Massachusetts and Connecticut, Cornish quarrymen – granite-cutters and stonemasons – found in the 1870s and 1880s that their ethnic and craft credentials actually smoothed the way for acceptance by other groups. Already members of the Operative Stonemasons' Society in Constantine and other quarrying districts in Cornwall, they were welcomed in New England by the Granite Cutters' National Union of America as fellow workers. As Horst Rossler has explained: 'craft tradition, union membership and ethnic background combined to earn the Constantine and other Cornish granite stonemasons a privileged position in an atmosphere in which immigrant labour was often viewed with hostility'.[101]

This tradition of trade unionism was taken to the goldfields of South Africa by Cornish miners from America. Prominent among them was Tom Matthews, originally from Newlyn in Cornwall, who had mined on the Upper Peninsula in Michigan and at Butte, where he had been president of the Miners Union of Montana. In 1907 Matthews led a strike at the predominantly Cornish Knights Deep mine on the Rand, protesting against the health risks posed by pneumatic rock-drills (the notorious 'widow-makers', which produced lethal clouds of dust) and resisting new rules in which skilled miners would now be expected to supervise three drills rather than the customary two per team. Matthews' tireless agitation resulted in two Miners' Phthisis Acts being passed by the

Transvaal government, designed to improve conditions in the gold mines of the Rand. Ironically, Matthews himself died of phthisis, or 'miner's complaint' as it was known in Cornwall, a result of inhaling quartz particles underground, expiring in 1915 aged only forty-eight.[102]

By the Great War, the 'Great Emigration' had all but run its course. In the aftermath of the decline of copper and tin, Cornwall was no longer considered the pre-eminent reservoir of hard-rock mining skills and experience – that mantle had passed long since to the more modern mines of America, Australia and South Africa. But by now the Cornish had already made their mark across the globe, not least in industrial relations. The 'Cornish radical tradition', which had emerged so strongly in the first half of the nineteenth century, had been taken abroad by Cornish emigrants in the second, finding a home wherever the Cornish settled in any numbers – especially in the mining districts – taking root and adapting to local conditions. But nowhere did this have such an early and enduring impact than in South Australia.[103] Here the Cornish played a significant role in moulding the State's own radical tradition, their lasting influence detectable in the Labor movement until after the Second World War, and even beyond. It was, as Don Dunstan claimed, an influence that gave threads of continuity and coherence to the story of Labor and the radical tradition in South Australia.

PART TWO
COPPER AND ORGANISED LABOR

Chapter 3

1848 and All That – Antipodean Chartists?

In the first half of the nineteenth century, as we have seen, Cornwall was the acknowledged centre of the hard-rock metalliferous mining world. Copper was the dominant metal but for centuries Cornwall had been associated with the extraction of tin, hence the popular designation 'tinner' for the Cornish mine-worker. Iron, silver-lead and, increasingly, china-clay were also won, further enhancing Cornwall's reputation as an unrivalled repository of mining skills, and central to this enviable reputation was the Cornish miner himself.[1]

The myth of Cousin Jack

By the 1840s this reputation had acquired a significant transnational dimension. In the years after 1815, as the Cornish made their mark in the rapidly developing international mining frontier – first in Latin America, and then in the United States – there emerged the 'myth of Cousin Jack'. Here the Cornish were seen as indispensable in the rush to open up new mining districts, their expertise in deep hard-rock mining and associated steam engineering an essential component in the armoury of British capital as it sought to exploit newly emergent opportunities across the globe.[2] The Cornish were at the forefront of the burgeoning international mining labour market, and they colluded in their new-found myth, asserting a transnational ethno-occupational identity which insisted upon their innate superiority in mining matters, not least when compared to potentially competing ethnic groups. 'They plainly tell me that I am obnoxious to them because I was not born in Cornwall', complained the youthful Robert Stephenson in Mariquita, Colombia, in December 1825: 'they tell me it is impossible for a North countryman to know anything of Mining'.[3] It was an opinion that sometimes offended, as Stephenson's testament indicates, but it was also highly persuasive, encouraging British investors – such as the Colombian Mining Association, formed to develop Andean copper and silver mines – to accept that Cornish skills were essential if their overseas enterprises were to prosper. Cornwall led the world in hard-rock mining, it was agreed, and the Cornish, it was acknowledged, should likewise lead the practical development of the world's mineral deposits. As D.B. Barton has observed, 'by 1850 Cornishmen had more experience of deep mining, and with it deep pumping, than the rest of the world put together'.[4]

Although, as Robert Stephenson experienced, the assertion of Cornish superiority could be blunt, even confrontational, the myth of Cousin Jack'was essentially positive, emphasising the Cornish miner's many attributes. 'The Cornish are remarkable for their sanguine temperament, their indomitable perseverance, their ardent hope in adventure, and their desire for discovery and novelty', wrote one admiring observer in 1859, and 'to this very cause has science to boast of so many brilliant ornaments who claim Cornwall as their birthplace'.[5] Integral to this enviable status was the Cornish reputation (deserved or otherwise) for religious piety, an opinion encouraged by the Cornish themselves, and evidenced (it was argued) in a society dominated by Methodism in its Wesleyan, Bible Christian, Primitive Methodist, and other denominational forms. Methodism encouraged sobriety and order and gave men (and sometimes women) responsibility, co-opting them as local preachers, Sunday-school superintendents and the like, instilling self-discipline and promoting self-improvement. Individuals were exhorted to make the most of their talents, as the New Testament demanded, and among the improving causes embraced by Methodism was emigration, contributing to an 'emigration culture' that characterised nineteenth-century Cornwall and encouraged would-be emigrants to seek new and better opportunities abroad. In this way, Methodism was an essential ingredient in the myth of Cousin Jack, lending it religious authority and moral content.[6]

Henry Ayers, the South Australian Mining Association
and the Burra Burra mine

However, as we have seen (in Chapter 2), Cornwall in the English popular imagination in the 1840s was still 'West Barbary', the wild land of food riots, smuggling and wrecking. Indeed, the Hungry Forties in Cornwall, with the failure of the potato crop (a Cornish staple, especially in the mining districts), had precipitated a new round of rioting, with the tinners routinely demanding fair prices for bread and attempting to halt the export of wheat and barley from Cornish ports. Behind the virtuous mask of Cousin Jack, many feared, lurked the ever-present lawless tinner For those overseas mining companies who sought to recruit Cornish miners, the alarming propensity of these tinners to resort to riotous behaviour had to be weighed carefully against their undeniable reputation as skilled hard-rock men. James Vetch, a Scotsman engaged in the 1820s by the mining magnate John Taylor to develop the silver-lead mines at Real del Monte in Mexico, had no illusions about the Cornish. They were not 'steady and submissive characters', he complained, but were 'of the lowest class ... the most difficult we have to manage ... and the most ungrateful'. As Vetch concluded: 'I must express disappointment with the miners sent out from Cornwall'.[7] They were insolent, disobedient, dissatisfied, often violent and sometimes drunken. 'Of this the pitman Treweek is a powerful example', claimed Vetch: 'No man brought so many recommendations and none so unworthy of them'.[8]

Henry Ayers, secretary of the South Australian Mining Association (SAMA), which owned and managed the mighty Burra Burra copper mine, discovered in the colony 1845, was one of those acutely aware of this conundrum, and understood the difficulties faced by men such as James Vetch. Ayers' task, as he saw it, was to seek a balance, acquiring all the benefits that a Cornish workforce would confer, while at the same time seeking mechanisms to limit the worst excesses of Cornish behaviour. Like other mining companies across the rapidly expanding international mining frontier, SAMA had sought Cornish expertise to develop its mine, recruiting Cornish mine workers and adopting Cornish technology and mining methods. Cornish miners were among the earliest European settlers in South Australia, and had played an important role in opening and developing the Glen Osmond silver-lead mines in the Adelaide Hills in 1841. As early as 1846, SAMA had written to the Colonial Secretary in Britain, urging special arrangements for the procurement of Cornish miners, and in the mid-1840s most ships arriving at Port Adelaide did indeed carry sizeable contingents of Cornish emigrants. The *Isabella Watson*, for example, arrived from Plymouth in April 1845, with nearly 120 passengers of whom thirty were identifiably Cornish. The surgeon's return for the *Rajah* in 1846 indicated that out of fifty-five passengers, thirty were Cornish, a number, including Uriah Scoble, Peter Spargo and John Trenowith, listed specifically as recruits for the Burra mine.[9] In November 1846, when the *Princess Royal* dropped anchor at Port Adelaide, its emigrants were said to be 'chiefly from the mining districts of Devon and Cornwall'.[10] The *Britannia* and the *Hooghly*, other arrivals during 1846, carried further groups of Cornish miners.[11]

In 1846, specimens of the dazzling Burra Burra ore – malachite and azurite – had been sent to J.B. Wilcocks, the agent in Plymouth for HM Colonial Land and Emigration Commissioners, their richness said to 'exceed those from the far-famed mines of South America'.[12] These copper specimens caused great excitement throughout the mining districts of Cornwall and western Devon, stimulating further interest in emigration to South Australia. Wilcocks himself, appointed in the late 1830s, went on to develop a close relationship with Henry Ayers, carefully selecting miners for SAMA. Thus the miners despatched in the *David Malcolm* in 1846 were, he reported, 'as fine a body of people as ever left England'. John B. Tregea was a 'very superior miner', James Rundle a 'good wheelwright, miner, carpenter and excellent character', and William Spargo 'an excellent [mine] captain'.[13] In January 1847 it was reported that the *Theresa*, then in Plymouth Sound, carried 'upwards of 230 emigrants, for the very prosperous colony of South Australia . . . most on board were from this [Devon] or the neighbouring county, Cornwall . . . they consist principally of miners, agricultural labourers and female servants'.[14] The exodus continued through 1848, reaching a highpoint in 1849 when, for example, half of the 336 passengers in the *William Money* were Cornish, as was a similar proportion in the *Pakenham*. The *Prince Regent* carried sixty Cornish emigrants, the *Eliza* forty-two, the *Himalaya* fifty-three, and so on. When, in 1850, the Cornwall

Henry Ayers, Secretary of the South Australian Mining Association.
[Courtesy State Library of South Australia, B10797]

and Devon Society was founded in South Australia to promote emigration from Cornwall and western Devon to the colony, Henry Ayers was delighted to lend his support to the initiative, approving the appointment of Captain Henry Roach – chief captain at the Burra mine – to the Society's committee. Intriguingly, the Society argued that miners should be sought exclusively from Cornwall and Devon, as 'early association and knowledge of each other's habits and character are calculated to preserve the best moral restraint on the conduct of all'.[15] Here was the myth of Cousin Jack in action.

Although Henry Ayers readily accepted the need to recruit Cornish miners, he found aspects of Cornish solidarity alarming, and privately he may have doubted the Society's optimistic assertions. He was suspicious, for example, of the relationship between the Burra mine clerk, H.M. Boswarva (a Cornishman, as his name suggests), and the mine's employees. In April 1846 Boswarva was reprimanded for being over familiar with the miners and of adopting too informal a manner in administrative matters, an offence for which he was finally dismissed in November 1847.[16] Ayers was also keen to exert what control he could over the behaviour of the workforce through the provision of company housing. Cottages for mine officials were built in the mine area itself, and by 1846 houses were being constructed for company employees in the SAMA township of Kooringa. A visitor to the Burra in 1851 reckoned there were more than 100 of these cottages, a 'great number of small houses ... we were told that they belonged to the Company'.[17] Some employees resorted to excavating their own homes in the banks of the Burra creek, a practice disapproved of by SAMA, but the company did allow, albeit reluctantly, miners to construct their own makeshift timber-paling cottages on the hillsides around the mines. Moreover, Henry Ayers was anxious that company land be donated, or leased at a peppercorn rent, to religious denominations seeking to erect places of worship. Religious observance, he imagined, not least the moral code of Methodism, would be the surest restraint on the conduct of the local population. As yet unaware of the increasingly radical dimension of Cornish Methodism, Ayers actively encouraged the 'civilising' and ostensibly conservative impact of organised religion.

James Blatchford, for example, a Cornish miner and Bible Christian local preacher, arrived from Cornwall in 1847. At first he and his wife Charity held services in their own cottage, until SAMA provided land for a chapel, affording a more permanent focus for the denomination's activities.[18] Likewise, in 1847 the Revd Daniel J. Draper could write to the *Wesleyan Methodist Magazine*, published in England, explaining that:

> I have ... the pleasure to inform you that a new Wesleyan Methodist chapel has been opened at the famed Burra Burra Mine, one hundred miles north of Adelaide. The proprietors leased me an acre of land for ninety-nine years, and I laid the foundation stone of the chapel in March last. Since that time ... the cause has improved through the labours of Local Preachers and the zeal and piety of the members ... Many of them are from Cornwall, a considerable number of whom were members of our society at home.[19]

It was an assessment that might have reassured Henry Ayers, an indication of the positive attributes of Cousin Jack routinely exhibited at the Burra. However, despite his efforts to provide company housing and to assist denominational development, Ayers was also aware that the lawless tinner was still very much alive in their midst, a serious and not always latent threat to law and order. In October 1846 one report alleged that at the Burra 'drunkenness exists ... to a frightful degree', with wages so high that 'men have the means of gratifying their worst passions'.[20] There were no fewer than thirteen public houses in the locality, names such as the Ancient Briton, the Miners' Arms and the Cornish Arms, more than a clue to their frequenters' identity. As Johnson Frederick Hayward noted in his diary in 1847, at one of these hostelries:

> The toughest characters congregated, breaking windows, singing and fighting, and ... the landlord used a cricket bat to clear his house at night – on pay nights, Saturday, fights would be coming off all afternoon and evening, and the ring formed and kept by two policemen, who were powerless to do anything but see fair play – on Sunday mornings also there were often 8 to 10 matches (pugilistic) come off at the back of the Inn, the house being closed on that day.[21]

As Henry Ayers no doubt reflected, it was possible, even likely, that some of these rollicking miners, recruited during the Hungry Forties, had been participants in the recent riots in Cornwall, forcing fair prices for corn at Wadebridge, Helston, Penzance, and elsewhere. In 1847 William Allen, an emigration agent at Penzance, had reported that 'there is great excitement in this county and neighbourhood. Many persons in the Penzance district are preparing to emigrate to South Australia, and among them a fair proportion of first rate miners'. In distant Adelaide, the *Register* echoed his assessment, explaining that 'Mr Allen says business was dull in Cornwall, and as the potato crop in his neighbourhood participated in the general failure, much distress was felt and anticipated'.[22] This 'excitement' and 'distress' came to a head in June 1847 in the so-called 'Penzance rising', an immense gathering of tin and copper miners from as far west as St Just and eastwards towards Marazion. The tinners, said to be 3,000 strong, marched through the streets of Penzance and held a mass meeting on the Eastern Green, outside the town. In anticipation of violence, premises had been locked and shuttered, with 200 special constables sworn in and a detachment of soldiers sent to help keep the peace. But, the miners having aired their grievances, the meeting broke up quietly enough.[23] The Penzance authorities had been rattled, however, and looked for ways to assist the hungry masses, in March 1848 proposing a local rate to meet the cost of emigrant fares.[24] 'Fortunately, at this juncture', as D.B. Barton put it, 'came the further spur of massive copper finds in south [sic] Australia, opening up a whole new world for dissatisfied Cornish miners'.[25] Vivid memory of all this 'excitement' and 'distress' was surely brought to the Burra by at least some of the newly arrived miners and their families, their experience of the demand for fair prices still at the forefront of their minds. It was, indeed, something for Henry Ayers to ponder.

The Burra Strike

When, in September 1848, the authority of Henry Ayers and SAMA was suddenly challenged at the Burra by striking miners who effectively took control of the mine, his worst fears appeared to be realised.[26] Overnight, the lawless tinner was in the ascendancy, replicating in South Australia the 'riotous' behaviour so recently exhibited in Cornwall. In fact, trouble had been brewing at the Burra for some time, a result of discrepancies in the ways in which the miners' ore had been assayed. Among the aspects of Cornish mining practice adopted at the Burra mine, was the 'tribute' and 'tutwork' system of employment. Organising themselves into small groups or 'pares', the miners competed among themselves to work sections of the mine, engaging in downward bidding to secure their contracts, valid usually for a month. Tribute 'pitches' were keenly sought after, where 'pares' were rewarded according to the value of ore won during the contract period or 'take', while 'tutwork' contracts were concerned with the volume of dead ground removed in the driving of tunnels or sinking of shafts. Tributers and tutworkers were responsible for purchasing their own tools, candles, powder and timber, and for contributing to the compulsory club and doctor fund. Accurate assaying was crucial in determining the value of ore won, and thus the level of remuneration

Underground in the Burra Burra Mine, 1848, from a print by S.T. Gill.
[Courtesy State Library of South Australia, B69728/3]

awarded a tribute pare, and the process was keenly observed by both the miners themselves and the captains who oversaw their work.

In June 1848 suspicion emerged of collusion by some tribute pares and the 'grass' (surface) captain, Captain Samuel Penglaze, in which assays of copper ore samples provided by the miners were consistently over-estimated. The rules were tightened but the discrepancies persisted, leading on 8 September 1848 to the dismissal of Thomas Burr, SAMA superintendent, the man ultimately responsible for the accuracy of the assays. Burr refused to go quietly, and a SAMA delegation, headed by Henry Ayers, made its way northwards from Adelaide to remove him in person. When they arrived at Kooringa, the company township, on 13 September, Ayers and the SAMA delegation were horrified. They found that the miners had struck in support of Burr and, in Ayers's estimation, had effectively taken over the mine. He sent an immediate express message to the Governor in Adelaide, containing the disturbing news and describing:

> acts of the most violent character and actual force having taken men up from the shafts tied together and carried them off the mine ... [warrants were issued] against two of the ringleaders but the police prevented from making the capture by a mob of about one hundred and sixty men. The total number now in revolt is about three hundred. The men have virtual possession of the Mine and have prevented ore from being carted away. The only work permitted to go on is the Whim [pump] at the Water Shaft which they threaten to stop ... unless means are taken to stop this ... the Mine will be ruined ... This being the first time that anything like this has occurred in the province the Deputation feel that it is necessary to act with energy and decision or otherwise we should be entirely in the hands of the people.[27]

The news was greeted with dismay. The *South Australian* announced solemnly 'Revolution at the Burra Burra Mines', exaggerating the already sensational tone of Ayers' dramatic report. 'On Saturday', the newspaper explained, 'the good citizens of Adelaide were astounded with the information that three hundred of the Burra miners had taken possession of the mine, stopped the whims for raising water, and all the other work ... There had been some rioting'.[28] Meanwhile the *Register* reminded readers that 1848 had been a Year of European Revolution, one correspondent noting 'the convulsed state of affairs in various parts of Great Britain, Ireland, and the Continent' and suggesting that readers 'observe and compare the growing coincidence of matters on this distant side of the Atlantic [sic]'.[29] Again, there was an air of exaggeration. But the revolutionary events of 1848 in Europe had not gone unnoticed in South Australia. Dislocation and upheaval on the Continent had caused a fall in the world price of copper, with implications for the colony, and Henry Ayers was already looking for ways to cut costs at the Burra mine, not least through closer scrutiny of assays.[30]

If the colony's capitalists had been unsettled by European disturbances, the Burra miners also appear to have taken note of the spirit of 1848, although it is difficult to determine the degree of this influence, not least as news from Europe travelled slowly to Australia in the days before the telegraph. Prior to the arrival of Ayers and his delegation, the striking miners had called a mass meeting, at which they elected a strike committee and voiced their grievances. They condemned the 'aggression on the part of the *monied* capitalists on their subservients', advocating instead a 'reciprocal return' to redress the balance, and invited their colleagues – 'fellow-sufferers' – to 'give language to their opinions in this ... all-important subject'.[31] This sophisticated talk was the rhetoric of political radicalism, an echo not of the supposedly inarticulate lawless tinner but of Chartism, then at the height of its influence in Britain, not least in Cornwall. Moreover, its advocates at the Burra were Methodist local preachers, determined to impose order, discipline and, above all, purpose on the strike. One of their measures, significantly, was the prohibition of alcohol for the duration of the strike, a decision applauded by the editor of the *Register*, John Stephens, who welcomed 'the pastoral efforts of the various Reverend Gentlemen for having drained the flocks in so admirable a manner'.[32] Stephens, a Methodist and of Cornish descent (his father was born in St Dennis, near St Austell), was a brother of the prominent British Chartist Joseph Rayner Stephens, himself a Wesleyan Methodist minister. Stephens had been associated with radical activity in South Australia since his arrival in the colony in January 1843, not least as editor and then owner of the *Register* newspaper and its sister publication the Adelaide *Observer*. Sympathetic to the Cornish miners, and to the tenets of Chartism as well as Methodism, John Stephens lent the Burra strikers consistent and vociferous support throughout the crisis.

Following the alarming 'express' message to the Governor, and the sensationalist reports in the press, the colony's Commissioner of Police and twenty-six armed troopers were despatched to the Burra. When they arrived, they found that Ayers had exaggerated the situation, which was more peaceable and orderly than the public had been led to expect. The strike committee had offered to meet the SAMA delegation to discuss the grievances but Ayers refused, insisting that the company would only deal with individual tributers, those with him whom it had individual contracts. The miners called a further mass meeting, which reaffirmed the decision to strike, and descended on the mine to persuade any who were hesitant. Two 'recalcitrants' were tied back-to-back on a handbarrow and paraded from the mine to the township, 'exposing them to the gaze and ridicule of about 1,800 laughing souls'.[33] It was a good-natured occasion, and the *Register* emphasised that it 'was done in perfect good humour – there was no quarrelling, rioting nor violation of the law throughout the proceedings'.[34] But it was, perhaps, an echo of the rituals of the Captain Swing disturbances that had swept southern Britain in 1830. Although the Swing outrages barely impinged upon Cornwall, there were wage riots in mid-December in parishes around Launceston and Callington, followed shortly after by threatening letters (a hallmark of the Swing disturbances) against tithes and threshing machines at St Neot (on the southern slopes of Bodmin Moor) and at Morval, near the port of Looe.[35] At the very least, the Burra handbarrow incident was strikingly reminiscent of Swing ritual, where luckless individuals would routinely be wheeled out of the parish in the parish cart and dumped at the boundary, to the approval of the accompanying crowd. There was, for example, the humiliating experience of one 'unfortunate Abel', an assistant overseer in the parish of Brede in Sussex, who was pushed out in the parish cart and deposited across the border 'by a crowd of labourers wearing ribbons in their hats, led, it was said, largely by smugglers, and applauded by several of the farmers as well who treated the labourers to beer to show their appreciation'.[36] So successful was the 'punishment', that it was immediately copied in half-a-dozen or more neighbouring parishes, and later adopted further afield, as news of its effectiveness spread.

The Burra handbarrow incident, then, may have been a further legacy of rural radicalism, introduced from Britain by the miners and their families, part of the anatomy of 'the crowd', collective action in direct response to their ring-leaders' rhetoric. Sensibly, G.S. Dashwood, the Commissioner of Police, catching the mood of the moment, intervened before the situation could deteriorate further, convincing SAMA of the wisdom of a meeting with the newly appointed strike committee. Under pressure Ayers relented, and in the subsequent negotiations the miners, as well as raising the assay question, complained to SAMA about the level of deductions for the club and doctor fund and the high charges for tools, fuses, powder and candles. By and large the miners got their way, especially with regard to the assays, where new procedures suggested by the tributers were accepted by the SAMA delegation. The miners returned to work, and the contingent of police troopers set off for Adelaide. Shortly after, the coach conveying Ayers and the SAMA Directors back to the capital left the Burra Hotel. Starting at too vigorous a pace, the coach appeared to run out of control, and promptly overturned, much to the amusement of onlookers. There were a few minor injuries but Ayers escaped unscathed, save for his embarrassment.

The strike renewed

Brooding, perhaps, on the cost implications of the agreement, Ayers redoubled his commitment to cut expenditure at the Burra mine. For some time he had considered the general labourers at the mine to be overpaid. In 1846, for example, he had written to the mine superintendent with firm advice: 'You will please understand that the Labourers are to have £1 per week only ... this being the very best wages which are given throughout the colony, and if the men choose to leave I can soon replace them by others to any extent you may require'.[37] Now, having reached agreement with the tributers, on 20 September 1848 Ayers suddenly announced a general cut in wages for day-labourers, carters, blacksmiths, sawyers, mechanics and other grass (surface) workers. There were certainly Cornishmen among these surface workers but it is unlikely that they were a majority. Nonetheless, the tributers and tutworkers struck in 'solid consideration' of their colleagues, refusing to bid for tribute pitches and tutwork bargains at the next survey, and demanding the restoration of existing rates of pay for all 'miners, labourers, carriers on the mine, whim boys, and ore-pickey boys'.[38] Their memorial to the directors – signed by John Davey Hailes, Malachi Deeble, Charles Read, Richard Trezize, Richard James, William Mitchell, James Hosken, Hugh Bowden, Richard Cocking, William Moyle, James Wallis, and Charles Burns 'with a long list of other signatures' – was duly published in full in the *Register* by John Stephens.[39] Ten days or so later, Stephens received a curt note from Henry Ayers: 'Sir: I am required by the Directors of this Association [SAMA] to request that you will discontinue advertising in the *South Australian Register* newspaper, any notices, etc. having reference to this Company'.[40]

Perhaps as many as 600 mineworkers were now out on strike, to be joined shortly by the teamsters who drove the bullock drays conveying the ore for export. The bullockies' leader was an Irishman, self-styled 'Captain' William Chace, but among his teamster colleagues was more than a smattering of Cornish – James Grylls from St Buryan, William Escott from St Ives, Henry Pinch from St Mabyn, James Thomas from Ludgvan, and various others – with ethnic sentiment once more an ingredient of class solidarity.[41] Raising the deliberately provocative Red Flag at Sod Hut, about ten miles from Burra on the Adelaide road, the teamsters set up a blockade, preventing any traffic from moving in or out. In the press, many correspondents expressed sympathy for the striking miners and bullockies. 'The "rights of labour" are even more to be respected than the "rights of capital", insisted one writer, 'for as labour is the foundation of all wealth, it follows ... that no wealth can be created without labour.'[42] Another, anticipating the workers' victory and its spread to Kapunda and other localities, was delighted that 'the public may see, at a *coup d'oeil*, the "Union, Strength, and Communion" which now so happily reign throughout the mining districts of the colony'.[43] John Stephens was less sanguine, however, and railed against the SAMA directors for exercising 'their limitless power ... by which the honest labourer of South Australia will be brought down to the level of home [British] drudgery and starvation from which he hoped he had escaped when he touched our free shores'.[44] As another correspondent put it: 'Workmen what did you come here for? You came here, I presume to escape the bondage and the serfdom that labour is under capital in Europe.' Explaining that 'the exaggeration of capital in a few hands is an embodiment of tyranny as sordid as it is powerful', he called on the workers of South Australia to 'Awake, arise, or be for ever fallen'.[45]

This time, however, SAMA was in no mood for compromise, and its response to such audaciously radical language was to stand its ground, or, as John Stephens saw it, 'to grind the faces of the poor'.[46] The directors continued to act with indifference, and on the next survey-day (11 November), when underground contracts were let, SAMA offered only seven tutwork bargains and fourteen tribute pitches (instead of the usual seventy or eighty), with the direction that any others miners seeking employment at the Burra would have to work on a daily-wage basis – a calculated affront to their professional standing.[47] Not surprisingly, the assembled miners, 400 strong, refused all such offers and reaffirmed their decision to continue the strike. However, on 22 November 1848 the teamsters' strike suddenly collapsed, and the bullockies grudgingly returned to their duties. Thereafter, there was a steady trickle of desperate miners, persuaded to return to work as their money ran out and shops refused them credit. Some of the more disgruntled tributers had already left for the copper mine on Kawau Island in New Zealand, confident in the knowledge that there would be a ready demand for their skills.

Meanwhile, SAMA had drawn up a list of 'Obnoxious persons' who would be barred from employment in the future and given notice to quit the company's cottages.[48] Two days before Christmas, Ayers relented somewhat, agreeing that Joe Trevean, A. Penna, Thos. Cocking, M. Rogers and F. Polkinghorne were to be offered the chance to return to work on tribute or tutwork. Similarly, Messrs Hailes, Mitchell and Moyle were told that they might be re-employed at a later date. But Messrs Bosance, Robins, Hoskins and Stephens were instructed to vacate their cottages immediately.[49] Those miners who had erected their own makeshift dwellings around the mine, with the tacit approval of the company, were now told to tear them down. By January 1849 it was all over. SAMA presented the outcome as a victory but in reality it had been shaken by the events of the previous three months or so, not least the cohesion shown by the miners. Ayers had been unable to recruit replacements from newly arrived Cornish emigrants, despite accosting them with offers of jobs as they left their ships. As Mel Davies has observed, the 'Cornish miners refused to scab on their fellow countrymen ... the [SAMA] directors ... underestimated the solidarity among the Cornish immigrants'.[50] Thereafter, there was a noticeable change in attitude, with SAMA readier to consult its skilled workforce on matters concerning the mine's management. But Captain James Trewartha, the colonial government's mineral surveyor and one of the colony's leading mine agents, was not impressed, insisting in an indignant letter to the press six months later that the position of a worker at the Burra was 'not a whit better than that of the Cornish miner' at home in Cornwall.[51] John Stephens, predictably, mourned the fate of 'The Burra Burra Martyrs'.[52]

The rest of the colony had followed the progress of the strike with great excitement. The conservative *South Australian* was generally critical of the miners, in contrast to the radical *Register* and *Observer*, and there had been some animosity towards the Cornish. William Stevens, a resident of Brown Street, Adelaide, wrote angrily to the *Register*, explaining that he wanted 'my brother Cornishmen [to] ... know how disparagingly they are spoken of by some persons in Adelaide'. According to his account, Stevens had visited a store in the city in the hope of selling shovels. The storekeeper, referring to recent events at the Burra, retorted: 'There's not a d...d Cornishman ... in the colony that would use them, for they are too lazy.' Stevens, suitably outraged, snorted in turn that 'Cornishmen, "one and all", are a match for any other countryman any day, and more than a match for the best counter-jumper [storekeeper] in the colony'.[53] But there was also much support for the Burra miners in the capital: 'here's Five Guineas for your cause my old friends Cousins Jackey', wrote one sympathetic observer.[54] At Kapunda, where many of the employees in the copper mine were also Cornish, the miners had demonstrated the 'proof of their unity in the common cause' by preparing to send £100 or more to 'our brethren' at the Burra.[55]

Aftermath – a lasting impact

Reflecting on the strike, one newspaper correspondent reckoned that 'one thing is certain, that to a great extent, a species of "Trade Union" has been established among the miners of several mines'.[56] It was an overestimation. No permanent trade structure emerged from the strike, and in any case the gold rushes – in New South Wales in 1850, and more importantly, Victoria in 1851 – lured many of the recent strikers away to the neighbouring colonies. Among them, for example, was William Moyle, one of the blacklisted ringleaders, a Wesleyan local preacher who on the goldfields earned a reputation as a pious man of God but a poor gold-digger. As one report put it, 'Good father Moyle was always richer in grace than gold'.[57] He toiled first at Bendigo, moving on to Ballarat in 1853, and later returned to South Australia, where he found work in the Moonta mine. Such was the exodus from the Burra mine, that operations were suspended for a time, as many of the miners followed Moyle's example, and as late as 1853 the local Bible Christian minister, Revd James Rowe, could still lament that 'We are yet suffering from the absence of our Local Preachers and members who are still at the Gold Diggings'.[58] The following year, however, as more miners returned from the neighbouring colonies and newcomers arrived from Cornwall, Rowe could report that the 'cause here has recovered from the shock it received from the discovery of the Victorian Gold Fields. The congregation is good'.[59] Henry Ayers, for his part, had written to J.B Wilcocks in November 1852, explaining that SAMA had 'for many years past experienced the benefit of your judicious selection of Cornish and Devonshire Miners', adding that 'We could find employment for a thousand hands consisting of Miners, Smiths, Engineers, Carpenters and others employed at Copper Mines – at wages varying from £6 to £10 per month. Such wages as these', Ayers quipped, 'should be sufficient inducement to the thousands in your district who cannot in the best of times expect to make much more than a third of this'.[60] A month later, and Ayers wrote again: 'We are still thirsting for labour.'[61] Subsequently, Ayers offered Wilcocks a personal bounty of £2 per head for up to 500 miners. Wilcocks responded magnificently to Ayers' gesture, despatching over 1,600 Cornish emigrants, mainly miners and their families, to South Australia during 1854 and 1855.[62]

Meanwhile, notwithstanding the exodus to Victoria, Burra emerged as a centre of the radical Political Association, as did Kapunda. First formed in 1850, with the expressed intention to 'win a South Australian Charter', the Political Association and its explicit embrace of the Chartist cause provoked much excitement in the aftermath of the events of 1848.[63] George Pearce, a Primitive Methodist local preacher, was one of those who continued to entwine religious teaching and political rhetoric. His vivid imagery ensured his popularity with the Burra miners, although he was sometimes unsure of his Biblical allusions, on one occasion looking forward to the Second Coming of Christ: 'Then shall that glorious Scripture be fulfilled, "Jack's as good as his master".'[64] However, like much else, the Political Association eventually fell victim to the gold rush, and disappeared from view until revived in July 1859. Then, paradoxically, men who had witnessed the surge of egalitarianism on Victorian goldfields, including the Eureka Stockade episode, returned to South Australia with their radical credentials burnished anew.[65] The *Register* reckoned that 'things were ripe at the Burra for the foundation of a Branch Association', and one was duly formed in November 1859, its chairman George Vercoe, a Cornish miner who had worked in Ireland and Wisconsin before arriving in South Australia in 1845.[66]

The Burra branch attracted widespread interest, the *Weekly Chronicle* in February 1860 noting that a recent meeting at the Pig and Whistle public house in Kooringa was 'crammed to excess, chiefly of the working class ... a great number joined the Society [*sic*]'.[67] Lobbying the colony's Parliament and politicians, the Political Association pressed for payment for parliamentary members, equal rights for all, freedom of speech and the press, an end to immigration, law reform, taxation of unimproved lands alienated from the Crown, and a belief that the 'happiness and well-being of the mass is paramount to the aggrandizement of the few'.[68] Adapted to South Australian conditions, it was, as Jim Moss has observed, a political creed that continued to bear the stamp of the Chartist movement in Britain.[69] Unafraid to take sides in parliamentary elections, the Political Association entered the fray in the 1860 contest in the Burra and Clare constituency, assisting in the toppling of the existing member and his replacement by a radical candidate. Such was its influence, albeit momentarily.[70]

Although the Political Association declined once more and disappeared during the 1860s, as economic conditions improved, its practice of lending organised support to progressive candidates survived intact in the mining towns until the emergence of the Labor Party in the 1890s. In 1868, for example, James Penn Boucaut (a Cornishman) was returned unopposed as member for Burra Burra, having been invited to stand by the miners and farmers of the locality.[71] In similar fashion, concerted action by the Kapunda miners ensured the election of Captain John 'Mochatoona' Rowe as the member for Light in 1862. Earning his nickname as a result of his management of the Mochatoona copper mine in the Flinders Ranges (he had also mined in New

Zealand and in Queensland), Rowe was born at St Agnes in Cornwall in 1816 and was a respected Methodist local preacher. As the *Northern Star*, published at Kapunda, observed, he could hardly fail to win the miners' votes. He championed 'the poor man', it was explained, and was 'well up in his political catechism' – support for free and secular education, opposition to immigration, payment of parliamentary members. Moreover, he 'is a tolerably good speaker and deeply versed in Scriptural history'.[72]

In the Political Association and its influence we see the lasting impact of the Burra strike of 1848. Although the strike did not lead to the imminent establishment of a trade union movement, as at least some of its observers had hoped, it had evidenced a mood of political radicalism among the mine's predominantly Cornish workforce. The strike borrowed from the wider rhetoric of 1848 – the Year of European Revolution – in Britain and Europe, co-opting particularly the language and ideology of Chartism. It drew too from the emergent radical movement in Cornwall itself, and mirrored the venerable tradition of the lawless tinner and riot as a means of achieving fair prices, a tradition tempered now and given direction and moral authority by a new class of politically aware Methodist activists. Henry Ayers, the SAMA Secretary, had recognised the ostensibly oppositional reputations of Cousin Jack and the lawless tinner. He was keen to benefit from the acquisition of Cornish skills but the Burra strike had appeared to confirm all Ayers's worst fears, explaining his overreaction in calling for the Governor's intervention and the despatch of armed police troopers. Yet the strike was largely an orderly affair, managed carefully by Methodist local preachers. Intriguingly, despite Ayers's apparently firm line throughout the strike, SAMA's stance softened in the years ahead, while Ayers himself continued to lobby for the emigration of skilled Cornish miners to South Australia. Ultimately, the myth of Cousin Jack proved more persuasive than the reputation of the lawless tinner, at least as far as Ayers and SAMA were concerned, but already political radicalism was a force to reckoned with in the mining towns of South Australia.

The Cornish would continue to arrive in large numbers after the discovery of further major copper deposits in the colony, this time on northern Yorke Peninsula at Wallaroo in 1859 and Moonta in 1861. Here they joined with miners from Burra and Kapunda, and others from the Victorian goldfields, some of whom no doubt remembered the heady days of 1848. Indeed, as we shall see in subsequent chapters, just as the Burra strike gave voice to an incipient Cornish radicalism, so the emergence of a trade union movement and an attendant Labor Party at Wallaroo and Moonta represented the consolidation and flowering of the Cornish radical tradition in South Australia.[73]

Chapter 4

Moonta, Wallaroo and the Rise of Trade Unionism

The Burra strike of 1848, with its entwinement of rhetoric, ritual, mass meetings, Methodism, Chartism, and Cornish sentiment, caused a sensation in that Year of European Revolution and caught the imagination of the South Australian public. It was a heady mix that was to provoke similar excitement when exhibited in like fashion a decade and a half later at the Moonta and Wallaroo mines on northern Yorke Peninsula. As Peter Bell has observed, the 1864 strike at Moonta and Wallaroo demonstrated the same 'strength of union and community solidarity', underpinned by a deep conviction of 'being morally right', and was characterised by 'disciplined organisation, superb public relations, and a strong sense of theatre, consciously sharpened by references to Cornish and Wesleyan cultural distinctiveness'.[1]

As at the Burra in 1848, the strike at Moonta and Wallaroo was precipitated by shortcomings in the mines' management, exacerbated by personality clashes and individual failings. Bell considers, therefore, that it is 'difficult to assign it a place in the overall picture of Australian industrial history', and that the strike's contribution to the development of a wider Labor history is unclear.[2] But such an assessment is only possible if the strike is treated as an isolated incident, unrelated to subsequent events. Moreover, it does not give sufficient weight to Cornish and Wesleyan cultural distinctiveness as an enduring agent of industrial and political action, as this chapter will show.

'Cornish and Wesleyan cultural distinctiveness'

Significant copper deposits were discovered on northern Yorke Peninsula in 1859 and 1861, the first on the Wallaroo property of the pastoralist Walter Watson Hughes, and the latter at neighbouring Moonta. A small mine, Wheal Mixter, had been worked for a time on the beach at Port Wallaroo, where, it was said, specimens of copper ore could be 'picked up freely'.[3] The spectacular discovery of 1859, however, was made a few miles inland at a place swiftly dubbed Wallaroo Mines, alongside which grew up the new township of Kadina. Together with Port Wallaroo (or plain Wallaroo as it was routinely known), where the copper smelters were soon located, Kadina and the equally new township of Moonta (and its satellite settlement Moonta Mines) formed a vibrant community that by the 1870s was some 25,000 strong, dominated by Methodism and far-famed as 'Australia's Little Cornwall'.[4] Cornish miners and their families were drawn from the Burra, Kapunda, Callington, Kanmantoo and other mining districts of South Australia, as well as from the Victorian goldfields, with many more recruited from Cornwall itself. Between 1862 and 1870 some 3,235 Cornish emigrants arrived in the colony, almost 25% of the total number of immigrants, and of the male migrants in that period for whom occupations were recorded, 36% were miners and many others were in allied trades such as blacksmithing. In 1865 some 42.5% of people arriving in South Australia were from Cornwall: 211 out of 315 on the *Queen Bee*, 214 out of 358 on the *Lady Milton*, 242 out of 388 on the *Gosforth*, and so on. The stream continued into 1866 and 1867, as the Cornish copper industry collapsed, and the last significant recruiting drive was as late as 1883 when Captain Richard Piper was sent to Cornwall, returning with 408 'new chums' for Moonta and Wallaroo.[5]

One effect of this constant migration stream was the continual refreshment of northern Yorke Peninsula's Cornish and Wesleyan cultural distinctiveness, together with a symbiotic dialogue between Cornwall and the Peninsula which kept each locality abreast of developments in the other, an important element of a transnational identity which insisted that 'if you haven't been to Moonta, you haven't travelled'.[6] But Cornish skills and technology were also pivotal in the rapid exploitation of northern Yorke Peninsula's copper deposits, so that, as Peter Bell put it, the region became 'a dominant force in South Australia's economy for the next three generations'.[7] As early as 1863, J.B. Austin in his *The Mines of South Australia* had noted the existence of hundreds of 'promising mines', as he termed them, on Yorke Peninsula, although he reckoned that 'not more than half a dozen' showed any real signs of being successful in the long term.[8] Ten years later, the *Yorke's Peninsula Advertiser* could still list no fewer than fifty-three separate mining ventures in the vicinity.[9] But, as Austin had predicted, the number of smaller remunerative mines could really be counted on the fingers of two hands – Yelta, Poona, Hamley, Matta Matta, Kurilla, New Cornwall, Devon Consols, Wandilta, Wheal Hughes – while they in turn were overshadowed by the big two, the mighty Moonta and Wallaroo mines.

The efficient application of Cornish skills and technology in the interests of the rapid development of Moonta and Wallaroo was one of the key issues that lay behind the strike of 1864. Intriguingly, the concern to apply Cornish know-how effectively was expressed by neither the mine owners nor the mine management but by the working miners themselves. It is this, perhaps, that makes the strike difficult to categorise. As Peter Bell has shown, the boards of both mining companies were dominated by Scottish financiers and pastoralists (including Walter Watson Hughes), who together represented the colony's capitalist class but collectively knew very little about mining operations. The nearest any of them came to being 'a Cornish Wesleyan' was George Marsden Waterhouse, who happened to have been born in Penzance when his father – a Methodist minister from Yorkshire – was stationed there.[10] Instead, they relied upon the apparent expertise of three Cornish mining captains – the Warmington brothers, Eneder, James and William – who had mined in Cornwall and America before arriving in South Australia in 1857 to work at the Burra. They were appointed to senior managerial positions at Moonta and Wallaroo on the recommendation of Captain Henry Roach at the Burra, and were responsible for the early development of the Peninsula mines. Eneder was made Chief Captain of the Wallaroo mine in 1860, shortly after it opened, and James was appointed to the same position at Moonta in April 1862, with the not inconsiderable salary of £250 per annum, together with a rent-free house, free firewood, free water for domestic use and a further £25 for miscellaneous expenses.[11]

'The impropriety of Captain Warmington's conduct'

However, just two months later, on 16 June 1862, James Warmington tendered his resignation, citing 'ill-health'.[12] Reluctantly, the Moonta directors accepted his decision, and began to look elsewhere for a replacement. Yet only a few weeks later, after the directors had already interviewed for the position, an apparently recovered James Warmington was writing to ask for his job back. The directors agreed but placed on record their annoyance at his 'hasty manner' and expressed their 'dissatisfaction at the inconsiderate way in which he has acted'.[13] Three months later the directors found cause to dismiss James, replacing him with his brother William. As they noted: 'Captain William Warmington had been appointed Chief Captain at the [Moonta] Mines in place of his brother James who had been discharged in consequence of misconduct.'[14] However, William soon fell out with his deputy, Captain Osborne, who had only recently been brought out from Cornwall at considerable expense, and the directors found it necessary to intervene in what appeared an increasingly ugly situation. Meanwhile, at the Wallaroo mine, Eneder Warmington was also in difficulties. He had acquired a financial interest in several of the northern Yorke Peninsula copper mines, without informing the Wallaroo directors or seeking their permission. When they found out, the directors were outraged. One threatened to resign from the board in response to 'the impropriety of Captain Warmington's conduct', and Eneder Warmington was warned that he would be dismissed if he did not relinquish his holdings forthwith.[15] Although protesting that the investments were trifling and of little value, he did as he was told.

Eneder Warmington's performance at the Wallaroo mine was also called into question. When J.B. Austin toured northern Yorke Peninsula, collecting material for his book *The Mines of South Australia* (published in 1863), he visited the Wallaroo mine. He was surprised to find that Smith's Shaft 'will not be used at present for want of sufficient drainage to carry off the water'. Admitting that drainage was a problem at all the local mines, he felt that at Wallaroo 'unless some prompt action is taken in the matter it will become very serious'. Not only were the deeper workings in danger of becoming inundated, but the inability to pump water in sizeable quantities meant there was insufficient at the surface to facilitate ore washing. Incredulously, Austin observed that 'Captain Warmington informs me that he has just been obliged to discharge twelve boys in order to allow of a pair [*sic*, i.e. group] of tributers washing their Ore', and that 'this need not to have been the case had the drainage been such as to admit of arrangements being made to enable the boys and tributers to work at the same time'. Thus, Austin concluded, 'the poor lads are thrown out of employment, and the Mine is deprived of the benefit of their services'.[16] Although he noted with satisfaction that a large sixty-inch pumping engine, recently imported from Cornwall, was shortly to be erected, the tone of Austin's report was critical, not least of Eneder Warmington himself.

The tributers forced to compete with pickey-boys for scarce water resources were no doubt among those increasingly disgruntled miners who were themselves critical of the Warmington regimes – at both Wallaroo and Moonta. They may have taken their cue from colleagues at the Kapunda mine, where in May 1862 a dispute had emerged between the mine manager William Oldham (an Irishman) and the tributers, the latter complaining of poor assaying, delayed payments and other inconveniences. A memorial, signed by seventy-one miners, was presented to Oldham, detailing the tributers' grievances, and two public meetings were held at Kapunda to air the issues.[17] Threatening letters had been sent to Oldham, it was reported, and there was much speculation about the identity of their authors. The Cornish and the Irish (of whom there were several employed in the mine) eyed each other suspiciously, prompting several speakers at the meetings to express their collective opinion that the writer was 'neither a Cornishman or an Irishman'.[18] Oldham, for his part, accepted that there had been delays and other difficulties, and undertook to respond to the tributers' complaints. Widely reported in the South Australian press, the Kapunda dispute would no doubt have caught the attention of the miners at Moonta and Wallaroo, where there was also considerable difficulty in the management of tribute and tutwork.

In December 1862, the *South Australian Register* noted that Cornish miners, only recently recruited to the Peninsula mines, were already making their way back to the Burra, exasperated by the failure of Moonta and Wallaroo to introduce the tribute and tutwork system effectively. 'A few of the miners at this place [Moonta] are returning to the Burra', the *Register* reported, 'and a great many who are practical miners urge that the tribute system should be introduced into the workings of the mines on the Peninsula'. This would be the key to the more efficient management of the mines, the paper insisted: 'doubtless, in the case of the Moonta, hundreds of pounds would fall to the share of the men, [and] thousands would go to the proprietors more than the present yield would admit of'.[19] A year later a contributor to the *Register* complained (in the unfortunate language of the period) that the Warmingtons were capable of nothing more than 'nigger-driving', their hectoring manner a mask for their managerial incompetence. 'An intending Cornish mining emigrant would', it was asserted, 'on looking at our public reports of mining, suppose that its miners were paid according to the mining usages of Cornwall. But have the lessees of Wallaroo and Moonta so paid their men? Yes and no'.[20] Yes, in that some short-term development work had been done on tutwork, but no in that the tutworkmen were later employed as day-labourers. Moreover, it was alleged, not one tribute pitch had yet to be offered.

In fact, as Peter Bell has observed, 'the Warmington brothers were not sufficiently skilled to recognise productive ground, and [were] too obdurate to negotiate a reasonable bargain'.[21] When they did offer tribute pitches, it was for worthless ground where the miners wasted their time and energy and made no money, forcing them to fall back on 'subsist' (an advance on earnings) which they would then have difficulty repaying. By early 1864, further Peninsula miners were returning to the Burra, said to be 'dissatisfied with the wages'. Later, others 'returned disgusted' from Moonta, complaining about 'the annoyances they had to suffer from the captain [William Warmington], who was a short time ago one of themselves'.[22] Matters came to a head in March 1864, when miners at both Moonta and Wallaroo came out on strike. At the Wallaroo mine a group of timbermen had been instructed by Eneder Warmington to repair some shaft work over the Easter long weekend, so that the shaft would be fit for haulage after the break. Insistent that the Monday was part of the religious holiday, the timbermen demurred. As Ephraim Major, a Cornish miner who witnessed the unfolding crisis, later recalled: 'the men refused to do it, and when they returned to work on Tuesday [29 March] there was a notice on the dry [changing room] door to the effect that the men who had refused to repair the shaft would be fined'.[23] In fact, the twenty-one timbermen were summarily dismissed by Eneder Warmington.

'Incivility to the men'

An impromptu meeting was held, Ephraim Major remembered, and the miners 'decided to petition the directors to dismiss the manager, and they then formed in a line and marched to Moonta Mines'.[24] The Wallaroo men, 130 strong, waited for the Moonta miners to come to 'grass' at the end of their core [shift], knowing that feeling against the Warmingtons was equally strong among their fellow workers at their sister mine. A mass meeting of 300 miners was held outside the Moonta mine office. It was addressed by Reuben Gill, a Cornish miner who, like many of those present, had previously worked at the Burra. Significantly, he was a Bible Christian local preacher. A skilful orator, he would shortly become a favourite speaker at strike meetings. According to one contemporary report, 'Mr Gill's style of speaking was extraordinary. Jumping upon the platform as though propelled there by a catapult, he would jerk his head from side to side, and instantly let loose his eloquence at a tremendous rate'.[25] Biblical allusion peppered his address, lending it moral and religious authority, but he also sought to moderate the men and to clarify their objectives. Here was an echo of the Burra strike a decade and a half before, and of the food riots in Cornwall in the 1840s, where Methodist intervention had tempered the behaviour of the lawless tinner. 'In his advocacy of the working-men's claims', it was observed, Reuben Gill was 'very zealous'. However, it was added, 'he was much more moderate than others who took part in the proceedings'. Indeed:

> when the miners were wrought up to take extreme measures, Reuben, by his good-natured addresses and jocular remarks, caused them to be less unreasonable in their demands. He was a good tempered and earnest speaker. His rough eloquence would fall from his lips in rapid stream, and apt metaphor and racy contemporaneous rhyme follow each other with lightning-like rapidity, while the attention of his audience would remain enchained throughout his speech.[26]

Suitably enthused by Reuben Gill's stirring performance, the Moonta and Wallaroo miners agreed to form a union to press their claims, and voted to strike at both mines. A strike committee was formed, with one of the Moonta men, Thomas Collingwood Kitto, elected chairman. Mr Knowles, another Moonta miner, was given the task of drawing up the memorial demanding the Warmingtons' dismissal. Surface workers and beam-engine drivers joined the protest, submitting their own memorials, and later in the strike they were joined by men at the Wallaroo smelting works. Intriguingly, the miners' memorial made no mention of the sacked timbermen. Instead, it demanded a general rise in wages, an increase in 'subsist', and 'that the present Mining Agents [the Warmingtons] should be dismissed on account of their incivility to the men'.[27] This incivility included physical abuse, according to some miners – slapping, punching, throttling – and Eneder Warmington was accused of flogging three apprentice boys who had left the Wallaroo mine's employ and then had the temerity to ask to be reinstated. As the price of re-employment, the three boys 'were compelled to receive a dozen lashes each on their backs, which punishment was inflicted by Captain Warmington'.[28] On another occasion, it was alleged, Eneder Warmington had forced a young boy to shovel out of a hot limekiln, resulting in serious burns. When the lad's father complained, he was dismissed from the mine's employ. Infuriated by such stories, the miners hardened their attitude towards the Warmingtons. At Moonta, despite Reuben Gill's call for moderation, there was some intimidation, men gathering outside William Warmington's office to beat empty kerosene drums and fire pistol shots into the air. The local police offered protection but William Warmington declined, insisting that 'the Cornish people were law abiding and would do no harm to him or the mine'.[29]

Commenting on the background to the strike, the *Register* explained that 'the present agents [the Warmingtons] have not the knowledge which they ought to possess when letting [tribute] bargains of this kind'. The newspaper also noted the Warmingtons' curious and uncompromising method of offering tribute contracts. The men 'are compelled to take [them] when they know they cannot get the half of 35s per week' but 'if they refuse a bargain they are not allowed to work in any other place on the mine ... at Wallaroo and Moonta'.

As the *Register* concluded, the 'strike did not take any one by surprise resident on the Peninsula, for the grievances and ill-usage which the miners have been subject to for the past two years was such that the only surprise is that it had not occurred earlier than it has'. Indeed, the general opinion on the Peninsula was that the 'working process in the Wallaroo [and Moonta] Mines is quite 20 years behind time', such was the extent of the Warmingtons' incompetence.[30]

Meanwhile, the strike had entered what Peter Bell has called a 'more theatrical stage', the miners staging a 'monster meeting' at Bald Hill, a local landmark roughly halfway between Kadina and Moonta and visible on the horizon from both the Moonta and Wallaroo mines. The theatre that Bell detected echoed the time-honoured ritual of the tinners' mass meetings, evidenced earlier in Cornwall in the 1840s and more recently at the Burra. Indeed, a telling reflection of the Bald Hill demonstrations would be witnessed less than two years later in Cornwall at mass meetings of striking copper miners on Caradon Hill, stage-managed by Methodist local preachers and featuring the customary hymns and prayers.[31] As Bell remarks, the drama of the Bald Hill meetings was heightened by the lighting of huge bonfires, which could be seen across the Peninsula, the miners gathering there after dark to listen to speeches, air grievances, sing hymns and offer prayers. Impressive, moving occasions, the torchlight meetings humbled observers from outside the region. 'Never in the annals of strikes was there more order or greater unity among a body of men', exclaimed one commentator: 'a more respectable, quiet, sober, and industrious set of miners I never saw gathered together as there is at Moonta and Wallaroo'.[32] As the Adelaide *Observer* explained, the strikers 'wished to obtain all they wanted by respectful remonstrance – by comporting themselves in a peaceable and orderly manner'.[33]

'Captain Warmington could write, but little'

As Peter Bell adds, bonfire rituals were a 'long-standing Cornish cultural practice', most commonly observed on St John's Eve (Midsummer), 24 June, each year.[34] According to the *Wallaroo Times*, on Midsummer's Eve, 'as Cousin John [Jack] still persists in calling it', scores of bonfires were lit across the Peninsula 'according to Cornish custom'.[35] In 1867 there were fifty bonfires at Moonta alone, and at Wheal Hughes there was a great blaze when an abandoned bough-shed was set alight. Although St John's Eve was now imbued with Christian meaning, there were those who recognised that the celebratory bonfires reflected a much earlier cultural inheritance. As the *Yorke's Peninsula Advertiser* remarked: 'Our Midsummer fires, or rather Midwinter fires at the Antipodes, are in all probability lingering remnants of the ancient Druidical rites of Britain'.[36]

Be that as it may, 'the Wesleyan spirit', as Bell terms it, permeated the Bald Hill meetings and bonfires. Collingwood Kitto insisted that the miners should refrain 'from intimidation and violence', and praised the 'unanimity and order still prevailing amongst them', praying that 'it would still continue while the strike prevailed'.[37] Committed as ever to self-help and mutual improvement, the Methodist local preachers running the strike were concerned that the men should use their time wisely, rather than idling. Recognising that illiteracy was widespread among the workforce, Kitto explained that 'during the strike they were going to try and remedy this defect'. He added that they 'were going to start a school', and he 'imagined that there was sufficient talent amongst them to enlighten the most ignorant and illiterate in the ranks'.[38] It was an initiative of which the miners approved, although at least one striker was anxious to point out that the 'ignorant and illiterate' included the Warmingtons: 'Mr Tresize said Captain [William] Warmington could write, but very little.'[39]

Reuben Gill and the other strike leaders also took their grievances to Adelaide, a shrewd public relations move, and won an important political ally when the prominent politician James Penn Boucaut expressed his 'entire sympathy' with the miners of Moonta and Wallaroo, a declaration that was greeted with 'loud cheers'.[40] A Cornishman to boot, Boucaut had been associated with the radical Political Association in the 1850s and, as we shall see, was to remain an outspoken champion of the colony's copper miners, in1868 being returned unopposed as the Member of Parliament for Burra Burra. Boucaut's regard for the miners extended to their religious affiliation, for although he had been brought up an Anglican, he was always keen, as he explained in the *Bible Christian Magazine*, 'to express my sympathy towards the Nonconformist churches, partly from my own natural feelings and greatly from old family associations'.[41] Born in Saltash in 1831 and educated at Mylor, near Falmouth, Boucaut was pleased to call himself 'Cousin Jackey', and, claiming common cause with the miners, was reckoned a proud 'son of Cornwall . . . [as] he has more than once boasted . . . on public occasions'.[42]

Back on northern Yorke Peninsula, the strikers also lobbied the local business community, for whom an extended strike would be a calamity, and the shopkeepers and merchants of Wallaroo, Moonta and Kadina submitted their own memorial to the mine proprietors, expressing their sympathy for the miners. Meanwhile, the Moonta and Wallaroo directors had been pursuing their own agenda. Instinctively, they interpreted the strike as a clash between capital and labor, and defended the *status quo*. The strikers' demands were considered unacceptable, and the directors determined to nip the miners' solidarity in the bud by easing the ringleaders out of the companies' employ once the present difficulty had been resolved. They also attempted – with a singular lack of success – to recruit strike-breakers from elsewhere in South Australia, and from neighbouring colonies. As Reuben Gill had observed, the 'name of Warmington was known throughout the length and breadth of the colonies' and he was certain 'that none of the miners resident elsewhere when they heard of this strike would come to take their place'.[43] Gill's prediction proved correct, and there was an air of quiet desperation in the letter despatched by the Moonta company secretary, T.F. McCoull, to the mine's agents in London. 'You will learn from the Adelaide papers that the miners at Moonta and Wallaroo Mines are now out on Strike', he wrote: 'this circumstance coupled with the fact that considerable difficulty has been experienced hitherto in getting really good hands, has induced the Directors to send to Cornwall through you for fifty men to be brought out under the Assisted Passage Regulations of the Government'.[44] Not long after, the London agents, A.L. Elder, were requested to find another 200 Cornish miners, and although the resultant recruits were not employed as blacklegs, their arrival after the strike was over no doubt served the mines well as they moved into a new period of development and prosperity.[45]

'It would be expedient to accept the resignation you have placed in their hands'

Having earlier insisted that they would hear no complaints against their managers, the Warmingtons, the Moonta and Wallaroo directors began at last to shift their ground. Mindful that the strikers enjoyed widespread support across the Peninsula community, and had now won the public relations battle in Adelaide, the directors looked more closely at the charges levelled at the Warmington brothers. In mid-April two Cornish captains – Captain Thomas Prisk of Kanmantoo, and Captain Trestrail of Magill (near Adelaide) – were engaged to sound out the mood of the miners and to inspect the underground workings at Moonta and Wallaroo, the latter carried out with the grudging assistance of the Warmingtons. A month later, and the directors were sufficiently worried by what they had heard from Prisk and Trestrail to summon Eneder Warmington to appear before them. He resigned the same day, 13 May 1864. His decision to quit was, no doubt, influenced by his continuing ill-health (he died from stomach cancer a few weeks later) but the triumphant miners saw his sudden removal as an admission of guilt. Sensing victory, the Wallaroo men indicated their willingness to return to work, but only after the equally unpopular William Warmington had been likewise unseated at Moonta.

By the end of May, as the miners had calculated, William Warmington's position had become untenable. He was duly suspended, and Captain Matthew East, from the nearby New Cornwall mine, was appointed temporary manager. At the same time, Thomas Collingwood Kitto was appointed captain at the neighbouring Yelta mine; 'probably to keep him out of the way'.[46] Subsequently, in a successful career on the Peninsula, Kitto went on to manage the Wheal James, Parra, Challa, North East Moonta, North Yelta, Euko, and Wallaroo Beach mines, before moving on to South Africa where he became a prominent mining engineer.[47] Drawing upon his experiences at Moonta and Wallaroo in 1864, he acquired a reputation as a moderating influence in industrial relations in South Africa, insisting that miners were 'partners, not hirelings' in the Rand goldmines, and interceding where possible between managers and men.[48] Alas, Thomas Collingwood Kitto died in suspicious circumstances in the Plume of Feathers public house in Redruth, Cornwall, in 1909. As Richard Dawe noted, there 'was speculation at least in two Cornish newspapers that one of the finest mining engineers in the world had somehow committed suicide'.[49] If the reports were true, it was a sad end to the inspirational local preacher who had cut his teeth on Bald Hill before taking his newly honed skills as a leader of men to the mines of South Africa.

But all that lay in the future. For now, Captain East was busy arranging new tribute contracts at Moonta, while the directors agreed to the general increases in rates of pay and subsist demanded by the miners. On 10 June 1864 the men returned to work at both mines, having achieved almost all of their aims in the ten-week strike. The only outstanding issue was the status of William Warmington. In the face of considerable public hostility, on the Peninsula and in Adelaide, and under investigation by the Moonta company, William decided that he had no alternative but to offer his resignation. The Moonta directors thought it prudent to accept, the company secretary writing to William Warmington to explain that 'although they [the directors] believe you have served there [Moonta] to the best of your ability, they have reluctantly come to the conclusion that it would be expedient to accept the resignation which you have placed in their hands'.[50] The next day, 28 June 1864, William Warmington was given one month's pay in lieu of notice, together with an *ex gratia* payment equivalent to three months' salary. Clearing their collective conscience, the directors agreed that they had 'dealt liberally' with him.[51]

It was the news that the miners had been waiting for, their triumph now complete. They had been planning a massive celebration at Bald Hill to coincide with the midsummer/midwinter bonfires when, as the *Observer* explained, 'the whole population of Moonta and Wallaroo [would] meet to commemorate the strike'.[52] But news of William Warmington's resignation had come too late for St John's Eve, the *Register* reporting that the festivities were now postponed to July.[53] If the directors had 'dealt liberally' with William Warmington, then they also behaved graciously towards the miners. All talk of sacking the ringleaders was quietly forgotten, and instead the Moonta company donated ten guineas to the educational institute set up by the miners during the strike. In a situation remarkably similar to the resolution of the Burra strike, the Moonta and Wallaroo directors had acquired a more nuanced understanding of their workforce, the two companies – like the South Australian Mining Association after 1848 – now much readier to consult the miners on management and practical issues. Indeed, following recommendations from Captains Prisk and Trestrail, the directors announced a comprehensive overhaul of tribute and tutwork contracting at both mines.[54] By February 1865, the Wallaroo mine was offering seventy-two tribute pitches and 107 tutwork bargains at survey-day, with an expectation that the number of tribute contracts would increase still further in the near future. In December 1866, the Wallaroo directors recruited Captain John Tredinnick from the large North Downs copper mine in Cornwall to take charge of their underground workings. Recommended by his brother-in-law, Captain Edward Dunstan, who was already at Wallaroo, Tredinnick was reputed to be 'especially conversant with Tribute work'.[55]

Captain Hancock at the helm

The departure of the Warmingtons opened the way for the highly successful managerial regime of Captain Henry Richard Hancock, first at Moonta and later at Wallaroo, with a vigorous program of expansion and development. Hancock combined all that was best in Cornish mining practice with an eye for innovation and modernity, blending tradition with novelty, and presided over the growth of two mighty Cornish copper mines in the Antipodes when those in Cornwall itself were already in swift decline. In 1898 the two mines combined to form the Wallaroo and Moonta Mining and Smelting Company Limited, the largest mining company in Australia. In the aftermath of the 1864 strike, with Hancock at the helm at Moonta, both companies took steps to recruit Cornish miners from neighbouring Victoria and from Cornwall, and in the attendant atmosphere of optimism and reconciliation, the miners' union that had organised itself so effectively appeared to fade.

Yet it would be wrong to assume that the miners basked in uncritical contentment in the years after 1864. As early as August 1864, only weeks after the Warmington crisis had been settled, there was talk of forming an Anti-Butchers Association to deal with the high price of meat on the Peninsula. This

"Only one-and-six tribute, Cap'n? Why that edden nuthin'."
"Better take un, boays, nuthin's better than nuthin' 't all."

Discontent with the tribute system, as sketched by Oswald Pryor
in his *Cornish Pasty: A Selection of Cartoons*, Adelaide, 1976.
[Courtesy National Trust of South Australia, Moonta Branch]

smacked of incipient trade unionism, and in the October the Moonta directors warned that the miners might 'fully persist in going on with this Union'.[56] In August of the following year, the Wallaroo miners submitted a memorial demanding a Saturday half-holiday. But by then international copper prices were falling, and the directors' response was a general reduction of wages at both mines. At Moonta they posted a notice explaining that 'in the present depressed state of the copper market the Directors find it necessary to reduce the rate of Wages on the Moonta Mines from and after 1st October next'.[57] Suitably outraged, the miners countered with a memorial demanding higher tribute rates, only to be informed that the new team of captains engaged recently by Captain Hancock to facilitate the mine's rapid development had already agreed to lower salaries than those originally indicated in their contracts. Grudgingly, the men felt that they had little choice but to follow the example of their superiors, and accepted the cuts. A crisis had been averted.

Yet the price of copper continued to fall. Some miners left the Peninsula for Victoria and Queensland in search of higher wages, and there was tension at the mines when an anonymous notice was posted threatening Captain Hancock with physical violence. In May 1867, unsettled by news of continuing low copper prices, and worried that legal disputes concerning ownership of the Moonta mine might affect their jobs, the miners met again to air their grievances. 'Here's five thousand Cornishmen will know the reason why!', they thundered, echoing the catch-cry of their patriotic ballad 'Trelawny', and deploying Cornish cultural distinctiveness once more to express their continuing solidarity and resolve.[58] Far from being forgotten, the rhetoric and the lessons of the 1864 strike remained important elements of the miners' repertoire as they sought mechanisms to voice their disquiet. In August 1867, the Moonta miners met to compose another memorial to the directors, again requesting improved rates of pay. The response was not slow in coming. A rise was impossible, it was explained: 'The price of copper is now lower than it has been for many years; and in consequence of the existing depression numerous mines (among them the Burra Mine) have recently been closed.' Moreover, in a classic display of divide-and-rule tactics, the directors informed the Moonta workforce that 'Any advance of wages now must have the immediate effect of closing The Wallaroo Mines, upon the working of which so large a body of Workmen depend for their daily bread and for the maintenance of their Wives and families'. Indeed, the directors added, if they 'had consulted only their own interests they would long ago have largely reduced the number of hands employed at Moonta ... [and] would have brought the operations at the Wallaroo Mines to such a point as must, in the present circumstances in this Colony, have entailed great distress upon the Mining populations of Yorkes Peninsula'. Furthermore, they argued, the 'average payment at last "Take" at Moonta was Tutworkmen 35/- to Tributers 42/- ... these rates are better than wages paid at any other Mines in the Colony'. Besides, 'Flour and meat are unusually cheap'.[59]

On a more conciliatory note, the directors explained that the current low copper prices were largely a result of competition from Chile, something they were powerless to affect. But they assured the men that they would 'always be ready to listen to reasonable suggestions of their Workforce on any subject'. However, they warned that 'the good feeling which ought to exist between employers and employed is only weakened by threats of violence by recourse to which no good result can under any circumstances be obtained'.[60] These were persuasive arguments, the miners felt, and they duly withdrew their demands. Unaware that at that very moment the directors had feared that the continuing leach of miners to Victoria and Peak Downs in Queensland would lead to a shortage of skilled labour on the Peninsula, the miners had underestimated their bargaining power. In the absence of a permanent trade union structure, the men had been outmanoeuvred by their employers. Yet there was a mood of reconciliation in the face of a perceived mutual adversity and external threat. When Reuben Gill, who had tactfully sought employment elsewhere on the Peninsula after 1864, was very publicly re-employed by Captain Hancock as an underground miner at Moonta, the conciliatory spirit appeared to triumph. As the directors put it, 'the threatened strike may be considered at an end'.[61]

However, discontent continued, not least when there was another small reduction in wages in 1870, and in 1872 the Moonta directors were irritated when Reuben Gill suggested in a letter to the *Register* newspaper that they had improperly influenced the casting of votes in recent elections to the colonial Parliament. The allegation was also evidence that Gill, and no doubt other activists, was beginning to consider the issue of parliamentary representation and how best the workers' interests and aspirations might be expressed. A meeting at the Moonta Institute in May 1872 undertook to petition the colonial Parliament for a separate constituency to represent the 'mining interests' of northern Yorke Peninsula, and in the following October the electoral district of Wallaroo was duly created. In the same month, perhaps energised by this significant development in democratic representation, seventy miners met at the Globe Hotel in Moonta to debate the possibilities of founding a Moonta Miners' and Mechanics' Association. A few weeks later, the Association was born.

The Moonta Miners' and Mechanics' Association

From the first the Moonta Miners' Association (as it was generally known) was seen as irremediably Cornish by both its supporters and detractors. One early critic complained that 'as Britain is made up of England, Ireland, Scotland, and Wales', so 'I consider a mistake was made ... forming the [Association] committee by selecting all Cornishmen'.[62] Another opponent, alarmed by the supposed ethnic exclusivity of the Association, announced that he 'would now seek refuge in some place where Cousin Jack has no existence'.[63] Founded upon 'the principles of Christian equity and charity', the new Association also reflected the Methodist allegiances of its members, especially its leaders who to a man were prominent local preachers.[64] Reuben Gill, a veteran of the 1864 strike, was a Bible Christian, admired as the 'Billy Bray of South Australia' in a flattering comparison with the famous Cornish preacher.[65] John Visick, from the parish of Kea in Cornwall, had arrived in South Australia in 1857 to work at the Burra mine, before making his way to northern Yorke Peninsula. A Wallaroo miner, he was appointed President of the Moonta Miners' Association in a deliberate attempt to widen its appeal across the Peninsula. The son of a schoolmaster, he was a 'radical all his days' and a committed Wesleyan.[66] The Secretary of the Association was John Prisk, 'a lay preacher of the Gospel in connection with the Bible Christian Church', and until recently a beam-engine driver at the Bingo mine near Kadina.[67] In June 1874 the *Yorke's Peninsula Advertiser* was moved to describe 'the Holy Land of Moonta under the able leadership of their modern Gideon, Mr J. Prisk', an allusion to the ethno-religious solidarity evident in the community, as well as to Prisk's prominence in the Association itself.[68] Here again were all the ingredients that Peter Bell identified as characteristic of the strike of 1864, and which had also been apparent as far back as the 1848 Burra strike.

Some members saw the new Association as merely a co-operative society, and hoped that it would open a store to be run in the interest of the miners and their families. Others, however, insisted that it was nothing less than a fully fledged trade union. A three-week strike by Cornish miners at the Blinman copper mine in the Flinders Ranges over the method of setting tribute contracts, when 'the tributers, "one and all", refused to take their tribute pitches', excited such ambitions.[69] As one Association activist wrote:

> We invite the young and old
> To join our miners' band;
> Come and have your name enrolled,
> And join us heart and hand.
>
> Cornwall was never conquered yet,
> By men of mighty powers;
> And shall we all in silence it
> And show ourselves like cowards?
>
> We have the motto 'one and all';
> This coat of arms is ours;
> Then let us rise both great and small
> To carry out our endeavours.[70]

Here once more was a call for workers' solidarity through the medium of Cornish distinctiveness. There was the appeal to 'one and all' (the Cornish motto), allusion to the Cornish coat of arms (which depicted a miner as well as a fisherman), and the time-honoured insistence that 'Cornwall was never conquered yet', a deeply held belief among the Cornish at home and abroad. As the Association grew in strength, so another, yet more evocative verse appeared in the Peninsula press, the old catch-cry which formed the chorus of the Cornish patriotic anthem 'Trelawny'. Its blend of collective defiance and Cornish sentiment seemed tailor-made for the new trade union:

> And have they fixed the where and when?
> And shall Trelawny die?
> Here's twenty thousand Cornishmen
> Will know the reason why![71]

An early indication of the Association's growing strength, and of its new standing in the community, was its election of the new bal-surgeon (mine doctor) at Moonta in December 1872, a duty devolved by the mine's directors.

Acknowledging that this was *de facto* recognition of the fledgling trade union, the directors at once regretted their decision. But the 'ring meeting' held to conduct the election showed that the Association had yet to win over sceptics who remained suspicious of the new responsibilities in the community that it claimed. One miner, for example, objected that 'he would sooner be attended by a dear Cornish woman than by doctors (Hear, hear)'.[72] Later, in December 1873, the *Yorke's Peninsula Advertiser* warned the community of the dangers of untrammelled trade unionism, recalling the 'damaging effects' of the 1864 strike and of recent disturbances in Britain and America. A few days later, the same newspaper published a detailed report on the 'Camborne riots' in Cornwall, with the inference that the same collapse of law and order might occur on northern Yorke Peninsula if due caution was not exercised by the Association and the community at large.[73]

'Where Cousin Jack stands like a king ... now Cousin Jenny is no fool'

Perhaps the *Yorke's Peninsula Advertiser* detected a new, more sombre mood on the Peninsula. The prevalence of infant mortality, especially on the Moonta Mines settlement, had taken its toll during the preceding year (as it would in 1874), while financial difficulties at the mines had once again became apparent.[74] This time the directors failed to take the Association into their confidence, with the result that when summary notice at both Moonta and Wallaroo of immediate wage reductions was given on the morning of 2 April 1874, there was considerable dismay. Remembering the heady days of 1864, miners converged on Bald Hill, just as they had done a decade before, which became a regular meeting point over subsequent days as hundreds of men met to air grievances and to hear the latest news. At Moonta a 'ring meeting', said to be 1,200 strong, readily agreed to strike action. Reuben Gill, theatrical as ever, 'mounted the buggy amidst vociferous cheering'.[75] As one observer put it:

> And soon they met at Elder's Shaft;
> The 'Ring' was form'd, the glo'rous ring,
> Where Cousin Jack stands like a king;
> And freely to each thought gives vent,

As to his brain each thought is sent,
In eloquence, that's all his own,
He thunders forth in manly tone;
States his opinions quick and clear,
Nor will he yield to force or fear,
Nor will he back from anything
He states when standing in the 'Ring'.[76]

Taken aback by the speed and strength of the miners' response, the directors moved swiftly to prevent the impending strike from damaging the mines. Fearful that cessation of pumping would allow the underground workings to flood, with calamitous results, they persuaded the beam-engine drivers to stay at their posts, even as the other workers downed tools. However, recognising that stopping the pump engines was the key to winning early concessions from the directors, the Association decided that direct action was needed to remove the 'scabs' from their engine houses. In an extraordinary development, this task fell to the women; to the wives, daughters, and sisters of the striking miners. The deployment of women would disconcert the strike-breakers, it was calculated, who would be at a loss how to respond to their advances, when similar action by the men themselves would have provoked ugly confrontations and perhaps violence. The ready acquiescence by the women in what was to prove a challenging role, was a further insight into the strength of community solidarity and its cross-gender dimension. It was also an indication of the status of women in the community. The Bible Christians (in contrast to the other Methodist denominations) had always allowed women to occupy positions of responsibility in their church and encouraged them to preach, implying an equality in this world as well as before God. Moreover, the 'myth of Cousin Jack' (see pp. 55–56) had its female equivalent in a 'myth of Cousin Jenny', where emigrant Cornish women were seen as uniquely equipped to confront the rigours of the frontier, bringing domesticity and order where lesser women might fail.[77] Now Cousin Jenny was set to become a secret weapon in the armoury of the Association.

'There is a rumour', John Prisk (a Bible Christian) is reputed to have told a meeting of local women, 'that you're going to sweep all the nuisances out of their engine-houses'.[78] Suitably enthused, the women promised 'to do their best with their mallee poles' – brooms made from sticks of mallee scrub – and, as Prisk had urged, swept the blacklegs from the engine-house, bringing the pump engines to an abrupt halt.[79] As the *Yorke's Peninsula Advertiser* explained, the 'women went vigorously to work with their brooms, charging in all directions':

> The females attached to the sweeping regiment numbered about a hundred strong … carrying, many of them, their brooms, poles and pine branches. Never before, perhaps, was such an extraordinary spectacle witnessed as here presented itself. The space between Bower's and Ryan's [shafts, at Moonta], an area covering acres of ground, was alive with people of all classes, miners, mechanics, tradesmen and travellers, boys and girls, women (some with children in arms) excitedly talking, shouting, laughing and hurrying towards the engine house.[80]

At Wallaroo mine the women acted likewise. Despite pleas from Captain Higgs that they should take no action 'for which they would suffer to their dying day', they set to with the same enthusiasm of their sisters at Moonta. They marched first to the Matta Matta mine, at Kadina, whose engine-house was closest to the 'meeting ring' at Matta Flat where they had gathered, ejecting the drivers, firemen and boiler-tenders, and then proceeded to all the other pump engines in the locality. One engine-driver who resisted was threatened that he would have his 'brains knocked out' by the enraged women, and his hat was sent flying by a mallee broom. At another engine-house a woman was reportedly wrestled to the floor by a cornered driver, despite earlier assumptions that no physical resistance would be offered to the 'fair sex'.[81]

Be that as it may, the women were spectacularly successful, forcing the cessation of pumping throughout the mines. It was an event that entered local folklore, an important part of collective memory on the Peninsula, and a device that the women would not be frightened to threaten again in the future. As one versifier put it:

Now Cousin Jenny is no fool
She does not work by red-tape rule,
But by the glorious rule of right –
Not recognising wealth or might,
God bless her! She's a little Queen
For every one she swept out clean.[82]

When in 1898 W.G. Spence, representative of the Amalgamated Miners Association (which the Moonta Miners' Association had recently joined) visited the Peninsula from union headquarters in Creswick, Victoria, to resolve a looming industrial dispute he was surprised to find that Cousin Jenny's exploits were still fresh in memory, some fifteen years after the event. As Spence discovered, however, in the intervening period, as the episode was mythologised, so that memory had become blurred. For some, the events of 1874 and the earlier strike of 1864 had become conflated, a confusion in which women were reckoned to have also played a distinctive part in the action of 1864. Returning to his hotel at Kadina after a day of negotiations at the Moonta mine, Spence met the landlord, who explained that local women were preparing to play a dramatic role in any impending industrial unrest. He 'told us', Spence recorded, 'that a big Cornish-woman had just been there to borrow his stable broom because, she said, "it had plenty of wood in en" and she "might want to sweep Captain Hancock out"'.[83] Muddling the events of 1874 and 1864, the hotel landlord insisted that Captain Hancock's predecessors, the Warmingtons, had been swept out of town in like fashion by Cornish women. Fortunately, Spence was able to diffuse the situation in 1889, averting a strike, so the brooms were not needed. But in the same year at Broken Hill, where many miners and their families from Moonta and Wallaroo had moved recently, women were prominent in the strike that had erupted in the local silver-lead mines. According to the *Barrier Miner* in November 1889, a self-styled Women's Brigade, the 'daughters of the union', had marched 400-strong to the mines armed with brooms and mops, where they swept the mines clear of blacklegs, in some cases stripping them of their underwear.[84] So successful was the tactic, that it was deployed again by the women in a further disturbance at Broken Hill in 1892.[85]

Leader of the Womens Brigade

Cousin Jenny with her mallee mop – a tradition of women's action established
at Moonta and Wallaroo and later taken to Broken Hill.
[Reproduced from *Pictorial Australian*, November-Christmas 1889]

'See the Conquering Hero Comes'

But all that lay in the future. For the moment, at Moonta and Wallaroo,
the strikers appeared to have the upper hand, as water began to rise in the
mines, albeit slowly. John Prisk, chairman of the hastily convened strike
committee, thought it timely to approach the directors to seek a meeting. The
directors declined, however, despite the potential damage to their mine from
imminent inundation, denouncing the men (and women) for going beyond 'the
legitimate course of striking' by 'forcibly stopping the engines [and] expelling
the Mechanics from the Workshops'.[86] It was a calculated snub. Infuriated,
the miners and their supporters met again at Bald Hill in another 'monster
meeting', said to number 5,000 strong, a 'grand sight' according to one
observer. 'Cheer Boys, Cheer!' thundered the brass bands, as one local Primitive
Methodist minister urged the strikers onwards.[87] 'One and All, stick to it my

'Assaulting a blackleg.' It is unlikely that there was this degree of physical violence at Moonta and Wallaroo in 1874, although there may well have been later at Broken Hill, as depicted in this illustration.
[Reproduced from *Pictorial Australian*, November-Christmas 1889]

men', he exhorted, 'you have principle and right on your side and angels look down upon you men who are longing to do right'. Be fearless, he said: 'The God of nations will defend you, trust in God; nothing will harm you, you will come out on the right side presently. God bless you!'[88] As before, the moral force of Methodism was important in legitimising and validating the strike, as well as giving it firm direction.

At the same time, remembering the lessons of 1864, the strikers went on a public relations offensive. They enlisted the support of the local business community, as they had done before, arranging for the storekeepers to lobby the directors on their behalf, and, again as before, took their case to the colonial capital, Adelaide. Among those to publicly express their support for the miners' cause was the prominent politician James Penn Boucaut, who had spoken up for them in 1864, and his declaration of solidarity with the strikers was critical in convincing the directors that they were fast losing public sympathy – in the capital as well as on the Peninsula. Reluctantly, they announced that in

The Moonta and Wallaroo Delegates in the Great Strike of 1874.
From the top left to bottom right: Joseph Nottle, Thomas Rodda, John Visick,
G.N. Birks (representing tradesmen of Kadina); Martin Edwards, John Prisk
(Chairman of committee); L.L. Furner (Mayor of Moonta); F.W. Gurner
(Mayor of Kadina); John Uren, N. Thomas, John Anthony.
[Courtesy State Library of South Australia, B45105]

'deference to a generally expressed opinion that the Miners were taken by surprise by the absence of previous Notice of the intended reduction in wages, the Directors will pay the late rate for the next two months'. There was an important caveat, however, for they explained that, after that two-month period, 'unless the price of Ore should improve, a reduction will take place'.[89] But the latter was ignored by the triumphant miners, and the strikers' delegation – John Prisk, Thomas Rodda, John Anthony, J. Uren, John Visick and Martin Edwards, Cornishmen all – were welcomed home to the Peninsula as heroes. At Bald Hill they were met by cheering crowds, as the brass bands played 'See the Conquering Hero Comes', celebratory bonfires blazing from Moonta Mines to Port Wallaroo in their honour.

The men returned to work on 20 April 1874 but the situation remained fraught. Captain Hancock reported dissatisfaction at the rates offered to tributers and tutworkmen at the next survey day, and John Prisk delivered a letter in which the Moonta Miners' Association demanded that in future one month's notice should be given of any planned reduction in wages. Testily, the directors responded that they would only give a fortnight's notice. The bad-tempered exchange typified the tense atmosphere that now prevailed on the mines, the Moonta Miners' Association determined to stamp its authority as a vibrant trade union, capitalising on its recent success, the out-manoeuvred directors anxious to recover their prestige. Put simply, the mines of northern Yorke Peninsula were now about to embark upon a new era of industrial relations, as organised Labor began to plan for the future, looking ahead even to a time when it might elect its own representatives to the colonial Parliament.

Changing attitudes were reflected in the gradual erosion of deference. As in 1864, the early days of the 1874 strike were marked by careful protestations of loyalty. 'We have not anything against our Managers or Captains', it was explained at one strike meeting, 'but on the contrary we respect them'.[90] Yet the mood altered swiftly, as the men observed the intransigence of the directors and began to see their captains as merely mouthpieces for the two companies. Particular hostility was reserved for Captain Hancock and his second-in-command, Captain Malachi Deeble. The latter was the same

Malachi Deeble who had been a ringleader of the 1848 strike at the Burra, and there were no doubt those who saw him as a turncoat and a traitor. Captain Hancock, meanwhile, was reviled for not being a proper Cousin Jack, having been born just across the Devon border at Horrabridge. The 'manager of the Moonta is a Devon Dumpling!', the miners reminded themselves in times of tension.[91] There were other jibes. 'Sometime since in a parish in Devonshire', added another miner, 'there was an old cripple' – a thinly disguised allusion to Captain Hancock which was much appreciated by those in the 'ring', who responded with cheering and hoots of laughter. One observer was surprised to note 'the threatening attitude of the Cousin Jacks lately', and at a ring meeting at Moonta a miner named Tonkin – an enthusiastic striker who hoped now to perpetuate the atmosphere of confrontation – proposed that the 'men will not work again under Captains Hancock and Deeble'.[92] The motion was defeated (Hancock and Deeble were more formidable opponents than the Warmingtons, as most recognised) but there was sympathy for Tonkin's position.

Methodists criticised Hancock and Deeble for their 'un-Christian' attitude and actions (although the more charitable in their ranks thought this going too far), and John Prisk was alleged to have exclaimed on one occasion that the 'best news I have for you is that Captain Higgs [Captain of the Wallaroo mine] is spitting up blood'. He was also accused of having urged the miners to pray for the deaths of Hancock and Deeble. Prisk's hardening language typified the decline of deference – Hancock was now merely 'Warmington No. 2' in the miners' estimation. Later, in September 1879, Prisk could add that if 'Captain Hancock knew how much the men spoke against him ... he would be ashamed to look the men in the face'. Hancock, Deeble and the other captains would be long remembered, he predicted, for their 'dirty tricks and new-fangled schemes'.[93]

Along with the new attitudes was an anxiety to professionalise the Moonta Miners' Association and to achieve greater focus for its aims and objectives. Despite all the recent progress, there were still, as one frustrated unionist complained in 1878, 'a portion of [Association] members ... aiming to make the Union a mere co-operative store affair'. Likewise, it was alleged that 'Cornish men do not understand the true principles of Unionism and never will during the present generation'.[94] Such impatience was a reflection of the progress that the Association had achieved already, and it may be that newcomers recently arrived from Cornwall found it difficult at first to adjust to the recent advances. An amusing dialect tale was published in the *Yorke's Peninsula Advertiser* in January 1876, a supposed letter from 'A New Chum to his Friends in Cornwall, near England' in which a newcomer expresses his confusion. He thinks instinctively of 'the Union' as the poor-law union in Cornwall, the workhouses to which paupers were consigned, and grapples with the alternative meanings he has encountered on the Peninsula. As the new chum explained:

> Sum time ago when the waages was cut ere, the men ad a strike, and thare was sum fine doins wat I can heer; and ever sense they av got a Union. Now a Union out here esnt zaccly like a Union es some, for ome tes for peepel wen they do git ould an caant git a livin for to go in. You knaw ould Jan Rekerd an Maary Tommas and Maary Joans went in the Union wen they got ould an cud only crawl bout. But this ere Union out ere in Munta es a different kind or thing – tes a kind of club in wich men do pay sum munny evry week (wot for, I doant zaccly knaw).[95]

Elaborating further, the new chum added wryly that some reckoned such subscriptions were to 'keep a good place for a man they do call a Prisidunt – that es a little king'. And yet, he continued, 'sum do say tes for to git cheep things, for the shopkeepers es too deer, and sum do say tes for to ave munny to strike agen wen they do cut the waages, but I doant knaw myself'.[96]

But if some newcomers seemed naively ill-informed, there were others whose arrival had a radicalising effect on the Association and its aspirations. In February 1877, for example, one astonished new chum wrote to relations in Cornwall: 'no doubt you will be surprised', he said, 'when I tell you that the system of five weeks' pay which the miners not only in our mine but of almost every mine in Cornwall fought so valiantly to crush is in operation in this far-off land'.[97] For those who needed persuading of the merits of trade unionism, there remained the appeal to Cornish patriotism. John Anthony, one of the Association leaders, urged the men to remain solid 'in the grand old Cornish motto "One and All"'.[98] Another unionist put it this way:

Tell me not, ye horrid grumblers,

That unity's an idle dream;

If we firmly stand united,

We are stronger than we seem.

Let us all, then, be united,

Be our motto – 'ONE AND ALL',

Firm as rocks when bound together,

But divided, down we fall.[99]

'The establishment of an union on a firm basis'

In May 1874, in the immediate aftermath of the Great Strike, as it was now called, J. McArthur was appointed secretary of the Moonta Miners' Association. His clear opinion was that now was the time 'for the establishment of an union on a firm basis ... it was necessary that they would do so if they would resist tyranny and oppression'. Others had urged that 'immediate steps ... be taken to form a trades Union embracing the whole of the Peninsula having Moonta for its centre'. But the Wallaroo men, led by John Visick, wanted their own Association. This was grudgingly agreed to by the Moonta men, although John Visick was angered when it was insisted that the new Wallaroo organisation should adopt the rules and constitution of the Moonta Association. Workers from the two mines had co-operated harmoniously during the strike, as they had in 1864, and Reuben Gill warned the two groups not to fall out. If they squabbled, he said, the directors would divide and rule – they would 'analyse, tantalise, scandalise and pulverise them if they could'. These were wise words, as McArthur would soon find to his cost.[100]

For the moment, however, McArthur was keen to press ahead. Looking for political guidance, he turned to James Penn Boucaut, the Adelaide politician who had lent the Peninsula miners crucial public support in 1864 and 1874, and had been a friend of the erstwhile Political Association. Briefly Premier of South Australia in 1866–67, he was *de facto* leader of the Opposition in Parliament when approached by McArthur, and went on to become Premier again in 1875–76 and 1877–78. He was also a justice of the Supreme Court from 1878 to 1905, and was knighted in 1898. Boucaut had first entered Parliament in 1861, forming an early political alliance with another radical member, Philip Santo from Saltash in Cornwall (and formerly clerk at the Burra Burra mine), whom he considered a 'liberal nonconformist' in the Cornish tradition.[101] Santo was also a political ally of James Crabb Verco, originally from Callington in Cornwall, the two men enjoying parliamentary reputations in the 1860s as 'great lovers of political and religious freedom'.[102] In the fluidity of the South Australian Parliament, before the emergence of clear party politics, Boucaut was a natural partner in such a grouping. As he explained, he had been encouraged to enter politics 'by friends who knew my democratic sympathies', and 'I have always stood by my counties [sic] motto "One and All" and contemn and despise mere money shoddy aristocracy'.[103]

Responding to McArthur's approach, Boucaut was at pains to impress upon him that 'I wish you to believe that I do not profess liberal sentiments in order to gain power. I should have more power if I were to hold contrary sentiments'. His political enemies had branded him a 'Red Republican'. Boucaut countered that 'I have been accused of setting class against. That is absurd'. As he explained:

> Class was against class long before I came into the world. Such an accusation is a very common thunderbolt launched by capital. I have never heard a man accused of setting class against class who advocated the cause of capital. This is because capital is true to itself while labour is too often true neither to itself not to its friends who become marks for sneering until few men have courage left to face it.[104]

Yet times were changing, he insisted. 'A great struggle between capital and labour is commencing all over the world', he believed: 'Labour was once enslaved. It now demands liberation, and that labour shall no longer be considered so much animal clay.' His vision for the future was entirely social democratic: 'There is no reason why the man whose industry makes the article should not look forward to the time when he will be on a perfect equality with in every respect with the man whose capital aids him in doing it.'[105]

In offering advice to McArthur, Boucaut emphasised that 'I differ from those who think that the Union should be dissociated from politics'. But he criticised the Moonta Miners' Association because it exercised its power 'in fits and starts which is bad both for the country and yourselves'. Moreover, the Association 'had no settled principles and no cohesion'. He urged the Cornishmen not to be divided by sectarian prejudice: 'if a Wesleyan vote against a Bible Christian because he is of a rival Church both suffer'. Importantly, he also advised the Moonta unionists to forge links with like-minded groups in Adelaide and elsewhere in the colony, recognising that organised Labor needed to co-ordinate its efforts if it was to realise its potential to drive political and social reform. His main recommendations were that the Association should concentrate on political education for its members, so that in argument and debate they could compete on equal terms with their capitalist opponents, and on the achievement of payment for parliamentary members. As soon as Members of Parliament received a salary, rather than serving without financial reward as they did at present, it would be possible for Labor candidates without private means to stand for election. As Boucaut concluded: 'everything comes back to payment of members and education. These are your two great necessities'.[106]

This was excellent advice. But at the same moment that McArthur sought to professionalise the Association, so the directors moved to stifle the emerging trade union structure on the Peninsula before it could entrench itself yet more fully in community life. They were encouraged by press reports critical of the miners, some of which had adopted a distinctly anti-Cornish tone. There was reference to 'Cousin Jack's childishness' and 'despised Cousin Jack', and assertions that 'the councils of Cousin Jack are hasty and sudden'.[107] As Boucaut had predicted, there were attempts to provoke inter-denominational rivalry. Wesleyans were sometimes seen as belonging to 'the bosses' chapel' – Hancock himself was a leading Wesleyan local preacher at Moonta Mines – and this was a distinction that was firmly but unobtrusively encouraged, not least because it was a vehicle for restoring deference and obedience. An exasperated McArthur warned his membership against religion getting 'mixed up with copper and wages'.[108] Extraordinarily, given earlier efforts to develop Moonta and Wallaroo as model Cornish copper mines, and to recruit almost exclusively from the ranks of Cornish miners, the directors thought briefly to employ workers of other than 'Cornish nationality' (as they described it), and in early 1875 decided to try to find Scottish and Irish miners in a bid to undermine the Association's ethnic exclusivity.[109]

The directors also decided that they would reduce the number of tribute pitches and tutwork bargains offered at survey days, a means of shedding 'undesirable' characters as well as to effect savings. In June 1874, in the immediate aftermath of the strike, Hancock had advised the directors that he could afford to shed 200 'or more' men at Moonta, 'without damaging the mine to a parlous extent', although he soon had second thoughts, fearing what the Association's reaction might be to such drastic action. Yet the directors were determined to ease out the core of Association activists, thought to number about fifty, and were soon complaining to Hancock that 'the number thrown out of employment is only 15 as yet'. Accordingly, at next survey day some fifty or sixty miners were left without contracts and were effectively dismissed. Hancock reported nervously that 'great excitement and anxiety prevailed at the mine', with John Prisk asserting (no doubt correctly) that the discharges were done to create dissension in the Association's ranks. At the Wallaroo mine, where there were also cutbacks, the directors disingenuously rejected similar accusations put forward by the miners' representatives, David Edyvean and Stephen Spargo: 'they most distinctly repudiate the allegation that they have been in any way instigated by motives or feelings of retaliation'.[110] At both Moonta and Wallaroo the captains bore the brunt of the miners' ire: years later Stanley R. Whitford, a prominent Labor politician brought up at Moonta, could still write of 'the iron heel the Hancocks [Captain Hancock and his son, H. Lipson Hancock] had for Unionists'.[111] As a precaution, the directors had notices posted at the mines, pointing out that the sackings were not Captain Hancock's fault but were a consequence of the current economic climate.

As the tension continued, Hancock decided that 'certain leaders of the Union will never settle down contentedly to work as long as they remain at the Mine'. Accordingly, the directors acknowledged the 'advisability of getting rid of rowdy characters', emphasising that they would 'not retain in their service men who attempt to interfere with the Management of the Mine'. Thus Messrs Tonkin (who had expressed particular hostility to Hancock and Deeble), Sleep and the appropriately named Strike were immediately dismissed. Taken together, the recent round of dismissals had shaken the Association, as the directors had intended, and soon Hancock could report with satisfaction 'that the better class of Men were withdrawing from the Union'.[112] Tragically, one of these was J. McArthur, the far-sighted strategist who had sought Boucaut's advice. Among those recently discharged from the Moonta mine, McArthur had written a pitiful letter to the directors 'requesting to be reinstated in the Company's employ as a Miner'. He admitted that he 'had made a grave mistake in joining the Union and therefore determined to shake free of it'.[113] The directors were delighted to re-employ McArthur as an example to the rest of the men. Reuben Gill denounced him as a Judas and a traitor but soon he too was forced out.[114] He found employment for a time at the nearby Hamley mine, an independent working in the vicinity, and ended his working days in Adelaide – first as a mechanic, and then trying to sell insurance.

These were grievous set-backs for the embryonic trade union, and there were the inevitable recriminations. John Visick, leader of the Wallaroo miners, fell out with John Prisk, blaming his Moonta-centric outlook for the failure to establish the proposed sister Association at Wallaroo: 'though his mismanagement the Kadina [sic] Union is defunct'.[115] Yet the Peninsula's trade unionists was determined to make progress, aiming to achieve a 'closed shop' – full unionisation of the workforce – and, in the manner advocated by Boucaut, they began to formulate a clear political strategy. As Boucaut had urged, they campaigned for free and compulsory education for all and demanded payment of parliamentary members. The Association, betraying its Methodist leanings, also called for a prohibitory liquor law, and sought an end to immigration, which was seen as driving down wages, despite the impact this policy might have on kith and kin in Cornwall. As John Prisk explained later in September 1879, men should 'be writing to their friends in Cornwall ... to give them a truthful account of how things are here ... it would keep others from coming out to swell the numbers of unemployed'.[116]

'Labor is bought below a nominal figure'

As the miners adopted increasingly collectivist attitudes toward industrial and political questions, so they began to revise their attitude towards the tribute and tutwork system of employment. Earlier, as we have seen, the miners at Moonta and Wallaroo had fought to secure the effective establishment of tribute and tutwork and, following the demise of the Warmingtons, saw the system as the foundation of their working relationship with the management. Here the proudly 'independent' tributer or tutworkman could claim entrepreneurial status alongside the directors and shareholders, an equal in the process of wealth creation. However, as the mines grew ever larger, so the miners considered that this status had been gradually eroded, the directors increasingly inclined to treat them as mere labourers, despite their jealously guarded reputation as skilled hard-rock men. Moreover, they argued, tribute and tutwork had shifted from being the means by which the enterprising miner might maximise his income, to a mechanism through which the directors conspired to keep earnings artificially low. The foundation of the Moonta Miners' Association had been tacit recognition of this situation, and thereafter, in a remarkable reversal of their earlier opinion, the miners began to press for the abolition – or at least radical restructuring – of tribute and tutwork contracting.

After the Great Strike in 1874, criticisms of tribute and tutwork had become more frequent, including the 'five week month' adhered to by the directors in determining pay periods (also a bone of contention in the early 1870s in Cornwall itself). The inherent disadvantages of the system were as apparent as they were in Cornwall. For example, while it was true that a tributer working an apparently indifferent piece of ground on a favourable contract might suddenly encounter a 'sturt' – an extremely valuable ore deposit – and thus earn a significant amount during that particular 'take', it was equally likely that apparently rich ground would fail unexpectedly, leaving the disappointed miner considerably out of pocket. In such circumstances, miners might resort to desperate measures to make good their losses. In 1865, for example, the Moonta directors dismissed two tributers for stealing ore, and a fortnight later another pare was sacked for the same offence. Over the years, similar patterns were repeated, as various malpractices came to light. In 1889, for example, two tutworkmen (Simmons and Trebilcock) were suspended for six months for failing to adequately timber their workings. Responsible for purchasing their own timbers, the tutworkmen had cut corners in a (dangerous) attempt to save money.[117]

In 1879 the Association stepped up its criticism of tribute and tutwork contracting, and in response the Moonta and Wallaroo companies replaced the time-honoured method of 'open bidding' – where groups (pares) of miners competed publicly for tribute pitches or tutwork bargains – with 'private tendering'. This new procedure required miners to tender for their preferred pitches or bargains by submitting their offers on pieces of paper. Although this reduced the confrontational competitiveness sometimes apparent at open bidding, as rival pares fought to secure a particular contract, it did not adequately address the trade unionists' concerns. As one frustrated observer put it in April 1880:

> Cornishmen are generally of an envious disposition, the characteristic principle being a dislike to see a neighbour advance a step ahead, and so with tendering. I have heard a remark passed when a miner has heard another is tendering for the same job. 'Ef 'ee d'get un 'll have tew tender some law', hence they all tender low and labor is brought below a nominal figure.[118]

That this was so was graphically illustrated in 1878, when tenders were invited for a tutwork bargain to sink four fathoms of a shaft at the East Moonta mine:

> T. Williams £26 per fathom (accepted); S. Stephens, £28; J. Angove, £28 5s; J. Rowe, £28 2s; R. Hancock, £29; W. Pengelly & Co., £34; J. Bray, £37; H. Stephens, £38; J. Murrin and S. Samson, £44 15s; Samuel Richards, £90 for the first two fathoms and £100 for the next two fathoms.[119]

In other words, while Richards' pare believed the job could only be done for £190, the contract went to the Williams team, which had tendered £104.

In the same year, one 'old miner, what do belong to Cornwall' wrote to a local newspaper to complain that tribute and tutwork were 'good for the

Cornish miners at the Moonta mine, c.1880s. [Author's collection]

company, but not so good for the workmen'. As another put it: 'The fact is that we miners cut each other, hence we bring down the price of labor.' As he explained, 'it is to be feared that our price is often far below the captain's price [the guide price for a particular pitch or bargain, set by the relevant underground captain], which is cutting wages with a vengeance'.[120] There was a brief strike over the matter in 1884, as such agitation continued, and in 1886 there was more serious unrest following the abolition of 'subsist' – an advance on earnings – for long-term contracts. The latter had been introduced in 1877, and could span several months, the miners considering it essential to draw subsist during this period if they were to feed their families. Now, however, subsist was to be replaced by a 'percentage retained' policy. Instead of applying for subsist when their funds ran low, the miners were now paid a weekly rate, the amount being calculated as a weekly average of the estimated total earnings over the contract period. However, a percentage of this weekly rate was retained by the companies in case the miners did not realise their estimated income, the retained money being paid out on the expiry of the contract. In principle, it was a good idea. But the percentage retained was manipulated by the companies, a device to reduce the amount paid to the miners on a weekly basis. By March 1888 the percentage retained had risen to 25%, which the Association considered unacceptably high. In the face of apparent managerial indifference, the miners struck. Hastily, the directors agreed to reduce the percentage retained to 12.5%. But the men remained on strike until Captain Hancock also awarded a general increase in the weekly rate. Later it was decided, again in deference to union pressure, that a percentage would only be retained if average weekly earnings were above £2 2s 0d per week.[121]

An intriguing feature of the March 1888 strike, as a journalist on the Adelaide *Advertiser* observed, was the continuing prominence of local women in the deliberations. 'It is astounding the amount of interest evinced by the female population in the matter', he reported: 'Members of the fair sex turn out at all meetings and discuss the question in a most animated manner. Several informed me today that rather than their husbands should give way they would start taking in washing themselves.'[122] Variations in the percentage retained would directly affect a family's weekly budget, often managed by women, ensuring the 'female population's' close attention to developments. But the willingness to share the burdens of strike action, and to devise economic strategies (such as taking in laundry) to cope with loss of income, was striking evidence of continuing cross-gender and community solidarity.

'We have born the evils too long'

Subsequently, attitudes towards tribute and tutwork contracting hardened further, and in February 1889 a memorial was submitted to the Moonta company demanding the abolition of the system, the miners insisting that 'we have borne the evils too long for the comfort of our homes and our own peace of mind'.[123] When this was rejected out of hand, a more moderate proposal was submitted by Messrs Peters, Pascoe and Rowe, 'requesting the Board's assent to a list of rules dealing with underground contracts'.[124] Again the directors were unmoved, their intransigence setting the scene for several years of hostility and unrest. By now the Peninsula miners were routinely in contact with miners' trade unions across Australia, and in 1889 the strategic decision was taken for the Moonta Miners' Association to merge with the Amalgamated Miners Association of Australasia (the AMA). Formed in 1884, when the Amalgamated Miners Association of Victoria had joined with other unions, notably the New South Wales coalminers, the AMA was now recognised as the peak body for trade unionism in the mining industry. The Moonta Association was reformed as a branch of the AMA, and sister branches were inaugurated at Port Wallaroo (for the smelting works) and at Kadina (for the Wallaroo mine). By May of 1889 most of those employed in the northern Yorke Peninsula copper-mining industry had joined one of the three branches. Emboldened by their membership of the mighty AMA, the Peninsula miners were now committed to further collectivist action. As W.G. Spence, one of the original architects of the AMA, recalled in his book *Australia's Awakening*:

> The Cornish miner is generally a man who can do his share of grumbling, and reckons he knows how to run a mine better than the manager, so when Unionism caught on [on Yorke Peninsula] they realised that many injustices might have been remedied years ago had they been organised and pulled together, instead of merely growling as individuals.[125]

Indeed, the men seemed to be spoiling for a fight. The Moonta directors having rejected proposed changes to underground contracting, and both the Moonta and Wallaroo companies having announced a general lowering of wage rates in response to falls in the international price of copper, the Peninsula AMA branches felt they had little choice but to threaten industrial action. The smouldering situation caught public attention across Australia (reports appeared in the Melbourne *Argus*, for example), and on 13 May 1889 the men stopped work.[126] However, before formally declaring a strike the miners sought the permission of AMA headquarters at Creswick, in Victoria, which at once despatched an AMA delegation – including W.G. Spence, the union secretary – to Yorke Peninsula to investigate the situation.

As he had anticipated, Spence found the influence of the trade unionists on northern Yorke Peninsula curiously uneven. Despite the new air of militancy, and the undeniable progress made by the erstwhile Moonta Miners' Association, there was much evidence of outdated practice. 'In the detail of the Moonta trouble', he reported, there were 'several instances ... of what will be found in all industries where men are not [properly] organised'.[127] For example:

> We found in charge of pattern-making in the foundry a first-class tradesman working for 7s. per day. He was a very superior tradesman, with a considerable genius for invention. He was of the type who take a keen interest in their work for work's sake, and but little in what they receive for it. Quiet and unassuming, and content with a living wage, his only ambition was to excel in the quality of his workmanship.[128]

Likewise, Spence noted, he 'found grown-up men working from 2s. 6d. to 4s. 6d. per day, and in more than one case they were married. Starting as boys, it was apparently forgotten by all concerned that they had grown older as time went on'. As he put it: 'As their producing power increased, so their share of wealth decreased.'[129] This was partly the fault of the trade unionists, he inferred, whose impact had lacked consistency. But he also felt that the patriarchal managerial regime of Captain Hancock had begun to atrophy and that Hancock's grip on the detail had begun to fade. Spence thought Hancock 'a rather nervous, elderly gentleman' but concluded that he was reasonable and open to suggestions. He asked 'our advice ... [and] honestly carried out our recommendations', Spence acknowledged, although the directors rejected a suggestion that a 'sliding scale' of wages – reflecting the price of copper – should replace tribute and tutwork contracting.[130] But Spence and the other AMA delegates were allowed to inspect the companies' accounts, and reluctantly came to the conclusion that the financial position was more parlous than the trade unionists had imagined, and that in the current economic climate neither a general increase in wages nor radical restructuring of the system of employment was feasible.[131] Spence had the unenviable task of breaking the news to the miners – and to the women, who were ready with their brooms, as Spence had already discovered in his discussion with the Kadina innkeeper. As he later explained:

The delivery of our report and ultimatum to the miners was a scene never to be forgotten. Excitement ran high. The brooms were ready, and their plucky owners equally so. No sooner had the signal bell rung for knock-off work at 5pm than the men assembled around the platform of the tramway, from which we were to speak. All hands came just as they were. The women stood generally in the outer circle of the crowd. They left the work of decision to the men, but were prepared to loyally carry it out, whatever it might be, even if it meant going hungry in order to secure justice.[132]

However, to Spence's evident relief, 'the meeting fully accepted our recommendation [not to strike] ... and later [the miners] were specially glad that no strike had eventuated, and that there had been no need for that broom with "plenty of wood in 'en"'.[133] But, as Oswald Pryor put it in his local history *Australia's Little Cornwall*, nothing 'could convince the Primitive Methodist radicals that the Moonta mine was now working at a loss'. Local trade unionists such as 'Uncle Joe' Goldsworthy, John Prisk (hero of 1874), and Jimmy Peters (Moonta Branch secretary), 'almost to a man Methodist local preachers', continued to agitate for industrial action.[134] During July and August of 1889 they demanded further concessions from the companies, and in the December there was a brief but successful strike by moulders and fitters demanding a 'closed shop'. In February 1890, the union forced the directors to honour the 'percentage retained' agreement. In the March, 500 men at the Wallaroo struck – without official sanction from AMA headquarters – and stayed out until winning yet further concessions from the newly amalgamated Wallaroo and Moonta company. Yet the directors still refused to address the miners' fundamental grievance, the system of employment itself. There were further negotiations in July and August 1891 but little progress was made. Finally, in the September, the Moonta Branch of the AMA declared a strike.[135]

The Primitive Methodist minister told the miners he could see victory in their eyes but the reality was rather different. As much as £8,507 was sent to the Peninsula by sympathetic miners at Broken Hill, Bendigo and Charters Towers, as well as from fellow trade unionists in Adelaide. But many families went hungry, and some miners ran up credit at local shops that they could never hope to repay. Moreover, the AMA struggled to maintain its own strike payments, and after eighteen gruelling weeks the strike was broken by desperate men going to the mine office to plead for work. The AMA conceded defeat, and in return the company promised it what it termed 'substantial modifications' to the employment system.[136] Those unfortunate men who had caused the strike to collapse were ostracised by the local community and vilified as '92ers' – the strike ended in February 1892 – a pejorative label they carried and were known by wherever they went, even on the Western Australian goldfields where many Peninsula miners had gone to find work in the 1890s.[137] However, despite the defeat, agitation against tribute and tutwork continued. Partly in response to this continuing unrest, numerous adjustments were made to the method of letting contracts. This culminated in 1903, when the time-honoured practice of 'captain's prices' was replaced by a 'sliding scale' – based on fluctuations in the price of copper – in which the contractor participated directly in the company's profits.[138] Ironically, this was exactly what W.G. Spence and the AMA delegates had recommended back in 1889.

By the turn of the twentieth century, industrial relations in the copper-mining industry of northern Yorke Peninsula had changed almost beyond recognition since the heady days of 1864. The quaint deferential attitude of the men (and women) had diminished (although it had not yet disappeared entirely), and the faltering, fledgling trade union structure of the early days had been transformed by its incorporation into the modernising and powerful Amalgamated Miners Association. Most of all, attitudes to tribute and tutwork had changed utterly, although the new 'sliding scale' continued to offer individual contractors a certain independence of action and a place in the entrepreneurial function. Yet amidst the change there were important continuities. Methodism still guided the moral sensibilities of the mineworkers and, as in the early days, inspirational Methodist local preachers remained the backbone of the miners' leadership, their authority undiminished. Those qualities that Peter Bell detected in the 1864 strike – the 'strength of union and community solidarity' and the pervading influence of 'Cornish and Wesleyan distinctiveness' – remained vitally important at the turn of the century, and had underpinned the experience of trade unionism as it had developed on the Peninsula in the preceding four decades. As one local unionist put it in March 1895, echoing the sentiments of those early days: 'Cornishmen, my advice to you is to be true to each other; and let your motto be "One and All" ... let the spirit of your fathers animate you on to freedom and justice.'[139]

PART THREE

RISE AND FALL

RISE AND FALL

Chapter Five

Towards Parliamentary Representation

Richard Cox, writing in 1979, thought that early trade unionism in South Australia in the 1870s and 1880s was confined to a small number of craft associations in the capital, Adelaide. In the rest of the colony, he argued, 'the irregularity of employment precluded the establishment of country union branches'.[1] But, as we know, this is to ignore the rise of trade unionism in the copper-mining industry of northern Yorke Peninsula, not least the foundation of the Moonta Miners' and Mechanics' Association in 1872 and its eventual metamorphosis into three local branches of the powerful Amalgamated Miners Association of Australasia, which for a time were important enough to constitute a 'colonial district' of the AMA in their own right.[2] Cox's failure to note the emergence of this important centre of trade unionism reflects, perhaps, the Adelaide-centric perspectives of many historians, where, as R.J. Holton observed, 'South Australia is effectively likened to a city-state'. The concentration of institutions – political, cultural, social, economic, educational – within the central confines of a relatively small capital has inevitably drawn the historian's gaze, sometimes to the exclusion of other parts of the State. As Holton put it: 'Such public spaces are animated by a powerful *geist*, distinguishing Adelaide as the centre-point of South Australia from other Australian city-states.'[3] Viewed in this partial way, there is sometimes a tendency to overlook the vast hinterland beyond. For example, South Australia was seen by many to have come late to industrialisation, considered a product of the twentieth-century Playford years, conveniently overlooking the State's copper-mining and smelting industry which was for a time the largest of its type in Australia.

Alongside this metropolitan focus, was the fact that the copper industry had collapsed dramatically in the aftermath of the Great War, and had then disappeared quickly from view. This relative invisibility increased with the passage of the years, so that the earlier significance of the industry could easily be forgotten. Geoffrey Blainey might devote generous space in his *The Rush That Never Ended: A History of Australian Mining*, first published in 1963, to South Australian copper but Labor historians were not always as insightful.[4] Brian Dickey, for example, writing in 1975, described 'the declining copper mines of Moonta, Wallaroo, and Burra' in the 1890s.[5] Burra had been abandoned long since (it was closed in 1877) but Moonta and Wallaroo were by no means in long-term decline in the 1890s. Indeed, they were shortly to enjoy a renewed era of prosperity, with considerable modernisation and investment, followed by soaring demand for copper during the Great War years. Perhaps too, for some historians, there was an inability to take Moonta and Wallaroo seriously, an unfortunate side effect, maybe, of the folksy, quaint portrayal of 'Australia's Little Cornwall' in Oswald Pryor's eponymous book, articles and Cousin Jack cartoons.[6] As Holton admitted, it was 'all too easy to make sport' of such 'celebratory local histories'.[7]

However, as John Hirst has hinted, another possible reason for Adelaide-centric writers to overlook the significance of the Yorke Peninsula copper industry was the simple fact that the Amalgamated Miners Association and its predecessor on the Peninsula were far more intimately linked with mining communities elsewhere in Australia, rather than with the trade unions and Labor movement in Adelaide itself.[8] The Peninsula miners looked to AMA headquarters in Creswick (Victoria), to Broken Hill, where many of their kith and kin had settled, and in the 1890s to Boulder and Kalgoorlie on the Western Australian goldfields. Only rarely, despite James Penn Boucaut's advice to the fledgling Moonta Miners' Association (see p. 104–106), did they look south to claim common cause with fellow trade unionists in Adelaide. In this way, two narratives of the Labor movement in South Australia have emerged, one which

"Capital! What IS Capital?"
"If you was to ask we to come 'n' 'ave a drink, lad, that would
be capital."

Scepticism of Marxist rhetoric, caught by Oswald Pryor in his
Cornish Pasty: A Selection of Cartoons, Adelaide, 1976.
[Courtesy National Trust of South Australia, Moonta Branch]

locates 'its origins in the trade union movement of Adelaide in the 1880s',[9] and
one (such as this) which attempts to cast the net wider and earlier, capturing
the mining industry and its important ethno-occupational and ethno-religious
characteristics, incorporating these into the broader synthesis presented here.

Broken Hill and Yorke Peninsula

An important illustration of the Peninsula trade unionists' cultivation of links
with other mining districts, was the close symbiotic relationship developed
between the three Peninsula towns and Broken Hill in the 1880s and beyond.
As early as 1867, miners from Moonta and Wallaroo had been drawn to the

Barrier Ranges by reports of gold. But it was the more substantial discovery of silver-lead at Silverton and nearby Umberumberka that precipitated the first significant movement, such as when in November 1885 Captain Luke sent down to Moonta for twenty miners and a blacksmith, 'and had no difficulty in securing the number'.[10] The discovery of Broken Hill itself in 1884 opened the way for a yet more substantial migration. Situated just across the border in New South Wales, Broken Hill was more akin to South Australia than the colony of which it was formally a part. As one observer noted in 1888, Broken Hill belongs 'geographically to New South Wales, but commercially to South Australia', while the 'great majority of the people are South Australians, with families and friends in South Australia'.[11] It was an opinion echoed by the Broken Hill correspondent in the Moonta *People's Weekly*, who in December 1893 was keen to explain that 'a very large proportion of our [Broken Hill] population have connections in Moonta, Kadina, and Wallaroo'.[12] Later in the month, the same newspaper reported that during the Christmas break 'there is no other town in Australia from which there is a greater exodus than at Broken Hill, and on this occasion there is quite the usual number leaving for the well-remembered sights of Kadina, Moonta, and Wallaroo'.[13] Two years later H. Lipson Hancock, general manager of the Wallaroo and Moonta Mining and Smelting Company, expressed anxiety at the potential shortage of experienced miners on the Peninsula as a result of 'men . . . leaving the district for Broken Hill'.[14]

As Brian Kennedy noted in his social history of Broken Hill, many of these migrant miners were also Methodists, 'in accord with Cornish and South Australian traditions'.[15] In 1890 the Blende Street Primitive Methodist Church was composed almost entirely of miners and smelters and their families, with Jacob Burrows from Moonta reckoned to be 'an effective preacher to the Cornish miners'.[16] As on the Peninsula, Methodist local preachers at Broken Hill emerged as trade union leaders and advocates, purveyors of the 'moderate, liberal traditions of trade unionism from South Australia'.[17] For example, explains Kennedy, there was William Rowe from Moonta, 'a Wesleyan Cornish miner who was opposed to working on the Sabbath'.[18] In March 1890 Rowe became district president and Broken Hill vice-president of the

Amalgamated Miners Association, and he was one of the first trade unionists to urge Labor representation for the Barrier region in the New South Wales Parliament. Likewise, there was Josiah Thomas, 'another Cornish miner', who had toiled in the Umberumberka, Purnamoota and Broken Hill South mines before becoming a member of the local AMA executive and Broken Hill branch president in 1892.[19] He too was a Wesleyan local preacher – a teetotaller and a non-smoker.

Especially significant was John Henry Cann. 'Almost a Cornishman', as Kennedy described him, Cann was born in 1860 at Horrabridge (also the birthplace of Moonta's Captain Hancock), a village in the mining district of west Devon, close to the Cornish border.[20] As a youth he left to work in the coal mines of Northumberland, and from there emigrated to New South Wales in 1887 where he became a coal miner at Kembla. In the following year he moved to Broken Hill, and in September 1889 became a local preacher at the Blende Street Primitive Methodist Church. A self-avowed Christian Socialist, advocating 'evolution and not revolution', Cann believed in the power of moral and religious persuasion rather than coercion, a conviction that 'social evils stemmed from human nature rather than some uniquely vicious system of oppression'.[21] From this perspective, even the most intransigent capitalists could be persuaded to see the error of their ways, while whole communities could be moved to pity – and thus reform – by the exposure of poverty, injustice and inequality in their midst. Cann was elected president of the Broken Hill branch of the AMA in 1890, and in January 1891 became Labor member for the Sturt constituency in the New South Wales Parliament. He went on to enjoy several ministerial appointments and for a time was Speaker. However, like many Methodists, he became estranged from the Labor Party over the conscription controversy during the Great War, and was eventually expelled from the party.

John Henry Cann made explicit the intimate connection between his religious and political beliefs (his Sunday sermons were on subjects such as 'Poverty: Its Causes and Cure').[22] So too did the *Barrier Truth*, founded in Broken Hill in January 1898 with financial support from the AMA. The newspaper aimed to promote socialism as 'the practical application of the principles laid down by Christ', and championed trade unionism as 'continuous mission work', the vocation of 'the moralist' and the 'altruist'.[23] Its Christmas story 'Union by Love', published in 1901, was a Christian Socialist allegory whose sentimentality no doubt appealed to its local readership. In the story 'a young Scotchman, Allan Campbell' arrives in Broken Hill and soon falls in love with Marian Tregellas, 'a Cornish Barrier Lassie', whose father is a committed Methodist local preacher and trade union activist. In church, Marian's father takes as his text John 12:21, telling his congregation that 'Jesus Christ was the greatest of Socialists, and His Sermon on the Mount teaches Socialism in its brightest and noblest character'. Allan and Marian's courtship blossoms but eventually Allan leaves for the Western Australian goldfields in search of work, taking along his chum, 'a jovial young Cornishman, Charles Pentreath'. However, it transpires that Charles is infatuated with Marian, and when Allan falls desperately ill with typhoid, Charles leaves him to die in the bush. Having struck it rich on the goldfields, Charles then returns to Broken Hill a wealthy man, and courts the heartbroken Marian, who in the meantime has also lost her father. Marian agrees to marry Charles Pentreath but at the critical moment a miraculously recovered Allan Campbell appears in the Wesleyan church, stopping the wedding and claiming his true love. The final act is when the duplicitous Charles himself contracts typhoid, and promptly expires, a lesson to us all.[24]

If the tale of Allan Campbell and Marian Tregellas captured the hearts of Broken Hill's Christian Socialists, it was exactly the type of sentimentalism calculated to frustrate and infuriate Tom Mann, the famous English socialist and leader of the 1889 London dock strike who was engaged by the AMA in 1907 to help better organise the workers at Broken Hill and in the associated Port Pirie smelting plant in South Australia. Having spoken in Adelaide on 'Religion and Socialism', Mann wished out-loud that something could be done 'to relieve the Holy City of some of its feeble Religio-Liberalo-Laboro attitude which would fail to achieve a revolution in a thousand years and most of whom would rather go to a prayer meeting than a socialist demonstration'.[25] Likewise, in opening the new Trades Hall at Broken Hill in March 1908, his colleague Ben Tillett detected 'a tendency towards conservatism' in the local Labor movement, a reflection of its religious sensibilities, and predicted that 'a reaction was bound to come, a reaction in favour of wider reform and more vigorous movement'.[26] In fact, the reaction came a decade later in the conscription crisis of the Great War when Broken Hill became a hotbed of anti-war and anti-conscription agitation. The Industrial Workers of the World (the 'Wobblies') became a major presence at Broken Hill, and IWW members or supporters, including figures who would rise to national notoriety, such as Percival Brookfield and 'Mick' Considine, were soon in open confrontation with the Labor old guard. Men like John Henry Cann and Josiah Thomas were marginalised and estranged from the movement they had so recently led, as the militants took control. As Brian Kennedy observed, Broken Hill became 'a community divided against itself', and Methodism, once a vital force on the Barrier, retreated into 'a narrower world of piety and patriotism', thus removing a 'powerful moderating influence' on the local Labor movement and propelling it to the left after 1916.[27]

'A deliberately organised conspiracy against Labor'

Richard Cox, in attempting to explain the origins of social democracy in nineteenth-century South Australia, considered that the moderate, reformist, evolutionary 'socialism' which emerged in the colony was a result of the politically cautious craft associations, with their narrow and self-interested objectives. These contrasted strongly with the aims of the new industrial trade unions elsewhere in Australia, he argued, so much so that in 'comparison with the eastern States, the search for early South Australian working class interest in socialism is almost fruitless'.[28] If Cox had cared to lift his gaze to South Australia's copper-mining industry, his opinion might have shifted. It would have shown too that the moderate evolutionary socialism that came to characterise South Australia was a function – as Tom Mann understood – not just of cautious craft association but of the pervasive influence of Methodism and religious Nonconformity in the Labor movement. Based on Christian rather than revolutionary principles, it believed, like John Henry Cann, in the fundamental goodness of human nature and the ability of organised Labor to create 'a superior moral society'.[29]

At a practical level, the influence of northern Yorke Peninsula on Broken Hill trade unionism was also apparent. As the *Yorke's Peninsula Advertiser* reported in May 1887, a 'number of old Moonta miners and others are having difficulty with the management of the Broken Hill Company'. As the paper explained, the 'difficulty there as here [the Peninsula] appears to be about the contract system, which is not popular with the men up there [Broken Hill] any more than in Moonta Mines'.[30] To this familiar difficulty was added that of plumbism, or 'getting leaded', a deeply unpleasant feature of underground work in silver-lead mines such as those at Broken Hill. As the *Burra Record* noted in March 1892: 'Big stalwart men who left the Burra and Moonta Mines just a year or two ago to toil in the silver mines of the Barrier, are now in many instances past recovery, and the rest of their days apparently must be spent in helpless misery.'[31] Together, hostility towards the contract system and concern over the effects of plumbism, became the twin pre-occupations of the Amalgamated Miners Association at Broken Hill.

In 1889 there was talk of the Broken Hill branch of the AMA combining with those on the Peninsula to form one giant 'colonial district', and in November that year Broken Hill trade unionists wrote in public support of industrial action then being taken by colleagues at Moonta and Wallaroo.[32] Jimmy Peters, secretary of the Moonta branch, explained this intimacy by noting that AMA 'members were continually coming and going between the two towns [Moonta and Broken Hill]'.[33] This solidarity was further evidenced in the volatile events of 1891 and 1892. When the miners at Moonta and Wallaroo were out on strike during that fateful summer, AMA brethren at Broken Hill sent funds to support them. Likewise, when the first 'Big Strike' erupted at Broken Hill in 1892, South Australian unionists were swift to offer their assistance to the striking silver-lead miners.[34]

Precipitated by the cynical dismissal from the mines of William Rowe, Josiah Thomas and other AMA leaders when they were absent from Broken Hill on union business in early 1892, the Big Strike was a reaction against what appeared to be a determined attempt to break the power of the union movement. The Moonta *People's Weekly*, observing the events at Broken Hill, detected 'a deliberately organised conspiracy against Labor, and first and

Women in action again, Broken Hill 1892.
[Reproduced from *The Leader*, 3 September 1892]

foremost against Unionism as its strongest citadel'.[35] To the dismissals was added the mine employers' controversial decision to reintroduce competitive 'stoping [mining] by contract', despite a recently negotiated settlement to the contrary.[36] Setting worker against worker, contracting was seen as a device to undermine the miners' solidarity. It would lead to a reduction in wages, the AMA argued, as well as encouraging dangerous practices and increasing the incidence of industrial disease, as miners were forced to cut corners to keep their costs low. On Sunday 3 July 1892, a mass meeting of miners and their families voted for strike action. The few 'blacklegs' who remained in work were later swept from their posts by the enraged women, just as they had been in disturbances at Broken Hill in 1889. Here, of course, was an echo of the Great Strike at Moonta and Wallaroo in 1874 – popular remembrance and re-enactment of an epic 'story . . . now part of a [Broken Hill] tradition'.[37]

David Morley Charleston, a Cornish Methodist and prominent Labor leader, travelled up to Broken Hill from Adelaide to address strike meetings, and when several AMA officials were arrested on charges of conspiracy, the Revd R.J. Daddow – Primitive Methodist minister at the Burra – declared that these 'martyrs' had shown great 'self-sacrifice, self-control and moral courage'.[38] But rhetoric was not enough to prevent the strike from collapsing. Just as at Moonta and Wallaroo in early 1892, desperate men had begun to trickle back to work. The mine companies had managed to maintain production by recruiting blackleg labour from Melbourne, effectively ignoring the strikers and their demands. The AMA eventually called off the strike on 6 November 1892. The immediate aftermath was catastrophic. The AMA was no longer recognised by the mine companies at Broken Hill, and some ringleaders were refused employment thereafter. As on northern Yorke Peninsula, those unfortunates who had pleaded for their jobs back were ostracised as '92ers'. Yet in the longer term, the workers turned from industrial action to political organisation to achieve their ends, heralded by the return to the New South Wales Parliament of four Labor members for local seats in July 1894. The *Barrier Truth* became the voice piece of the emergent Labor Party at Broken Hill, and for a revivified trade union movement.

'To send John Prisk to Parliament / He'd beg from door to door'

Meanwhile, back in South Australia, there had also been a graduation from industrial action to political organisation as a means of securing reform and social change. As early as 1874, after the Great Strike on northern Yorke Peninsula, there was talk of the Moonta Miners' Association sponsoring its own Labor candidates. John Prisk, one of the strike's heroes, was keen to put his name forward. He was, as one local poet acknowledged, a man with an outstanding reputation in the community:

> John Prisk, the Union President
> Of credit and renown,
> And eke he was a Citizen
> Of famous Moonta town.

As the poet recognised, there would be many who would support his election to parliament:

Then up jumped Reuben Gill,
And he stanked on the floor
To send John Prisk to Parliament
He'd beg from door to door.

And Brother Strike would do the same,
(Bold Rodda cried 'hear, hear')
The Union would support the cause,
Of that there was no fear.

Yet others were hesitant:

Then up jumped bold John Anthony,
And he swore by his word
To send John Prisk to Parliament
Was really quite absurd.

Then there were words of fierce debate,
And voices loud and high,
Till 'Junius' moved for peace's sake
Adjournment *sine die*.[39]

Behind the petty politicking evident in the verses, was the plain fact that the Moonta trade unionists had yet to devise a coherent strategy on parliamentary representation. They settled down, therefore, to lobbying and vetting other candidates, rather as the Political Association had done before (see p. 73–73). In February 1875, for example, the Moonta Miners' Association declared 'in favour of Mr Richards'. Born in Helston, Cornwall, in 1843, John Richards was a captain at several of the Yorke Peninsula mines, and a regular contributor on mining matters to the *Register* newspaper and the London *Mining Journal*. The Association supported Richards because he approved of Boucaut's railway policy (designed to penetrate far-flung corners of the colony), defended 'the mining interest', and, crucially, was a keen supporter of payment of parliamentary members and an advocate of the principles of trade unionism.[40] Winning the miners' backing, Richards was elected a member for Wallaroo in 1875 but stepped down in 1878. His personal fortunes deteriorated rapidly thereafter. He spent several periods in gaol on account of non-payment of debts and for fraud, and in 1881 could be found sleeping rough in Adelaide. He died in the Adelaide Destitute Asylum in 1919.[41]

The Association also lent its formal support to William Henry Beaglehole, born in Helston, Cornwall, in 1834. A builder by trade, Beaglehole had constructed many houses in Moonta, Wallaroo and Kadina before moving to Adelaide in 1874, where he purchased the Lion Brewery. Later, he also bought a brewery in Broken Hill. A small-time capitalist, and presumably not a teetotaller, he nonetheless appealed to the Peninsula miners, no doubt because of his local connections. He was elected member for Wallaroo in 1881, serving until 1884, and from 1884 until 1887 was member for Yorke Peninsula.[42] By now, however, the Association felt ready and able to sponsor its own Labor candidates. The merger with the well-organised AMA in 1889 redoubled this conviction, as did the long awaited introduction of payment for parliamentary members in 1890, and in May 1891 the three AMA branches on the Peninsula adopted Richard 'Dicky' Hooper as their own Independent Labor candidate. In a by-election that month, Hooper was duly returned as member for Wallaroo, topping the poll by winning more than twice as many votes as his nearest rival, and in the process he became the very first Labor member of the House of Assembly in the South Australian Parliament.[43] Born in Cornwall in 1846, Hooper possessed all the credentials necessary for popularity on the Peninsula, not least as Methodist local preacher and past president of the Moonta branch of the AMA. According to the versifier 'Old 'Un' (Revd Charles Martin), Hooper worked hard for his constituents and, although a miner, was careful to consider the interests and aspirations of other workers in the colony:

> Tho' a Democrat strong, with some Socialist leaning,
> [Hooper] is no demagogue given to cranks,
> Tho' a champion of Labour, he gives it a meaning
> That includes every toiler in Labour's broad ranks.
>
> The worker in factory, business or farm
> Has few truer friends on North Terrace [i.e. in parliament] than he;
> And the farmer is coming, though slowly, to calm
> His fears and to trust the true Labour MP.[44]

Richard 'Dicky' Hooper, the first
Labor member of the House of
Assembly in the South Australian
Parliament, 1891, illustrated by
Oswald Pryor in his *Australia's
Little Cornwall*, Adelaide, 1962.
[Reproduced courtesy of the National
Trust of South Australia, Moonta
Branch]

The United Trades & Labor Council and the Maritime Strike

'Dicky' Hooper was wise to lift his view beyond simply 'the mining interest', for
a parallel movement for parliamentary representation had likewise emerged
in Adelaide. The arrival of permanent payment for parliamentary members
had also galvanised the trade unionists of the United Trades & Labor Council
(UTLC) in the capital. Like the unionists on northern Yorke Peninsula, the
UTLC had been groping its way for some time towards the prospect of political
action. Formed in 1884 and representing some 6,000 workers, the UTLC
was an umbrella for a variety of craft associations and trade unions that
had grown up in recent years. They tended to be Adelaide-centric; indeed,
as Hirst has pointed out, the first union to join Adelaide members with large
numbers of country workers was the Railways Mutual Association, founded
in 1887.[45] Agitation for an eight-hour day and for early closing had led to a
plethora of associations. Bakers, cooks and stewards had organised as early
as 1875. The Suburban and Port Road Drivers were unionised in 1877, and
the United Boilermakers' and Ironshipbuilders' society was formed in 1880.

The Typographical Society was established in the same year, and teachers, clothing trade workers, and coopers formed their own associations. There was a saddlemakers' union, a Port Adelaide Workingmen's Association (established in 1873), a Seamen's Union (1874), and a Shearer's Union (1886) with branches in Adelaide and Port Augusta. Many of these associations stressed their status as friendly societies, and expressed moderate aspirations as well as conciliatory methods. One optimist interpreted this as evidence of 'that noble fusion of capital and labour under which each man will work for all and everyone will work for his fellow'.[46] This was certainly in contrast to the more robust unionism demonstrated on the mines of northern Yorke Peninsula (and its offshoot at Broken Hill). It was also challenged by the events of the Maritime Strike of 1890, when Adelaide's unionists began to focus more clearly on their rural hinterland, as well as expressing a new-found solidarity with workers elsewhere in Australia.

In May 1890 the UTLC in Adelaide received a telegram from the Australian Labour Federation in Brisbane, requesting support. 'Big struggle pending', it warned presciently, 'threatening to involve all labour organizations ... the support and sympathy of your Council is earnestly solicited. Please call special meeting and reply at once'.[47] The UTLC immediately cabled its solidarity. There was similar declaration of support for the Sydney wharf labourers, who were agitating for better working conditions, and on 12 June the Port Adelaide branch of the Maritime Labour Council (MLC), taking its cue from its more militant eastern colonies colleagues, announced that henceforth its members would cease to work with non-unionists.[48] In similar mood, shearers at Port Augusta, Strathalbyn, Blumberg [Birdwood] and the Burra indicated that in future they would not shear 'non-union wool', a move supported by the UTLC.[49] The much anticipated 'big struggle' finally broke on 15 August 1890, the catalyst being the collapse of the long-running negotiations about conditions of employment between the Mercantile Officers' Association and the Steamship Owners' Association of Victoria, not least over whether the Association should be allowed to affiliate with the Melbourne Trades Hall. The strike would soon engulf Australia and New Zealand, as workers in other unions – seamen, wharf labourers, even coalminers – became embroiled, and was a prelude to the bitter shearers' strike of 1891. At its height, the Maritime Strike involved some 50,000 workers across Australasia, mobilising whole communities in which women as well as men (shades of northern Yorke Peninsula and Broken Hill) would play active parts.[50]

In Sydney, on 15 August 1890, a number of officers from ships of the Adelaide Steamship Company handed in their resignations in solidarity with their Victorian colleagues. Representatives from the Melbourne unions arrived in Adelaide shortly after to address members of the MLC, seamen and wharf labourers. Suitably enthused by what they had heard, a large crowd of workers gathered at the wharf at Port Adelaide to jostle and jeer when the *Adelaide* sailed on 20 August with non-union officers. Likewise, when the *Ferret* arrived from Port Lincoln, its officers promptly tendered their resignations. The same day, 24 August, wharf labourers at Port Pirie stopped work. As the *Advertiser* newspaper reflected, the visiting union delegates from Victoria had had a profound impact upon local opinion: 'Port Adelaide instead of being a weak spot in the struggle is now a tower of strength that will greatly supplement the powers of the colonies.'[51] It was also a struggle that the UTLC was prepared to back formally, interpreting the refusal of the steamship companies to reach an agreement with ships' officers as tantamount to a capitalist denial of the rights of the working people of Australia. 'Have the marine officers the right to combine for their mutual protection?' asked the UTLC rhetorically: 'This is the question that has caused the capitalist to throw down the gauntlet and defy the united workers of Australia.' The UTLC continued:

> What charge can the capitalist make against the officers of the Australian coasting vessels? They are men of skill, education and courage, placed in arduous positions of trust where they must maintain appearances and are expected to consider the interests of big companies before their own life or limb. But how have they been treated? For many years, they have been unorganized and consequently the worst paid and most inconsiderately treated of maritime men.[52]

As the UTLC explained: 'Instead of their non-unionism being recognized, and fairness being specially remembered in dealing with them, the companies have paid them often worse than their subordinates and brow beaten them at the slightest provocation.' Significantly, the UTLC was prepared to raise its gaze far beyond the parochial confines of Adelaide, speaking now to fellow workers across the continent: 'Fellow Australians, this is your hour of trial ... This conflict is not of our making but seeing that it is inevitable we are resolved to fight it out once and for all to the bitter end.'[53] This was fighting talk, and in South Australia its effect was palpable. Maritime workers at Port Augusta joined the strike, and the shearers' union at Port Augusta donated £363 to the strike fund. Railwaymen raised £1,222 and the 1,200 members of the AMA's Wallaroo branch gave an immediate payment of £50 and agreed a weekly levy of one shilling per week each to support the strikers. Similar funds were forthcoming from the miners at Broken Hill. Soon inter-colonial shipping was at a standstill, and the economy began to grind to a halt as a result. Flour mills at Port Adelaide closed for want of supplies, and the smelters at Dry Creek (outside Adelaide) and Port Pirie ceased production. The *Advertiser* vented the frustration felt by many: 'That the complete dislocation of the industrial machinery of Australia should be threatened by the failure of a few capitalists to agree with their employees on a point of trifling moment would be laughable were it not such a grim reality.'[54] Frustration was also evident when the *Blair Drummond*, about to sail from Port Pirie with a cargo of wheat bound for Britain, was crewed by non-union men brought in from Melbourne. Scuffles broke out, and the majority of the crew was persuaded to abandon the ship, several joining the union instead.

There were similar scenes at Port Adelaide as the strikers' blockade of shipping was expanded to include oceanic as well as coastal vessels. The deployment of a large body of police was condemned as 'quite uncalled for' by the *Advertiser*, which felt that its presence would only make matters worse.[55] Certainly, police protection for strike-breakers provoked an angry reaction. Stones were thrown and ships were stormed to prevent them from sailing with non-union crews. On one occasion a strike-breaker drew a revolver. The police confiscated the weapon but allowed its owner to go free, although arresting three strikers who had attempted to disarm the gunman. The incident precipitated three days of rioting at Port Adelaide, together with further arrests. The crisis now seemed intractable, and had metamorphosed from a specific grievance surrounding treatment of the Mercantile Officers' Association to a much broader conflict reflecting a wide range of workers' discontents. Moreover, as David Morley Charleston claimed, the strike had assumed the character of class conflict. As he explained: 'The present trouble was a very difficult matter to settle, it had resolved itself into a question of capital versus labour.'[56]

The employers themselves had not been idle, and were also organising, the self-styled Employers' Union co-ordinating strategy and seeking to win over public opinion. As public goodwill for the strikers began to falter, so the unions' strike funds ran low. In November the Mercantile Officers' Association reached a compromise. The ship-owners would recognise the Association but, in return, the Association was barred from affiliating with the Melbourne Trade Hall, effectively isolating it from the wider trade union movement in Victoria. Thereafter, the nation-wide strike began to unravel. Strikers at Port Pirie returned to work on 2 November 1890, to be followed the next day by those at Port Augusta. The Port Pirie men had won a reduction of the working day from ten to eight hours. But when, after a total of fourteen weeks on strike, the Port Adelaide unionists reluctantly went back to work, they had nothing to show for their pains. Instead, they were forced, like other strikers across Australia, to accept the employers' right to employ non-union labour and to insist on 'freedom of contract', that wage bargaining would take place between employers and individuals rather than collectively with trade unions. Overall, the Maritime Strike had ended in defeat. But it had led to a heightened sense of class identity, in South Australia as elsewhere, among working people. Moreover, it redoubled the growing conviction that trade unionists should be more intimately involved in politics, and that this would be the route to lasting social reform.[57] As Nick Dyrenfurth has put it, rather dramatically: 'From the ashes of this industrial holocaust arose the unionist Phoenix – a Labor party determined to prevent a repeat of these shocking events.'[58]

Birth of the United Labor Party

In fact, as we have seen, unionists had for some time been attempting to enter – or at least influence – the political arena, before the extraordinary events of

1890 spurred them to greater efforts. The UTLC had set up a Parliamentary Committee for the purpose in 1885 and, mirroring the stance of the Peninsula miners, had decided upon a policy of vetting and endorsing those candidates it considered sympathetic to social reform and the principles of trade unionism. In the 1887 elections to the South Australian Parliament, the UTLC endorsed Andrew Kirkpatrick, charismatic leader of the Typographical Union, as well as several 'liberal' candidates. In August 1890, no fewer than fourteen of the nineteen 'liberals' endorsed were duly elected, although David Morley Charleston – past president of the UTLC – was unsuccessful in Port Adelaide. None of the 'liberals', however, felt the need to acknowledge any formal due or allegiance to the UTLC after the elections – on the contrary, they were concerned to retain their 'independence' and immunity to outside interests.[59] Recognising the limitations of its arrangements with the 'liberals', mindful of the new opportunities offered by permanent payment of parliamentary members, and determined to learn from the trauma of the Maritime Strike, the UTLC decided that now was the moment to sponsor its own Labor candidates.

Accordingly, in December 1890 the UTLC Parliamentary Committee resolved that a public meeting be called, to which all its affiliated bodies would be invited, designed to 'bring about unity of action to secure the return of bona fide labour candidates at the forthcoming Legislative Council elections'.[60] The meeting was duly held on 7 January 1891, at the Selbourne Hotel in Pirie Street, Adelaide. A campaign committee was formed, and from this emerged the United Labor Party (ULP) of South Australia. Pondering its strategy for penetrating the conservative upper house in the upcoming election, the campaign committee selected three ULP candidates: David Morley Charleston, Robert Guthrie and Andrew Kirkpatrick. As Jim Moss has observed, it was a shrewd choice, neatly appealing to different components of the electorate:

The three personified the trends existing in the labour movement. Charleston, the craft unionist, was a member of the Amalgamated Society of Engineers, a sponsor of single [land] tax, a Rechabite, and a Cornishman. Guthrie, a Scot and Rechabite, represented the seamen and the mass unions affiliated to the MLC [Maritime Labour Council], such as waterside workers, carters, smelter workers and mill workers, and labourers. Kirkpatrick, already a veteran of the labour movement, was a foundation member of the Typographical Society. He was not limited by the boundary of craft concerns but showed dedication to the broader objectives of the industrial and political labour movement.[61]

The decision to pierce the Legislative Council was also shrewd, as well as courageous and far-sighted. As the ULP recognised, the Legislative Council had almost equal powers to the lower house, the House of Assembly, and had not been afraid to use that power to frustrate legislation of a progressive nature. Looking to the future, the ULP understood that any reformist legislation it might promote in the Assembly would likely fall foul of the Legislative Council. It was necessary, then, to dent conservative dominance of the Council before further progress might be made. Additionally, as Brian Dickey has explained, the elections of 1891 were the first for the fully reconstructed Legislative Council under the Act of 1881. Henceforth, South Australia would be divided into four Council electorates, each of which was to return six members. These would be elected at three-yearly intervals, with eight members retiring each time. In 1891 the last three members of the Legislative Council for the whole of South Australia would retire, together with two members for the colony's Central District and one from each of the other three electoral divisions. In other words, there would be eight vacancies to fill on this occasion.[62] The United Labor Party aimed to secure three of them.

In the run-up to the Legislative Council elections in May 1891, the United Labor Party articulated its policies carefully and campaigned hard. Advertisements were placed in newspapers, circulars distributed, how-to-vote cards printed, and an exhausting round of speeches and meetings was held by the three candidates and their supporters. The ULP platform ranged from a progressive tax on land values, a comprehensive Workshops and Factory Act, and Redistribution of Seats Bill (to reduce the rural bias) to the demand for a State Bank, an Eight Hours Bill, and opposition to free and assisted immigration. Overall, the 'emphasis was on social justice', as Dickey has commented, a program that was practical rather than revolutionary.[63]

As Dean Jaensch has observed, this approach was to become a defining characteristic of the new party. The ULP professed adherence to democratic socialism, Jaensch noted, but the 'emphasis [was] on "democratic" rather than "socialism"'.[64] 'From its beginnings', he added, 'South Australian Labor was a moderate movement, practical rather than ideological in its outlook and essentially pragmatic in its activities'.[65] In 1898 Michael Davitt, the Irish land-league agitator, had thought much the same. Reflecting on his recent visit to South Australia, Davitt observed that ULP activists 'were eminently practical, rather than eloquently visionary'.[66] It was a stance that appealed to the electorate, and all three ULP candidates were returned, Charleston and Guthrie in the Central District and Kirkpatrick in the Southern, the first of the so-called 'Labour wedge' in the Legislative Council.[67] As Ross McMullin has mused: 'The infant ULP had exceeded its wildest dreams. Charleston dared to hope a new era was dawning. His excited supporters were sure of it.'[68]

'The Labour Wedge'

As Jim Moss has argued, the newly elected members were a good cross-section of the Labor movement. David Morley Charleston was born in St Erth, Cornwall, in 1848 and was, according to the *Cornishman* newspaper (published in nearby Penzance), imbued 'with characteristic Cornish fervour and enthusiasm'.[69] As a youth he learned engineering at Harvey & Co., the great iron foundry at Hayle that, among other things, built beam engines for the copper mines of South Australia, and in 1874 he travelled to San Francisco. From California he ventured to China, eventually arriving in Sydney, Australia, in 1884. In 1887 Charleston found employment at the English and Australian Copper Company's smelting works at Port Adelaide, and it was there that he became involved in the Amalgamated Society of Engineers. He was president of the UTLC in 1889–90. The Adelaide *Observer* considered him an attractive character likely to appeal to the electorate, and his religious principles enjoyed the support of the *Christian Weekly and Methodist Journal*, which wrote approvingly that the 'ideals of labour were consistent with Christianity'.[70] He was, according to the *Register*, a fair and reasonable man; he was 'no demagogue, smashing here, there and everywhere without rhyme or reason'.[71]

'To love and be loved', reported the admiring *Cornishman*, was Charleston's highest aspiration: 'To dream of perpetual bliss, and feel the union of souls in the one great love for Nature.'[72] More prosaically, Charleston's own opinion was that to 'obtain happiness is the end and purpose of life in high and low

David Morley Charleston, one of the so-called 'Labour Wedge'
in South Australia's Legislative Council in 1891.
[Courtesy State Library of South Australia, B58972]

degree', a Utilitarian liberalism which likewise underpinned his declared support for 'broad liberal Unionism'.[73] Yet he also called himself a socialist, and there was a strong socialist strand to his personal political thought. He believed, for example, that the 'State . . . should, if Democracy means anything, completely control Production and Distribution, thereby carrying to its conclusion the co-operative system'.[74] This would, however, be an evolutionary rather than revolutionary process, and here Charleston linked his political thinking to that of the 'gradualist' social democratic Fabian Society in Britain, founded in 1884 by Sidney and Beatrice Webb. A committed Methodist, Charleston added that 'Divorce, except for proven adultery ... I shall oppose'.[75]

Charleston played a prominent role in the ULP as a pioneering member of the Labour Wedge. Unfortunately, however, he fell victim to suspicions and uncertainties within the embryonic party. The Amalgamated Society of Engineers accused elements of the ULP of plotting against Charleston, and he in turn expressed his frustration with the ULP's parliamentary caucus, reporting that at its meetings 'a great part of the time was spent in frivolous talk and barracking'.[76] Eventually, feeling that he lost the confidence of his party, Charleston resigned his seat and left the ULP. He fought the 1897 election as an 'independent liberal' and was returned with a substantial lead over his ULP rival. Thereafter, he continued to drift to the right of the political spectrum. He remained a member of the Legislative Council until 1901, was a Federal Senator from 1901 to 1903, and was later active in organising the conservative Farmers' and Producers' Political Union.

But all that was in the future. For the moment, Charleston was a key ULP presence in the Legislative Council. So too was Robert Storrie Guthrie, born at Partick, near Glasgow, in Scotland in 1857. A seaman, he had first arrived in Australia in 1878. From 1888 he was secretary of the Port Adelaide branch of the Seamen's Union, and in 1890 was president of the Maritime Labor Council (MLC) at Port Adelaide, and thus intimately involved in the great Maritime Strike of that year. Guthrie was reputedly a Presbyterian but he was also a district ruler of the Independent Order of Rechabites in South Australia, which, according to Dickey, 'means, almost certainly, that he was a Primitive Methodist'.[77] As a trade unionist and as a politician, Guthrie was concerned ('obsessed', according to his detractors) with working conditions and safety in the maritime industry. Following Federation and his elevation to the Senate, he served on the Royal Commission of the Navigation Bill, 1904–07, which resulted in the so-called 'Guthrie Act', with Guthrie himself hailed thereafter as the 'Australian Plimsoll'. A Labor Senator, he split with his party in 1916 over the conscription issue (he was a supporter of conscription, and lost two sons in the Great War), and like his close friend W.M. 'Billy' Hughes, helped form the Nationalist Party. Guthrie spoke with a distinct Glasgow accent, and

Hughes remembered him as 'a real sailor' who always 'woke at … 4.a.m' and 'rolled heavily in his gait'. Although a moderniser, Guthrie was said by Hughes to have had 'the poorest opinion of steamships'. He was knocked down by a tram in Melbourne on 19 January 1921, and died the next day.[78]

Robert Storrie Guthrie, second member of the Labour Wedge.
[Courtesy State Library of South Australia, B12166/6]

The third of these historic figures was Andrew Alexander Kirkpatrick. Born in London of an Irish father and English mother in 1848, Kirkpatrick emigrated to South Australia in 1860 with his mother, his father having died when he was only a year old. He was employed in the Government Printing Office before later starting his own printing business. He was a foundation member of the Typographical Society (in 1874), and helped form the UTLC, of which he was president at the time of the Legislative Council elections in 1891. Guthrie lost his seat in the Legislative Council in 1897 (the Southern district was not reckoned a likely Labor stronghold) but returned triumphant in the election of 1900. In 1909 he resigned to become Labor's first Agent-General for South Australia in London, a position for which he had been recommended by John Langdon Bonython, the radical liberal sympathiser and owner-editor of the *Advertiser*, who helpfully assured the government that Kirkpatrick (despite his Irish name, presumably) was a Protestant.[79] Following his stint in Britain, Kirkpatrick returned to Adelaide in 1914, and was promptly elected member for Newcastle in the House of Assembly 1915–18, before returning in 1918 to the Legislative Council, where he remained until his death in 1928. An accomplished parliamentarian, he held ministerial office during Tom Price's premiership in 1905–09, and again during the Labor governments of John Gunn in 1924–26 and Lionel Hill in 1926–27. An enthusiast for constitutional reform, Kirkpatrick introduced his (unsuccessful) Franchise Extension Bill in 1894 – the 'most radical private bill introduced by a ULP member', according to Jaensch – and later agitated for the establishment of wages boards.[80]

Together, the three founding members of the Labour Wedge had a profound effect upon the conduct of politics in South Australia. To begin with, their victory was a spectacular vindication of the UTLC's decision to sponsor its own Labor (ULP) candidates. The Labour Wedge was part of a ULP strategy that would soon witness a substantial Labor presence in parliament, and help to introduce and sustain a lengthy period of reform under the Radical Liberal Premiership of Charles Cameron Kingston, from June 1893 until November 1899, leading ultimately to the appointment of South Australia's first Labor Premier, Tom Price, in July 1905. The Labour Wedge was also a significant first step in the emergence of party (as opposed to faction) politics in South Australia, not only heralding the growth (and permanency) of the ULP but also prompting the establishment of an oppositional National Defence League (NDL). The NDL began life as a parliamentary grouping but soon moved to town and country. By the end of 1892 it had no fewer than 49 branches across the colony and more than 2,500 members. According to the *Observer*, the NDL was 'distinctly opposed to the extremists of the Labor Party' and was determined to 'oppose all undue class influence in Parliament'.[81] Despite the latter aim, the NDL began to sponsor its own parliamentary candidates but with little immediate success, in the long-term becoming one component of the Liberal Union that emerged in South Australian politics after Federation.[82]

Alexander Andrew Kirkpatrick, the third of the 'Labour Wedge'.
[Courtesy State Library of South Australia, B38840/1]

The ULP and Independent Labor

Following hot on the heels of the Legislative Council successes in May 1891, came the elections of April 1893. The ULP was well-placed to exploit the prevailing conditions. Economic depression gripped the colony, exacerbated by a series of bank failures, an indifferent harvest, and the impact of the miners' strikes on northern Yorke Peninsula and at Broken Hill. No fewer than three ministries had come and gone during 1892, and the last of these, Sir John Downer's premiership, offered the electorate only a spell of 'rest and quiet'.[83] It was hardly a rallying cry likely to inspire the voters of South Australia. In the ensuing elections, the first to the Assembly contested by the ULP, Labor captured ten seats, together with a further seat to add to the Labour Wedge on the Legislative Council. The ten Assembly seats included Wallaroo, held by Dicky Hooper, who had first captured the mining constituency as an Independent Labor candidate in a by-election in 1891, and the outback constituency of Flinders. The latter was won by Alex Poynton, secretary of the Port Augusta branch of the shearers' union, standing, like Hooper, as an

145

Independent Labor candidate. By contrast, each of the seats won by the ULP proper was in metropolitan Adelaide, in areas with a strong UTLC presence. Hooper and Poynton were invited to attend parliamentary Labor Party caucus meetings, and generally identified with the ULP. But they signed no pledges, and remained outside the formal ULP structure. The same was true when, in 1896, Ernest Roberts was returned as an Independent Labor member for the country seat of Gladstone. A wharf labourer at Port Pirie and member of the local Workingmen's Association, Roberts had narrowly failed to take the seat in 1893 but was successful in 1896 and again in 1899. He too supported the ULP in parliament but remained independent of its organisation.

Although the understanding with the Independent Labor members worked well enough, at least in the short term, the dichotomy between Labor's metropolitan and country representation was plain for all to see. The ULP hoped to raise its visibility (and popularity) in country districts, and in the 1896 elections approved five candidates to contest country constituencies. But these were all Adelaide residents – the party's rural 'missionaries', as they patronisingly thought of themselves – and they were effectively asking country voters to accept absentee candidates and a political program devised in Adelaide with metropolitan interests in mind. Yet this was a time when dire economic conditions had hit rural workers as much as they had their metropolitan counterparts. At the Burra in January 1894, for example, there was a worrying report that of 'late the town has been visited by a lot of men out of work. The poor fellows seem to be in the most wretched conditions, and are camped in unoccupied houses, whilst others may be found sleeping under bridges'.[84] The ULP did not effectively address the question of rural representation, and the establishment of country branches, until after the turn of the century.[85] For the moment, it remained an Adelaide-centric party.

One result of this dichotomy was that the Labor Party on northern Yorke Peninsula, as it developed, retained its status as an 'ally' of the ULP in Adelaide and resisted full integration into the party structure.[86] This institutional independence slipped sometimes into independence of action, such as in the debate on Federation that emerged in the 1890s. Here the Peninsula miners adopted their own strategy, in direct opposition to the formal ULP position

146

devised in Adelaide. The ULP argued that Federation of the Australian colonies was not in the interests of the working class. The proposed Federal Senate was dismissed as 'undemocratic', while the additional tier of government made necessary by Federation would mean – it was asserted – extra taxation. South Australian manufacture would be hit, it was argued, by the removal of inter-colonial tariffs, while the lucrative Broken Hill trade (so important to the South Australian economy) would be siphoned off by New South Wales. None of this impressed the Peninsula miners. They were convinced that inter-colonial free trade – a foundation principle of Federation – would be a significant boost to the region's copper industry, and said so loudly. In the Federation referendum in 1898, the Peninsula voted accordingly, producing an overwhelming endorsement of the Federation Bill. As R. Norris observed, 'where class and regional interests clashed, the latter triumphed'.[87]

The Kingston years

Overshadowing the relationship between the ULP and the Independent Labor members of parliament, was the wider relationship between Labor and the Radical Liberals. In the aftermath of the April 1893, Charles Cameron Kingston took office as Premier. The strict Methodist strand within the Labor ranks might have been calculated to raise an eyebrow or two at 'Charlie' Kingston's private life. He was rumoured to have fathered at least six illegitimate children with various women, and was the butt of many scurrilous stories, such as that which insisted that he was once found *in flagrante delicto* with one of the maids in Parliament House by members searching for him to vote in a crucial division. According to Don Dunstan, on another occasion, when he was addressing a boisterous meeting outside Adelaide Town Hall, Kingston was interrupted by a heckler who shouted: 'didn't you get a wharf labourer's daughter with child – and didn't she bear your bastard?' Kingston pulled out his handkerchief, and sniffed 'Alas, it's true', as he burst into tears. When the resultant furore had died down, he put his handkerchief away and pointed directly at his accuser: 'But let he who is guiltless cast the first stone.' As Dunstan told it, 'his biblically educated audience burst into applause and cries of, "good on you Charlie"'.[88]

Be that as it may, the ULP readily lent Kingston its support. He had spoken enthusiastically on many occasions about trade unionism, and the UTLC in particular, and 'took positively pro-working class – or at least radically Liberal – positions on a number of issues'.[89] The *Advertiser* newspaper, which was the voice of liberal opinion in South Australia in the 1890s ('the fearless exponent of liberal and progressive policy[90]', according to one observer), saw no conflict between the program of the new ULP and the views of Kingston and his allies, and had no doubt that they could work together: 'There is much in the rest of the comprehensive [ULP] platform with which a moderate Liberal can warmly sympathise . . . we fail to detect any trace of undue radicalism in the proposals.'[91] The owner-editor of the *Advertiser*, John Langdon Bonython, was personally sympathetic to both the Radical Liberals and ULP. For example, in 1887 he had briefly toyed with the prospect of being a UTLC sponsored parliamentary candidate, and he had actively supported the radical John Cockburn during his brief premiership in 1888–89, whose progressive (but unfulfilled) program included bold initiatives such as votes for women.[92]

As John McConnell Black, *Hansard* reporter on the *Advertiser* from 1886 to 1911, argued in his memoirs, Bonython the newspaper magnate 'was the power behind the throne that dominated several South Australian Ministries, notably those of Cockburn and Kingston'.[93] As Jean Prest has observed, despite being a practising Methodist, Bonython, like his other co-religionists, was prepared to overlook Kingston's 'life of wild and erratic behaviour' because the flamboyant politician offered the best prospect of stable government and an attractive program of legislation.[94] Bonython was also a friend and colleague of David Morley Charleston. They were both long-serving members of the Council of the South Australian School of Mines and Industry, and were present together when the School was opened formally in June 1889. They also saw each other socially as members of the Cornish Association of South Australia. Inaugurated at a glittering banquet in Adelaide Town Hall on 21 February 1890, when all the capital's grandees sought to marshal their Cornish credentials to celebrate the intimate links between Cornwall and South Australia, the new-found Cornish Association proudly proclaimed 'that South Australians and Cornishmen were synonymous terms' – an extravagant conceit that Bonython and Charleston (and Boucaut, the Association's president) were prepared to sign-up to, not least in terms of their political fraternity.[95]

Personal relationships and the patronage of the influential *Advertiser* helped cement the ULP–Kingston understanding. Kingston's six years as Premier saw the enactment of much radical legislation, including women's franchise. New Zealand had been the first to give women the vote. But South Australia went one step further, enabling women to sit in parliament too. The sincerity of Radical Liberal commitment to women's suffrage was evident, for example, in a hustings speech in 1894 by John George Bice, yet another Cornish Methodist, a former Moonta Mines blacksmith, and a Kingston ally. 'I am in favour of Adult Suffrage', he told his audience, 'and because I believe that women are equally as intelligent, equally as capable of studying political questions, and of recording their vote as we [men] are, I think they should have the same privileges as men in this respect'. Moreover, he added, 'without representation there is no right of taxation and under our present laws women are entrusted with the rights of property and are subjected to taxation – consequently they are entitled to rights of representation'.[96] No ULP candidate could have put the case more concisely or convincingly, and Bice was duly elected to the Legislative Council.

In addition to votes for women, there was also much else to please the ULP – industrial arbitration, a State bank, factories legislation, working-men's lien, and various other pieces of progressive legislation. Kingston's public works program helped to alleviate the worst effects of the economic downturn, and he made it plain that, like the ULP, he believed in increased governmental intervention to secure greater social justice. Yet the ULP members were clearly little more than factional junior partners, and only one piece of legislation – the *Marine Board Act* of 1894 – was actually originated by Labor parliamentarians in the period 1893–1900. Tom Price, later to become Premier, characterised the ULP strategy in these years as achieving 'a little, and then a little more of what one wanted'.[97]

The Labour Wedge in the Legislative Council reached its high-water mark in 1894, a total of six seats (it was steadily eroded thereafter). Among those newly elected was Henry Adams, an active Methodist (the son of Cornish immigrants), and a former pattern maker at the Moonta mine, another product of Peninsula trade unionism. In 1894, the year he was elected to the Legislative Council, he was also president of the UTLC, having worked for some years as a carpenter for the Ways and Works Department at Glanville, a suburb of Adelaide. Adams remained a pillar of ULP representation in the Legislative Council until his eventual defeat in 1902.[98] In the House of Assembly the ULP won twelve seats in 1896, and eleven in 1899. Its share of the vote had held steady but there was frustratingly little sign of growth. Economic prospects had brightened, and, ironically, taking their cue from Labor's earlier successors, conservative candidates had begun to mobilise their own support more effectively. To this was added the negative publicity surrounding David Morley Charleston's resignation from the ULP in 1897. Moreover, there was the first whiff of sectarian tension, a brief foretaste of what would emerge much later during the Great War. Despite the strong Methodist and Nonconformist influence within the ULP, ULP activists had tried to keep their religious scruples separate from practical politics, as their attitude to Kingston demonstrated.

However, in the election campaigns of 1896 and 1899, State aid to religion had emerged as an issue. Nonconformists in early South Australia had campaigned successfully for the separation of church and State, and part of this separation was the establishment of the principle of non-State aid to church schools. This secularisation was seen by some critics as 'Protestantisation' by the back door. Hitherto sympathetic to the ULP, the Roman Catholic newspaper *Southern Cross*, published in Adelaide, began to take a more critical line. In 1897–99, responding to pressure from the new Catholic Archbishop (O'Reilly), the *Southern Cross* became overtly hostile to much of Labor's program, and during the 1899 election campaign O'Reilly himself vigorously attacked the ULP, alleging that 'the tyranny of the Labor leaders was the worst tyranny from which Catholics suffered in South Australia'.[99] This sparked a war of words between the *Southern Cross* and the Labor-supporting *Weekly Herald*, which may have had the effect of alienating some working-class Catholic voters from the Labor Party and its largely Nonconformist leadership. Ironically, the editor of the *Southern Cross* during this period of estrangement was W.J. Denny, who would later join the ULP and serve in several Labor administrations.

At the same time, the dynamics of the Kingston alliance had begun to change. ULP leaders in parliament, including Tom Price, became more critical of Kingston's leadership and accused him of running out of radical steam. Perhaps in response, Kingston became more active on Legislative Council reform, a subject close to the ULP's heart. However, a bill for its reform, passed in the Assembly in 1898, was rejected by the Legislative Council, and a second bill passed by the Assembly in 1899 appeared to be heading the same way. Anticipating the bill's rejection by the Legislative Council, Kingston sought a pre-emptive double dissolution of both Houses of Parliament. But the Governor refused to co-operate, and there was further uproar when on 28 November 1899 two of the Independent Labor members, Roberts and Poynton, hitherto loyal supporters of the ULP, crossed the floor to vote with the Opposition, thus bringing Kingston's premiership to an end. Although apparently turncoats, Roberts and Poynton may actually have been expressing increasing Labor frustration with Kingston, which their independent status gave them the opportunity to vent. Additionally, as they explained, they had never signed a pledge, and were representatives of country districts far removed from the metropolitan world of the ULP and the UTLC.

Turning points

Kingston, sensing that the moment had come for him to change course, bowed out gracefully, accepting an appointment to join the delegation to London to negotiate the Commonwealth of Australia Bill, the instrument of Federation. It was truly the end of an era, of the longest ministry thus far in the political history of South Australia. The year 1899 was also a turning point for the ULP. It marked the rise of Tom Price as parliamentary leader of the ULP, who in half a dozen years would gain distinction as the first Labor Premier of South Australia. An 'ardent Methodist all his life', as Brian Dickey described him, he was thus 'representative of a significant proportion of the ULP in South Australia'.[100] He was also responsible for crafting the political characteristics that would mark the ULP in the first decade of the twentieth century, as the party gained increasing influence, although he would die at the age of only fifty-seven, his baton passing to his successor, John Verran, another staunch Methodist.

Chapter Six

Labor in Power –
Tom Price and John Verran

Shortly after Kingston's departure, William Holder, sometime owner-editor of the *Burra Record* newspaper, assumed the premiership of South Australia. Long regarded as Kingston's lieutenant, Holder was elevated to the position following the remarkably short (a mere eight days) ministry of Vaiben Solomon. Promising to pursue reform of the Legislative Council, Holder won the cautious support of the parliamentary United Labor Party, which acquiesced when its leader, Egerton Lee Batchelor, was appointed minister of education in the new administration. But handing over the leadership of the ULP was the price of Batchelor's elevation, and in his stead Tom Price was elected as Labor leader by the party's caucus.

As we have seen (p. 18), Tom Price was born in Wales in 1852. Like many of his compatriots from industrial north-east Wales, Price grew up among the Welsh community in the poorer districts of neighbouring Liverpool, where he attended the local Wesleyan Methodist Sunday School and became a Rechabite. As a youth he was apprenticed to a stonecutter, and gained a more formal education through night classes at the Liverpool Mechanics Institute. Like many of the working-class Labor men of his day, Price was an autodidact, taking advantage of whatever educational opportunities that came his way, attending public lectures and reading widely. He was also politicised at an early age, claiming later that one of his forebears had been a Chartist activist, thrown into gaol for 'fighting for his principles'.[1] He joined the Liverpool

Tom Price, first Labor Premier of South Australia, with his wife Annie and their children. [Courtesy Stephanie McCarthy]

Reform Association, and soon earned a reputation as a gifted orator. In 1871 Tom Price completed his apprenticeship, and was duly admitted into the Liverpool Masons' Society. Conscious of his identity as a Welshman, he also became a member of the Order of Ancient Britons. He was likewise aware of a Celtic affinity with Ireland, and joined the radical Irish Home Rule League, insisting that 'the sons of Old Erin have been sold, betrayed and sacrificed by the superior ruling classes [in England]', and arguing later that 'Ireland, Scotland and Wales are as capable of governing themselves as Australia, Canada and South Africa'.[2]

In April 1881 Tom Price married Annie Lloyd, the beginning of a formidable partnership, Price later describing his wife as the 'instigator of all his best work'.[3] As Stephanie McCarthy has observed in her 2015 biography of Tom Price, Annie 'was no fool'.[4] Alongside her staunch support for her husband, she was active in her own right in political and civic life, later becoming vice-president of the United Labor Party in South Australia, as well as the British Empire's first female Justice of the Peace. Less than two years after their wedding, Tom and Annie Price emigrated to South Australia in January 1883, arriving in late May. It was a bad time to land in the colony, as it was slipping into recession. Price wisely abandoned plans to try his hand at farming in marginal lands in the far-north or south-east, joining the Operative Masons and Bricklayers Society (OMBS) and finding employment with James Shaw, a building contractor for whom Price was to work for seven years.

'The rushing eloquence of the young Welshman'

By 1887 Price was president of the OMBS and active in both the Cambrian Society and the Adelaide Democratic Club. He also joined the Mitcham Literary Society, with its model parliament, where he earned a reputation as a 'frequent and favourite speaker ... the Celtic fire, untempered by experience, burned high, and the rushing eloquence of the young Welshman was a source of delighted wonder to many'.[5] Increasingly politically active, Price found himself working on the new Parliament House on North Terrace in Adelaide in 1889, helping to craft its elegant steps and classical pillars, an activity that seemed to herald the prominent role the building would play in his life in the years ahead. For the moment, however, he looked to give up his trade as a stonecutter – he recognised the signs of encroaching silicosis – and was appointed Clerk of Works at Islington railway workshops, outside Adelaide. But his affiliation with stonemasonry endured, and in 1890 he was chosen to represent the OMBS on the United Trades & Labor Council (UTLC).

The disastrous Maritime Strike (see pp. 134–7) also occurred in 1890, and Tom Price was one of those many trade unionists who decided that its trauma should never again be repeated, believing now, as Stephanie McCarthy has put it, 'that the only real solutions were to be found in the seats of parliamentary power'.[6] He was, therefore, one of the first to join the newly fledged United Labor Party. He put his name down as a potential ULP candidate for the April 1893 House of Assembly elections, but in the plebiscite to decide who would run he narrowly missed being chosen. Astonishingly, others who had been successful stood aside, recognising his talent, and Price was adopted as a ULP candidate after all, contesting the large parliamentary district of Sturt. Equally extraordinarily, he topped the polls in Sturt constituency by a single vote, and duly became one of the ten Labor men returned to Parliament in that election.

This was to be the era in which the ULP broadly supported Kingston's regime, and the party used its influence constructively to help Kingston implement his progressive policies, demonstrating to an expectant public that Labor in Parliament would be responsible, trustworthy and reliable. As Price himself explained, 'as a Labor member ... I believe, not in revolution, but in gradual progress – indeed in the Fabian system of going slow'. David Morley Charleston, elected earlier to the Legislative Council, had also declared himself a Fabian socialist (see p. 142), in favour of evolution not revolution, and, as we have seen (p. 149), Price summarised the agreed approach of those early ULP members in Parliament as 'to get a little, and then a little more of what one wants'.[7] As Nick Dyrenfurth has observed, for many thinking Labor men, socialism was the natural extension of Australia's democratic struggle.[8] In 1891, the South Australian Fabian Society put it thus: 'Socialism may be brought about in a quiet and constitutional way, thanks to our democratic institutions; and the leaders of thought are rapidly giving their adhesions to socialist principles. Few now believe Socialism to be impracticable.'[9]

One of the more radical Kingston initiatives that the ULP had supported was the establishment of communal settlements along the River Murray. Deciding that he was now a 'State Socialist', Kingston had asserted 'the right of the State to interfere with the few for the good of the many', and on this principle gave land to Adelaide's unemployed and homeless, many of whom were living rough on the city's parklands.[10] It was a utopian scheme almost bound to fail (it had largely petered out by the turn of the century), not least because most of those selected for the settlements had no experience of farming whatsoever, while others resisted the communal ethos underpinning the experiment. When Michael Davitt, the Irish Land League activist, toured Australia in the 1890s, he visited the 'communes'. His commentary is an illuminating insight into the scheme and its limitations – and his informant's reservations may even have reflected the private opinions of more cautious ULP members, in and out of Parliament. As Davitt explained, while journeying from Pyap to New Residence he encountered a Cornish fisherman, who was 'a sturdy individualist, as most Cornishmen are at home and abroad'. When asked his opinion of the commune settlements, the fisherman replied:

> Am I a 'Commonist' [*sic*]? Not much! I works for myself, and them there 'bush lawyers' up at Pyap will be all for themselves in a short time – that's sartin. It's all very well to talk and read about this Commonism, but it's another when you come to work it out with a pick and shovel or fishing-boat. I'm no believer in these new-fangled idees, I'm not. I'm a Cornishman, I am. I have enough to do to work by my missus and myself. No sir, I'm no Commonist. Good-bye.[11]

Yet Tom Price seems to have shared none of these doubts. Remembering, perhaps, his earlier aspiration to become a farmer, he welcomed this opportunity for those with little (or no) resources to till the land themselves, and as a socialist he approved of the communal basis on which this was to be undertaken. He saw the scheme as a chance to redress the imbalance in land ownership created by the Wakefield system, not least the iniquitous 'special surveys' that earlier in the century had subverted Wakefield's original intentions and created a South Australian landed gentry (see p. 22). However, although Price defended the Murray settlement experiment, he was appalled by the conditions endured by the settlers, which he saw for himself when he visited the communities, and he was an active member of the Village Settlement Select Committee in Parliament which enquired into their plight.[12]

'I am going to be Premier of South Australia'

In these his formative parliamentary years, Price also emerged as a vocal champion of women's rights, and eagerly supported the extension of the franchise to women in December 1894. By now he was making a name for himself as an effective MP but he also attracted the attention of those who feared his reforming zeal. In a widely reported speech at Mitcham in January 1895, in which he tackled the subject of corruption, he made allegations about the activities of Cave & Co, owned by the wheat and shipping businessman William Cave, a powerful figure in the colony. Cave retaliated immediately by issuing a libel writ against Price. Price duly appeared in the Supreme Court, charged with Criminal Libel, but after a brilliant defence, following which the jury was unable to agree a verdict, the charge was dropped.[13] The *Herald* newspaper passed its own judgement, with palpable but defiant relief: 'Wealth plays a powerful part in the everyday affairs of the world, but wealth is not going to crush the Labor party, and as a member of that party we congratulate Mr Price.'[14] But Price was not yet out of trouble, and in a second case brought by John Langdon Parsons, whom he had also named, he was ordered to pay damages of £100 plus costs – a vast sum for a man of modest means. Two years later, however, Tom Price was vindicated when a Royal Commission examining the affairs of Cave & Co substantiated everything that he had alleged. It had, nonetheless, been an unnerving as well as financially costly experience, evidence of the powerful forces ranged against Labor and the personal animosity towards Price himself.[15]

Sometime during the second half of 1896 Price was walking home in the early hours of the morning after an all-night sitting in the House, accompanied by a *Hansard* reporter. Suddenly he stopped, and self-mockingly tongue-in-cheek announced that 'I am going to be Premier of South Australia one of these days'.[16] It was half in jest but also a prescient insight, although it would be another nine years before he achieved such high office. But he would become Labor leader in the House just three years later, in the aftermath of Kingston's departure. In the preceding period, from January 1898, he deployed an anonymous nom-de-plume 'Tom Jones, Working Man' to write a series of lengthy letters to the *Herald*, a vehicle (among other things) for expressing Labor's increasing frustration with Kingston's ministry. Although Price tried to keep 'Tom Jones' anonymous, he was rumbled eventually, and Stephanie McCarthy has argued convincingly that there are so many tell-tale details and glimpses in 'Tom Jones' 'as to make any author other than Tom Price impossible'.[17] The letters attack Kingston's uncritical embrace of Federation (Price was equivocal on the matter), and regret the airs and graces that the Premier had increasingly adopted. 'There is an aroma of greatness and a flavour of condescending patronage', 'Tom Jones' protested, 'we [ULP supporters] like you not because of your colossal greatness … but rather because of your courage, generosity, and the happy knack you have of making

September 25, 1897.   THE CRITIC.   11

WITH HIS BLOOMING HONORS THICK UPON HIM.

Now that he is such a tremendous swell, Premier Charley will surely want to shake off that common little party.

Charles Cameron Kingston begins to acquire airs and graces.
[*The Critic*]

us feel you are one of us'.[18] The goading, criticism, friendly banter, faint praise and gratuitous advice continued until at last Kingston was forced from office, 'Tom Jones' urging him to don 'a set of false whiskers and hair, an old suit of clothes, and go and register his name at the Labor Bureau as an out-of-work . . . and then sit on the steps or kerbstone at the back of the Government offices and hear what the unemployed think of him'.[19]

In his first speech to the House as Labor leader in December 1899, Tom Price denounced the political manoeuvrings of recent weeks, including the intrigues that had led to the embarrassingly short ministry of Vaiben Solomon, and hoped that in future Parliament would adopt 'a nobler way of doing things'.[20] Whether noble or not, the next few years were difficult ones for Labor. Learning from the independent actions of Roberts and Poynton, who had crossed the floor to defeat Kingston, ULP caucus discipline was tightened, and all those attending its meetings were required to sign a pledge of loyalty. There was also the question of Federation. Labor continued to campaign for a more democratic constitution, to enshrine full adult suffrage and one vote–one value across Australia. The ULP and its counterparts elsewhere in the country likewise hoped to achieve significant representation in the new Federal Parliament, and sought well-known candidates with strong records to run as candidates. A ULP plebiscite in South Australia decided that Gregor McGregor and Andrew Kirkpatrick would stand for the Senate, while Egerton Lee Batchelor and Tom Price himself would contest seats in the House of Representatives. Electioneering was fierce in the run-up to the Federal election on 29 March 1901, the *Herald* reminding voters of Labor's crucial role in securing women's suffrage, and warmly endorsing the Labor candidates. Tom Price was recommended enthusiastically for 'his earnest, homely oratory which never fails to reach the hearts of the people; Kirkpatrick with his easy address, pleasant manner and convincing argument; Batch with his lucidity and grasp; and canny Scot McGregor with his logic, his humour and his emphatic Scottish style'.[21]

When the count was declared, McGregor had succeeded in winning a Senate seat and Batchelor had been similarly successful in the House of Representatives. But Price and Kirkpatrick had both missed out. There were mixed feelings in Labor ranks, no doubt, when Charlie Kingston topped the poll for the House of Representatives, and the victory of Radical Liberal John Langdon Bonython would have been some small consolation, although

Bonython himself (who came second after Kingston) complained that: 'If the Labor Party had been quite true to me I should have been at the top.'[22] But what Price, Kirkpatrick and indeed the entire ULP membership would have found difficult to swallow was that the 'rat' Charleston (standing as a Free Trade–Labor candidate, making him 'the biggest political hypocrite on earth',[23] according to Price) and the 'turncoat' Poynton had both been elected to the new national Parliament. For Price, one lesson to be drawn from the Federal election experience was that he should redouble his opposition to the Legislative Council, seeking reform where Kingston had failed, denouncing the 'House of Landlords' whose members were 'the bosses of the destiny of South Australia'.[24] Now that there was a bi-cameral Federal Parliament, he argued, there was no need for the State's upper house, and it should be abolished, saving South Australia £15,000 a year. He reminded his fellow members of the House of Assembly that 'they, the representatives of the people, were controlled by a body [the Legislative Council] elected on property qualification and a restricted franchise'.[25] It was a theme Price would return to as Premier, but for now one unfortunate consequence of Federation for Labor in South Australia was that the membership of the House of Assembly would be reduced from fifty-four to forty-two.

To this disadvantage was added the increasingly conservative nature of the Jenkins ministry that followed Kingston and Holder, together with the ceaseless anti-Labor rhetoric of the National Defence League, much of it echoed in a hostile press. In this atmosphere, the old understanding between Labor and the radical and independent liberals faltered and finally collapsed, many of the erstwhile Kingstonian liberals shifting to the Jenkins camp. But there was a small group under Archibald Henry Peake which, anticipating the major change to party contestation that would emerge in subsequent years, distanced itself from the Jenkins government. As Peake warned: 'The [Jenkins] Government, therefore, must not be surprised if not only labour but other members who favoured liberal legislation turned their backs upon it.'[26] Price in turn, writing this time under his new nom-de-plume 'Peerer', praised Peake unreservedly as 'an honest man', evidence perhaps that he felt they could do business together.[27]

'You are a most desirable acquisition to the Labor Party'

This incipient re-alignment began to work itself out in the State election of 1902, when all seats – in both the Legislative Council and the House of Assembly – were vacated. Peake's liberal group campaigned as a separate entity, advocating reform of the Legislative Council, and Price emphasised the gulf between the ULP and the Jenkins government, attacking it 'for abandoning liberal principles'.[28] Tom Price approached the 1902 election with his usual passion and energy, the *Herald* reporting one typical campaign meeting: 'Barely has the Welsh orator been heard to better advantage, and at times his audience rose and waved their hats and cheered again and again. It was a splendid effort – a masterly and convincing speech.'[29] Avoiding ideological rhetoric, Price and his team campaigned on eminently practical issues, in the ULP manner, of which the most contentious was the proposal to create a unicameral parliamentary structure. The ensuing election, however, was 'nothing less than a slaughter' for Labor, as Stephanie McCarthy has described it.[30] Price came close to losing his seat in the District of Torrens, and overall Labor representation in the State Parliament was reduced dramatically from eleven to five. This reflected in part the fewer seats available for contestation (forty-two as opposed to fifty-four previously) but, as Frederick Coneybeer complained, 'many of the working class did not take the trouble to turn out and record their vote'.[31] Among those who survived alongside Price were the ULP stalwarts Archibald, Coneybeer and MacGillivray in the House of Assembly, and Guthrie and Kirkpatrick in the Legislative Council. But there was one newcomer to the now very small Labor parliamentary team, John Verran, who had been elected for the seat of Wallaroo on northern Yorke Peninsula.

John Verran's victory was significant in a number of ways. His seat, Wallaroo, was the only one won by Labor in the country beyond Adelaide, saving the ULP from appearing an increasingly marginalised metropolitan party. Indeed, in the capital itself, Labor's position seemed parlous. In 1899 it had held half of the seats in the city but in 1902 it won only one third. Verran's victory, then, was a wake-up call to the party, demonstrating that the ULP needed to pay far more attention to the country districts as well as to the city. Moreover, the accession of John Verran to the ULP caucus at last brought

John Verran, first Premier of a majority Labor government in South Australia.
[Courtesy State Library of South Australia, B669/12]

the twin Labor movements of metropolitan Adelaide and northern Yorke Peninsula much closer together, strengthening the party's base, credibility and appeal beyond the capital. Hitherto, the relationship had been informal and distant but Verran recognised the importance of bringing the Peninsula Labor movement more firmly within the structure of the ULP. As he explained at a 'monster meeting at Moonta', local people would benefit enormously 'through the formation of a branch of the United Labor Party in Moonta, and steps would be taken at an early date to finalise matters in this respect'.[32] Tom Price also understood the importance of bringing the metropolitan and Peninsula movements closer together, and warmly welcomed John Verran's arrival in Parliament.

Writing as 'Peerer', Price revealed his personal affection for Verran. They were like-minded men from similar working backgrounds, one Welsh, the other Cornish, and both were Methodists. 'My dear Verran,' wrote Peerer:

162

'One has only to talk to you for a few moments to discover that you are a full-blooded Cornishman.' Light-heartedly, Peerer explained that 'You call everything "he" except an inyun (engine) and a tom-cat, which by some unexplainable contrariety you and your kinsmen designate as "she"'. Revealing his pan-Celtic knowledge and sympathies, Peerer added that 'Scottish Highlanders have the same peculiarity when speaking of mere man'. Recalling his own modest background, no doubt, Peerer described Verran's childhood at Kapunda, observing that 'Shortly after your removal to Moonta Mines, like many others, you had to bid good-bye to an imperfect schooling and start the real battle of life at the mines'. Aged twenty-three, Verran 'went on the plan as a local preacher', and 'taught the first adult class for males in the Primitive Methodist Church'.

Moreover, Peerer continued, Verran 'early felt it your duty to look after the social as well as the spiritual welfare of your fellows', and this had led him to become both a Rechabite and 'one of the pioneers of unionism in the district'. He progressed from the 'humbler position of steward ... to be president', although Peerer had 'sad recollections of the strike of '92, which lasted for twenty-four weeks and terminated without gain to the men'. But Verran had pulled the union together in the face of defeat, and brought about 'the amalgamation of the various A.M.A. [Amalgamated Miners Association] societies into the Colonial District of South Australia, a federation which meant increased strength'. And finally there some advice from Peerer for John Verran, the novice MP. 'It is quite evident the people of Wallaroo and Yorke's Peninsula have a high opinion of your character when they placed you at the top of the poll by a thumping majority of about 400 votes at the late election. Do not let that give you a swelled head', Peerer implored, 'for you have a lot to learn in the House yet.' Nonetheless, he concluded, 'I congratulate you for telling the electors in the country portion of your district that you were standing as a straight-out Labor man ... You are a most desirable acquisition to the Labor Party'.[33]

As Price (writing as Peerer) acknowledged, Verran had demonstrated that Labor could appeal to farmers and others beyond the urban areas, as he (Verran) had done in the rural parts of Yorke Peninsula. It was a lesson that the ULP took to heart, and during 1903–04 the party's fortunes began to revive. At the Federal elections in December 1903, Labor won all three South Australian Senate vacancies, a significant boost to party morale. In January 1904 a ULP committee was established for the specific purpose of founding country branches, and in the March the committee recommended the inauguration of an annual conference to decide Labor policy. This would be held during the Adelaide Show week in early September to encourage country members to attend. The first annual conference was convened on 8 September 1904. Among the delegates attending were those from nineteen district branches and fourteen representing organisations outside Adelaide, evidence that country voters, especially small farmers, were now being courted in earnest. Much effort was devoted to hearing and acting upon the country point of view.[34] Earlier, in May 1904, metropolitan Labor leaders were careful to attend the annual meeting of the Moonta Miners' Trades and Labor Association, supporting Verran and demonstrating visibly that the ULP was indeed active in areas far beyond Adelaide. Guthrie, Archibald and Tom Price himself were among those who spoke.[35]

Meanwhile, within the State Parliament things had also begun to change. Premier Jenkins had lost half a dozen of his supporters in the 1902 election, and his reaction was to move further to the political right, seeking the active endorsement of the conservative National Defence League, now reconstituted as the Australian National League (ANL), 'the instrument of metropolitan capitalists and absentee landlords', as Dean Jaensch has described it.[36] Archibald Peake, in response, in July 1902 formed what he termed the Liberal Party of the House of Assembly. It had no formal structure beyond Parliament, but was part of what Peake described as 'the formation of a genuine opposition in place of a bogus one'.[37] Moreover, Peake and Price were now talking, and Peerer took the view that Peake should 'rise higher than ever and gather up the Liberal fragments lying around the Chamber and piece them together into a consolidated whole ... there is nothing to prevent the defeat of today becoming the victory of tomorrow'.[38] Peake needed little encouragement, his parliamentary team eventually becoming the focus of a new party, the Liberal and Democratic Union (LDU), which appealed to 'Farmers, graziers, miners

[and] other workers . . . interested in the progress and welfare of the State', and pursued a 'liberal and progressive policy', which included such elements as a progressive land tax, expanded franchise for the Legislative Council, and public ownership of all railways, tramways and wharves.[39] It was a political program not far removed from the aims of the Labor Party, and would provide the basis for future co-operation.

Labor too had called for public ownership of railways and trams, for a progressive land tax, and for provision for State repurchase of large landed estates for redistribution. It had also decided that, should abolition of the Legislative Council prove impossible, then it would settle for universal adult suffrage for both Houses. It also planned a conciliation and arbitration bill, and other proposed measures included conservation of the River Murray for irrigation and navigation (designed to appeal to country voters), amendment of the *Food and Drugs Act* to safeguard public health, and a tightening of the *Landlord and Tenant Act*. Armed with such proposals, Tom Price and the ULP looked forward to the forthcoming 1905 elections. Indeed, in November 1904 Labor joined forces with Peake and his Liberals to vote twenty-one to seventeen in favour of reforming the Legislative Council, the bill failing because it did not gain the requisite absolute majority of the whole House.[40] Jenkins, increasingly beleaguered, resigned ahead of the election and went to London as agent general, to be replaced as Premier by Richard 'Dismal Dick' Butler, who continued the government's drift to the right.[41] Sensing Labor's growing confidence, Jenkins and Butler's conservatives had deployed the bogey of 'red socialism' but Tom Price was having none of it. He insisted that the 'policy of the Labor Party was one of development and progress, and they would not be frightened by the nonsense that had been talked about Socialism'. As Price explained, the 'Labor Party stood for expansion of business as far as South Australia was concerned, and they meant to bring about prosperity and good government . . . [the] misstatements of their opponents would not impede the triumph of the Labor Party'.[42]

The 'future Premier of the State'
In an effort to appeal to voters across the State, Price visited Mount Gambier

in the south-east, and then journeyed northwards to Port Pirie and Quorn in the southern Flinders Ranges. At Quorn, Price spoke on what was perhaps his favourite subject, Christian Socialism, explaining the relationship between politics and religion, and insisting that socialism was nothing less (and nothing more) than the practical implementation of Christianity. He had always stressed 'the morality of the Nonconformist conscience',[43] and at Quorn his message was warmly received. As McCarthy has observed, the 'trip was a triumph, and Tom [Price] spent eight Sundays in a row lecturing on Christian Socialism in a tenacious attempt to counter the conservatives' injurious claims about the aims of Labor'.[44] Later, at a meeting of the newly formed Renmark Labor Party, Price and two colleagues were introduced ironically as 'three dreadful Socialists who, according to certain persons, were bringing ruination to the country'. It was an amusing start but the chairman continued in more serious mood to hail Price as the 'future Premier of the State', while Price spoke the next day in the local Congregational Church on 'Temperance Legislation and the Evils of the Drink Trade'.[45] Labor was both broadening its appeal and affirming its roots.

The long-anticipated election took place on 27 May 1905. As it had hoped, the ULP performed strongly, winning fifteen seats (including all but one of the twelve metropolitan constituencies) to become the largest party in the House of Assembly. Peake's Liberals took six seats, while the ANL was reduced from seventeen to ten, and the newly formed Farmer's and Producers' Political Union (FPPU) won five. Ominously, however, the ANL continued to dominate the Legislative Council, with Kirkpatrick the sole Labor representative. In the Assembly, Butler was defeated twice by Labor voting in tandem with Peake's Liberals, and duly resigned. Price was called to form a government, and he introduced himself as Premier in the House of Assembly on 27 July 1905. It was an auspicious moment – Price had become the first Labor Premier in South Australia's history. But it was not a majority government, and Price governed with the goodwill of Peake and his group in what was effectively a Labor–Liberal coalition. Moreover, the ULP did not regard the arrangement as a formal coalition. Although the parliamentary Labor Party approved the deal, and was delighted that Tom Price was Premier, it made it clear that Price (and

Kirkpatrick – chief secretary in the new administration) would have to resign from caucus, just as Batchelor had done. At the very moment that Price, the Labor leader, became Premier, so he relinquished the leadership to Archibald, his successor in caucus. It was an awkward situation, and was explained thus: the 'Labor Party accepts no responsibility for ministerial actions ... there is no more official connection between Party and Ministry than there was between the Party and the Kingston team'.[46]

As Brian Dickey has observed, from Peake's point of view it was an excellent bargain. He had acquired two of the four cabinet posts, despite the disparity in size between the ULP and his Liberal group in the Assembly, and it was his plan to reform the Legislative Council on the basis of a £15 franchise that was adopted by the new government. Jim Moss judged this to mean that from the first 'Price was forced to compromise with the Peake liberals'.[47] But Dickey offered a more nuanced interpretation when he pointed out that it 'was reform of the Legislative Council which provided the common ground [between Labor and Peake] in the elections and for the coalition'. Moreover, the new government's decision to prioritise the Legislative Council issue actually 'suggests the anxiety of the P[arliamentary] L[abor] P[arty] to secure immediate reform of the Council', a measure of its influence (not weakness, as Moss inferred) in the new parliamentary arrangement.[48]

The Price–Peake government was right to be pre-occupied with the Legislative Council. The Council would only amend, not accept, the crucial reform bill, watering down its provisions. Moreover, while a small number of minor Acts were passed during the 1905 session (one being for the protection of pigeons!), the Council threw out bills on compulsory re-purchases, factories, judicial appointments, land value assessment, taxation, and municipal tramways, and allowed to lapse others on the State Bank and an increase in the number of government ministers.[49] The *Herald* fumed that the Council had 'kicked out the factory Regulations [and] rejected the factory bill on the point of the same big boot ... one by one the progressive and humane measures go up from the people's House, and one by one they are kicked out by the [Australian National] League of surplus wealth and stifled wisdom'.[50] Not surprisingly, the 1906 session of Parliament was convened early, to pick up the pieces and restore momentum, and the reform bill was presented once more. Equally unsurprisingly, the Council once more rejected reform, leaving Price with little choice but to seek from the State Governor a double dissolution of both Houses, to take the question directly to the people. The dissolution was duly granted, with the election set for 3 November 1906. It was to be an important test of public opinion.

'He knew what to do, and what to leave undone'

In fact, the ULP achieved its greatest success so far. It won nineteen of the forty-two seats in the Assembly, including all twelve metropolitan seats, two of three seats in each of the Victoria and Albert, Wallaroo and Stanley constituencies, and one of three in Burra Burra. Additionally, Peake's Liberal and Democratic Union (LDU) – having been given immunity by the ULP – retained its nine country seats, and secured a tenth.[51] In a House in which, for the very first time, every MP was a member of a political party, the Labor–Liberal alliance could muster an impressive twenty-nine votes. However, the ANL continued to dominate the Legislative Council and, far from accepting the election result as a mandate from the people, made it plain that it would continue to oppose reform. In the encroaching impasse, the government threatened a further double dissolution. The ANL decided that it was in its interests to compromise, and offered a £17 property franchise (a vote for any adult paying £17 rent), not far from Peake's proposed £15, together with the right to vote for the Legislative Council extended to a small group of respectable worthies, such as ministers of religion and postmasters. 'To the annoyance of the caucus', Jaensch has observed, 'Price accepted the compromise offer rather than continue the fight for Labor policy'.[52] As Dickey has acknowledged, 'Price was disappointing the party' and the result was far short of Labor's aspirations (Price himself would have preferred abolition).[53] Yet it was the first time since 1856 that an expansion in the franchise for the Legislative Council had been achieved.

Despite the deep unease over the compromise in Labor ranks, it would be wrong to assume, as Marxist historian Jim Moss did, that Price's 'strategy of ... "little at a time" had in fact achieved very little'.[54] Brian Dickey has offered an alternative conclusion – that the 'achievements of the Price–Peake government were ... considerable'.[55] Moreover, John Hirst has pointed out that Peake's Liberals were persuaded by Price to adopt 'socialistic proposals' on a range of issues during the period of coalition government.[56] The 1907 budget, for example, had introduced a minimum wage for all government workers of seven shillings a day. Plans to privatise the tramway system were reversed, establishing the Metropolitan Tramways Trust, and there was legislation to enable inspection of scaffolding and sheepshearers' accommodation. Prosperity had increased as Price assumed office, and this allowed him to spend money on a variety of major projects, including new government railways, weirs on the River Murray, and the development of Outer Harbour to enable much larger ships to navigate the Port River. Especially significant was the introduction of free secondary-school education, and the attendant appointment of Alfred Williams as director of education. Born at St Ives, near Callington, in South Australia, the son of Cornish migrants, Williams grew up at Moonta (where his father was a miner), and became a pupil-teacher at an early age. In a life devoted to education, he was motivated by a 'belief in social equality', attributable to his 'Methodist working-class background', and worked hand-in-glove with Price to develop education provision – one of his innovations was the teaching of Australian history in schools.[57]

The Price–Peake arrangement seemed set fair to continue. But beneath the surface there were tensions. Labor, sensing its rising popularity with the public, let it be known that it might not offer immunity to the LDU members in the forthcoming 1910 election, much to their chagrin and discomfort, prompting Peake to make preliminary overtures to the FPPU. Moreover, there were signs of discontent within Labor ranks. The concerted efforts to woo country voters, especially small farmers, had irked the more militantly left-wing trade unions, led by the Australian Workers Union (AWU) and the United Labourers Union (ULU), which had grown in size and influence in recent years. Indeed, some of these unionists were critical of the ULP more generally, frustrated by its pragmatic approach and demanding a more overtly socialist agenda. Foremost among these critics was Frank Lundie, secretary of the AWU and president of the ULU, who, according to Hirst, looked forward to an early and 'spectacular improvement in the lot of the workers and the humbling of the capitalist class'.[58]

However, the collapse of the Labor–Liberal understanding, when it came, was a result not of these rumblings but of the untimely death of Tom Price on 31 May 1909, aged only fifty-seven. Price had been suffering ill health for some time. His stonecutting days had left him with silicosis, and latterly he had been diagnosed with Bright's disease, a painful and debilitating affliction of the kidneys, often linked to diabetes.[59] Tributes poured in from across Australia and the Empire but it was the Adelaide *Advertiser* which best caught the spirit of the man and the mood of the moment. 'One of the most remarkable feats that Mr Price accomplished', the newspaper opined, was that of 'securing general confidence without sacrificing avowed principles'. Thus:

> He was too clear-headed to be led away by fantastic schemes for revolutionizing society, but he allied himself with progressive movements ... [his] sympathetic interest in his fellow-workers was developed as a necessary consequence but he never lowered himself to the level of demagogue. He knew what to do and what to leave undone, how far to go, and when it was good policy to accept a compromise.[60]

'The typical Cornish miner, with his burley frame'

The ULP lost no time in electing John Verran to succeed Tom Price as leader. By now well known in South Australia and beyond, Verran was characterised by John McConnell Black, the diarist, as 'the typical Cornish miner, with his burley frame, his goatee and general exuberance'.[61] There can be little doubt that Verran's working-class, Cornish–Methodist background accounted for his popularity on Yorke Peninsula and beyond, and his reputation as a firm trade unionist appealed to the ULP's traditional supporters. As the *Advertiser* put it, 'Mr Verran is the more popular at the Peninsula towns because only nine years ago he was working with his three sons at the 360 fathom level at Taylor's Shaft at Moonta'.[62] Indeed, Verran had shared all the exertions, dangers and vicissitudes of those he represented in Parliament. In 1889 he had a narrow escape in Taylor's Shaft, when he fell a distance of about five fathoms but fortunately managed to catch hold of a rope, which broke his fall and probably saved his life. As the *Kadina and Wallaroo Times* reported, Verran 'escaped with only a few cuts to his hands, caused by friction of the rope'.[63] Almost exactly a decade later, Verran had another close brush with death when he was caught in a rockfall underground – his helmet was smashed, and he suffered a severe gash to the head.[64] 'Those who can't schemey must louster', Verran was fond of repeating, using the Cornish dialect of northern Yorke Peninsula to explain that 'those who can't use their brains must do hard manual work', and he was proud to count himself among their number.[65]

Verran lived cheek-by-jowl with his constituents in a modest miner's cottage in Ballarat Row on Moonta Mines, experiencing the rough and tumble of life on the mineral leases where makeshift homes had been erected in *ad hoc* manner among the paraphernalia (and dangers) of the mining industry. Largely law-abiding but lively and often boisterous, the community had its fair share of mishaps – drownings in water tanks, accidents with heavy machinery, 'falling away' in shafts, and occasional epidemics, such as the 'colonial measles' which in the 1870s had decimated the infant population.[66] Again, the Verran family was not immune to these hazards. For small boys the mines were adventure playgrounds, the detritus of the mining industry providing instant materials for outdoor games. In April 1897 there was a 'sad accident', as the *People's Weekly* reported it, 'to a son of Mr John Verran', when a playful boy threw a piece of glass 'which struck the unfortunate lad over the eye, destroying his sight'.[67] Infant mortality, prevalent on the Mines, had also touched the Verran family. John and his wife Catherine (nee Trembath) lost their son James in December 1894, when he died aged a mere three weeks. Their daughter Ida, born at Ballarat Row on 14 May 1896, survived just one month before expiring on 16 June that year.

Methodism provided a bulwark and a comfort in such circumstances. Brought up in the Primitive Methodist church, John Verran had tried to apply Christian values to daily life. When he was eighteen years old, for example, he had briefly visited the Queensland goldfields, where he was lucky enough to strike a rich patch which yielded him a return of £500. In an act of filial duty and faithfulness, he generously handed this amount to his father on his return to Moonta, a manly demonstration of Christian charity that was still remembered with admiration many years later.[68] Moreover, as Tom Price had noted, Verran's Methodism had social and political implications. The *Westralian Worker* considered that Verran 'is essentially a man of religion, and is proud of it'. As the newspaper explained, the 'Bible, says John Verran, is the greatest power for good in the world and next to it stands trades unionism'. Verran was 'a man of the people', the paper continued, adding wistfully that the Labor 'movement could do with a few more John Verrans'.[69] It was an assessment that Verran himself was quick to acknowledge, telling the *Methodist* (published in Sydney) that he was only a rough man but that 'God wants some rough men ... Rough men have purposes to fulfil, and I have mine'. Furthermore, he insisted, the 'Christian Churches needn't hang back from politics'. As well as seeking political action to tackle 'a drink evil and a gambling evil', churches should also condemn the 'sweating evil' where men (and sometimes women and children) were forced by unscrupulous employers to work long hours in appalling conditions for a pittance.[70]

In the pulpit, John Verran consciously mixed religious teaching and political debate, an article in the *Plain Dealer* in 1911, for example, noting that in a sermon delivered in Wallaroo Mines Methodist church, Verran had used the parable of the Barren Fig Tree to criticise 'modern commercialism'.[71] On numerous occasions Verran explained 'that his MP (Membership of Parliament) was due to his PM (Primitive Methodism)'.[72] When he eventually became Premier of South Australia, it was claimed that 'had not Methodism first made him a preacher, politics could not now know him as Premier'.[73] To those who objected that religion had no place in politics, Verran retorted:

> Religion is citizenship, and the relationship between religion and politics is very close ... When we come to justice and righteousness and truth these are great elementary principles of religion which affect the basis of our manhood. Religion is not a question of going to heaven. It is a question of living and making the world better for having been in it.[74]

Like Tom Price, John Verran espoused Christian Socialist values. Caution, conscience, compassion, charity, patience and persuasion were important tenets, he believed. When the Revd Brian Wibberley spoke at Moonta Mines in May 1904 on the subject of 'Christian Socialism', none cheered louder than John Verran when the materialist, anti-Christian, revolutionary socialism of Karl Marx was condemned.[75] As the *Barrier Miner*, published at Broken Hill, put it, Verran was a 'genuine out-and-out member of the working class'. But there was 'nothing of the revolutionary socialist about John Verran', it was explained, 'and those who fall down and worship that particular kind of Joss will find that their praises ... of John Verran will stick in their throats'. Verran, the *Barrier Miner* concluded, 'is not about to bring about the red flag revolution, he has too much sense for nonsense of that sort'.[76]

'Jack, there are certain things that must be done'

Nonetheless, in what was almost a death-bed handing over of the Labor baton, Tom Price had urged John Verran to do what he would 'not live to do'. When he saw the ailing Premier for the last time, Verran explained, Price had said to him: 'Jack, there are certain things that must be done. You will be there. For my sake, carry on the battle.'[77] Among the unfinished business was further reform – or even abolition – of the Legislative Council, Price considering his compromise deal a first step, perhaps, on the road to more far-reaching legislation. Verran certainly thought so, and his forthcoming premiership would prove, as R.J. Miller wrote, the 'most determined attempt to abolish the Legislative Council of South Australia'.[78] But first Verran had to acquire the reins of government.

The Labor caucus had made it clear that it would only continue the coalition arrangement with Peake's LDU if there was another Labor Premier to replace Price, theirs being the larger party. But Peake, already Acting Premier, refused, clinging precariously to power as he attempted to win over members from the political right. He formed a new ministry from among his own nine LDU members – 'the nimble nine', as they were known – and secured the support of Richard Butler's conservative Australian National League. The ULP was insistent that Peake had broken the terms as well as the spirit of the 1905 coalition arrangement, and the *Weekly Herald* protested that Peake had feathered his political nest as Acting Premier when Price was overseas.[79] Now the official Opposition, the ULP began preparing itself for the forthcoming 1910 election, with full adult suffrage for the Legislative Council, the next step on the road to abolition, being at the top of the agenda. Also prominent was the intention to extend free education for all, up to and including university level.

As the battle lines for the 1910 election were drawn up, the conservative *Critic* warned: 'It is a fight in the open. The objectives of each side offers no difficulty of choice. Liberal or Labor! Progress or Chaos! Freedom or Caucus domination.' At all costs, the 'irresponsible experiment-loving Socialists' must be defeated.[80] Verran countered that the ULP was committed to 'moderate measures of much needed reform', the launch of the eagerly awaited *Daily Herald* in March 1910 now providing a strong platform for Labor's voice.[81] The *Advertiser* also noted the ULP's moderate stance, explaining that although the party was 'so often defined as Socialist', its aims were in reality limited to concern for 'the social concerns of the people' and advocacy of 'the nationalization of industries when they become monopolies in private hands', all this a far cry from 'acceptance of the Marxian gospel'.[82] Indeed, as the *Methodist* explained, it was the gospel of Jesus Christ that motivated the ULP. 'Doctrinaire or extreme theories break down in presence of the practical needs of the country', the *Methodist* continued, and 'as the ideals and aims of the Labour Party are humanitarian, and look forward in the direction of bringing a larger share of the rewards of industry within the reach of toilers, we [the Methodist Church] are cordially with it'. Moreover: 'Nor can we forget that the foremost men in the political Labour movement in England are good Methodists.'[83]

In the ensuing election, on 2 April 1910, the ULP won all twelve metropolitan seats, and a further ten in the country, gaining a majority in the House of Assembly and was thus able to form a government in its own right. It was a truly historic moment – the first majority Labor government in Australia, and indeed the world, had come to power! As it was a Labor government, Verran and his Cabinet were not required to withdraw from the party caucus, as Price and Kirkpatrick had done, and in that strict sense it was John Verran who was the first fully fledged Labor Premier of South Australia. There was also a very strong sense of popular mandate, reinforced eleven days later when Labor won

The first Labor ministry in South Australia, 1910, 'elected from the first Labor
Majority of any Parliament in the History of the World'. [Author's collection]
Back row: C. Vaughan, W.J. Denny, J.P. Wilson
Front row: F.S. Wallis, J. Verran, F.W. Coneybeer

power in its own right at Federal level, with Andrew Fisher the first majority
Labor Prime Minister of Australia.[84]

John Verran was the man of the moment, and congratulations poured in.
He was the 'Local Preacher Premier' and the 'Miner Premier'.[85] The *Register*
detected similarities between Verran and his predecessor, the late Tom
Price. 'From miner to Premier is as far a cry as that of his former leader, who
rose from stonecutter to occupy the highest office in the Government', the
newspaper reported, and it could 'detect in Mr Verran passing glimpses of the
characteristics which distinguished the warm-hearted Celt who five years ago
assumed the responsibilities of State in very similar circumstances'.[86] The
Methodist also made favourable comparisons. 'Tom Price was honoured and
trusted as a loyal Methodist and Labour Premier', it was explained, 'and John
Verran (who succeeds him) has shown his quality as an uncompromising
enemy of drink, gambling, and lust'.[87] The *Australian Christian Commonwealth*
(published in Adelaide) exclaimed: 'Against fearful odds which would have

crushed a man of less heroic mould John Verran, by sheer power of personality, has fought his way to place and power.'[88] Mental and physical robustness were common themes in the laudatory press reports. 'Bluff, genial John Verran . . . is a portly, thickset Cornishman, with decided opinions', the *Register* announced: 'The new Premier is not a man who minces his words . . . Unlike Mr Price, who was frail in body, he has great physical strength, and can perform feats which would astonish a practised athlete.'[89] Among the many religious allusions, the *Observer* acknowledged Methodism as 'the cause of his [Verran's] integrity and sterling worth . . . and Moonta Methodism will shine in his reflected glory'.[90]

Indeed it did. 'Hoorah! Hoorah!', echoed the *Register*, as it reported Verran's triumphant return to his constituency following his victory: 'The cheering began at Kadina, was renewed at Wallaroo, and at intervals along the line, and culminated in a magnificent reception at Moonta.'[91] The conservative *Kadina and Wallaroo Times* thought that the demonstrations that greeted Verran were 'the most miserable specimens of his irresponsibility . . . Torches and bands and wild words, and gesticulations'.[92] But the Moonta *People's Weekly* had no such reservations:

> There could be no doubt as to the warmth of the welcome which the Cornish miners sought to give to their [trade union] President on being raised to place and power, and the gathering will be mark an epoch in the history of Moonta. Bunting was flying all over the town, and all Moonta and his wife were out to take part in the gathering. At Kadina and at Wallaroo hundreds of workers joined the train, and the scene at Moonta was an animated one. The Wallaroo town band and the combined Commonwealth and Model brass bands discoursed music as the train drew up in the platform.[93]

There followed speeches, cheering, and even the shedding of tears. Nine hundred people then sat down to tea in relays, as though it were a Methodist tea-treat, and that night there was a large gathering in the Agricultural Society's building at the showground. As Verran described his ascent from pickey-boy to underground miner, Methodist local preacher, trade union leader, and now Premier, he spoke in emotional and moving terms, and the 'tears rolled down his cheeks'. The evening wore on, and as it did so the meeting 'became distinctly evangelical, and cries of "Amen" and "Glory" came from all parts of the hall'. As Oswald Pryor later observed, it 'was one of the strangest political meetings ever held in Australia'.[94]

'Perhaps the weakest administration the State has known'

Alas, the honeymoon period was soon over. As T.H. Smeaton wrote in 1914, the 'path trodden by the Verran government was not a smooth one; beset as it was by snares skilfully laid by its enemies, as well as obstacles heedlessly cast there by its friends'.[95] The decision to place reform of the Legislative Council at the forefront of the government's agenda was interpreted by conservative opponents as nothing less than a revolutionary assault on the status quo. In the subsequent polarisation of opinion, the consolidation of party-political allegiance continued apace. This move towards 'fusion', as it was described at the time, was complete by October 1910 when Peake's LDU, the ANL and the FPPU merged to form a single party, the conservative Liberal Union (LU). Thereafter, the LU expanded rapidly, and by May 1911 could boast no fewer than 282 branches, fifty-two in the metropolitan area. By September there were 343 branches, comprising some 24,000 members. Price's erstwhile policy of appealing to farmers and country voters was gradually undone by the LDU's tireless campaigning and recruitment, and by Labor's increasingly exclusive identification, for better or worse, with the trade unions.[96]

Writing during the Second World War, J.J. Craig looked back pityingly on the Verran government, describing it as 'perhaps the weakest administration the State has known during the present century'.[97] Verran soon found himself assailed on all sides – by a conservative press echoing (and fuelling) increasing public disquiet, by a well organised and unified Opposition, by an intransigent Legislative Council, and – perhaps most wounding of all – by growing criticism and hostility within the Labor movement itself. Verran's first year in office was characterised by industrial strife, with more than half-a-dozen major incidents in Adelaide, each one an embarrassment for John Verran whose instincts and sympathies were often with the trade unionists, but who was under great pressure (not least from the Opposition) to maintain law and order.

He also knew that industrial militancy was undermining his government and its ability to deliver its reformist program. But prices were rising and, as unemployment fell in response to improving economic conditions, so increasingly empowered trade unions strove to maintain real wages and improve working conditions.

In September 1910 railway workers, members of Frank Lundie's ULU, struck over the overbearing attitude of a supervisor. The Verran government refused to intervene in the dispute, and as the strike spread, so did press condemnation. Verran, perhaps unwisely, insisted that the 'labor party of today cannot be dictated to by the revolutionary socialists of this state'.[98] Adopting the language (and confirming the fears) of his opponents, he also risked offending and alienating his supporters. The *Advertiser* warned of 'An Epidemic of Strikes', and even the supportive *Daily Herald* conceded that never before had the workers of South Australia 'exhibited such strong industrial feeling as has existed during the last few months'.[99] The *International Socialist*, published in Sydney, an avowedly left-wing paper, took an increasing interest in the unfolding events in South Australia, evidence that the Labor movement across Australia was watching the State closely. Displaying its decidedly hostile attitude to Verran, the *International Socialist* advised him to 'leave off reading his bible for a few moments' to attend to the real needs of the workers.[100]

In October 1910 the tarpavers' strike erupted in Rundle Street in the heart of Adelaide, where a hundred men ashphalting the road struck for an extra shilling a day. Again, these were ULU members, and Frankie Lundie, speaking in their support, criticised 'the so-called Labour Government' for its handling of the strike.[101] Strike-breakers had been brought in from Melbourne, and duly commenced work in Rundle Street. Meanwhile, a large crowd gathered to heckle the 'scabs', and as the strikers confronted the 'volunteers', so the police intervened, using their truncheons to devastating effect. There was a number of arrests, and subsequently several unionists were gaoled. 'Rioters Imprisoned', reported the *Kadina and Wallaroo Times* approvingly.[102] 'This is what you get from the Labor Government', protested J.M. Dale, secretary of the ULU, but Verran insisted that 'the police will do their duty in regard to the protection of persons and property'.[103] Eventually, the Attorney-General,

W.J. Denny, proposed a compromise deal, which was grudgingly accepted by both sides. The ULU objected that it had not achieved all it wanted, thanks to 'the strike-breaking tactics of the Premier', and the employers grumbled that Denny and the government had effectively intervened on behalf of the strikers.[104]

But if the government had brokered an agreement favourable to the workers, then this went unnoticed by its critics elsewhere in the Labor movement. 'John Verran: Strikebreaker' was the headline in the *International Socialist*, the introduction to a colourful article in which Verran – 'Cornish miner and Christian man' – was systematically vilified. The article described the 'curious scene … enacted in Rundle-street', explaining how a body of 'industrial derelicts' were 'pressed into service' to undertake the work abandoned by the strikers. It noted that 'the Labor Government had sent quite a large force of police to protect the scabs', and reckoned that the 'presence of the police itself was surely sufficient to incite trouble'. The paper continued: 'it is not surprising to read that a collision occurred between the people and the Labor Party's police. With a savagery worthy of – well, worthy of the Labor Party's police, the unionists were attacked, and beaten and battered with bludgeons carried by John Verran's administrators of Law and Order'. Thereafter, 'a large force of armed police patrol[ed] the streets of Adelaide', and 'unionists and peaceful citizens were insolently ordered to move on', while those 'strikers who dared to venture near the job where the blacklegs were working under the official protection of the Labor Government were, threatened with arrest and jail by the Labor Government'. Indeed, several unionists were imprisoned, the *International Socialist* reported, so 'brutal, so barefaced, was the Labor Government's treatment of the strikers', and the paper noted with disgust that the House had cheered loudly when Verran 'read them the villainous, cowardly instructions he had issued to the police'.[105]

'Where were the golden streets?'

There was worse to come. In December 1910 the Drivers' Union went on strike, an episode that was to be especially damaging to Verran and his government. The drivers demanded eight shillings a day for an eight hour day. Led by

179

John Gunn (later to become Labor Party leader), 2,000 drivers were soon on strike. J.M. Dale, the ULU secretary, spoke in their support, evidencing the new levels of solidarity and militancy that had been achieved in the trade union movement in recent months. 'They had miles of proof', Dale declared, 'that when Labor men got into power they had forgotten the class that put them there. For twenty years they had been urged to obtain Labor majorities. They had got those majorities but where was their heaven? Where were the golden streets?'.[106]

Virtually all commercial traffic in Adelaide came to a halt as the strike took hold. Shortages of key products were predicted, and there were rumours that famine was imminent. Again, there was violence and when strike-breakers (some of whom were armed) engaged by the Tramways Trust clashed with the strikers, rioting ensued, provoking police intervention. Critics suggested that John Verran was incapable of taking the strike seriously. John McConnell Black wrote that 'Jack Verran took a jovial interest in the strike and Gunn, the secretary of the union, used to stroll across Victoria Square [in the centre of Adelaide] from Trades Hall and consult with the Premier, who sat smoking his short pipe with his legs up on the fence of his boarding house in Landrowna Terrace'.[107] It was rumoured that Verran had been summoned to Government House for a dressing-down (and possibly a threat of dismissal) by the State Governor, and that a Naval gunboat would be sent to Port Adelaide to restore order in the city. In the end, the government submitted the dispute to the Court of Industrial Appeals. The strike was settled amicably enough, and the Drivers' Union achieved most of its demands. But John Verran's credibility had been further dented, as had that of his government.

The Opposition, in and out of Parliament, had been careful to exploit the situation to the full, and was given additional ammunition in the form of the State mining controversy that unfolded during 1910 and 1911. Verran had decided, apparently unilaterally, to acquire the near-defunct Wandilta, Yelta and Paramatta copper mines, all on northern Yorke Peninsula and located within his Wallaroo constituency, with a view to running them as State enterprises. As he explained: 'God had put the wealth in the earth for everyone and not just a few people.'[108] To his opponents this 'nationalisation' was seen as further evidence of Verran's commitment to 'advanced socialism', although Verran retorted that it was just sound business sense. It was a disgrace, he said, that promising properties 'should be languishing for want of capital'. At one of the ailing mines, he insisted, all that was needed was 'a good Cornish lift pump to get the water out.'[109] Unwisely, perhaps, Verran purchased the Yelta and Paramatta mines without reference to Parliament and, indeed, without consulting all the relevant officials within his own Department of Mines. As he snorted angrily: 'I am not going to officers who don't know as much about mining as I do'.[110] Although the Yelta and Paramatta mines had lost £200,000 in the eight years before July 1911, Verran reckoned that the Yelta had made a profit of £1,000 a month during the early 1900s, and argued that recent reverses were merely a result of bad management. He envisaged, he said, a return of about 4% on the capital invested, noting that the two properties had been purchased for only £6,000 and that the smelting plant at the Yelta was alone worth £20,000.

In the controversy that ensued, the Labor-sponsored *Daily Herald* supported the purchases, as might be expected, but the *Register* considered that Verran was 'wasting public money in a vain attempt to resurrect an abandoned property in his district'.[111] The public purse was being misused to fund a dubious project in Verran's political backyard, it was argued, a blatant attempt to curry favour with his constituents, a crass example of regional favouritism that voters elsewhere in the State could not fail to notice. On Yorke Peninsula itself, the locality supposedly set to benefit from Verran's initiative, the *Kadina and Wallaroo Times* voiced its condemnation of State ownership, while Captain Richard Cowling (a local mining expert) advised that Verran's estimation of the mines' worth was unduly optimistic.[112] Yet there were those who approved of the plan. William Polglase, a Cornish miner with sixty-six years' experience 'in different parts of the world', wrote to the *Daily Herald* in fulsome terms. Verran could be trusted, Polglase explained, because he was 'always honourable, honest and truthful . . . and loved by all'. Moreover, he continued, Verran was 'a first-class miner, a good judge of lodes and their worth'. Indeed, Verran 'did one great thing for this State when he started the Yelta and Parramatta [*sic*] Mines for the taxpayers'.[113] W.H. Trewennack was duly engaged as captain to run the mines but the experiment in State ownership did not last long, as the incoming government in 1913 took measures to close the properties.

The Legislative Council and Verran's downfall

Meanwhile, the attempt to reform the Legislative Council had worked steadily towards its climax. As R.J. Miller put it in his analysis of the unfolding crisis, the Verran government, with its majority in the Assembly, and believing it had the support of the people, was 'prepared to go all the way, even if it meant political suicide'.[114] The Legislative Council had thrown out an adult suffrage bill in 1910, and in September 1911 it rejected what was known as the 'Council Veto Bill'. Taking its cue from the concurrent reform of the House of Lords in the United Kingdom, which the British upper house had reluctantly accepted in August 1910, the Verran government sought now to limit the power of the Legislative Council in like manner. The 'Council Veto Bill' provided that whenever a bill had been passed by the House of Assembly in two sessions in one Parliament and then once again in a further Parliament, an election having taken place in between, then the bill might be presented for Royal assent without further reference to the Legislative Council. When the Legislative Council refused this provision, Verran turned to Asquith's government in the United Kingdom, requesting assistance so 'that the Constitution be so amended by an Imperial Act as to enable the matured will of the people of the people of South Australia on these and all other questions to become law'.[115]

Having already rejected or allowed to lapse more than a dozen bills, the Legislative Council, turning the screw yet tighter, now found an excuse to defer the government's Appropriation (Budget) Bill, effectively denying its supply and ultimately its ability to govern. The pretext was Verran's allegedly illegal practice of 'tacking', the attaching of new, hitherto undiscussed, public works to the Appropriation Bill – in this case provision for a State brickworks and timber yard. On 23 December 1911, the State Governor, on Verran's advice, sent an urgent cablegram to the British government, explaining that supply was running out and again requesting Imperial intervention. Three days later came the reply: 'interference of Imperial Parliament in internal affairs of self-governing State would not be justified under any circumstances until every constitutional remedy had been exhausted and then only in response to the overwhelming majority of the people, and if necessary to enable Government of the country to be carried on'.[116]

Intriguingly, Verran had also written personally to Ramsay MacDonald, leader of the British Labour Party, seeking whatever support he might be able to offer at Westminster. MacDonald's response is interesting, not only for its lack of attention to detail – his letter was addressed to 'W. Varran" and hailed John Verran as 'My dear Mr Varran' – but because it faithfully echoed the line adopted by the Asquith government. MacDonald was 'afraid that the Colonial office [sic] could not interfere at the present stage', and explained that a 'general election seems to be necessary and immediately after the election you should pass a resolution asking the Colonial Office to give you a new Constitution'. Offering a crumb of comfort, he assured Verran that such action 'would put your friends in this country in a position from which they could do some fighting for you'. He also agreed that 'Your Constitution is absolutely intolerable, and you can rely upon our doing everything to enable the democracy of your State to govern itself free from interference both of ourselves here and of your own "fat men" [capitalists]'.[117]

Faced with such unanimity of opinion, Verran had little choice but to seek the dissolution of the House of Assembly and thus a fresh election. On 16 January 1912 the Assembly was duly dissolved, and the brief election campaign that followed was described at the time as 'the most important and fiercest political battle ever fought in South Australia'.[118] Verran attacked Peake personally, calling him 'a political rogue' and condemning him and his 'so-called Liberals ... [for] turning from Democrat to Conservative'.[119] The Liberal Union, in turn, could insist that: 'It is NOT the people versus the Legislative Council (merely pretext). The real issue is the LABOR SOCIALIST POLICY versus the true interests of the whole community. We stand for the PEOPLE against SOCIALISM. Remember the Drivers' Strike.'[120] Verran's failure to reform the Legislative Council, together with his inability to get so many of his reformist bills through the obstructionist upper house, frustrated a large number of the government's increasingly disillusioned supporters.

Besides, as we have seen, many trade unionists had been dismayed by what they imagined to have been Verran's betrayal of Labor's principles. To this was added the Liberal Union's formidable organisation and its effective campaign against 'socialism' and the government's apparent incompetence.

Under attack from all sides, the Labor Party suffered a major defeat in the election on 10 February 1912, only sixteen ULP members being returned, against twenty-four for the Liberal Union. On 16 February, the first Labor government in South Australia came formally to an end, as the first distinctly Liberal Union government was formed under Archibald Peake. The only constituency not to register a swing against Labor was faithful Wallaroo, where all three seats were won by the ULP, contributing almost 20% of the party's remaining representation in the Assembly. As the *People's Weekly* reported, John Verran was still 'one of the most popular men in Labor circles in the mining district', despite what might have happened elsewhere, and was 're-elected as senior member for the Wallaroo Electorate'.[121] Also elected were J.T. Herbert and J.A. Southwood. Herbert was a native of Wallaroo, where he was born in 1863. A carpenter by trade, he had worked in the town before moving to Broken Hill in 1886, where he was employed in the Proprietary mine, returning to Wallaroo in 1900 to work in the smelting works. Southwood was a native of neighbouring Wallaroo Bay, where he was born in 1868, and had likewise spent time at Broken Hill, where he was a print compositor and became a foundation member of the Barrier Typographical Society. He later established the *Katoomba Times* in New South Wales, and in 1894 transferred his printing press to Kadina, where he founded the *Plain Dealer* newspaper. Together, Verran, Herbert and Southwood, with their solid local credentials, were a strong voice for the Peninsula Labor movement in the new Parliament, perpetuating a tradition that went back to the early days of trade unionism at Moonta and Wallaroo.

However, notwithstanding the strong affirmation of support on northern Yorke Peninsula, Verran's reputation had suffered. Significantly, despite his continued popularity at Moonta, Wallaroo and Kadina, the Methodist heartland, he had lost the hitherto unequivocal support of the Methodist establishment in South Australia. The *Australian Christian Commonwealth* had warned in February 1912 that Verran and his Cabinet colleagues had been too 'prepared to take their orders from the more violent and revolutionary forces in their party'.[122] Detecting a sinister Irish hand in this, the journal felt that 'efforts are being made to dominate the Labour Party by the Church of Rome'.[123] Here were the first signs of an estrangement of institutional Methodism from the United Labor Party, a distancing that (as we shall see in Chapter 7) became deeper and more profound during the conscription crisis in the Great War. Here too was an indication of the increasing sectarianism that would become a feature of religious and political debate during the war.

John Verran, no doubt, was touched by the demonstration of loyalty that he had encountered in his home constituency. But he had been distracted during the election campaign by his wife's illness. The *People's Weekly* reported on 20 January 1912 that Catherine Verran 'underwent a serious operation' in hospital. Although the paper added that she 'was getting on satisfactorily', it was soon plain that Mrs Verran was not a well woman.[124] Verran soldiered on as party leader but he found the task increasingly difficult and burdensome. By July 1913 he had had enough, and duly tendered his resignation as party leader, although signalling his intention to remain a member for Wallaroo. When asked his reasons for standing down, Verran replied that he had been party leader for five hard years, and 'he should take a rest'. Moreover, Catherine remained in poor health, and 'his first duty was to his wife and family'. It was also in the interests of the party, Verran added, that it should have a new leader, and Crawford Vaughan was unanimously elected to that position.[125]

Less than a year later, Catherine Verran was dead. Feeling tired after tea one evening, she went to lie down. 'Shortly afterwards', according to the *People's Weekly*, 'she came down to Mr Verran and her daughters in the dining-room, and startled them by the statement that she was dying, and within a quarter of an hour she had passed away'.[126] She was only fifty-four. John Verran 'never had a single angry word with his wife during their married life',[127] it was said, and while John forbade card playing and dancing, Catherine 'realised the boredom her family, especially her four sons, might suffer' and so 'encouraged a little relaxation at home' when Verran was away.[128] Years later, her daughter Ruby remembered that Catherine played the mouth organ well, and to the tune of 'The Wild Colonial Boy' taught her sons to tap dance by the fire at Ballarat Row. By all accounts it was a close-knit family, and Catherine Verran understood her husband and delighted her children with her bubbly sense of fun. Her passing left a great gap in family life, and none felt her loss more keenly than John Verran himself.

John Verran's grief explains, perhaps, the sadness and intense bitterness that he expressed with ever greater ferocity and emotion during the Great War years, not least over the conscription issue. It was a sadness made all the more grievous by the death of his brother-in-law John Thomas, killed in September 1916 in an underground accident in the Great Boulder Mine in Western Australia, and that of his own son Percy, who died the following year aged thirty-seven years from 'miners' phthisis', a disease contracted in the goldmines at Boulder. Especially painful was the tragic loss of Percy's only son Jack, John Verran's grandson, who had died in the Kalgoorlie Children's Hospital in October 1915, aged just four years and three months. So too was the death of Verran's twin sister Alice in September 1918.[129] Later, in 1922, Verran would look back on those times, reflecting 'feelingly [on] the death of some of those with whom he was intimately acquainted'. As the *People's Weekly* reported: 'Since the passing of his wife and son, his life had been restless.'[130] The Great War years were intensely difficult ones for John Verran personally, who felt increasingly bereft and beleaguered, just as they would be for the Labor Party more generally.

Chapter Seven

Labor and the Conscription Crisis

Crawford Vaughan, elected to the Labor leadership in South Australia in 1912, was cast in a different mould to that of Tom Price and John Verran. Price and Verran were largely self-educated, and had acquired their leadership skills in the Methodist church. Both were practical, working-class men – a Welsh stonecutter and a Cornish miner – and both had been born in Britain. The two men were firm trade unionists, and had come to the Labor Party by way of the unions. Crawford Vaughan, by contrast, was born in South Australia in 1874 (he was eighteen years younger than Verran), and had been educated at Prince Alfred College in Adelaide. He had worked as an office clerk and as a journalist, both 'white-collar' occupations, before entering Parliament in 1905. Treasurer in Verran's government, Crawford Vaughan had demonstrated that he was highly numerate and literate, and he emerged as the Labor Party's most able performer in parliamentary debates. These skills smoothed the way towards his leadership of the party. But he also represented a growing 'middle class' component in the party, known somewhat pejoratively in Labor ranks as the 'black-coat brigade'.[1]

Crawford Vaughan and the Great War

As leader of the Opposition, Crawford Vaughan was a robust and effective critic of Archibald Peake's Liberal Union government. Like Labor before it, the Liberal Union had turned its attention to constitutional issues. In 1913 it

Crawford Vaughan, Labor Premier in 1915,
pictured here in 1911 when a member of Verran's government.
[Courtesy State Library of South Australia, PRG280/1/44/398]

introduced a bill increasing membership of the House of Assembly from forty to forty-six, and the Legislative Council from eighteen to twenty members. This was opposed by Labor, mainly because the size and boundaries of the new constituencies were determined by the government itself, rather than an independent electoral commission, resulting in a deliberate weighting in favour of rural areas. The bill also tightened the qualification for suffrage for the Legislative Council, removing the extension of the franchise to 'worthies' such as policemen, postmasters and ministers of religion, concessions won in Tom Price's earlier compromise. These new measures were condemned as reactionary by Labor, the *Daily Herald* opining that 'the whole policy of the Conservatives [as it dubbed the Liberal Union] is manifestly one of fearing the people, and of taking every precaution, no matter how fraudulent it may be, to prevent the people governing themselves'.[2] There was also dismay and indignation when the Peake government pushed through coercive

Industrial Arbitration legislation, which imposed dire impediments on strikes.

To this was added the changing economic fortunes after 1912, when rising unemployment caused increasing anxiety and unrest, and deteriorating conditions were exacerbated by the drought of 1914–15. The latter was especially severe, with average rainfall falling by at least a half in South Australia and wheat yields diminishing accordingly. Hard-pressed farmers urged the government to introduce a 'complete grain purchasing scheme' but this was rejected. Fears of water shortages in Adelaide added to the disquiet, as did the government's decision to increase taxes as its revenue fell. The ULP, meanwhile, was experiencing an upturn in its fortunes. Shrewdly, the party focused much of its attention on the difficulties experienced by rural communities. Specifically, Labor policy now advocated the establishment of a Land Board, which would allot land with a greater emphasis on equality, the revenue from which would be devoted to debt redemption. Tax on personally earned income from the land would be abolished, with that on absentee landholders substantially increased. There would be a Land Court of Appeal to hear disputes, and a separate board set up to regulate and assist the wheat industry. All this was music to countrymen's and countrywomen's ears.[3]

By now Vaughan was on the attack. In July 1914, at the opening of the parliamentary session, he launched a motion of no-confidence against the Liberal Union government, condemning its electoral gerrymandering, its subservient deference to the Legislative Council, its failure to act in the countryside, and its partisan Arbitration Act. But as the motion was being debated, increasingly worrying news began to arrive from Europe. The ULP attempted to withdraw its motion, in acknowledgement of the grave situation that now faced South Australia and the British Empire, but Peake insisted on a vote. Labor promptly abstained, and both sides in the House joined in a rousing rendition of 'God Save the King'.[4] Yet any thought that bi-partisanship would mark the ensuing war years was swiftly disabused, as political controversy rose to new heights.

Initially, the outbreak of war in August 1914 exacerbated the State's economic difficulties. By 1914, in a deliberate policy of 'peaceful penetration' (a phrase that Australian soldiers would turn ironically against their German enemies on the battlefields of France and Belgium), several large German companies more or less controlled Australia's entire base metal industry.[5] The great bulk of the copper produced on northern Yorke Peninsula thus found its way to Germany. Faced with the abrupt closure of its German market almost literally overnight, the Wallaroo and Moonta Mining and Smelting Company had little alternative but to cease production immediately. As H. Lipson Hancock, the general manager, explained: 'in consequence of the outbreak of war in Europe, and the inability of the contractors [the Germans] to take delivery of our copper, it has become imperative to at once curtail operations'.[6] The pumps would be kept going to prevent inundation of the lower levels, and at the Moonta cementation works 'leaching liquors' would continue to be applied so that the treatment of recycled mine waste could be restarted if and when required. In all other respects, however, the mines were suddenly idle, some 2,000 men thrown out of work, and thousands more jobs put at risk in the regional economy of northern Yorke Peninsula.

The situation at Moonta and Wallaroo was replicated across Australia, and William 'Billy' Hughes, shortly to become Australia's wartime Prime Minister (but in late 1914 still Attorney-General in the Federal Labor government), intervened to ensure permanent national control over what were now vital strategic metals. This included the formation of an association of principal copper producers, designed to co-ordinate the supply of all copper surplus to Australia's requirements to Britain to facilitate the manufacture of munitions. On northern Yorke Peninsula these developments were followed closely by John Verran and the other local Labor MPs, and by the Amalgamated Miners' Association (AMA) which had been obliged to agree that, when production was resumed, 10% of its members' wages would be held back for the duration of hostilities, to be paid in full at the war's end. There was even a suggestion that an extension to 20% might become necessary, should things fare badly, a source of anxiety for local trade unionists. However, as Keith Bailey has shown, after the initial hiatus, the speedy return to work engineered by Hughes and the Federal government heralded a period of hectic production and renewed prosperity in the Peninsula mines.[7] The 10% retention was soon abandoned, and the back-pay refunded in full.

At the close of November 1914, the *Yorke's Peninsula Advertiser* could observe with satisfaction that, although the region was 'seriously affected on the outbreak of war by the closing of the Mines', the subsequent 'successful financial negotiations' undertaken by the Federal government had 'permitted and enabled our mining industry to resume'. The Moonta and Wallaroo company itself had exhibited its 'patriotic feelings in so actively dealing with the serious situation and restarting work', while 'the employees too assisted in the situation by willing co-operation'.[8] Here was an analysis that suggested a determination by all parties to work together for the common good and to support the war effort. In many ways it was an accurate assessment, at least in the short term, and the years 1915–18 were boom times in the Peninsula mines, the comparatively high wages paid to the mineworkers filtering through into the regional economy, which prospered as a result, despite the drought in its rural hinterland. However, as the AMA readily appreciated, the surge in demand for Australian copper, and the attendant rise in international copper prices, meant unprecedented returns for shareholders. There was a discomforting sense that investors were profiting unduly from the war.

Billy Hughes' especially generous treatment of corporate interests in the mining industry had raised eyebrows in the Labor movement throughout Australia.[9] In August 1914, on the outbreak of war, the *Register* newspaper had remarked reassuringly that: 'Although a "red-hot Labour centre", the Yorke's Peninsula mines have been remarkably free of labour troubles.'[10] After the bitter strike of 1891–92, there had indeed been a long period of industrial harmony on the Peninsula, the AMA using its influence to good effect in securing various advantageous agreements in return for supporting the company's ambitious modernisation plans at the mines.[11] However, beneath the veneer of continued co-operation in the Empire's interest, there was in the events of late 1914 a renewed suspicion of the Wallaroo and Moonta Mining and Smelting Company that would eventually manifest itself in a complex series of disputes in 1916–17, when, as we shall see, Labor issues would become inextricably entwined in wider conflicts involving conscription (to the armed forces), religion and ethnicity. For the moment, however, there seemed only goodwill and consensus, a desire for the Peninsula's mining industry to prosper in service of the British Empire.[12]

191

The Peninsula mines and smelters now back in full production, the greater part of the region's copper was purchased by the British government for Kynoch Ltd, the ammunition manufacturer in Birmingham, England.[13] This laid the foundation for the mines' wartime prosperity, and strengthened the belief locally that the Peninsula's economy was now contributing directly and significantly to the war effort, an important factor in the conscription debate that was shortly to emerge.[14] Likewise, at Broken Hill, initial dislocation was addressed by Federal government action. Tied in closely to that of South Australia, the downturn in Broken Hill's faltering economy had been felt keenly in Adelaide. South Australian railway receipts had declined dramatically, as had the provision of many goods and services by the State's industries, and the Port Pirie smelters were threatened with imminent disruption.

The North Broken Hill Mine, the Broken Hill South, and the Zinc Corporation – three of the largest mines on the Barrier – had hitherto sold almost all their lead concentrate to German smelters. Now they were summarily cut off from their main market, throwing them into crisis. The lead smelters in Australia – Port Pirie (South Australia), Zeehan (Tasmania) and Cockle Creek (New South Wales) – had the capacity to deal with only half of this additional volume. The solution was for the big three – the North, South, and Zinc Corporation – to acquire a controlling interest in the Port Pirie smelters (the closest geographically to Broken Hill), investing heavily to greatly increase their capacity. Zinc, also produced in large quantities at the Broken Hill mines, was likewise disrupted by the outbreak of hostilities. Before 1914, Zinc concentrate was sent by rail to Port Pirie, and from there by sea to the smelters of Belgium and Germany. The Port Pirie smelters were capable of treating only a tiny fraction of Broken Hill's zinc output, and huge dumps of unsold concentrate grew up around the mines. But zinc, with its corrosion-resistant qualities, was essential for the manufacture of munitions. Eventually, W.M. 'Billy' Hughes, as Prime Minister, persuaded Britain to purchase the existing Broken Hill concentrate, while Australia's principal zinc producers moved to adopt the new electrolytic process for producing metallic zinc developed by the Anaconda Copper Mining Company in America in 1914.[15] All this benefited South Australia's economy, and was welcomed by the AMA and other trade unions.

'Undying hostility to the conscription of life and labour'

Meanwhile, South Australia's election campaign had begun in earnest in February 1915. As before, Crawford Vaughan focused on economic issues and the State government's apparent inability to address them. Peake's inertia was contrasted with the robust intervention of the Federal Labor government to safeguard South Australia's copper industry. The election result was resounding. The ULP won twenty-six seats, an increase of ten, and the party duly took office for a second time, with Crawford Vaughan as Premier. Peake himself was humiliated, losing his seat in the election and only clawing his way back into to the Assembly at a by-election prompted by the opportune resignation of another Liberal Union member. Vaughan's program was ambitious. Bills ranged from financial advances to settlers (designed to provide easier credit) and revised industrial arbitration (removing the power to imprison and other disabilities), to raising of the school leaving age to fourteen. But the Legislative Council played its usual obstructionist role, so that not all proposed legislation found its way onto the statute book. Economic conditions remained difficult, despite the resumption of copper mining and smelting, and at the 1915 party conference there were rumblings on a number of issues. In particular, Frank Lundie of the Australian Workers' Union (AWU) successfully opposed the introduction of individual voting by all ULP members in pre-selection plebiscites because the trade unions 'would lose their hold of the political movement'.[16]

Lundie's concerns were prescient. In discerning a growing tension between the 'industrial' and 'political' wings of the Labor movement – the trade unionists and the politicians – Lundie anticipated the conscription controversy that was about to engulf the Labor Party, in South Australia and in the country as a whole. W.M. 'Billy' Hughes had become Labor Prime Minister of Australia in October 1915. His predecessor, Andrew Fisher, had supported the voluntary principle in recruiting for the Australian armed forces, and considered conscription unnecessary and undesirable. Hughes, however, was an early convert to the view that voluntary recruitment alone would not be enough to meet Australia's military manpower requirements. He left Australia for London on 15 January 1916, ten days before the introduction of conscription in

Britain (but not Ireland), and did not return home until more than six months later. Posturing as a great Imperial statesman, Hughes adjudged his London sojourn an unqualified success, and when he arrived back at Fremantle on 31 July 1916 he was met by cheering, flag-waving crowds. But by now he had declared his support for conscription. The *Australian Worker* warned: 'Welcome home to the cause of anti-conscription. Let him not mistake the popping of champagne corks for the voice of the people.'[17]

In fact, campaigns for and against conscription had already emerged by the time Hughes returned to Australia. Ostensibly, the divisions that appeared were on class lines – the middle-class generally supporting conscription, and the working-class against – but the reality was far more complex.[18] There were anti-conscriptionists who opposed conscription because they were against a 'capitalist war'. More numerous were those who supported the war but deplored the abandonment of the voluntary principle and the coercion implicit in conscription. There were also those, committed to the war, who felt that Australia's manpower could be harnessed more profitably in other ways to support the war effort – for example, in the mines and on the farms – and therefore also opposed conscription. There were even those who imagined that conscription would cause manpower shortages and open the door to foreign workers, forcing down wages and compromising the White Australia policy.[19] The pro-conscription lobby was equally diverse, ranging from those who insisted that conscription was a matter of honour (to show good faith with Britain and New Zealand, both of which had introduced conscription), to others who believed that only the full mobilisation of the Empire's manpower resources would defeat 'Prussian militarism'. There were those who criticised the 'slackers' and the 'shirkers' who had failed to volunteer, and who saw conscription as a means of getting these reluctant fellows into uniform. There were also diverse ethnic and religious factors at play in the conscription debate, and in some areas of Australia there was a clear distinction between town and country. There were likewise variations between and within States, and sometimes important regional issues were at stake.[20]

The Labor movement, in particular, was exposed to this complexity of opinions and influences, and was in imminent danger of splitting on the matter, its 'industrial' wing inclining to the 'Anti' cause (as it was known) and the 'political' more likely to be pro-conscriptionist. This was the case in South Australia, as it was elsewhere, although there were several Labor Assembly members (including John Price, son of Tom Price, newly elected in 1915) who became prominent 'Anti' supporters, to the intense irritation of Crawford Vaughan and his colleagues in government, and who worked hand-in-glove with the 'industrial' wing. As Jenny Stock has observed, the 'high level of Labour and Trade Union participation in the "Anti" campaign [in South Australia] made almost inevitable a public identification of the Labour Party with anti-conscription ... much to the chagrin of its "black-coat brigade".'[21]

The ULP had decided initially in December 1915 that it would only support conscription if it was accompanied by a parallel compulsory conscription of wealth, presumably to be levied on 'the capitalists'. But in January 1916 Crawford Vaughan, as Premier, announced his support for conscription, should its introduction become necessary, and thereafter the battle-lines hardened. By June 1916 the United Trades & Labor Council (UTLC) had decided to 'oppose conscription by all lawful means ... and to oppose all Labor members of parliament who supported conscription'. The UTLC then promptly circulated all Labor MPs, making it perfectly clear that it would confront 'any member of parliament ... who dares to support the pernicious policy of Conscription'.[22] A hastily convened Australian Trade Unionism and Conscription Congress declared 'its undying hostility to conscription of life and labour',[23] and the Labor parties in almost all States came out firmly against conscription – only Western Australia remained equivocal.

News of the Anzacs' exploits at Gallipoli had initially boosted voluntary recruitment in Australia. Enlistment in May 1916 was 10,656 but then dropped-off substantially to around 6,000 a month during June, July and August of that year. This decline may have reflected a growing 'war weariness', especially as the vast casualty lists of the Somme battles were published in July and August. But it was also evidence that the reservoir of eligible males was already decreasing. Accordingly, on 30 August 1916 Hughes announced a nation-wide referendum on conscription, claiming in the Federal Parliament that no fewer than 32,500 new recruits were required in September, with a further 16,500 each month thereafter.[24] The referendum announcement unleashed a torrent of pent-up fury, and cracks in society appeared suddenly in areas that only months before had appeared to reflect an almost comfortable consensus. Ostensibly cohesive communities were now ripped asunder as the argument raged.

'Particularly hard-fought in Wallaroo'

As Jenny Stock has observed, in South Australia 'the battle over conscription was particularly hard-fought in Wallaroo'. In the 1915 elections, contested within the newly redrawn boundaries, the constituency had returned two MPs – John Verran and J.T. Herbert – both of whom were Labor. However, both were also staunch pro-conscriptionists, in marked contrast to the miners, smelters and waterside workers of the district who rallied to the 'Anti' cause. The stage was set for confrontation, and the close-knit nature of the northern Yorke Peninsula community ensured that the debate would be vigorous and that a great many local people would become embroiled. As Jenny Stock explained, 'the three mining and smelting towns [Moonta, Wallaroo and Kadina] which made up the constituency were so large and in such close proximity that enormous crowds were able to gather at the frequent meetings'. Moreover, in contrast to other localities across the State, where pro-conscriptionist meetings predominated, 'only here [on northern Yorke Peninsula] did the number of 'Anti' gatherings equal the conscriptionist ones'.[25]

A taste of what lay in store was provided on 29–30 March 1916, months before the Somme offensive and with voluntary recruiting still running strong as the Australian Imperial Force was reinforced and trained in Egypt. To encourage enlistment, a special Recruiting Train toured South Australia, on this occasion making its way to northern Yorke Peninsula. Among its passengers was none other than Crawford Vaughan, Labor Premier and arch pro-conscriptionist, who had come to make a personal plea for all eligible males to join up. He was accompanied by one Corporal Evans, a veteran of Gallipoli, who would persuade local men to volunteer, or so he thought. The train arrived at Wallaroo Mines railway station, outside Kadina, at 9.40 in the morning, with a brass band playing and Boy Scouts forming a guard of honour. The Wallaroo and Moonta Mining and Smelting Company had made it clear that it would not frustrate the ambitions of those who chose to enlist, and its employees were given time off work to attend the Recruiting Train and listen to the speeches.[26]

The Recruiting Train incident, Wallaroo Mines, March 1916.
[Courtesy Keith Bailey]

Corporal Evans addressed the assembled mineworkers, urging them to step forward. Nobody moved. He redoubled his exhortation, and still no one budged. Expressing his disappointment, Evans confessed himself more surprised by this lack of response than he had been by the Turkish reception at Gallipoli. More significantly, he had a stark warning for the mineworkers. 'Don't you think it better to go now, voluntarily', he asked, 'than have a recruiting sergeant calling for you with a squad of fixed bayonets?'. Would it not be more honourable to enlist as a volunteer, he implied, than to wait until conscription was introduced, with its inevitable coercion into the armed forces of the unwilling. Exasperated, a clearly disconcerted Corporal Evans turned to Crawford Vaughan. 'It's no use, Mr Premier', he exclaimed, 'I can't shift them!'.[27] In the end, only a handful of men came forward during the two-day visit to northern Yorke Peninsula: four at Kadina, two each at Moonta and Wallaroo, four from the small agricultural settlement of Paskeville, and ten at outlying Port Wakefield.

However, as Keith Bailey has argued, this reluctance was hardly a measure of the mineworkers' patriotism. Together, they had already contributed some £12,000 to the various voluntary organisations supporting the troops, along with another £13,000 to the Federal government's War Loan Fund. They had also supported fundraising activities, such as a Miners' Carnival in Kadina, and held their own charity 'hammer and tap' display at Kadina showground, where 'pares' (groups) of miners competed against each other to see who could drill six inches into a hard-rock slab in the time allotted.[28] But their patriotic sentiment did not extend to volunteering for the armed forces – except on those occasions when there were calls for skilled miners to join specialist tunnelling units.[29] Rather, the mineworkers saw their place of duty as the mines and smelters, and considered that they were already making a significant contribution to the Empire's war effort, much of their output going to assist munitions manufacture in England. Indeed, many felt that their individual contribution as a skilled miner or smelter would far outweigh anything they might achieve as a soldier in uniform. Additionally, after the initial dislocation on the outbreak of war, there had been a tacit understanding between the miners' trade union (the AMA) and the mining company, in which they would both strive together to maximise output. In this way, industrial disputes were kept to a minimum. The men benefitted from this arrangement – comparatively high wages and secure employment – but there was no sense that mining was a soft option, for it was hard and hazardous work.

Moreover, as Corporal Evans and Crawford Vaughan were now painfully aware, there was already grassroots hostility in the Labor movement towards conscription as a concept. Instinctively opposed to government coercion and supportive of the voluntary principle, the trade unionists of northern Yorke Peninsula – like their colleagues elsewhere in the State (and across the border at Broken Hill) – voiced their opposition to conscription. The Recruiting Train episode looked uncomfortably like a step in the direction of coercion, and the Premier's presence only heightened fears that conscription was imminent. The miners' reaction, and their firm rejection of Corporal Evans and Crawford Vaughan, was a portent of things to come. By October 1916, when John Verran spoke in favour of conscription at a rowdy meeting at Kadina, it was clear that the ULP was in trouble, and that a great rift had opened between Labor's rank-and-file and many of the party's politicians. Verran warned the hostile crowd at Kadina: 'You are striking at the very roots of your trade union principles [compulsory membership as a means of securing group solidarity] and by making this a party question you are assisting to drive a wedge into the Labour movement which will go a long way to destroy what has taken many years to construct.'[30]

Although by no means sympathetic to the ULP, the Wallaroo and Moonta Mining and Smelting Company tried to perpetuate a sense of community harmony in the face of the divisions that were now appearing. H. Lipson Hancock, as general manager, had put the mines and smelters on a war footing, and had courted the trade unionists with favourable conditions of employment. Integral to this was the 'Betterment Principle', as Hancock dubbed it. Developed in the years after 1912, the Betterment Principle built upon the existing Club & Doctor fund, founded on traditional Cornish practice, to create a modern and highly innovative welfare system, which reached its apogee during the Great War. Hancock proudly described the Betterment Principle in an explanatory article 'Welfare Work in the Mining Industry' in October 1918, and a lengthy report on its operation and features subsequently appeared in the *South Australian Department of Mines Mining Review* for the half-year ended June 1919.[31] The latter praised the general atmosphere of 'tidiness, space and light' at the company's plants. At the Wallaroo smelting works, it was explained, there were baths and changing-houses, and at Wallaroo Mines the company had provided for public enjoyment a sports pavilion, croquet lawn, hockey pitch, and bowling green with twelve rinks and a 'good club house'.[32] There were similar facilities at Moonta Mines, including a billiards room, recreation hall, rotunda, tennis courts, and children's playground. The company's Club and Medical Fund (as it was now termed), provided generous sick pay for employees in return for modest subscriptions.

The Betterment Principle mirrored the mutual improvement ethos that characterised Methodism on northern Yorke Peninsula, and drew upon a long-standing sense of community solidarity. Additionally, it reflected H. Lipson Hancock's own Methodist convictions, although Hancock also recognised that the Betterment Principle was an important device for encouraging community cohesion and trade union support during the war years. In the same way, Hancock sought to deploy religious observance as a similar device, mobilising northern Yorke Peninsula's overwhelming Methodist identity as another agent of community cohesion. In 1905 he had become Superintendent of the Moonta Mines Methodist Sunday School, and had lost no time in importing the rigorous 'Rainbow System' of Sunday-school instruction developed at the Marion Lawrence School at Toledo, Ohio, in the United States.[33] In the years before the Great War, Hancock made Moonta Mines Sunday school an exemplary model of best practice that was emulated across the Peninsula and beyond. By 1918 no fewer than 7,000 visitors had been received at the school to observe its methods first-hand, while the Rainbow System had been embraced by other Sunday schools in the locality – at Yelta, Agery, Paskeville, Greens Plains West, and Wallaroo Mines.[34]

The Rainbow System was highly structured, its authoritarian, methodical approach and inherent discipline no doubt attractive to many Methodist practitioners during the Great War years. At Moonta Mines the Sunday school was divided into ten grades or departments, ranging from the 'Cradle Roll' (for children from infancy to three years) to the adult 'Home Grade' for those too old or infirm to attend the school itself. Although the emphasis was naturally on the youngsters – there were Beginners', Kindergarten, Primary, Junior, Advance Junior, and Intermediate grades – there was also a 'Senior Grade' for those from sixteen to twenty-three years old, together with an 'Adult Grade' for people aged over twenty-three.[35] In this way, the Rainbow System comprehensively touched the lives of individuals and families across the community. There were no fewer than twenty-two different committees to administer the system at Moonta Mines, among them the Prayer and Visitation Committee, the Statistical Department Committee, and the Mothers' Meeting

Institutional Methodism – the 'Rainbow System' in action in the
Primary Department at Moonta Mines Methodist Sunday School.
[Courtesy State Library of South Australia, PRG280/1/44/398]

Committee. The Rainbow course of instruction itself followed a prescriptive syllabus, commencing with 'Lesson 1: The Bible and how we got it' and culminating in 'Lesson 100: The Call of China'.[36]

As H. Lipson Hancock explained in 1919, it was imperative that all Rainbow instructors should have a firm grasp 'of the principles that underlie the statements of scripture', and be able to 'Guard against teaching anything that will not bear the strictest examination'. Any error, he warned, placed scholars 'in danger of moral shipwreck'.[37] Similar unblemished conduct was expected of the scholars themselves. As one visitor to Moonta Mines observed: 'A large card suspended before the superintendent's [Hancock's] desk bore the legend "I am early". A minute or two prior to the opening of the service this was replaced by another bearing the words "I am only just in time"'. Finally, the visitor added: 'When the service began, a third card appeared announcing "I am late" ... Among the mottoes on the walls, "Study to be quiet" was prominent.'[38] Hancock himself explained the strict discipline that

201

was a central feature of the school's opening formalities. 'After removal of hats and coats, under supervision', he wrote in 1916, 'the different sections are formed into a line, headed in each case by the leader of the day'. Then, he continued, the 'procession, to the accompaniment of music, passes through the Kindergarten room on its way to the main hall for the opening exercises, a junior teacher taking a place after every third scholar. One teacher or helper should be available, if possible, for every three scholars, but at least one for every four or five scholars'.[39]

'Mark the difference between Romanism and the Evangelical faith'

In this way, as Hancock intended, institutional Methodism sought to exercise its authority on northern Yorke Peninsula during the Great War, providing moral certainty in uncertain times. A further mechanism was the *Australian Christian Commonwealth* magazine, published in Adelaide, which enjoyed a wide circulation on the Peninsula (John Verran was a subscriber) and was popular among Methodists elsewhere in the State. Its editor for the majority of the war years was Revd Octavius Lake. A Welshman, Lake had been a Bible Christian minister before Methodist union in 1900, and had been active on northern Yorke Peninsula, where he claimed affinity and common cause with the Cornish miners and Welsh smelters and their families. He had, for example, worked closely with the miners' trade union in tackling poverty on the mineral-lease settlements at Moonta Mines and Wallaroo Mines.[40] When war broke out in 1914, Lake was already seventy-three years old, an elderly man of firm convictions, which he expressed as President of the Methodist Conference of South Australia in 1915–16 and through the pages of the *Australian Christian Commonwealth*. As early as March 1915, the *Australian Christian Commonwealth* had predicted that conscription would become necessary, and in the December Octavius Lake had expressed editorial support for the current 'recruiting campaign', urging 'men who are fit to go forth as soldiers in our nation's defence, and in defence of small nations like Belgium and Servia'.[41] By March 1916, Methodist support for the recruiting campaign had hardened into a demand for conscription. As the *Australian Christian Commonwealth* put it, explaining its position, the typical anti-conscriptionist, seeking now to evade his responsibilities, 'combines the heart of a sheep with the face of a lion. He mistakes the pleading of his self-love for the protests of his conscience'.[42] When, in the August, Hughes announced his conscription referendum, institutional Methodism in South Australia was right behind him, as Octavius Lake's ironic 'Anti-Conscription Song' made clear:

> We don't want to fight,
> But by jingo if we do,
> We'll stay at home and have our fun
> And send the brave Hindoo!
>
> We don't want to fight,
> Perhaps the Russians do:
> Then let us hire the poorer types
> For just the Russian screw.
>
> Or look to Africa,
> The lusty, large Zulu;
> Let him be trained to fight the Huns
> Instead of me and you.
>
> We're in an awful funk,
> Believe us, friends, 'tis true;
> Before this close conscription call
> We kept it out of view;
>
> But now unless the 'Nos' –
> The rash, red-raggers' crew –
> Can show themselves to save their skins,
> What will the Slackers do?
>
> We do not want to fight,
> We are a peaceful crew;
> To races, pubs, and movey shows
> We'll stick, dear pals – like glue.[43]

Nonconformist hostility to Roman Catholicism also informed the Methodist stance on conscription in South Australia. As early as 1911, the *Australian Christian Commonwealth* had detected a malign Romish influence in John Verran's Labor government (W.J. Denny, erstwhile editor of the Catholic *Southern Cross* and hitherto a critic of the ULP, was Verran's Attorney-General).[44] Such fears were reinforced by the Easter Rising in Ireland in 1916. Irish nationalists active in Australia were now observed more sharply for evidence of republican sympathies, while Irish–Australian opinion was shocked by the harsh summary punishments meted out to the rebels in Dublin. In the eastern States, especially in Victoria, where there was a strong Irish–Catholic influence in the Labor movement, there seemed a real risk of subversion and unrest. Octavius Lake warned that 'Sinn Feiners are out to establish "The Irish Republic"'. Yet he dismissed the aspiration as a 'screaming farce', and asked his readers if they could 'imagine the Scotch or the Welsh embarked on such an enterprise'.[45] A few weeks later, he returned to his theme, inquiring: 'Why do not the Welsh break into rebellion ... Why are the Welsh so different from the Irish? They are both of Celtic origin.' The answer was straightforward, he explained: 'Mark the difference between Romanism and the Evangelical faith and then you will know.'[46]

Such polemic was designed to bolster the pro-conscriptionist cause, playing upon the prejudices of the largely Protestant rank and file in the Labor movement in South Australia, not least on Methodist northern Yorke Peninsula. For John Verran and his ilk, these Nonconformist arguments were sound. But for increasing numbers of workers, whatever their religious convictions, such rhetoric was simply irrelevant in considering the merits and demerits of conscription. The trade unions representing largely unskilled workers – the Australian Workers' Union (AWU) and United Labourers' Union (ULU) – were especially vociferous in their opposition to conscription and in their criticisms of Labor politicians who did not share their opinions. Frank Lundie, deeply involved in both unions, crossed swords frequently with Crawford Vaughan, their exchanges duly reported in detail in the *Daily Herald*.[47] The ULP annual conference was held in Adelaide on 9 September 1916, only six weeks before the referendum on 28 October. The *Daily*

Herald noted that the conference agenda 'bristles with motions regarding conscription', and the presence of none other than W.M. Hughes heightened the sense of drama and confrontation.[48] Although the conference resolved to support Hughes in his role as Prime Minister, including his calling of the referendum, it nonetheless decided that it was 'against conscription of human life'.[49] If there seemed here a whiff of compromise, then this was promptly dispelled when the ULP Council met on 21 October, a week before the referendum. Making its position entirely clear, it resolved that 'this Council emphatically and definitely declares that the resolution approved at the Conference absolutely binds every member to oppose conscription, and that we declare that any member favouring conscription is disloyal'.[50]

On northern Yorke Peninsula, the Council's decree was heeded by large numbers of trade unionists and their families. Among those who had risen to prominence in the conscription debate in South Australia was Robert Stanley Richards – known variously as 'R.S.' or 'Bob' – who only recently had been seen as an ally and confidante of John Verran. As late as April 1916 he had shared the rostrum with Verran and H. Lipson Hancock at recruiting campaign events on the Peninsula.[51] Now, however, Richards was firmly in the 'Anti' camp. A former miner, he worked as a moulder and carpenter in the Wallaroo smelting works. A budding trade unionist and (paradoxically, perhaps) a Methodist local preacher, he was also an aspiring ULP politician and increasingly the voice of radical opinion in the mining towns. Born at Moonta Mines in 1885, the son of two Cornish emigrants, Richard Richards of Camborne and Mary Jeffery from neighbouring Tuckingmill, Richards was noticeably to the left of Verran and the earlier generation of mineworkers, and exercised a ready appeal for the likeminded second and third generations born and raised on the Peninsula.

There was, for example, Stanley R. Whitford, later to become a prominent Labor politician in South Australia, who was born at Moonta in 1878. Proud to be counted among the 'Cousin Jacks from Moonta' (he spoke with a pronounced Cornish accent), he was also a committed Methodist.[52] And yet, as he explained, he was 'opposed to conscription because it violated my ideals as a follower of the International Socialist movement'. Such language, redolent of the Industrial Workers of the World, to which John Verran was implacably opposed, placed Whitford on the left of the Labor movement. Reflecting the shifting attitudes in the Peninsula mining towns in 1916, Whitford condemned Verran as 'robust, good looking, good voiced but ignorant ... [one] in whom I had no trust ... I placed him among my list of damned old humbugs, and he never reinstated himself in my estimation'.[53] Others had reached similar conclusions. When Norman Makin, one of the many ULP activists campaigning for a 'No' vote in the Referendum, visited northern Yorke Peninsula he was struck by the strength of feeling, and could not fail to note the paradox – an overwhelmingly Methodist people vehemently opposing the Methodist church's declared position on conscription. Years later, aged ninety-two, Makin could still recall with some bemusement 'a meeting in Kadina Town Hall where the fervour against conscription was so strong as to have the flavour of an old-fashioned [Methodist] revival meeting'.[54]

'I renounce South Australia as my mother State'

Despite such evidence, John Verran, like Premier Crawford Vaughan and other pro-conscription Labor politicians, continued to anticipate a 'Yes' vote, so wedded were they to their own propaganda. For them, the referendum result came as a nasty shock. South Australia – like Australia as a whole – voted against conscription: 119,236 (or 57.5%) to 87,924. Paradoxically, in that part of South Australia where Methodism was strongest – northern Yorke Peninsula – the 'No' vote was among the highest recorded: 78.5% in the Moonta subdivision, 75.8% in Wallaroo, and 72% in Kadina.[55] It was a result that indicated the extent to which institutional Methodism, despite the best efforts of H. Lipson Hancock, John Verran and others, had failed to mould local opinion in this crucial debate. The unpalatable reality, as Arnold Hunt has explained, was that the Methodist 'church's capacity to influence the thinking of its members on this issue was very limited, and in some areas (such as Moonta) was virtually non-existent'.[56] Despite the historic links on northern Yorke Peninsula between Methodism and the Labor movement, on this significant occasion many people had cast aside their religious affiliations to put their weight behind the ULP's increasing hostility to conscription. It was a situation replicated across South Australia, and beyond.

In Western Australia – which had voted comfortably in favour of conscription, by 94,069 votes to 40,884 – the conscription debate proved less damaging, as Labor struggled to maintain a semblance of unity. Nonetheless, the controversy was often as bitter as elsewhere in Australia, with the 'Anti' camp enjoying the support of the metropolitan working class in Perth and the miners' union at Kalgoorlie, Boulder and Coolgardie. There would be defections and expulsions, as there would be in the Labor parties in other States, and among the casualties was Jack Scaddan, Labor Premier on two occasions between 1911 and 1916 and architect of what he called 'state socialism' in Western Australia.[57] Born at Moonta in 1876, Jack Scaddan had much in common with John Verran. He too was convinced of the intimate relationship between religion and politics, insisting that the 'Trade Hall is my Church and Labour is my religion'.[58] Although he had spent his working life on the Victorian and Western Australian goldfields, where he was employed in the mines, he was especially proud that he was a 'Moontaite' and had been born in South Australia of Cornish parents. In 1913, when Premier of Western Australia, he had paid a visit to Cornwall, where he explained to all and sundry that he was 'of Cornish stock' and that 'in Moonta, South Australia, where he was born, at least 80% of the population were Cornish or of Cornish descent'.[59]

A firm Methodist and teetotaller, Scaddan was, like Verran, a passionate advocate of conscription, and this brought him into conflict with many in his party, with the accusation that he was 'allying himself with the enemies of Labor'.[60] Although Scaddan had felt vindicated by the referendum result in Western Australia, it was (as the *People's Weekly* put it) the 'big adverse vote in the Peninsula mining towns' that really disturbed him.[61] His reaction was as furious as it was unconventional. A bemused *Yorke's Peninsula Advertiser* was taken aback by the ferocity of Scaddan's verbal assault upon the 'peaceful town of Moonta', an 'unpleasant surprise' that had taken the form of a strongly worded telegram to Crawford Vaughan. 'I desire to notify you officially', Scaddan announced, 'that from today I renounce South Australia as my mother State unless Moonta proves to be of true metal'.[62] This formal estrangement remained in place from October 1916 until May 1917 when Scaddan, approving of the outcome of the Federal general election, cabled

Crawford Vaughan: 'You may now officially re-enter my acknowledgement of South Australia as my mother State.'[63]

Jack Scaddan's outburst was indicative of the trauma suffered in now deeply divided communities across South Australia, not least on northern Yorke Peninsula. The bad blood between John Verran and R.S. Richards was harrowing for those who recalled them as intimate friends and allies. Richard Williams, for instance, born at Moonta of Cornish parentage and later to become head of the Royal Australian Air Force, remembered John Verran fondly as his Sunday school teacher and as 'a stalwart of the Labor movement . . . I was often taken by my father to his political meetings'. Likewise, there was 'Another Labor supporter nearer my age with whom I played cricket and football when the team was otherwise short in numbers'. This 'was R.S. ('Bob') Richards', Williams explained, 'who subsequently became Premier of South Australia'.[64] That such men should now be sworn enemies, pulled apart by the conscription controversy, was deeply distressing, as Revd Gordon Rowe, one-time president of the Methodist Conference of South Australia, observed in his memoirs. When Rowe had first arrived on northern Yorke Peninsula he had been struck by the warmth of his welcome and the strength of community spirit. It was said that in his first sermon in the district he had 'thanked the Lord that he was amongst brothers and sisters from Cornwall. That set the seal on his popularity at Moonta'.[65] It was also reckoned that he could 'tell a Cornish story exceptionally well'.[66] Likewise, he was embraced whole-heartedly by the local Labor movement, of which he was a staunch supporter. In a widely reported visit to Britain in 1892 he had lectured in the London suburb of Bermondsey on 'Life and Labour in South Australia', stressing the unity of interests of British and Australian workers.[67] No wonder, then, that he should have been so dismayed by the fracture in the ULP in 1916 and 'the intense bitterness engendered locally by the conscription issue'.[68]

'Expect there will be a big split in the Labour movement'

This bewilderment was shared by many. William Humphrey Harvey, born in Moonta in 1869 of Cornish parents (John Harvey and Margaret Eathorn), had been elected as Labor member of the Legislative Council for the Central division in 1915. Employed hitherto as a moulder in the Moonta mine, and a past secretary of the Moonta branch of the AMA, he was seen as a rising star of the parliamentary ULP.[69] But, like many of his parliamentary colleagues, he was firmly in favour of conscription, bringing him into conflict with the trade unionists who were so recently his friends and supporters. His discomfort was echoed by his son Leonard, now serving with the Australian Imperial Force and training at Larkhill on Salisbury Plain in England, where he followed the conscription debate closely. Initially, like his father, Leonard Harvey was confident of a victory for the pro-conscriptionists in the forthcoming referendum. Writing home in August 1916, he reckoned that, 'going by the paper this morning, conscription in Australia seems inevitable'.[70] A fortnight later, he added breezily: 'We read a lot about Billy Hughes and his [conscription] policy in the English papers. To all account the English think him possible of doing anything'.[71] Yet less than a month later, it seemed that not only was Hughes not infallible after all but that conscription might fail in Australia, with dire consequences for the Labor Party. 'Dad', wrote Leonard Harvey in worried tones, having just read in the papers of the growing animosity between the grassroots Labor movement and the Prime Minister, 'what do you think of the Labour Party in N.S. Wales in connection with Hughes?'. With prescient insight, Leonard added: 'Expect there will be a big split in the Labour movement.'[72] He noted too that 'the majority of the Moonta population are against conscription. This was shown by one of the meetings J[ohn] V[erran] had there'.[73] When news of the referendum result reached Leonard Harvey in England, followed eventually by Australian papers reporting the outcome, he could report to his father: 'I have just read the piece in the [Adelaide] *Advertiser* on the Labor split. Seems as though there will be a big rumpus before it is settled.'[74]

Indeed there was. At an acrimonious special meeting of the ULP in November 1916 to discuss the outcome of the referendum, thirty-one State and Federal parliamentarians were condemned as disloyal. Even more significantly, the meeting recognised just seven ULP members – Lionel Hill, John Gunn, Ephraim Coombe, John Carr, James Jelley, T. Butterfield, and John Price – as the legitimate South Australian parliamentary Labor Party. Crawford

Vaughan, John Verran, William Harvey and the other pro-conscriptionists were disowned. To make matters worse, a plebiscite to select candidates for the forthcoming 1918 elections was brought forward, and when the results were made known in January 1917, none of the pro-conscriptionists was successful. A last ditch attempt at reconciliation was sought at another special meeting in February 1917 but, if anything, attitudes had hardened. There were no fewer than twenty-eight representatives of the AWU (of which Frank Lundie had now succeeded W.G. Spence as national secretary), which gave them a dominant voice in the proceedings. As Brian Dickey noted wryly: 'Some of the delegates came from branches heard of neither before nor since (for example, Mount Gambier).'[75]

Reluctantly, the pro-conscriptionist parliamentarians had been admitted to the meeting by Lundie and his associates. But they refused to sign a declaration to the effect that they would adhere to all conference decisions in the future, and left the meeting in high dudgeon. Thereafter, all executive posts in the party were declared vacant, and in the ensuing ballot Frank Lundie was elected as chairman of the ULP. As Dickey put it: 'The victory of the anti-conscriptionists was complete.'[76] In response, the censured parliamentarians formed themselves into a new political grouping, the National Labor Party, leaving a mere five members as the rump parliamentary ULP. At Moonta, John Verran announced the formation of a local branch of the National Labor Party, seen as a direct challenge to the recently formed Moonta Anti-Conscriptionist League, a further indication if any was needed that the solidarity and consensus that H. Lipson Hancock and others had worked hard to maintain in the district had broken down irretrievably.[77] Archibald Peake, observing the disarray in Labor ranks, saw his opportunity. Crawford Vaughan's suggestion that a government of national unity should be formed with him as Premier, was rejected by Peake. Equally, Vaughan refused to serve under Peake's leadership. Accordingly, on the first day of the 1917 parliamentary session, Peake took control of the House of Assembly on an adjournment debate (the ULP abstained), prompting the resignation of Crawford Vaughan's government.

On 14 July 1917 Archibald Peake formed his third ministry, and the Liberal Union was once more in power in South Australia. However, Peake's position was precarious, and, despite the failure of earlier overtures, he admitted two 'Nationalists' (as they now termed themselves) into his Cabinet, the prelude to a formal Liberal–National coalition. At the Federal level, the National Labor Party, with Hughes at the helm, had clung onto power with the backing of the Liberal Party. In February 1917 the two parties merged formally to form the Nationalist Party, with Hughes continuing as Prime Minister, and – with the Labor Party in chaos – the Nationalists were swept into office in the Federal general election of May 1917. Imagining (erroneously) that electoral victory would translate effortlessly into a 'Yes' vote, Hughes decided on a second conscription referendum, to be held on 20 December 1917. All the rhetoric of the previous year was dusted off, to be deployed again in yet more vociferous terms.

Once more Octavius Lake championed the support of institutional Methodism in South Australia for conscription, exclaiming in the *Australian Christian Commonwealth* that among the many foes facing the Empire none was more dangerous than the enemy within. 'The venomous snakes of treason lift their heads in many parts of our wide-flung dominion', he insisted, 'but their warmest, most crowded nests are in Ireland and Australia'.[78] It was a theme that Lake would make his own. 'This is not only Germany's war; it is Rome's war too' he could still declare as late as July 1918.[79] Indeed, during the 1917 conscription campaign, Lake took particular aim at the Irishman Dr Daniel Mannix, Roman Catholic Archbishop of Melbourne. Seen by detractors and supporters alike as sympathetic to Sinn Fein, Mannix was vehemently opposed to conscription, wedding the 'Anti' case to the cause of Irish nationalism, and encouraging the Labor Party in its anti-conscriptionist stance. Across the border in South Australia, Mannix's authority and influence in neighbouring Victoria, not least among the many Catholic members of the Labor movement, was seen by Octavius Lake and others as deeply subversive. Lake offered his readers clear advice:

Speak plain at the next Referendum
Reply by a thunderous 'Yes!'
And show Dr Mannix' Sinn Feiners
They cannot – yet – answer for us.

The manifold pro-German crew,
That tricks for betraying the soldiers,
Have no inch or quarter with you.[80]

As before, such attitudes cut little ice with the grassroots Labor movement in South Australia, not least on northern Yorke Peninsula where agitation by R.S. Richards had further hardened attitudes. As the erstwhile regional consensus broke down, so the mineworkers became increasingly suspicious of the vast profits made by the mining company and the fat dividends paid to shareholders. Moreover, they sought to construct new patterns of solidarity, increasingly willing to seek alignment with workers in trade unions beyond the mining industry. Initially, there was a demand for higher remuneration, led by the Moonta men who were becoming dissatisfied with their terms and conditions. In part, this was resentment that much of the recent investment and development by the company had been in the Wallaroo mine, not least when a number of Moonta men was moved across to Wallaroo, where they were required to live in 'batching quarters' (a boarding house) built for the purpose.[81] However, the real cleavage that would develop during 1917 was over the proposed merger of the Amalgamated (now Federated) Miners Association with the AWU.

The AWU and the 'Bogies'

John Verran was aghast at the suggestion. It was the AWU (and ULU) that had given him such trouble during his time as Premier, and its national secretary was now none other than Frank Lundie, one of those who had made life extremely difficult for the erstwhile Verran government. More recently, Lundie had been a leading architect of the ULP's effective expulsion from the party organisation of Verran, Vaughan and the other parliamentary pro-conscriptionists. Verran's fear that, should the merger go ahead, 'We will lose control of industrial matters locally', disguised a deep animosity and loathing for both the AWU and Frank Lundie.[82] But the merger did go ahead. Its leading advocate was R.S. Richards, by now Verran's nemesis, who became president of the Moonta Branch of the AWU at its foundation, as well as national president of the AWU's mining section.[83] The contest between Verran and Richards had become damagingly personal.

Verran reacted to the merger with characteristic anger and flourish, swiftly launching his own alternative trade union structure, officially the Yorke's Peninsula Miners' and Smelters' Association, but known to its detractors as the 'Bogus' union. Against the background of the acrimonious split caused already by the conscription dispute, this new fissure brought further recrimination and heightened the sense of antagonism within an already divided Labor movement and wider community. It was rumoured that the Wallaroo and Moonta company was victimising the militants who had orchestrated the AWU merger, while the 'Bogies' (members of Verran's alternative Bogus union) were in turn picked on by the AWU men and ostracised by many in the mining towns.[84] Verran, dismissed now as the play-thing of H. Lipson Hancock and the mining company, was attacked bitterly for causing 'so much distress in many homes in this district'.[85] But, as ever, Verran was unrepentant, riposting that the AWU was 'led by Pommies who came out from England to escape conscription'.[86] In so doing, he reinforced the complex entwinement of the conscription and merger controversies that had already divided the community. As Revd Gordon Rowe observed years later, the enmities thus created 'so seriously disrupted fraternal relations among the [mines'] employees ... that confusion, distrust and abuse grew to such proportions that the spirit of co-operation and sweet reasonableness – which the condition of the industry eventually required – became impossible'. Indeed, he reflected: 'During this turbulent period many good families, fed up with the state of things, packed up and left the district.'[87]

Meanwhile, the progress towards the second referendum had been marked by growing industrial unrest, across Australia as a whole and in South Australia. The Wallaroo and Moonta company refused to meet AWU representatives to discuss grievances, aggravating the sense of uneasiness in the community, and a lengthy nationwide coal strike caused further uncertainty at the mines and smelters as stocks dwindled. When the strike ended, the shortage of coal was perpetuated by the Seaman's Union, which refused to ship coal supplies. When, eventually, a vessel laden with coal did arrive at Wallaroo in October 1917, the local wharfies refused to touch it. Only with great difficulty were they persuaded to unload the precious cargo, after Hancock had warned that the mines and smelters faced imminent closure through lack of coal. Yet, despite these operational difficulties, the Wallaroo and Moonta company remained hugely profitable, as the AWU observed. Turnover was down on the record year of 1916, but production was up, and annual profits for 1917 stood at £126,736, with a healthy £80,000 paid in dividends.[88]

John Verran, attempting to regain the initiative, emerged as an important spokesman for the new Nationalist Party, which had subsumed the short-lived National Labor Party. 'The civilized world is engaged in the greatest struggle of all ages, fighting for Liberty and Democracy against Military Despotism', explained his advertisement in the *Yorke's Peninsula Advertiser*. Readers were asked to remember the sacrifices made 'by our brave soldiers – the men of Gallipoli and Pozières. Remember that the interests of Australia and Empire are one. The National[ist] Party stands for Empire, for a decisive victory'.[89] Likewise, northern Yorke Peninsula was again the target for the State Recruiting Committee, the *Yorke's Peninsula Advertiser* reporting on a recent visit to Moonta Mines and across the border at Broken Hill. Both localities, it was noted with regret, 'contain a much larger percentage of eligibles [for enlistment] than the average throughout the State'. Moreover, in both areas, 'especially Broken Hill', there was 'opposition to recruiting which is political'. Indeed, at Broken Hill, 'a great many persons ... would not stand during the singing of the National Anthem'.[90] As before, there was an insistence that those supporting a 'No' vote in the forthcoming Referendum were:

men who are playing Germany's game in our midst, Sinn Feiners, members of the I.W.W., syndicalists, men of the type responsible for the [coal] strike which paralysed Australia's industries, men responsible for the rebellion

214

in Ireland, the kind of men who, to-day, are in Russia and are offering Germany a separate peace.[91]

In addition to the well-worn mantras, new arguments were sought. On northern Yorke Peninsula, where the debate continued to be intense, there was a novel appeal to the 'Electors of Wallaroo, Kadina, and Moonta'. It was acknowledged that 'You are doing Great War Work. Your mines are helping to provide munitions of war'. However, it was explained, 'munitions are useless without men to use them'. But this was not, it was added hastily, an argument for Peninsula men to enlist: 'Yours is a necessary industry. It must be protected. Labor will be exempted to carry on.' Rather, here was an insistence that conscription was necessary if optimum use was to be made of the Peninsula's copper output, but with local miners and smelters exempted as reserved occupations. The mineworkers, therefore, should 'Vote YES'.[92] It was not only, of course, the State's mineworkers who had argued that their contribution was vital to the war effort. Farmers had increasingly articulated their fear that conscription would deprive the countryside of vital agricultural labour. As one newspaper advertisement asked rhetorically: 'One Conscript Equals Five Tons of Wheat. Which Will We Send?' Or, put another way: 'To equip a transport carrying troops from Australia to Europe means sacrificing tons of dead-weight cargo space for each man carried.' The message was explicit: 'Keep Australia Free. Send Foodstuffs to the Allies. Vote "No".'[93]

Verran versus Richards

And so the arguments raged, and Australia did indeed again vote 'No'. Much to the chagrin of Vaughan, Verran, Harvey and the other pro-conscriptionists, the nationwide 'No' majority had actually increased to 166,588. There was small comfort in the slight reduction of 'No' votes in South Australia (from 57.6% to 55.1%) but on northern Yorke Peninsula the 'Anti' vote had held up well – 69.7% at Kadina, 77.9% at Moonta, and 78.2% at Wallaroo. William Harvey's son Leonard, now serving on the Western Front, was braced for the result this time, and had anticipated the reluctance of the mineworkers to enlist. 'It will take a lot to move some of the young fellows [in the mines]', he wrote to his father, 'especially if there has been a good year and wages are good'. However, he was dismayed when he heard about the demands for higher remuneration: 'Fancy the fellows putting such requests to the Coy. I think they are making a big mistake, especially as everything is at so critical a period.'[94] He was also disturbed by the news that R.S. Richards had broken ranks with John Verran. 'Didn't expect that of Bob R.', he exclaimed in disbelief, but he thought that Richards would have little chance if he decided to contest John Verran's seat in the forthcoming elections in 1918: 'fancy he would get a bit of a knock if he stood against JV'.[95] It was a theme that Leonard Harvey returned to again in October 1917, writing to his father from France. 'Things seem a bit mixed in Moonta', he wrote. 'Fancy Bob Richards opposing J. Verran, probably he is after something higher. I should guess he would not have much of a chance to defeat John.'[96] By early 1918, Leonard's mood had changed to one of exasperation. Not only had the Peninsula rejected conscription once more but there was a new air of militancy on the mines, consequent upon the AWU merger. 'What's gone wrong with the peaceful Moonta miners?', he asked his father: 'The affairs of the union have taken a big turn in the last two years. I can't quite understand Bob Richards ... I should judge Robert is out to gain a seat in Parliament ... Mr Verran must be heartily sick of them all from that part.'[97]

Leonard Harvey was right on both counts. R.S. Richards was intent on winning a seat in the South Australian Parliament, and John Verran was by now exceedingly weary of him and his associates. Indeed, in the State election in April 1918 there was a sensation when R.S. Richards and John Pedler (also of Cornish descent), standing as official Labor Party candidates, defeated both John Verran and John Herbert in the Wallaroo constituency. Their victory marked the ascendency on the Peninsula of the anti-conscriptionists, the AWU and the anti-Hughes Labor Party. It was also the end of an era. Richards would go on to represent the district for more than fifty years, while Verran's political career was effectively over. Revd Gordon Rowe, an admirer of Verran, would later claim that it was 'adherence to principle that cost him [Verran] his seat in 1918'. As he recalled: 'The election campaign was very bitter. Labour leaders from Adelaide, and even from Tasmania, addressed meetings in the district against Verran, and the State labour [*sic*] paper "The Daily Herald" turned its guns on him.'[98]

Verran and Herbert were not the only ex-Labor casualties. Crawford Vaughan retired from South Australian politics, with the Nationalist Party winning just six seats in the House of Assembly. But the Liberal–Nationalist coalition won a total of twenty-eight seats, giving it a comfortable majority. The Labor Party, with the likes of R.S. Richards promising a fresh start and a new trajectory, achieved seventeen seats in the Assembly, an extremely credible performance, given that by the eve of dissolution it had dwindled to only three remaining members. However, as Brian Dickey has observed, the widespread support that Labor had enjoyed in 1915 had shrunk now to the 'hard core of industrial centres' – the working-class precincts of suburban Adelaide, the smelting town of Port Pirie, and the mining district of northern Yorke Peninsula. Moreover, Dickey concluded, 'it is doubtful whether the party regained the breadth of community support it had in 1915 until, perhaps, 1962'.[99]

Interviewed shortly after his defeat, John Verran was defiant. 'I don't say that I am defeated as a Labour man in any way', he insisted: 'It was a case of Labour fighting Labour, and we were defeated on the question of conscription.' He had simply stood by his principles, he said, and had 'had to pay the penalty'. Moreover, he added, he had never reneged on the party. 'It does seem unfair', he complained, 'especially when you remember that there are no charges against me. If a man had violated the Labour platform or been unfaithful to the party, I could understand him going out'. Asked about his record, especially as Premier, John Verran was emphatic. It was the obstructionist Legislative Council that had brought his government down after only twenty-three months 'but during that term, brief as it was, I had reason to be proud of our accomplishments'. He had achieved early closing for shops, and had forced through the Steam Boilers Bill, which had been before the House thirteen times before it received Assent. 'Then', he continued, 'I got through the Bill for the amendments to the Workingmen's Compensation Act, which provided for men working in places like the Port Pirie smelters and at Wallaroo getting compensation for lead-poisoning and so on'. As he concluded, 'I claim to have done more for the workers of this State than any other Premier'.[100]

'Have you any thought of your future?', the interviewer asked Verran guardedly. 'Yes', he replied at once, 'roll up m' sleeves – and at it. I am not ashamed to go to work again. There is no dishonour about it . . . I don't intend to go underground again, but I shall seek some sort of manual job. I can't do anything else'. As the interviewer rose to leave, Verran whispered 'I shall come again'. 'How soon?', was the parting query: 'When the mists have rolled away'.[101] In the short term, Verran continued in his role as chairman of the Railways Standing Committee. But, outside of Parliament for the first time since he was elected in 1901, he hankered to return. His local power base by now seriously eroded, he looked to win new sources of political influence. Earlier in the war, recognising that support for him was no longer solid, he had cultivated a vociferous anti-German stance. In August 1914, on the outbreak of hostilities, he had argued that it was necessary to crush Germany quickly, so that Europe could be cleaned up, 'just as the Cornish people like their general cleaning up at Christmas'.[102] He spoke strongly at the many farewell socials, designed to give volunteers for the front a hearty send-off, on one occasion turning suddenly mid-speech to confront a new recruit. Fixing the youth with his gaze, he said 'to put aside sickly sentiment and destroy as many Germans' as he could, predicting that 'the last German he would see in his travels would be a dead one'.[103]

'I am a Britisher and a Cornishman'

Likewise, Verran was active in the All-British League, founded in February 1916, which expressed hostility to South Australia's sizeable German community.[104] In September 1916 the League presented a petition to the government with 49,000 signatures, calling for for the disenfranchisement of all those of German descent in the State. Verran introduced disenfranchisement bills in 1916 and 1917 (both narrowly failed to make their way onto the statute book), and in August 1916 declared in the House that it was 'deplorable to allow those with German blood in their veins to vote in this country. No matter what they cry out, they must have a bias for Germany. I am a Britisher and a Cornishman, and no one can take away my feelings for my country'.[105] He was scathing about those Germans who anglicised their names to avoid scrutiny or to demonstrate their loyalty: 'Just fancy a German going through Australia calling himself Jack Verran.'[106] Equally, he was careful to use parliamentary privilege to denounce prominent Germans in the community. When Verran attacked the well-known Mr Schomburgk, it was pointed out that actually the poor man's father was a Dane and his mother English, and that he himself had been born in South Australia. Verran quipped: 'They all have some such excuse as that.'[107]

Now out of Parliament, following his defeat, Verran redoubled his anti-German efforts. To some extent he was successful. The workers on the Port Adelaide waterfront refused to work with their German colleagues, and one approving supporter wrote to the *People's Weekly* to ask: 'Who but a Hun would not say that Mr Verran is one of the most popular legislators in the State?'[108] After the war, as the troops came home, Verran tried to perpetuate the German question. He objected to servicemen of German descent being allocated land for soldier-settlement, and 'protested against Germans being allowed to enter into competition with [other] returned soldiers in securing such land'. As he explained: 'Many of these Germans retained the grin of the Kaiser when they bested the returned men.'[109] Moreover, he told the returning troops that in their absence 'he had been dropped out of political life'. Part of the conspiracy against him, he alleged, had been by the State's German community and its sympathisers. 'While the soldiers were dealing with the Germans overseas', he said, 'he had been endeavouring to deal with them at home, and when he was defeated as a politician they held an early prayer-meeting to thank God for it'.[110]

Embittered in defeat and politically marginalised, Verran identified the returned servicemen and women as a new constituency to which he might appeal. He aligned himself with the concerns and rhetoric of the Returned Sailors' and Soldiers' Imperial League, and at one homecoming social in June 1919 advised the newly returned soldiers 'to associate themselves with the R.S.&S. Imperial League ... to establish a new brotherhood which could never have been conceived of before the war'.[111] Verran embraced the returnees as 'the gentlemen of Australia' but warned that 'they had come home from one conflict to another'. Strikes and industrial disputes, orchestrated by the likes of the AWU, were making Australia 'as near hell today as it could be', with 'the influence of the IWW [Industrial Workers of the World] and the spirit of Bolshevism abroad'. It was the duty of the returnees, he insisted, to help eradicate this malaise. 'These things ought to be run out of Australia', he said, 'and they were looking to the returned men to assist in wiping them out'. Verran envisaged 'a new brotherhood' of returned servicemen who would 'stand together and dictate their demands to Australia'. This brotherhood would bring 'new aspirations to Australia', and 'must make itself felt throughout the length and breadth of the land'.[112]

It was a brave attempt, but it was not enough. In the 1921 State elections, Verran stood as Independent Labor candidate for his old constituency of Wallaroo. He narrowly failed to regain a seat but his alienation from the mainstream Labor Party was now complete. Already drifting to the right of the political spectrum, in 1924 he again contested Wallaroo, this time as a Liberal. As Verran explained, he 'could not see how any country could accept socialistic proposals of socializing all means of industry'. Now openly critical of his erstwhile party, he 'considered the Labor Party ideals took away a man's fundamental rights which were the basis of our civilization. Home life went when communism came on, and he would never favour any policy which took away his right to build his house'.[113] Once more, Verran was rebuffed. With the exception of a brief spell in the Federal Senate from 1927 to 1928, when he was appointed to fill a casual vacancy, his career was finished. He died in 1932.

He 'has had a romantic career'

'Mention of the name of the Hon John Verran, their one-time idol, is anathema to them to-day', observed one newspaper report in 1922, reflecting the widespread hostility that now existed towards Verran among the workers in his old constituency.[114] Yet the *People's Weekly* could concede that he 'has had a romantic career',[115] and when Verran moved from Moonta to the Adelaide suburb of Unley in November 1922, there was an outpouring of goodwill. 'They might not agree with his politics', explained one trade unionist, 'but they could not help admiring him for his fearlessness and broadmindedness'.[116] Indeed, there were those who admired Verran especially for standing up to the AWU, first as Premier and later in the merger dispute on northern Yorke Peninsula. 'I am not, nor have I ever been', wrote one Verran supporter, 'a member of the AWU that caused so much trouble and sorrow in the mining towns. I was a member of the first AMA, formed at Moonta Mines, and the leaders were all Cornishmen, right up to the time of forming the AWU'.[117]

It was the conscription crisis, of which the AWU merger was an element, that had split the community irretrievably, and it had been Verran's undoing. Yet he was an inherently controversial figure and always likely to court dispute, whatever the situation. Some years before he became a politician, John Verran had considered becoming an ordained Methodist minister. But, so it was said, 'his mother, who was averse to the proposal, settled the matter for him by stating that if he wanted to cause a row in every Church he became associated with, it was the best thing he could do'.[118] He decided instead to go into politics.[119]

Chapter Eight

Between the Wars

It was in 1917, at the height of the conscription crisis, that the United Labor Party [ULP] changed its name to the 'Australian Labor Party [ALP], South Australian Branch'. It was a move that echoed similar decisions in other States, and was suggestive of a closer relationship with interstate parties and the adoption of a broader national perspective. It also indicated a fresh start after the acrimony, defections and expulsions of recent months, and reflected the party's apparent shift to the political left. The aim of the new-look ALP was thus defined:

> To secure the adequate representation in Parliament, and other public bodies of organised workers and producers for the purpose of securing to each person the full result of his or her labor, by the collective ownership and democratic control of the means of production, distribution and exchange, and to ensure to each person full religious, political and social freedom.[1]

As part of the new-broom sweeping-clean process, Norman Makin was asked to write *A Progressive Democracy: A Record of Reference Concerning the South Australian Branch of the Australian Labor Party in Politics*, which was published on behalf of the ALP by the *Daily Herald* in 1918. Part manifesto for the future and part historical retrospect, the booklet was produced in response to the current 'widespread political and industrial unrest' and, as Lionel Hill (President of the ALP South Australian Branch) put it in his introduction, to refute the utterances of 'renegade politicians and the enemies of democracy'.[2] The choice of Makin as author was significant. In many ways, he embraced both the 'old' and the 'new' in Labor politics. A Member of the craft Amalgamated Society of Engineers, he had worked in foundries at Kapunda and Gawler, and had first stood for the ULP in the State election of 1915. In 1919 he would be elected as a Federal Member, and would remain one for forty years. Jim Moss reckoned that Makin was a 'Cornishman and Methodist lay preacher', cast in the traditional South Australian mould.[3] Moss was right about the religious affiliation but in fact Makin had been born in Sydney in 1889, the son of two emigrants from Lancashire. Traditionalist and moderniser, Makin would play a major role in crafting the ALP at both State and national levels, and would eventually become Australian ambassador to the United States of America.

'The eternal laws of justice, liberty and equity'

Given the atmosphere of the times, in the immediate aftermath of the conscription debate, it was hardly surprising that Makin in his *A Progressive Democracy* should deal initially with 'the desertion of the previously recognized leaders from the Labor movement'. He sketched 'the traitorous conduct of many politicians', looking back to the days of Richard Hooper, the very first (Independent) Labor MP, who eventually decided that his views were not consistent with those of the ULP and so 'drifted into the wilderness of reaction'.[4] Then there was Crawford Vaughan and his infamous 'black-coat brigade', whose underlying discomfort with Labor principles was exposed (according to Makin) by the conscription issue, revealing 'the hypocrisy of many who claimed allegiance to the name of Labor'.[5] Vaughan, he said, along with Verran, Harvey, and all the others who 'left the good ship of Labor are now drifting in the sea of political uncertainty'.[6]

It was also no surprise that Makin should look forward to the end of the Great War. The blame for the conflict, he said, lay squarely with 'the Governments of Europe founded on class rule', who had failed the Christian stricture of 'Peace on earth and goodwill to all men'. As he put it: 'While the people suffer and die in millions, thousands of the ruling and privileged classes are amassing huge fortunes out of war profits.'[7] He applauded the Russian Revolution and wished to 'congratulate the people of that country upon their efforts to abolish despotic power and class privileges'. Indeed, he urged all 'workers of every land where similar conditions exist to follow their example with the same magnificent courage and determination'. Turning to the conduct of the war, Makin considered that complete Allied victory over the Central Powers could only be achieved 'by the further sacrifice of millions of human lives'. The answer, therefore, was an immediate International Conference. The conference would acknowledge the 'right of small nations (including Ireland) to political independence', and all disputed territories would be allowed to choose their own forms of government.[8] Remarkably, Makin called for all occupied countries to be evacuated unconditionally. Armies would be disbanded and formed into volunteer reconstruction services, while conscription would be everywhere abolished and the international arms trade suppressed.

More achievable, perhaps, were the plans for the repatriation of Australian men and women at the war's end. Here Labor's stance was unequivocal:

> The question of Repatriation is one in which Australia must give a lead to the world. We are blazing the track in the matter of making an organized effort to look after those who fought for us – to reinstate in civil life all those who are capable of being re-instated there, and to provide for those who have suffered either from wounds or illness and who stand in need of care and attention.[9]

There was a requirement, Makin added, to deal 'justly with those who have been subject to the horrifying experiences of warfare'.[10] All military pensions should be of equal value, irrespective of rank, and all returned soldiers should be kept on the government's payroll until provided with suitable alternative employment. Training schemes to resettle returned service personnel should be set up, while jobs for them would be found in public works projects, from road construction to re-afforestation.

Turning to more general issues, Makin described Labor's mission as an 'endeavour to transform human institutions to the eternal laws of justice, liberty and equity'. This would 'protect the people from the ravages of commercialism and finance, and . . . secure to them the full advantage of their labor'.[11] There were specific policies, such as adult suffrage for the Legislative Council as a prelude to its abolition, a longstanding Labor commitment, and land reform so that the State government could manage closer settlement and the use of land for public purposes. Government control of railways and wharfs was essential, and so too was conservation of the Murray River for irrigation and navigation. Capital punishment would be abolished, and there should be a vigorous State housing program.

Equal pay for women was also an important plank of Labor policy, it was emphasised. 'Woman in many spheres of life is quite as satisfactory and efficient as a man', Makin conceded, 'and at times is his superior'. The 'Australian Labor Party claims justice for women', he insisted, 'while recognising that the rightful domain of woman is in the home'. Uncomfortably, perhaps, Makin tried to explain: 'Because the circumstances of life call for her in factory or industry, let her dues be paid, and let equal protection and advantages be guaranteed.'[12] But if Makin experienced some difficulty as Labor groped its way towards a fuller understanding of women's rights, then there was no such hesitation over the White Australia policy.[13] Here traditional Labor hostility to non-white immigrants, who might force down wages and lead to deteriorating working and social conditions, was to be maintained at all costs – this was Labor's shibboleth, and it would survive until the days of Don Dunstan and Gough Whitlam.

In 1919, as outgoing President of the ALP in South Australia, Norman Makin looked back on the achievements of the old ULP. It had 'sought to exalt life', he said, 'to demand justice and opportunity for all who furnished creative service to the world. It protected the weak and destroyed the power of the arrogant'.[14] The new-look ALP would, of course, take these ideals forward. But as *A Progressive Democracy* intimated, the ALP appeared now more radical – even utopian – than the down-to-earth ULP, more secular in flavour, more internationalist, and bent on creating a new mythology to validate its origins and destiny. However, the continuities between the old ULP and the new ALP were stronger than perhaps many cared to admit. Makin himself personified this continuity – craft trade unionist and Methodist local preacher – even if he also embraced the new with a passion. Moreover, as John Lonie observed in his study of the inter-war period (see pp. 16–16), the continuities between the old and the new exhibited enduring qualities characteristic of South Australia, despite the recent trauma of the conscription crisis. The ALP's composition was still redolent of the 1890s, he argued, not least the 'very strong Methodist flavour', which derived originally from 'the mineworkers of Burra and Wallaroo who were of Cornish stock'.[15] This was all the more remarkable, as Lonie admitted, because the copper mines at Moonta and Wallaroo – one of three 'hard core' industrial centres of Labor support identified by Brian Dickey (see p. 217) – had themselves been abandoned by 1923. Despite their demise, their influence lived on, not least in the ALP.

'Much bitterness among the workless'

The mines of northern Yorke Peninsula had prospered as part of a war economy – before August 1914 as part of Germany's 'peaceful penetration' in quest of raw materials to fuel the expansion of its military-industrial complex, and thereafter in support of the British Empire's war effort. By the end of 1918, however, it was clear that the writing was already on the wall. In the August, anticipating the end of the war, the British government had terminated the contract for Peninsula copper. Timely intervention by the Prime Minister, Billy Hughes, secured an extension until the end of the year but it was only a reprieve.[16] On 1 January 1919 the Wallaroo and Moonta Mining and Smelting Company took the unpopular but, it argued, inevitable decision to reduce wages. The Moonta men, still smarting from their perceived loss of status attendant upon the relative decline of their mine compared to the Wallaroo, took particular exception, a mass meeting of 400 miners protesting loudly that the company was sitting on £250,000 of accumulated war profits.[17] Meanwhile, the price of copper had dropped alarmingly on the international market, while costs of production at Moonta and Wallaroo continued to climb. By now, the cost of producing one ton of Peninsula copper was an extraordinary £20 above its market price – a situation that could not endure indefinitely.[18]

In March 1919 activity at the mines was severely reduced, coming to a complete stop on 15 April, a renewed coal strike in New South Wales ensuring that Moonta and Wallaroo would lie idle during the winter months. The arrival at Wallaroo of a ship laden with coal in September 1919 signalled a return to production, but there was a further period of inactivity at the mines from January to March 1920. The continuing slump in international copper prices forced another shutdown over Christmas 1920, the mines lying idle once more from January through to August 1921. The Australian Workers Union (AWU) had approached the company on several occasions during this period, seeking negotiations with a view to re-opening the mines. But the management was resistant to talks, explaining that the shortage of coal made a resumption of operations impossible at present. Industrial relations on the Peninsula were about to take a turn for the worse.

R.S. Richards, the local MP who had ousted John Verran and masterminded the AWU merger with the Amalgamated Miners Association (AMA) on the Peninsula (see p. 213), supported the AWU in its approaches to the company – especially in its demand that any return to work should be at existing rates of pay. Verran meanwhile, with the encouragement of his 'Bogus' union, insisted that the men would happily take a further wage cut, if that was what was needed to get the mines going again. Here was a return to the internecine industrial warfare of earlier years: the personal feud between John Verran (no longer an MP) and R.S. Richards, and the continuing struggle for legitimacy between the AWU and the Bogies. As the *People's Weekly* reported, it was a situation that caused 'much bitterness among the workless'. There was particular hostility towards Verran, whom the unemployed suspected of 'being a "tool" of the company for preaching ... the doctrine of half a loaf is better than none'. As the arguments raged, the *People's Weekly* observed pityingly the plight of those without a job: 'squatting listlessly on their haunches at the street corners, [they] still hang out in idleness, though it be worse than a chronic illness to the average Cousin Jack'.[19]

Verran and the Bogies came close to a deal with the company but it was effectively blocked by the AWU, which made it plain that its members would only return to work on its terms. In the event, there was a return to

Robert Stanley Richards, arch rival of John Verran and later Labor Premier.
[Courtesy State Library of South Australia, B7457]

work – albeit briefly – on 22 August 1921. But the price of copper continued to tumble, and the mines were again idle from 15 February 1922 until the following August.[20] Then, in a renewed attempt to cut costs, the company announced that in future the jackhammer rock-drills used underground would be manned by one miner only, rather than the customary two.[21] There was outrage. The AWU scheduled a meeting at Kadina to discuss the matter but before it could be convened two miners at Moonta were sent 'to grass' (surface) for refusing to adopt the new working practice. This triggered a walkout by workers at both the Moonta and Wallaroo mines, a prelude to a short but bitter strike in which R.S. Richards issued his passionate call-to-arms and final denunciation of Verran and the Bogies. A leaflet was circulated urgently and widely throughout the district:

Starvation may drive us back into the Mines; man's inhumanity to man may make countless thousands continue to mourn; but, whatever the result, we will never forget those men who aided the oppressor, we will never forget those men who played us false, and when the Time comes to show our contempt for them, we will do so in no uncertain manner:

> We will speak out, we will be heard, though all earth's system crack;
> We will not bate one single word or take a letter back,
> For the cause that lacks assistance, 'gainst the wrongs that need resistance,
> For the future in the distance, and the good that we can do.

> R.S. Richards MP
> North Moonta.[22]

In fact, the dispute went to arbitration and a compromise was struck, the men grudgingly returning to work on 7 November 1922. Prompted by R.S. Richards, the State government undertook a local geological survey with the aim of supporting future development work at the mines. But the reality now was that there was no future. Some exploratory work continued at the Wallaroo mine during 1923, but on the afternoon of 23 October 1923 the National Bank foreclosed on the Wallaroo and Moonta Mining and Smelting Company.[23] There were those who blamed this sudden collapse on the AWU, and there were others who imagined that some perverse extremists were glad to see the company go into liquidation. Writing years later in 1960, Oswald Pryor could still recall vividly the events of that awful day:

Some hot-headed trade union leaders were pleased at the news. The company, they said, had kept up ornate offices in Adelaide, yet the miners had not received an adequate share of the huge profits . . . and if an industry couldn't, or wouldn't, pay a decent wage, let it shut up shop! To the Cornish community that had lived in Wallaroo and Moonta for three generations, however, the closing of the mines was a calamity. For a while some thought that the company was only bluffing – that the announcement was just a stunt, designed to scare the miners into accepting a starvation wage. But they were faced with the fact that, for the first time in the history of the mines, the pumps were idle, water was rising steadily in the workings.[24]

Melville Pethick, writing in 1974, thought likewise. 'It was the demands of the Unions that closed down Moonta Mines', he reckoned: 'The Unions thought at the time that if they held out long enough the mine owners would give in to them, but the price of copper fell and the mines filled with water.'[25] Revd Gordon Rowe offered a more philosophical assessment: 'I ... think it is doubtful if the Moonta Mines ... would have continued much longer, even under harmonious and co-operative working conditions.' Anything else, he concluded, was 'wishful thinking'.[26] Be that as it may, the comprehensive dismantling of the mines began almost immediately, with the wholesale destruction of buildings and plant. The sale of machinery, materials and stores was designed to offset the company's losses. Fred Botterill of Kadina, a former miner, expressed his dismay at the scale and thoroughness of the project. 'It is rather a pity that we cannot have one or two landmarks left', he complained: 'They are not content without they tear down everything they can. When the mine was going it was dividends for shareholders – now, when she is done, they try to see how much wreckage they can leave about the place.'[27] Graham Jenkin agreed. Nothing was 'preserved as a memorial to the thousands of people who had made such a mighty contribution to this state'. Instead, he said: 'Nothing was left ... The capitalists, in their orgy of destruction, got their money.'[28] In fact, several of the old Cornish engine-houses did survive, too difficult or expensive to demolish, and in time came to be regarded as significant monuments to South Australia's copper-mining history.[29]

Victory! The State election of 1924 and John Gunn's premiership
There was no doubt that the closure of the Peninsula mines was a severe setback for the trade union movement and ALP in South Australia. The district would remain a Labor area for a good while yet – the popularity of R.S. Richards saw to that – but as much of the population drifted away to find

work elsewhere, so its significance (political as well as economic) dwindled. Nonetheless, as John Lonie observed, the region's cultural legacy remained highly influential within the Labor movement, not least, as we shall see, at parliamentary level. The Liberals had won an overall majority in the 1921 State election (with a new leader, the capable Henry Barwell), and thereafter the ALP attempted to widen its appeal, broadening its efforts beyond its industrial heartlands (including the fast declining Peninsula mines) to reach out to the rural vote. In earlier times, the ULP had tried periodically to win support in the countryside, often successfully, but sustaining and nurturing that support was always difficult. Makin's rhetoric, aimed primarily at the urban working class, was likely to arouse suspicion in the country, and Labor's message was modified and tempered to find appeal in agricultural districts. As Michael Atkinson has argued, in the early 1920s, despite the ostensible move to a more overtly socialist agenda (exemplified in Makin's *A Progressive Democracy*), the ALP in South Australia had remained resolutely pragmatic in practice, as it attempted to win office.[30]

The new strategic thrust paid off, and the ALP won the State election in 1924 handsomely with a record twenty-seven of the forty-six Assembly seats, seven of these in country districts. The new Labor Premier was none other than John Gunn, leader of the Drivers' Union strike during John Verran's ill-fated ministry, who had first entered Parliament in 1915 as Member for Adelaide. Politically, he had matured during the subsequent decade. As the *Advertiser* put it, rather sourly: 'Since the days of the drivers' strike ... Mr Gunn's views have been modified by experience, and he now believes in adopting strictly constitutional methods for adjusting grievances.'[31] The Liberal Federation (as it was now called) won seventeen Assembly seats in the 1924 election, the recently formed Country Party Association gaining just two. Reform of the Legislative Council remained high on the list of Labor's priorities, and Gunn took his impressive victory at the polls as a popular mandate to deal with the Council. However, despite the recent expansion of the franchise to include all returned servicemen who had served overseas, the Legislative Council remained firmly in the hands of those vehemently opposed to reform. In fact, the ALP was unable to expand its representation above four of the available twenty Council seats in any of the eighteen elections between 1918 and 1973.[32] As before, Labor measures passed in the House of Assembly to extend the franchise and reform procedures for dealing with parliamentary deadlocks were unceremoniously thrown out by the Legislative Council.

John Gunn (left), from strike leader to Labor Premier.
[Courtesy State Library of South Australia, PRG280/1/45/45]

Gunn borrowed heavily to invest in roads, railways and trams, and one early initiative was the launch of the 'one thousand homes scheme'. Responding to a perceived shortage of housing in the metropolitan area, the government launched its plans to create a 'garden suburb' – Colonel Light Gardens – which would provide homes for predominantly blue-collar workers. The idea was resisted by the existing middle-class residents nearby, whose cause was taken up by the Liberal Federation, which argued against this massive government intervention in the housing market. To add to Gunn's problems, the contractor entrusted with implementing the plan soon found himself in financial difficulties, and the scheme was dogged by scandal and controversy. It was finally completed in 1926, under the auspices of the State Bank. In other areas, notably education, the government was more straightforwardly successful. Teachers' salaries were increased substantially, medical support in schools was enhanced, a system of junior technical schools was inaugurated, and the Urbrae Agricultural High School founded. Revenue from a strongly performing economy (notwithstanding the closure of the copper mines) helped Gunn to afford these initiatives.

However, in August 1926, at the height of his powers and to the dismay of his parliamentary colleagues, Gunn announced his resignation. He had been approached by the Prime Minister, S.M. Bruce, to join the newly created Commonwealth Development and Migration Commission. It was rumoured that Gunn had been deliberately lured away from South Australia to deprive the State of an exceptionally able Labor politician. But whatever Bruce's motives, the new Commissioner's salary was twice that of the Premier's, and Gunn's ambitious wife had urged him to accept the post. Alas, Gunn's life soon unravelled. The Commission was abolished by Scullin's Federal government in 1930, and although Gunn was transferred to another post, his contract was terminated in 1935. He separated from his wife, became estranged from his four sons and daughters, and suffered a nervous breakdown. Thereafter, he drifted from the scene. He died in poverty and obscurity in Waterfall, New South Wales, in 1959.[33]

Gunn was replaced as Premier by 'Lightning' (an ironic sobriquet) or 'Slogger' Lionel Laughton Hill. Seen as ponderous and slow-thinking by his critics, with little or no grip on economic policy, Hill has been comprehensively damned by historian Ross McMullin as 'one of the worst ALP leaders in the party's history', his two spells as Premier marked by his 'ineptitude, vanity and swift abandonment of Labor principles'.[34] Jim Moss has offered a similar assessment: 'Lionel Hill ... soon showed that his progressive wartime stand against conscription would not be transformed into positive government policies on behalf of the workers'.[35] Hill's situation was not helped by the fact that the postwar prosperity had begun to fade, growing unemployment a prelude to the Depression years that lay ahead. There was unrest – in November 1926 a deputation, representing the unemployed, marched to the Treasury in Adelaide, where they were met by the Premier. It was not a good

'Lightning' or 'Slogger' Lionel Laughton Hill.
[Courtesy State Library of South Australia, B4083]

meeting. Hill 'loafed as a worker and now loafed on the workers', was the dismissive opinion of one of the deputation members.[36] The next day 250 unemployed workers confronted the Premier as he laid the foundation stone at Thebarton Central School. 'Work! Work! What about Work!' they chanted, and there were scuffles with the police.[37]

Disaster in 1927 and the Waterfront War

Not surprisingly, Hill was headed for catastrophe in the March 1927 State elections. Worsening economic conditions added to Hill's unpopularity and apparent lack of vigour, especially when compared to his predecessor, John Gunn. Additionally, the Liberal Federation and Country Party had reached an accommodation, a pact in which the Country Party would contest six rural seats without Liberal Federation candidates, with the Country Party guaranteed a place in a non-Labor Cabinet. The *Advertiser* made no secret

234

of its hostility to Hill's administration, and offered its readership straight eve-of-poll advice: 'Citizens who desire sane finance, economy, avoidance of dangerous and costly ventures, development of resources, fair play to individual enterprises and sympathy with rational measures of social reform and amelioration, should know how to cast their votes today.'[38]

The result was a resounding defeat for the ALP, an almost mirror image of 1924. The Liberal Federation–Country alliance won twenty-eight seats in the Assembly and Labor sixteen, plus one apiece for an Independent and (in the hitherto safe Labor seat of Port Adelaide) an Independent Protestant Labor Party candidate. Labor had lost heavily in the country, where it was hard hit by the Liberal Federation–Country Party pact. Yet that alliance was short-lived, the Country Party splitting on the question of whether it should merge formally with the Liberal Federation. To address the potential for renewed conflict between the conservative parties in country areas, which would obviously benefit the ALP, the new Liberal Federation government (under R.L. Butler) introduced extensive electoral reform, implementing a new preferential system of voting in which individual parties could recommend how their supporters should allocate their preferences. In this way, the disadvantages of Liberal Federation–Country Party competition were reduced, especially in the country.[39]

However, like Hill before him, Butler as Premier was faced with deteriorating economic conditions, to which was added drought and a burgeoning State government deficit. Growing unemployment led to further unrest, especially among the wharf labourers – 'wharfies' – of Port Adelaide, Port Pirie and other South Australian ports. Wharfies were casual labourers, 'picked up' early each morning by representatives of stevedoring companies to be assigned work for the day. It was an uncertain occupation – in downturns many hopeful men would be turned away day after day – and the system itself was open to abuse, with favouritism, victimisation and bribery commonplace. It was not popular with the wharfies, who dreaded the ignominy and indignity of the 'pick up'. In early September 1928, the Federal Arbitration Court announced its eagerly awaited 'award' for waterside workers. To the wharfies' dismay, the award granted no wage increases but ordered that henceforth there should be two pick-ups per day, one in the morning and one in the afternoon. This was too much for the wharfies, who promptly went on strike. By 10 September 1928, 200 wharfies were locked out at Port Pirie and ten ships were lying idle at Port Adelaide. A week later the automobile manufacturer, Holden, laid off 3,700 workers, providing a pool of desperate men from which 'volunteers' were recruited as strike-breakers to work on the ships at Port Adelaide.[40]

As the strike spread to other groups of workers, there were those who feared that a general breakdown of law and order was imminent. Under the leadership of Arthur Blackburn, the Adelaide solicitor and war hero who had distinguished himself at Gallipoli and won the Victoria Cross at Pozières, the Essential Services Maintenance Volunteers (ESMV) was formed. Composed largely of professional men, small businessmen, farmers and students, ESMV, despite its prosaic, even innocuous title, was paramilitary in organisation and intent. Blackburn insisted that his volunteers would not be strike-breakers, but it was clear that they were there to protect strike-breakers. As he put it, the volunteers would 'Uphold constitutional government, maintain law and order and perform essential services'.[41] Years later, Blackburn's daughter, Margaret Forbes, added a further gloss, explaining that her father was worried above all about the plight of returned servicemen, whose employment prospects, he had imagined, were being threatened by the effects of the strike. She recalled 'that he was greatly concerned about the welfare of the ex-soldiers who were losing their jobs because of the actions of the few'.[42] Be that as it may, Blackburn offered his volunteers' services to Butler's State government, which gratefully accepted, and in response a group of unemployed workers formed their own Volunteer Labor Army for the protection of trade unionists. When the *Advertiser* carried its alarming headline 'Waterfront War Begins in Earnest' on 21 September 1928, there were indeed those who thought that violent clashes in the streets of Adelaide were now inevitable.[43]

Yet there were many who were alarmed that the situation might deteriorate further, and a mass meeting of 1,400 waterside workers at Port Adelaide only narrowly defeated a motion to return to work. It did, however, authorise a secret ballot to decide the issue. But as the vote was being held, a small group of wharfies rushed the ballot box, kicking it over and tearing up some of the slips, throwing others over a nearby fence. The *Advertiser* condemned this 'irresponsible' incident, blaming a tiny 'Red Element', although it did concede that the ballot was in fact unconstitutional, as sufficient notice had not been given.[44] Meanwhile, as many had feared, there were violent scenes as strikers confronted the strike-breakers. Some strikers pursued their victims on bicycles, and others threw stones at trains carrying strike-breakers to Outer Harbour. But by now waterside workers in Brisbane, Melbourne and Newcastle had voted to return to work, their example followed at Port Adelaide by drivers, storemen and packers, and mill-workers. On 26 September the Port Adelaide wharfies decided that they too would offer for work. However, they were ignored, and only strike-breakers were selected at the pick-ups, the stevedoring companies insisting that preference should be given to 'volunteers'.[45] Not surprisingly, the wharfies were infuriated, as no doubt the employers intended.

The next day some 4,000 to 5,000 workers marched on the wharfs, attacking strike-breakers working on vessels and evicting volunteer crews from tugboats. They prevented the afternoon pick-up, held up a train allegedly carrying volunteers, and at Outer Harbour broke through a line of mounted police. In response, 500 ESMV members were sworn in as special constables to form the Citizen Defence Brigade (or League), organised by the Police Commissioner, Brigadier Raymond Leane, another distinguished war veteran. Nicknamed 'Blackburn's Black and Tans' by their detractors, an unflattering comparison with paramilitary auxiliaries operating in Ireland earlier in the decade, the special constables were issued with rifles, bayonets and other military accoutrements. They were deployed in three battalions to Outer Harbour, Fort Largs and Port Adelaide.[46] Again, there were scuffles and skirmishes, and – in an echo of earlier times at Moonta and Wallaroo and at Broken Hill – women played a distinctive role in the action. Calling themselves, ironically, the 'Girl Guides', they confronted the police lines. One woman accosted a policeman attempting to move men on, telling him to 'leave the boys alone'. When he replied that she 'would do no good', she retorted: 'If someone was scabbing on you wouldn't your wife do the same?' Another woman told a policeman bluntly to 'take a walk', warning that 'We'll pull the scabs out. Just give us women a go at them'.[47]

Lionel Hill, the ALP Opposition leader, interceded with the shipowners and stevedoring companies, in the hope of negotiating a return to work with conditions advantageous to the workers. The best he could do was to receive an assurance that, while volunteers who had worked during the strike would continue to be given preferential treatment, there would be opportunities at the pick-ups for the those striking wharfies who deigned to return. Grudgingly, the men went back on 4 October 1928 but the animosity – and violence – continued, setting the scene for years of unrest and discontent.[48] Rising unemployment contributed to the growing unpopularity of Butler's Liberal government but its willingness to use armed auxiliaries had genuinely frightened many observers. One felt, for example, that South Australia was getting dangerously 'close ... to the regime of Mussolini', and objected to the use of 'barbed wire entanglement', 'armed men marching about' and the 'appearance of an active state of war'.[49]

The Premiers' Plan

As the 1930 State election loomed, Butler could promise little more than extra belt-tightening and the possibility of even more difficult times ahead. Lionel Hill, however, boasted that he would swiftly eliminate unemployment and lower taxes, painting an altogether rosier picture of the future. As a result, Labor was returned to power with a record majority, winning thirty of the forty-six Assembly seats, including fourteen of the fifteen metropolitan seats. The Liberal Federation won only thirteen seats, the Country Party two, and a solitary Single Tax candidate was successful in the outback constituency of Flinders. Yet the 1930 election also evidenced a discernible level of political uncertainty and volatility in the electorate, not least among Labor supporters. Election candidates that year had included Independent Labor, Independent Protestant Labor, and Communists.[50] The Communist Party itself had been founded in South Australia in 1921, and had grown in influence thereafter, especially in metropolitan Adelaide. Jim Moss sought to explain the appeal of the Communists. Notwithstanding Hill's recent landslide, the 'history of the Labor Party in Government with Tom Price as Labor Premier of a coalition in 1905–09, John Verran as Premier of a Labor Government in 1910–12, and

Crawford Vaughan as Labor Premier in 1915–17', Moss argued, 'had done little to inspire confidence'.[51] He had a point, perhaps. Or, at the very least, while prepared to give Lionel Hill's optimism a chance to prove itself, voters were ready now to look in other directions, and sometimes to flirt with new alternatives.

Nonetheless, Lionel Hill's majority looked impressive and seemed to assure the ALP a clear way ahead in implementing its policies. However, if the beleaguered workers of South Australia had imagined that the tide had turned for them, they were sorely disappointed. Once in office, Hill had discovered that there was little opportunity to keep his election promises. Indeed, taking his advice from local and national business leaders, together with Lloyd Dumas, conservative editor of the *Advertiser*, Hill adopted a severe deflationary economic policy. Salaries of all State government workers were reduced by 10%, government spending was cut back, and taxation increased. Moreover, the unhappy compromise that Hill had negotiated for the waterside waters had already unravelled. 'Volunteers' continued to flood the labour market, marginalising those wharfies who had struck in 1928, despite those assurances that Hill thought he had been given. Additionally, as Premier, Hill failed to honour his earlier promise to remove the police presence from the waterfront. In September 1930 waterside workers of all types at Port Adelaide struck against the continued use of volunteer labour.[52] A Strike Committee was set up to co-ordinate the efforts of the different groups – seamen, timber workers, storemen and packers, carters and drivers, mill-workers, and so on – and as before women played a prominent part in the proceedings. Two women delegates sat on the Strike Committee, others engaged in picketing, and, according to Gilbert Roper in an article 'Class Warfare at Port Adelaide', published in October 1930, women were 'quick to march in their hundreds to the Port Adelaide Central School in reply to the victimization of children for the use of the word "scab" and for marching in demonstrations'.[53]

As the situation threatened once more to become ugly, a deal was sought to bring the dispute to a close. Again there was a messy compromise, with the employers guaranteeing three days' work a week for volunteer labour, with the wharfie trade unionists allowed to pick up whatever might remain.[54] It was a stand-off rather than a resolution, and the atmosphere remained tense. Meanwhile, convinced by Brigadier Leane that South Australia was on the brink of a Communist insurrection, Lionel Hill rushed his *Public Safety Act* through the State Parliament. This gave the government the power to proclaim a state of emergency, while persons obstructing the police at Port Adelaide could be subjected to a £200 fine and six months' imprisonment. Lamely, Hill defended this suspension of civil liberties by alleging that the recent strike was 'only an excuse for a certain organization to get a fast hold on South Australia. I refer to the Communist movement'.[55]

Ross McMullin hardly exaggerated when he concluded that 'Hill was the puppet of conservative interests'.[56] Yet there was worse to come – the Premiers' Plan crisis. Sir Otto Niemeyer, a prominent British banker, had visited Australia to advise the Federal government on its financial response to the world-wide economic Depression. He prescribed a severe deflationary policy, such as Hill had already introduced in South Australia. However, Ted Theodore, Treasurer in the Federal Labor government, had been much impressed by the work of John Maynard Keynes, the British economist, and argued for the exact opposite – a *reflationary* policy, which would create employment and stimulate demand by increasing government expenditure. But Theodore's plan was rejected by the Senate and the Commonwealth Bank, and in June 1931 the Prime Minister Jim Scullin sought to construct an alternative plan with the co-operation of the several State Premiers during the Premiers' conference. Lionel Hill, who had just introduced deflationary measures in his home State, was asked for his views on the matter by Theodore. 'I can't really make up my mind', Hill replied, 'I don't know'. Suitably irritated, Theodore quipped: 'You bloody old woman, you haven't got a mind to make up.'[57] But one State Premier who did know his own mind was Jack Lang of New South Wales, who in February 1931 had come up with a plan of his own, which would include a suspension of interest payments on debts to the British government, and reduction of Australian government borrowing interest rates to 3% to stimulate the economy.

At their conference, Scullin and the premiers agreed (Lang very reluctantly) to what became known as the Premiers' Plan, whereby taxes would be increased, interest rates reduced, and a 20% reduction made in all Federal and State government expenditure – including wages and pensions. To many traditional ALP supporters across Australia, this appeared the antithesis of Labor policy, not least the cuts in wages, welfare and pensions. The ALP's Federal executive met on 18 June 1931 to discuss the Plan. The party's South Australian branch had instructed its delegates, Norman Makin and Harry Kneebone (of whom, more below) to oppose the proposals, which they did – vehemently. They were joined by other critics, and eventually a compromise was struck. Mindful that a conservative Federal government would introduce yet harsher measures, the several delegates recognised that it was important to keep Scullin's Labor government in power at all costs. Thus a compromise was agreed, and, in a collective attempt to feel better about the matter, the delegates admitted that the cuts were inherently distasteful, attacking the banks and Senate for their obstructionist tactics. When the Federal Parliamentary Labor Party subsequently ratified the Premier's Plan, there was a palpable descent into gloomy self-loathing, a sense that it had betrayed fundamental Labor principles but that there had been little alternative.[58]

Jack Lang, however, drawing a veil over the fact that he had actually signed up to the Premiers' Plan, launched a vigorous campaign against its implementation, in the process attempting to extend the influence of Lang Labor (as it was dubbed) beyond New South Wales into other States. Intriguingly, South Australia, alone of all the States outside New South Wales, returned Lang Labor candidates to its State Parliament, as the ALP split over the Premiers' Plan.[59] Indeed, the split consequent upon the acceptance of the Premiers' Plan – every bit as bitter as the Labor split over conscription during the Great War – was especially damaging in South Australia. Stanley R. Whitford reckoned that 'This debacle in the ranks of the Labor movement in this State [South Australia] was the worst of my experience'.[60]

Lang Labor and the Bardolph Brothers

Don Hopgood, in examining the curious case of Lang Labor in South Australia, has traced the State's distinctive experience back to the discontents of 1929. As Hopgood has remarked, that there was a great deal of dissatisfaction with the ALP leadership at that time was hardly remarkable. However, that these dissidents were well organised, with a weekly newspaper as their mouthpiece, was rather more so. Additionally, 'that these people should have had close links with Sydney Trades Hall, regarding it, rather than the local party machine, as their political lode star, is the unique factor in the situation'.[61] The 'guiding spirits' in this group, as Hopgood has described them, were two brothers, Doug and Ken Bardolph. Part of a large Catholic family, the Bardolphs were born in Sydney and, 'spiritually at least, never left it'. The family had moved to Melbourne during the Great War, journeying on to Adelaide thereafter. Here the Bardolph brothers swiftly became involved in Labor politics but remained committed to 'New South Wales methods', according to Hopgood, injecting a new perspective into the local political scene.[62] Doug launched two weekly newspapers. The *Unley News*, which he founded in 1918 was to last five years, whereupon he started the *South Australian Worker*, designed as the official ALP paper to replace the now defunct *Daily Herald*. Ken, meanwhile, had risen rapidly in the trade union movement, and by 1929 was president of the United Trades & Labor Council (UTLC). In little more than a decade, the Bardolphs had gained considerable influence over the ALP in South Australia.

In 1929, on the death of John Carr, there was a by-election for Central No. 1 District of the Legislative Council. This was one of the very few safe Labor constituencies in the overwhelmingly conservative Legislative Council, so much so that the Liberals rarely bothered to put up candidates. Among the eleven nominees putting their names forward for the Labor pre-selection ballot were Doug Bardolph and Stanley R. Whitford. Bardolph won, with Whitford second, but there were widespread allegations of irregularities and malpractice. One incensed trade unionist even invited John Verran, the former Labor Premier and now (albeit briefly) a Liberal Senator, to stand against Bardolph. Verran refused. However, Whitford, with the backing of AWU officials, decided to stand himself, and competing factions grew up around the two contending Labor candidates, Whitford's supporters styling themselves the 'ALP Defence Committee'. Bardolph's campaign was managed by A.A. 'Bert' Edwards, MP for Adelaide. Pondering the threatened 'split', the ALP machine decided, two weeks before polling day, to endorse neither candidate, and instead referred the allegations of malpractice to a special committee. By now, however, as Hopgood has remarked, the party was effectively 'split down the middle'. Bardolph's supporters tended to be 'younger and predominantly Catholic', while Whitford's faction was 'generally older and largely Protestant'.[63] There was a whiff of sectarian conflict here, the 'Catholic' flavour of Bardolph's campaign an import of eastern States' Labor politics, the 'Protestant' backlash an indicator of Whitford's Cornish–Methodist background. There was also a generational split, and while Bardolph presented himself as a radical opposed to Whitford's 'deflationist' stance, Whitford too sported his own radical credentials as a life-long admirer of the Eugene Debs and the Industrial Workers of the World.

In the event, Stanley R. Whitford won easily, with more than 50% of votes cast. Doug Bardolph, in a fit of pique, severed the link between his *South Australian Worker* and the ALP, claiming that the party was manipulated by a 'junta' and 'uncouth political crooks'.[64] In response, the ALP's special committee on the ballot box allegations found against Doug Bardolph, and subsequently both Bardolph brothers were expelled from the party. As Hopgood has observed, although the Bardolph faction as yet owed nothing to Jack Lang, it was nonetheless, with its New South Wales connections, an embryonic Lang Labor group in waiting.[65] The first suggestion that Jack Lang might be invited to Adelaide to outline his 'plan' appeared in the *South Australian Worker* in March 1931.[66] A 'Lang Plan Campaign Committee' was formed, with Doug Bardolph as president. In the same month a special conference of the ALP, held to discuss the abject failings of the Hill government, narrowly avoided expelling Lionel Hill and his supporters from the party, such was the level of discontent. It did, however, endorse Lang's plan for financial management and economic development. Meanwhile, the Federal conference of the ALP had expelled Lang's New South Wales branch! Lang responded with an Australia-wide tour to garner support for his position. In April 1931, he addressed three packed meetings in Adelaide, and at each resolutions supporting the Lang plan were carried.[67] When Lang spoke at the Exhibition Building on North Terrace, in the heart of the city, the 'Song of Australia' was drowned out by competing factions singing variously 'God Save the King' and 'The Red Flag'.[68]

Lang won the support of three State Labor MPs but the first real test of his appeal in South Australia was the Adelaide by-election in July 1931, prompted by the imprisonment of Bert Edwards (reputedly one of the several illegitimate offspring of the former Premier, Charles Kingston) for committing a homosexual act.[69] The ALP nominated UTLC president Frank Goring for what was hitherto a safe Labor seat but the Lang Plan Committee decided to run an alternative Lang candidate, M.L. Collaston, secretary of the Ironworkers' Union. That there were also Communist and Socialist Labor Party candidates in the by-election was a measure of both hostility to the Hill government and uncertainty within the Labor movement, not least in its attitude to the Premiers' Plan. Collaston, the Langite, duly won, causing shock waves to run through the ALP. There were expulsions from the party of Lang supporters, as the Langites moved to set up what was effectively an alternative structure, complete with branches. At a further by-election in October 1931 for Central No. 1 District, Doug Bardolph himself stood. He was beaten easily but so too was the official Labor candidate, Labor's first defeat in the district since before the war, the seat being won by an Independent.

At the end of 1931, the Federal Langites forced a general election: Scullin's Labor government was swept away and the new United Australia Party won a huge majority in the Federal Parliament. Labor's defeat was especially marked in South Australia (again, a measure of hostility to Lionel Hill), with Norman Makin (who had voted against the Premiers' Plan) surviving as the party's sole member in the House of Representatives. Yet Lang Labor had also performed badly in South Australia, many of those voters who had earlier demonstrated their inclination to support the faction now registering their strong disapproval that the Federal Langites had precipitated the destruction of Scullin's government. This poor showing provoked much in-fighting within Lang Labor in South Australia, including a falling-out between Doug Bardolph and M.L. Collaston, the recently elected Langite MP. Out of the quarrelling a new party emerged in May 1932, the South Australian branch of the Lang Australian Labor Party, separate from the extant Lang Committee, which shortly began endorsing its own candidates for the impending State election. Absurdly, there appeared now to be two competing Lang organisations in South Australia.

At the height of this confusion, in May 1932, Jack Lang was dismissed as Premier of New South Wales, removing his plan from 'the realms of practical politics', as Hopgood has described it.[70] A representative from the parent body in New South Wales arrived to adjudicate as to the legitimacy of the two alternative Lang parties in South Australia, and, not surprisingly, plumped for Bardolph's original Lang Committee. Meanwhile, the State ALP, thinking perhaps that the Lang threat was already on the wane, decided to readmit all those who had defected, except individuals who had been specifically expelled – this caveat being aimed at the Bardolphs. By now, however, the ALP had also expelled Lionel Hill and his government ministers for supporting the Premiers' Plan, adding to the disarray in Labor ranks. Hill himself had had enough, and engineered his appointment as South Australia's Agent-General in London. Leaving the country, he handed the premiership to his deputy, R.S. Richards, who knew that this was a poisoned chalice, and that he had little chance of leading Labor to success in the forthcoming 1933 State election. Despite solid support in his home constituency of Wallaroo – his campaign meeting in Wallaroo Town Hall went so smoothly that one observer quipped 'the Cousin Jacks must have thought it was an evening church service'[71] – elsewhere in the State Richards was vilified as a Hill associate and supporter of the Premiers' Plan. He was Premier for just sixty-four days.

'It is not I who ratted. It was Jack Lang'

Labor entered the campaign in 1933 split into three competing factions. There was the Parliamentary Labor Party (led by R.S. Richards) with twenty seats in the Assembly, the official ALP, with nine seats, and Lang Labor with one. In the ensuing election, Labor was trounced, with the Parliamentary Labor Party caucus reduced to four, the official ALP winning six seats and Lang Labor three.[72] That Doug Bardolph and two other Langite candidates were successful was, in the circumstances, a remarkable result. Collaton, meanwhile, who had returned to the ALP fold, lost his seat. At the declaration of the poll he was 'counted out' twice by the Langite crowd, and to cries of 'Rat!' he replied by insisting: 'It was not I who ratted. It was Jack Lang.' He sat down, according to an *Advertiser* report, 'amid tumult'.[73] The scale of Labor's loss was a measure of the split but the success of the Liberal and Country League (as it was now called), which won twenty-nine seats, was greatly assisted by the formal merger in South Australia of the former Liberal Federation and Country parties. No longer in competition, they had turned their combined strength against the weakened and divided Labor forces, with impressive results. As Nick Dyrenfurth and Frank Bongiorno have mused, in 1933 the Liberal and Country League (LCL) was presented with 'office on a platter'.[74] South Australia would not see another Labor Premier for more than thirty years, when Frank Walsh assumed the premiership in 1965.

Doug Bardolph relished his new role as a parliamentarian, asking questions, moving votes of no-confidence, and introducing private member's bills. But if he behaved as a party leader, his party was crumbling around him. Infuriated by his controlling manner, Bardolph's two parliamentary colleagues, Dale and Howard, distanced themselves from their 'leader' and, joining with other anti-Bardolph dissidents in the Langite camp, formed yet another group, the South Australian Lang Labor Party. Later in the year a third Lang group emerged, the New State Labor Party, leading the *Advertiser* to observe wryly that the Langites were fast heading towards the principle of 'one man, one party'.[75] Recognising the absurdity of the situation, and the fact that Lang Labor was unlikely ever to appeal beyond its Adelaide heartland, several trade unions, led by former Langite F.R. James, convened a Labor unity conference in 1934. Even Doug Bardolph was persuaded by the pleas for unity and, despite earlier resistance, was readmitted to a unifying ALP. But Bardolph was too much of an individualist and a maverick to remain in the ALP fold for long. In August 1935 he was declared to be 'outside the party' for non-payment of the parliamentary levy, and in 1938 and again in 1941 he was returned as an Independent Labor member for Adelaide.[76]

As Don Hopgood concluded, Doug Bardolph, although 'strongly imbued with the Labor spirit and beliefs', was 'at heart, an independent. He suffered no superior and brooked no equal'. Even if we take Bardolph's commitment to the Lang plan at face value, Hopgood has argued, it is difficult to avoid the conclusion that the Lang Labor Party in South Australia 'was primarily the personal political machine of Douglas Henry Bardolph'.[77] Lang Labor itself quietly disappeared, after its short but spectacular intervention in the State's politics, as the two-party system re-asserted itself. Critics in the ALP continued to condemn the Bardolph brothers as 'political adventurers', outsiders who had brought the destructive politics of New South Wales into South Australia. The ALP tightened its procedures to prevent elements of its organisation ever being hijacked again. This allowed the party a return at last to something like normality. But, according to Hopgood, it was 'peace bought at the price of, at least before the Dunstan era, a certain drabness'.[78]

Richards and the Radical Tradition

R.S. Richards became leader of the ALP opposition in 1938, and remained so for all of eleven years, until his resignation in 1949.[79] He continued to represent Wallaroo, which he had wrested from John Verran's grasp in 1918, and in many ways personified the enduring Cornish-Methodist influence in the Labor Party that John Lonie has identified. He remained immersed in the Methodist church (in later years he would become a director of the Methodist radio station 5KA), and in 1940 introduced legislation to allow religious education in State schools. He was active in the Cornish Association of South Australia, and remained intimately entwined in the social and cultural life of close-knit northern Yorke Peninsula. The two sisters of his first wife, Ada Maude Dixon, whom Richards had married in 1914, were wed respectively to Stanley R. Whitford, his Labor colleague, and Oswald Pryor, Cousin Jack cartoonist and later author of the well-known book *Australia's Little Cornwall*. This enhanced that sense of a pervasive 'Cousin Jack and Cousin Jenny network' in which these figures moved. Richards was never as ebullient or explosive as Verran but he was quick witted and, like Verran, a master of clever repartee. As a Methodist and Rechabite, Richards was opposed to gambling. On one occasion, with gaudily dressed bookmakers in his audience, he was asked 'What have you got against bookmakers anyway?'. His response surprised those who knew his views on the subject: 'Nothing at all, they give me great pleasure.' But then he added, with a Biblical flourish, 'they toil not neither do they spin, yet Solomon in all his glory was not arrayed as one of these'.[80]

Richards even made his peace with John Verran, and as early as September

1927 the two men had shared the platform at the Back to Moonta celebrations, Verran in his capacity as Senator and Richards as local MP and member of the event's organising committee. Designed to entice exiled Moontaites in Adelaide, Port Pirie, Broken Hill, Kalgoorlie and elsewhere back 'home' to commemorate Moonta's past (and express confidence in its future), Back to Moonta – four years after the disastrous closure of the mines – rekindled pride in the Peninsula's distinctive identity. An editorial in the *People's Weekly* enthused: 'The Celtic spirit is deep set in folk that hail from Cornwall, and they are Celts on an equality with the Scots, Irish or Welsh.' Moreover, it was explained, the Celts 'are clannish to a marked degree, and the love of home and the clan seldom loses its hold in the individual and never in the race, and Moonta people are mainly Cornish'. This was one opinion on which Richards and Verran could surely agree, an echo of the solidarity they had once enjoyed in the days before the conscription and AWU split. No doubt both men smiled when the train from Adelaide carrying the returning Moontaites arrived with its locomotive's headboard sporting the Cornish arms and motto, 'One and All', along with the slogan 'Dignity and Power' (designed, perhaps, to appeal to Labor sentiments) and the belief that 'The Soul of Moonta is Not Dead'.[81] Richards did not attend Verran's State funeral in June 1932 but there was reconciliation of a different sort when Stanley R. Whitford, hitherto a firm critic of Verran and now Chief Secretary in Hill's administration, represented the government at the occasion.[82]

As a former mineworker, Richards took a particular interest in the fortunes of the State's mining industry. After the closure of Moonta and Wallaroo in 1923, he had complained in Parliament, with some justification, that 'we have a Department of Mines, a Director of Mines, two Inspectors of Mines, and a Minister of Mines, but practically no mines'.[83] He did what he could, and in 1936 supported a brief attempt by the Kadina Mining Company to restart the long-abandoned New Cornwall, together with a forlorn attempt by W.J.L. Polmear – an old Moonta identity, born at Landrake in Cornwall, a former trade union activist – to work the Poona mine lease on his own account. Slightly more successful was the Moonta Prospecting Syndicate, a small outfit with an initial capital of £3,000 which worked steadily until

1926 when, with a rise in the price of copper and the help of R.S. Richards (he would later become Minister of Mines in Hill's second government), a form of 'subsist' (a Cornish term, used by Richards) was paid by the State as an advance on earnings. Richards even managed to attract Federal financial assistance for a time, subsidies being provided for the re-opening of the old Smith's and Bennett's shafts, although this support was withdrawn in December 1931. Richards, however, was able to keep the workings going by re-organising them on a co-operative basis, arguing that this 'was the most practicable way to relieve the serious unemployment amongst local skilled miners and tradesmen accustomed to mining work', especially given 'the interest and willingness displayed by the employees'.[84] Yet these modest attempts at renewal were doomed to failure in the difficult Depression years, with their precarious government funding, and petered out before the Second World War.

Close colleague of R.S. Richards for much of this inter-war period was Stanley R. Whitford who, as we have seen (p. 205–6), was born at Moonta and was especially proud of his Cornish roots. He proclaimed northern Yorke Peninsula 'our Cornish colony', cultivating his own Cornish accent (perhaps for political reasons), and observing that many other local residents did the same. 'You would think', he said, 'that they came direct from Cornwall when you listened to their Cornish brogue'.[85] Whitford began his working life as a blacksmith at Moonta, attending night classes at the Moonta School of Mines, before going to the Western Australian goldfields in 1899–1908, and then returning to Wallaroo. He found employment with South Australian Railways, first as a navvy and then as a porter, where he became a prominent trade unionist. He was president of the State branch of the ALP in 1919–20, succeeding Norman Makin. He won the Assembly seat of North Adelaide in 1921, only to lose it in the debacle of 1927, but from 1929 until 1941 he was a long-serving representative of that rare species – a Labor member (albeit 'Independent Labor' after 1933) of the Legislative Council – having soundly defeated Doug Bardolph in Central No. 1 District. In 1930 Whitford was briefly minister for immigration, repatriation and irrigation, and was minister of lands in 1930–33 and Chief Secretary from October 1930 until April 1933. He

Stanley R. Whitford, self-proclaimed Cousin Jack and scourge
of the Bardolph brothers. [Courtesy State Library of South Australia, B5889]

was applauded especially as architect of the humanitarian *Destitute Persons
Relief Act 1931.*[86]

Harry Kneebone – 'A Son of Little Cornwall'

Arising from the same tradition was Henry 'Harry' Kneebone, born at
Wallaroo Mines in 1876, the son of Cornish parents – Henry Kneebone senior,
a miner from Penponds, near Camborne, and Elizabeth Tonkin. Brought up
in the Bible Christian denomination before Methodist union, Kneebone later
became organist in Kadina Methodist Church. He left school at the age of
twelve, becoming a printer's compositor at the *Kadina and Wallaroo Times*, but
in 1894, like many young men from the Peninsula, decided to try his luck as
a miner in Western Australia, first in the Murchison district and then on the
Kalgoorlie–Coolgardie goldfields. He fared better, however, as a journalist
on the staff of the pro-Labor *Coolgardie Miner* newspaper, becoming its editor
in 1908, as well as secretary of the local Labor Party branch. Like Stanley R.
Whitford, Harry Kneebone's political views appear to have crystallised during
his spell in Western Australia, and he was able to give them full expression

through the pages of the *Coolgardie Miner*. According to his daughter and biographer, Joan Tiver, Kneebone always adhered to 'the Bible as his social conscience guidebook'.[87] As she explained, her father was:

> a socialist in the sense that he considered Jesus Christ a Socialist ... [he] was entirely democratic in outlook and did not believe that anyone can be born with 'bluer' blood than another. Although he would not have described himself as a Republican, he was not an ardent Royalist. He believed, however, that complete independence must come to Australia some day, as a child sheds it apron springs. He also believed that superiority, if it need be recognised, should spring from achievement by the use and development of one's God-given talents and mental powers, never the accident of one's birth or the inheritance of wealth.[88]

In 1910, the year of Verran's victory, Harry Kneebone was enticed back to South Australia to join the newly launched Labor paper, the *Daily Herald*, becoming its editor shortly after. In 1912, the year of Verran's defeat, the Federal Labor government, recognising Kneebone's journalistic skills, appointed him press officer at the Australian High Commission in London, and after the outbreak of war he represented Australia on the British Press Council. He also founded the 'Anzac Buffet', which provided Australian soldiers in Britain with free meals and entertainment. He visited Cornwall too, venturing as far west as the Levant mine in St Just-in-Penwith. In 1916, Kneebone returned to Adelaide to become managing editor of the *Daily Herald*. A committed anti-conscriptionist he soon found himself in conflict with both the Methodist church and his erstwhile political ally, John Verran, drawing closer to R.S. Richards instead. He also became an active trade unionist and Labor Party member, speaking regularly at the 'Labor Ring' gatherings in Adelaide's Botanic Gardens, and representing the printers' union on the UTLC, of which he became president.[89]

In 1924 Kneebone was elected as Assembly member for East Torrens, on a platform that embraced causes such as the nationalisation of banking and insurance, state ownership of utilities, the socialisation of industry, and universal education. He resigned his seat in 1925 to fight the Federal constituency of Boothby but was unsuccessful. He then worked for some years on the *Advertiser*, presumably not entirely congenial employment, given the paper's increasingly conservative stance. In April 1931, however, he was appointed to fill a casual vacancy in the Senate, giving him the taste of Federal politics for which he yearned, although only serving for less than a year. But he remained as a member of the Federal executive of the ALP, and was president of the South Australian branch of the Labor Party when the Premiers' Plan storm broke. Finding himself opposed now to R.S. Richards, he supported the expulsion of all State and Federal members who supported the Plan, such were the shifting sands of Labor allegiance in this period. Shortly after, he launched his own newspaper, the *Labor Advocate*. In all this, he remained a keen supporter of the Cornish Association of South Australia. He was, as Joan Tiver averred, a proud 'Son of "Little Cornwall"'.[90]

A measure of Kneebone's progressive and humanitarian thinking was his awakening concern for indigenous Australians. It was unusual in his time, even among Labor supporters. Shortly after the Great War, he was asked to contribute to *The Wonder Book of Empire for Boys and Girls*, published in London, Melbourne and Toronto, and produced a series of chapters on 'Sunny Australia: The All-British Continent'. In these pages, Kneebone demonstrated his affection for 'the aborigines who have yielded their country to the white settlers'. He identified qualities of selflessness and courage in the Aboriginal population, observing that 'they make excellent stockmen' and that – as first-class trackers – 'they have saved the lives of many wanderers in the wild parts'. Indeed, Kneebone explained: 'All over Australia aboriginals are attached to country police stations so their services may be available for tracking criminals or suspected or lost persons.' He also admired Aboriginal culture, and described spear-throwing, boomerangs and corroborees. It was a simplistic picture (the book was designed for children) and somewhat patronising. But it evidenced a genuine desire to celebrate Aborigines as the original Australians, and to express concern for their welfare and future. As Kneebone put it: 'Many interesting stories could be told of these folk, and for many reasons it is to be hoped that the efforts which are being made to keep them from dying out will be successful.'[91]

Sadly, Harry Kneebone died suddenly and unexpectedly on 22 December 1933, aged only fifty-seven. In its obituary, the *Advertiser*, for which newspaper Kneebone had worked previously, acknowledged that his 'interests were bound up in the [Labor] party and his powers of oratory and his ever flowing enthusiasm were always at the service of the party in any political flight'.[92] The Port Pirie *Recorder* agreed, describing Harry Kneebone as 'one of the most prominent members of the Australian Labor Party'.[93] Certainly, he had remained absolutely true to Labor principles throughout his career – most notably in the conscription crisis and in the Premiers' Plan controversy – and his demise was a sore blow to the party he had loved so well. Yet his legacy lived on, his son Frank Kneebone becoming a Labor member of the Legislative Council in 1961, and serving in both the Walsh and Dunstan governments from 1965 until 1975. It was a remarkable continuation of the Cornish-Methodist radical tradition of which Harry Kneebone had been so conspicuously a part.

Further evidence for the 'Lonie thesis'

Who else might be counted as part of this tradition in the inter-war period? It seems appropriate to include John Stanley 'Stan' Verran, son of John Verran, born at Moonta in 1883, who held the safe Labor seat of Port Adelaide from 1918 to 1927. He had begun working in the Moonta mine at the age of eleven, first at surface and later underground. Like Stanley R. Whitford and Harry Kneebone, he spent time on the Western Australian goldfields before returning to the Peninsula and then gravitating to Port Adelaide, where he was employed as a clerk. He participated in the formation of the Federated Clerks' Union, and became its State president.[94] Stan Verran was duly recognised as 'one of Port Adelaide's Labour sentinels' and, pointing to his illustrious father, the *People's Weekly* observed in 1920 that 'Moonta and Verran are identical terms'.[95] Yet when it was revealed that his nickname at school was 'Grub', this somehow detracted from the Verran lustre, and it was admitted that 'Stanley is but a faint pattern of his father. He lacks the native humour, and the ready repartee, and the quaint Cornish sayings of the pioneer Wallaroo member'.[96] And so it proved. Losing his seat in 1927, Stanley Verran's fortunes declined alarmingly thereafter. In November 1935 he, with two accomplices, was found guilty of theft and sentenced to fifteen months' imprisonment, having broken into a warehouse at Port Adelaide and stolen thirty-two boxes of handkerchiefs, twenty-four tins of tongues and twenty-two tins of fish, all the property of the Adelaide Steamship Company.[97] Fortunately, his father had not lived to witness this fall from grace.

More successful was the career of Thomas Gluyas, born at Moonta Mines in 1864, the son of a Cornish miner. He joined the railways, where he became a locomotive engineer, working first at Quorn in the Flinders Ranges before transfer to Adelaide, where he was employed in the Islington workshops. He became president of the Adelaide branch of Amalgamated Society of Engineers, and a Labor activist. In 1918 he became another example of that rare species, a Labor member of the Legislative Council, serving until his death in 1931.[98] Another success story was that of Albert Redvers Hawke, son of a Cornish miner, who was born at Kapunda in 1900. Legend has it that, a convert to the Labor cause early in life, he was dismissed from his job as a greengrocer's delivery boy for wearing an anti-conscriptionist badge.[99] Be that as it may, he represented Burra Burra from 1924 until he lost his seat in the disastrous election of 1927. Thereafter, he shifted his political career to Western Australia, later becoming Labor Premier of that State. He was the uncle of Bob Hawke, later to become Labor Prime Minister of Australia – another remarkable continuity. Thomas Tonkin Edwards, born in Cornwall in 1870, had also embraced Labor politics as a youth, when at the age of thirteen he found work at a milling company in the trade union stronghold of Port Adelaide. Later, as a Labor member, he represented Barossa in the House of Assembly from 1929 until 1933.[100]

In seeking further evidence for the 'Lonie thesis', it might be stretching a point to include Leslie Claude Hunkin, born in Tasmania in 1884, the son of a miner, who arrived in Adelaide in 1908 by way of Western Australia, seeking a dry clime to suit his ill health. Yet he was recognised for his 'Cornishness', according to Carol Fort, and his 'father's Cornish background was apparent in Hunkin's rather short frame, dark hair and clipped speech'.[101] Moreover, he was for a time at the heart of the Labor Party in South Australia. He was a founder of the local branch of the Federated Storemen and Packers' Union of Australia, and from 1922 until 1929 was general secretary of the Public Service Association of South Australia and editor of its journal, the *Public Service Review*. Hunkin was also Labor member for East Torrens from 1921 until the great defeat of 1927. He acted as speechwriter for Lionel Hill, and took a leading part in the doomed 1927 election campaign, attempting to persuade the electorate to overlook the government's shortcomings by promising deep drainage, road improvements, enhanced social services, better housing, action against monopolies, and adherence to the White Australia policy. As Hunkin put it: 'Vote Labor, and Rid South Australia of a Danger to the Purity of Our Race.'[102]

As is readily apparent, the electoral cull of 1927 somewhat diluted that sense of continuity identified by Lonie. And yet, as we have seen, R.S. Richards led the ALP until 1949, when he married his second wife, Mary Alison Hawkes, a librarian, and was appointed administrator of Nauru. But in the 1938 State election, despite reconciliation and reunification after the Premiers' Plan controversy, the ALP still managed to achieve only nine seats in the House of Assembly. There was, surprisingly, a large number (fourteen) of Independents returned that year, a measure perhaps of the electorate's wariness after the recent splits. Only slowly did the Labor Party recognise that parties given to schism deterred voters and that, whatever the factional differences within the ALP, unity had to be maintained if office was to be won. As Michael Atkinson put it: 'Only then [in the late 1930s], on the bones of its bum, did the Party discover that bad Labor government was better than the best Liberal government'.[103] But it was to be almost another three decades before the ALP would achieve victory at the polls in South Australia, with Labor seemingly cast irretrievably in the role of perpetual Opposition. R.S. Richards, meanwhile, the firebrand of the Great War years and the early 1920s, settled in for the long haul, the zeal of the radical tradition he had inherited fading into something like cosy complacency.

'Playmander' and Labor impotency

However, the problem for R.S. Richards and the Labor Party, was not merely a question of electability in the eyes of the public, nor the fact that the LCL was reaping the benefits of the easing of the Depression. Rather, a fundamental shift in the way members were elected in South Australia had placed the ALP at permanent disadvantage, or at least for the next thirty-three years. In 1936 multiple member constituencies were abolished and this, combined with preferential voting, meant that a candidate needed to achieve an absolute majority (after the distribution of preferences) to be elected. Under the old system, Labor had a fair chance of winning a seat in three-member rural seats, such as Burra Burra, where there were pockets of Labor supporters. Under the new system, this was simply not possible. Moreover, the 1936 Electoral Act had further entrenched the over-representation of rural areas. As part of its price for merging with the Liberals, the Country Party had demanded a minimum weighting of 2:1 against the metropolitan district. Indeed, the resultant malapportionment was to be a principal factor in creating and maintaining the record LCL government of 1938–1965.[104]

This exaggerated rural bias had been introduced by R.L. Butler, LCL Premier, but it was especially associated with the long ministry of his successor in LCL government, Tom Playford, earning the pejorative title, the 'Playmander'. In November 1938, Tom Playford became leader of the LCL and Premier of South Australia. It fell to him to govern the State through the years of the Second World War (and for a long time thereafter). In contrast to the Great War, there were far fewer political divisions. The ALP and trade union movement had set their combined face against Fascism as it had emerged in Italy, Germany, Spain and elsewhere during the 1930s, and now there was widespread support for the war effort. Moreover, there was general approval for John Curtin's conduct of the war, especially the Labor Prime Minister's 'turn' to America as the Japanese appeared to threaten invasion of Australia after the fall of Singapore. In an atmosphere of consensus, Playford was able to implement the LCL's plans for economic development, including a major shift from primary to secondary industry, in a way that might not have been possible in peacetime. He convinced the Federal government, for example, that

South Australia was especially suitable for arms and munition manufacture, paving the way for postwar industrialisation, especially in the western suburbs of Adelaide. His *Industries Development Act 1941*, a crucial element of the Playford plan, made public finance available for any project which the government deemed worthy of support.[105]

Playford's plans came rapidly to fruition under wartime conditions. By 1942 coal was being mined at Leigh Creek to facilitate an expansion of electricity production in the State, and steel manufacture had been established at Whyalla, with the Morgan–Whyalla pipeline completed by 1944. There was a massive expansion in State-sponsored housing and the construction of factories, together with increases in employment. Although Tom Playford was no socialist, he did face opposition from his more conservative colleagues, who were alarmed at his costly State interventionist policies. For the ALP, the position was more ambiguous. Faced with the overwhelming parliamentary strength of the LCL, not to mention the towering presence of Tom Playford himself, there seemed little point in opposing his social and economic policies – especially as these were measures of which Labor generally approved.

Accordingly, the Labor Party in South Australia contented itself with the conceit that Playford and the LCL were actually implementing its program. R.S. Richards promised that as 'long as the Premier continues to implement Labor's policy, I will give him 100% support'.[106] Lindsay Riches, Labor member for Stuart, thought the same. 'Playford', he exclaimed, 'was the best socialist who had ever occupied the treasury benches'.[107] Mick O'Halloran, who had succeeded Richards as ALP leader in 1949, went one step further, describing Playford's policies as 'more socialistic than Labor could ever hope to implement even if it was in office'.[108] There may, indeed, have been some pleasure in seeing Labor's policies implemented, albeit by the ALP's political opponents, but these were the voices of defeat – and defeatism. Years later, Don Dunstan was to put it this way: 'Many of the older Members congratulated themselves that some Labor policies were being put into effect by Playford, and therefore the life of opposition wasn't too bad. A comfortable lethargy had settled over our Parliamentary Party.'[109]

PART FOUR

THE NATURAL PARTY
OF GOVERNMENT?

Chapter Nine

The Dunstan Era

'In many ways South Australia has a unique political history', observed Dean Jaensch, writing in 1977: 'The "Paradise of Dissent" had no convicts and no gold rush, and it began self-government with the most progressive constitution of the [Australian] colonies.' But, he stressed, this sense of 'difference' was not confined to South Australia's more distant past. Instead, Jaensch argued, there was also 'a different contemporary history'. First there was the 'politically somnolent' period under Tom Playford, from the 1930s to the mid-1960s, when 'political change [was] ignored rather than resisted'. And then, remarkably, there was a new era of rapid change. 'By 1976', Jaensch explained, 'a virtual revolution had apparently occurred.' The Labor Party had been 'transformed, with the dynamism and charisma of Donald Allan Dunstan dominating political life'. Indeed, by the mid-1970s South Australia led 'the nation in progressive legislation, especially in social and individual behavioural fields'. Moreover, the 'once hegemonic' Liberal Country League had entered a new period of uncertainty, the Labor Party – Jaensch suggested – 'increasingly appearing as the "natural government"'.[1]

Labor in power – at last!
In fact, the ALP had been electorally more popular than Playford's LCL for most of the postwar era, and the LCL had been kept in government in this period mainly as a result of the 'Playmander', with its built-in rural bias

and gross under-representation of the Adelaide metropolitan area. The tired acquiescence of the Labor old guard had not helped, with its pretence that Playford was actually pursuing socialist-style policies of state intervention. Mick O'Halloran, Labor leader from 1949 to 1960, liked to present himself as Playford's 'junior partner', and Playford nodded approvingly, contrasting 'our Opposition' with those elsewhere which were 'critical without being helpful'.[2] In practice, the Labor challenge came from the people themselves. Ironically, this was one result of Playford's industrial development program, which had facilitated the spread of the industrial working class into hitherto strongly held LCL constituencies, with suburban sprawl intruding on rural areas, and Housing Trust development occurring in LCL or marginal electorates.[3] This was why the LCL was at last defeated at the polls in March 1965 (although it continued to dominate the Legislative Council), with Playford's resignation as party leader in the following year ushering in a period of self-doubt in LCL ranks. Frank Walsh came to power as Labor Premier with a twenty-one to seventeen majority in the House of Assembly. He was already sixty-seven years old, and led an 'inexperienced and decidedly senescent' Labor Cabinet, as Andrew Parkin described it, with Don Dunstan (aged thirty-nine) the only member under fifty.[4]

Yet it would be wrong to imagine that ALP organisation had been entirely ineffective in the early postwar years. In particular, learning from the debacle of the Premiers' Plan split in the 1930s, the Labor 'machine' in South Australia had sought to maintain unity and consensus at all costs. Two leading members of the party's South Australian branch, Clyde Cameron and Jim Toohey, played a central role in guiding the party in the decades after the Second World War. Both were Federal politicians – Cameron was a Member of the House of Representatives from 1949 until 1980 (and was a Cabinet minister in Gough Whitlam's government), and Toohey was a Senator from 1953 to 1971 – but they were intimately involved in running the party in South Australia. 'Together', as Malcolm Saunders has put it, 'Cameron and Toohey were able to more or less satisfy all factions within the branch'.[5] Most especially, working closely and in concert they were able to deflect the potential threat to Labor unity posed by the existence of the so-called 'Industrial Groups'.

Deflecting the DLP

In the immediate postwar era, as the Iron Curtain went down over Europe and the Cold War with the Soviet Union warmed up, so a wave of anti-Communist paranoia swept Australia. Communists had become involved in trade unions during the 1930s, and their influence grew during the Second World War when the Soviet Union was an ally. Now, in very different circumstances, the danger of Communist infiltration alarmed sections of the Labor movement, especially on the political right. Accordingly, in 1945 the New South Wales ALP conference formed its Industrial Groups, designed to contest union elections against Communist candidates.[6] Other States, including South Australia, followed suit. However, behind the 'Groupers' – as they were known – was a shadowy and (to its detractors) sinister organisation, the 'Movement'. Formally the Catholic Social Studies Movement, the Movement had the support of the Roman Catholic hierarchy, most especially the aged Archbishop Daniel Mannix, the erstwhile anti-conscriptionist and Irish nationalist of First World War days. Its leader was B.A. 'Bob' Santamaria, an 'anti-Communist zealot from Melbourne', as Nick Dyrenfurth and Frank Bongiorno have described him.[7] Only a minority of the Groupers belonged to the Movement, and Santamaria was never a member of the ALP, yet his influence was profound. Religious sectarianism again reared its head within the ALP, Don Dunstan noting that the Movement 'aimed to make the Labor Party the political instrument of Catholic social policy'.[8] Dunstan also claimed to detect the influence of the Movement in Norwood, for which constituency he would be selected as Labor candidate in 1952, and expressed his personal antipathy towards Santamaria, not least because, Dunstan alleged, he 'had written publicly in praise of Mussolini'.[9]

In Victoria, and to a lesser extent in New South Wales, the Movement gained increasing control over the ALP machines. In October 1954 this prompted the Federal Labor leader, H.V. 'Doc' Evatt, increasingly angry and frustrated by the antics of the Movement activists, to accuse the Groupers and the Movement of disloyalty to him personally and to the party in general. Moreover, Evatt added, the Groupers and the Movement had unscrupulously adopted the very tactics of the Communists they had claimed to oppose. Thereafter, all hell broke loose, unleashing 'the wildest political and religious passions', as the Labor Party begun to split asunder for the third time in the twentieth century.[10] Out of the confusion emerged what became known as the Democratic Labor Party (DLP), mainly Catholic in religious affiliation and determinedly anti-Communist. Although its strength was largely confined to the eastern States, the DLP was successful enough at the Federal parliamentary level to effectively keep the ALP out of office until Whitlam's victory in 1972.[11] Likewise, the schism kept the ALP out of government in Victoria and in Queensland, Labor not returning to power in those States until 1982 and 1989 respectively. In South Australia, however, as Dyrenfurth and Bongiorno explained, 'the firm but benign rule of AWU strongman Clyde Cameron and his ally, Jim Toohey, ensured that calm prevailed'.[12]

In fact, there were relatively few Catholics within the State Labor Party, and in 1951 Cameron had used his considerable influence in the trade unions to ensure that the Industrial Groups were banned by the ALP in South Australia, hoping to nip the Movement in the bud.[13] Yet the process was not as easy or as straightforward as some historians have assumed, nor was support for the Movement in South Australia as marginal as many had imagined. As elsewhere, the Movement had been the driving force behind the Groupers.[14] Moreover, for a time the Movement had enjoyed the active support of the Catholic Archbishop of Adelaide, Matthew Beovich.[15] Initially, Beovich had appointed Ted Farrell as the Movement's regional officer. A Catholic lay teacher, Farrell's brief was to 'bring influence to bear of the trade union movement, on the ALP, and, by propaganda, on the community, especially the working community'.[16] Specifically, the Movement's aims in South Australia were:

1. To de-louse four or five trade unions.
2. To strengthen the local committees in Adelaide and the suburbs.
3. To extend in scope and volume propaganda both literary and *viva voce*.
4. To begin, by lectures and study circles, the education part of the work.[17]

Armed with such guidance, the Groupers, although now formally dissociated from the ALP at State level, appear to have played a significant part in the overthrow in South Australia of the left-wing leadership of the Shop Assistants' Union and the Federated Ironworkers' Association in 1954 and 1955. A similar takeover of the Federated Clerks' Union was only narrowly avoided.[18] In 1950 the South Australian branch of the Movement could boast twenty-two branches. This was fewer than neighbouring Victoria, with its seventy-four branches, but, allowing for South Australia's smaller population and the State's lower proportion of Catholics, it was impressive nonetheless.[19] In a review, probably written in the mid-1950s by Farrell for Beovich, it was admitted that only three Movement members were in full-time trade union posts, although it was added swiftly that 'in a voluntary capacity, many other members hold executive and delegate positions'.[20] And, as Josephine Laffin has noted in her biography of Beovich, when Catholics assumed important roles within the trade unions, it was inevitable that their influence would extend to the ALP. By now, however, Beovich had become suspicious of Santamaria, considering that the Movement was seeking to tie Catholics too strongly to its political viewpoint. Moreover, Clyde Cameron (a Presbyterian) had himself warned Beovich 'that the Catholic Church was taking a great risk of arousing the sectarian passions of the Protestant majority ... if it came to the point, many non-Catholics would rather vote Communist than allow Catholics to take over'.[21]

Yet when Evatt issued his condemnation of the Groupers and the Movement in October 1954, Beovich was appalled, accusing Evatt of deliberately splitting the Labor Party. For the moment any uncertainty that he had felt was put to one side. In March 1955, for example, when opening a new Catholic school in the Adelaide suburb of Goodwood, Beovich had insisted that subversives in Australia were 'determined to smash our liberty and make us part of the Communist empire'.[22] However, when he returned from a six-month overseas tour in November 1955, he was distraught to learn that in his absence the Labor Party had indeed split, the Movement throwing its weight behind the breakaway Australian Labor Party (Anti-Communist), soon to be renamed the Democratic Labor Party. Beovich registered his formal disapproval with Farrell and other Movement leaders, but nonetheless the new party was launched in South Australia the very next day.[23] Beovich acknowledged that such a party might have some legitimacy in Victoria but was firmly of the opinion that a Catholic party was 'unwise' in South Australia, adding pointedly that no one standing for the State Parliament should claim the support of the Catholic Church. He also emphasised that Catholics were free to vote for any party they wished, except, of course, the Communists.[24]

In the Federal election of December 1955, the new anti-communist party in South Australia, just a month after its formation, attracted some 35,000 votes (8.7%), enough to prevent the ALP gaining a third Senate seat. Later, in 1968, it was thought that DLP preferences – which were directed to the Liberal and Country parties – may have contributed to the defeat of the State Labor government. However, the 1955 result proved to be the high point of the new party's penetration of South Australian politics.[25] Thereafter, as membership stagnated and finances dwindled, the DLP declined in influence and visibility. To all intents and purposes, the split in South Australia was only momentary. Despite the disproportionate influence that the Movement had exerted in South Australia, there were too few Catholics to sustain what was essentially a religious-based party, and in any case the anti-communist paranoia had never reached the levels exhibited in the eastern States. To this was added the steadying hands of Clyde Cameron and Jim Toohey. But the failure of Matthew Beovich to endorse the DLP was surely a vital factor in its swift decline.[26] As Josephine Laffin has observed, perhaps the strongest evidence for Beovich's role is the fact that the credible showing in the 1955 Federal election was achieved before his opposition to the new party was widely known publicly. When the Archbishop's disapproval became common knowledge in the Catholic community and beyond, support for the new party quickly died away.[27]

Cameron, Toohey and 'talent-spotting' Dunstan

In marked contrast to the Premiers' Plan debacle of the 1930s, the ALP in South Australia in the 1950s had deflected the unsettling intrusion of eastern States politics. Crucially, Jim Toohey had been president of the State branch in South Australia in the difficult 1954–56 period, striving to keep an even keel – in 1956 he was rewarded with the prestigious President's Medal for services rendered to a grateful Labor Party.[28] However, as Saunders has argued, both 'Cameron and Toohey were well aware that keeping the branch stable and united was not enough. Their ultimate goal was to restore Labor to the Treasury benches in South Australia'.[29] It was no easy task. In March 1950 one wry letter to the press had remarked ironically that 'many South Australians were unaware that the Playford Government had opposition in the State Parliament.' The same contributor added, with withering insight, that for 'the benefit of New Australians [recent migrants from continental Europe] I should like to point out that elderly people can remember the time when the Labor Party actually governed in South Australia'.[30] Suddenly, the days of Price, Verran, Vaughan, Gunn, Hill, and even Richards, seemed a world away.

Given the relative weakness of the ALP Opposition in South Australia, it fell to Cameron, Toohey and other Federal Labor politicians to mount the real party-political opposition to the Playford regime. As Jim Moss put it, together they provided 'the Cameron–Toohey leadership of the ALP' in South Australia in the 1950s.[31] Jim Toohey, in particular, as leader of Labor's Senate team, was tireless in his constant criticism of the LCL State government. He was also campaign director for most of the State elections during the 1950s and early 1960s, and, in the face of the Playmander, helped devise a strategy to erode LCL majorities in key marginals. One by one, Labor wrested these marginal seats from the LCL. In a by-election in August 1957, for example, the ALP regained the symbolic seat of Wallaroo, which had been lost in the aftermath of R.S. Richards' retirement and the continued leaching of the district's urban (and Labor-voting) population.[32]

As Don Dunstan was later to recall, the sitting LCL member for Wallaroo, Larry Heath, had tragically been killed in a road traffic accident. A local man, Lloyd Hughes, employed in the district at a fertiliser factory, was selected as Labor candidate for the ensuing by-election. He was a Methodist local preacher and a Rechabite, credentials which the party thought would play well with the Wallaroo community. 'Some of the Cornish people reacted with customary reserve', however, as Dunstan noted: 'I remember one old lady whose house I was visiting remarking, "Mr Hughes. Ye-es. I remember meeting him the first time about ten years ago at the Church, and of course I've met him since. But I can't say I really know the man."' Nonetheless, the 'Choose Hughes' campaign was spectacularly successful. As Dunstan explained, as well as selecting a local candidate likely to appeal to the electorate, the ALP concentrated on 'a simple theme' – the LCL government's neglect of the locality. 'Our campaign', Dunstan observed, 'drove home the point that while the Liberals talked about decentralisation of industry they were in fact opposed to it in any country area which they thought they could win electorally because industry brought workers who were likely to vote Labor'. Thus 'the old mining towns were getting no support for improving their employment opportunities'.[33] Neal Blewett and Dean Jaensch, in their analysis of the by-election, put it slightly differently. They noted that Wallaroo was one of those marginals in which the deciding factor in an election was whether the LCL dominance in the country areas would outweigh the ALP strength in the towns. For example, in 'the small rural Bute subdivision of Wallaroo the Liberal vote rarely fell below 75%, Labor success or failure depending on the size of its majorities in the old and declining mining towns of Moonta, Wallaroo and Kadina'.[34]

Be that as it may, as Neal Blewett and Dean Jaensch also observed, the victory in Wallaroo marked the turning point in Labor's fortunes, beginning an electoral trend against the Playford government that would not be reversed.[35] In the 1962 State election, indeed, Labor emerged as the largest party in Parliament, with nineteen seats to the LCL's eighteen, but Playford was kept in government with the support of two Independents. Thereafter, he tried to prolong his grip on power with an attempted tinkering of the Playmander. But, this ploy having failed, Playford's government was defeated in March 1965 when Labor won a further two seats, giving the party an overall majority in the Assembly for the first time since 1933. It was an auspicious moment, and was to mark a long-term change in Labor's performance in South Australia in the decades ahead.

Frank Walsh became the first Labor Premier of South Australia since R.S. Richards, having taken over as leader of the parliamentary party after O'Halloran's death in 1961. However, his premiership was always likely to be short because, already sixty-seven, he was bound by ALP rules to retire from Parliament aged seventy. A Catholic, like his predecessor, he was, according to Blewett and Jaensch, ill at ease outside his own relatively small circle. 'He distrusted the intellectuals in the party', they wrote, 'had little sympathy with the puritanism of the Methodist elements, and was out of touch with the

Frank Walsh, first post-Second World War Labor Premier, opens the
Bastyan Wing at the State Library in Adelaide in May 1967.
[Courtesy State Library of South Australia, B72587]

younger leaders in the trade union movement'.[36] Moreover, Walsh was one of
those who had enjoyed working with Playford rather than against him, and his
'lack of pugnacity' in dealing with the LCL unsettled his supporters. Damning
with faint praise, Blewett and Jaensch concluded that, a 'kindly, generous
and unpretentious man ... Walsh lacked administrative experience, and was
devoid of administrative talents'.[37] Worse still, he was 'incapable of directing
the Cabinet', routinely deferring and devolving to more powerful personalities
in his government, and was frequently obsessed with trivial details to the
detriment of the bigger picture. Moreover, in the new television age, 'Walsh
was a neanderthal figure ... halting, uncertain, and obviously uncomfortable',
and on TV he appeared 'puzzled and bewildered'.[38]

By contrast, Donald Dunstan was the Labor 'Government's chief
newsmaker'.[39] Dunstan had been nurtured by Jim Toohey, and his victory
in the Adelaide metropolitan seat of Norwood, wrested from the LCL in 1953,

was part of Toohey's grand strategy to conquer the key marginals. As Dunstan later admitted, the 'person who influenced me most in local [State] politics was Senator Jim Toohey'.[40] But Dunstan also owed much to Clyde Cameron, who had smoothed the way for his pre-selection in Norwood, Dunstan acknowledging that Cameron was a 'brilliant and effective' operator.[41] Together, Toohey and Cameron had 'talent spotted' Don Dunstan, and had laid the foundations for the new Labor era that would supersede both Playford and Walsh. As the youngest member of Walsh's new Cabinet, Dunstan was also the most energetic and the most visible – so much so, according to Blewett and Jaensch, that it was 'not uncommon to hear the Walsh Cabinet referred to as the Dunstan Ministry'.[42] Moreover, in marked contrast to Walsh, Dunstan 'excelled in his relationships with the electronic media', and even managed to win the positive attention of a traditionally conservative press.[43]

Dunstan was given the major portfolios of Attorney-General, Minister of Social Welfare, and Minister of Aboriginal Affairs. His *Social Welfare Act* of 1965 completely overhauled the provision of social welfare in South Australia, and as Minister of Aboriginal Affairs he ushered in a stream of legislation to provide what was described by John Summers as 'far ahead of anything else in Australia at that time'.[44] As Summers explained, Dunstan's 'policies of "self-determination" for Aborigines and recognition of Aboriginal land rights were rejected by all other governments in Australia in the mid-1960s'. And yet, a decade later 'these policies had become accepted at national level by both major political parties'.[45] Dunstan's *Aboriginal Lands Trust Act*, for example, had created a dedicated trust in which State Aboriginal reserves could be vested. The trust could also acquire Crown Land, or purchase other property. Dunstan's *Prohibition of Discrimination Act* – the first of its type in Australia – made it illegal to discriminate on the grounds of race, national origin or skin colour in the provision of goods and services.[46]

It was due largely to Dunstan's energy and initiative that the Walsh government achieved its impressive legislative pace. In 1965, Parliament sat for sixty-five days – the most since 1931 – with many bills still queuing to be considered. But, as ever, the Legislative Council played its reactionary role. In language that would have been familiar to Kingston, Price, Verran,

Vaughan and Gunn, the Legislative Council obstructed a succession of bills on the grounds that it was 'acting impartially in the interests of the people of South Australia', that it was saving the State from 'radical moves that would not be the permanent will of the people', and was guarding against 'class legislation'.[47] Bills were delayed, amended or sometimes simply thrown out. Dunstan recalled that during Walsh's term the Legislative Council had 'laid aside or rejected eleven Government Bills, most of which contained major proposals of Government policy, and had succeeded in imposing major and politically partisan amendments in twelve others'.[48] In a compelling case of *déjà vu*, one of the bills thus rejected was an electoral reform bill for full adult franchise for the Legislative Council.

Ushering in the Dunstan Decade

To the frustration of Legislative Council obstruction was added the brief economic downturn of 1967, which the government's opponents gleefully blamed on Labor policies. By now the LCL had a new leader, the aging Playford having been replaced by thirty-eight-year-old Steele Hall in July 1966. Plainly, it was also time for Walsh to go. This was accomplished in a gentle coup orchestrated by Clyde Cameron. Detecting that a reluctant Walsh would have to be pushed, Cameron let it be known quietly among ALP branch members that Frank Walsh wished to retire but that all should keep this news secret, so that it could be announced at the forthcoming State Council meeting. When the Council met, Cameron poured fulsome praise on Frank Walsh, highlighting three particular achievements. The first was forming the first Labor government in South Australia for thirty-two years, the second was the bold decision to build the Gidgealpa–Moomba gas pipeline, and the third was the equally courageous decision to step down from the premiership to make way for a younger person. As Geoff Stokes tells it, a 'stunned Frank Walsh was greeted with a standing ovation from the Council and he had little choice but to meekly accept'.[49]

As Cameron had anticipated, Don Dunstan won the parliamentary caucus election for the leadership, although it was a close-run thing, with Des Corcoran proving a strong opponent. Nonetheless, Dunstan's personality and image were seen now as symptomatic of the government and party – 'progressive, professional and middle-class' – and this was to be the characteristic style of Labor in South Australia for the years ahead.[50] Moreover, as Richard Cox has observed, in the public mind Dunstan would be associated personally with much of the reform program that followed. 'Many of the reforms', Cox explained, 'such as liberalisation of censorship, consumer protection, promotion of the arts, conservation, protection of civil liberties and legislation designed to facilitate the advancement of aborigines [*sic*] and women', were attributed personally to Dunstan'.[51] Although Dunstan's charisma appealed to young, well-educated professionals, who were readily enticed into the Labor fold, he was met with some suspicion in traditional Labor circles, especially among trade unionists. In an echo of critics of Crawford Vaughan's 'black-coat brigade' earlier in the century (see p. 187), there were those who resented the intrusion of 'trendy' middle-class intellectuals into what they viewed as working-class politics. In October1968, for example, the Plumbers' Union warned the ALP State Council meeting: 'be advised that his [Dunstan's] promotion of an image of intellectualism for the Labor Party could lose the support of those of the working class upon whom the Party has traditionally relied for electoral and financial support'. Indeed, the Union added ominously 'that a realistic appreciation [should] be accorded to basic working class outlooks and that such outlooks might very well conflict with intellectual outlooks on certain matters'.[52]

It was a timely caution but in reality Labor's share of the vote had held up well in the State election earlier in the year. Far from losing working-class votes, Labor's campaign in its traditional heartlands was highly successful. It won 52% of the primary votes across the State, a clear majority, and an estimated 54% of the two-party preferred votes. That the Dunstan government lost office in March 1968 was not a result of working-class disaffection, nor even a loss of preferences to the DLP. Rather, it was due to the continuing operation of the inequitable boundary system, the Playmander. The iniquity of the electoral system was now plain for all to see, and Dunstan made the most of it by not resigning until formally required to do so by Parliament, affording him six weeks to mobilise popular outrage and maximise LCL discomfort.

There were demonstrations, and adverse comment in the interstate press added fuel to the controversy. When Steele Hall finally became LCL Premier on 16 April 1968, he was already on the back foot.[53]

Hall recognised that some form of electoral reform was now inevitable, and he, along with his Attorney-General, Robin Millhouse, led the newly emergent 'progressive' wing of the LCL, their arch-conservative critics clustered for the most part in the Legislative Council. Despite strong misgivings in the latter, Hall was able to push through a reform bill which, while perpetuating an element of rural over-representation, fundamentally shifted the balance towards a fairer apportionment. As Hall understood, it was simply no longer possible to defend the malapportionment of the Playford era. But in ushering in reform, he had in effect signed the death warrant of his own government at the next election, unless there was a strong swing to the LCL from Labor. Significantly, Hall attempted to tread where Dunstan had trod before, partly in an attempt to make the LCL appear more progressive and electable and partly, perhaps, to steal Labor's clothing. In Aboriginal affairs and social welfare, Hall continued where Dunstan had left off, and Millhouse introduced a ground-breaking abortion reform bill.

Hall's electoral reform, achieved with the reluctant acquiescence of the Legislative Council, had succeeded where Labor would surely have failed, and was obviously to Labor's benefit. Additionally, Hall's perpetuation of progressive legislation had helped to enhance South Australia's growing reputation as the 'progressive' State, again to Labor's advantage. But in 1970 Hall alighted upon an issue that just might, he thought, produce the swing from Labor that he needed. The River Murray Commission had recommended that the proposed Chowilla Dam on the Murray, located in South Australia, be abandoned, to be replaced with a plan for a new site at Dartmouth in Victoria. The LCL government agreed. However, sensing strong support for the South Australian dam, Labor immediately championed the Chowilla option. Hall needed parliamentary ratification for the Dartmouth plan, and in April 1970 it was duly put before the House of Assembly. The House divided on party lines but the Speaker, Tom Stott, an Independent who had hitherto supported the LCL, on this occasion voted with the ALP. Hall's government fell, with an election set for May 1970. It was only the second occasion in more than fifty years that a South Australian government had failed to live out its full term.[54]

In terms of votes cast, the outcome in 1970 was very similar to that of 1968, Labor winning 51% of first preferences. But in numbers of seats in the House of Assembly, the result was radically different, the ALP gaining twenty-seven to the LCL's twenty. At last the long period of LCL dominance appeared to be over for good, and commentators dared to talk of the likelihood of a 'Dunstan decade'.[55] Indeed, the phrase caught on and passed into popular parlance, later lending itself to the title of Andrew Parkin's and Allan Patience's edited volume *The Dunstan Decade: Social Democracy at the State Level*, published in 1981, an attempt to offer a scholarly evaluation of the Dunstan era.[56] If one counts his time in office before 1968, then Dunstan did indeed preside over South Australia for a decade and more. But in this, his second and more substantive period as Premier, he was in power for almost nine years, the ALP for eight months shy of the elusive decade. It was an era of 'policy innovation probably without emulation in this country', Andrew Parkin ventured in 1986. [57] But it was also marked by ever growing public fascination with Dunstan's 'flamboyant' style, often seen as outrageous in conservative circles, and behind the scenes there was also Dunstan's turbulent private life, ultimately with its own political ramifications.[58]

'Dunstanism', as it was sometimes termed, comprised an exhilarating mix of public enterprise, social reform, a greater professionalism in the State public service, increased investment in education, equal opportunities for women and ethnic minorities, Aboriginal rights and welfare, and a 'personal vision of inner Adelaide as a centre with prospering artistic facilities, pedestrian walkways, lively streetlife, al fresco eateries and other continental embellishments'.[59] There was also Dunstan's libertarian agenda, with relaxed rules on censorship, liquor licensing, gambling, and even nude sunbathing on Maslin beach. A glimpse of Dunstan's wider vision was given in his popular illustrated *Don Dunstan's Australia*, published in Adelaide in 1978 (when he was thought to be at the height of his powers) and which later informed his *Australia: A Personal View*, the latter appearing in 1981 to accompany a series of television documentaries.[60] There were chapters on Australian national identity and its relationship to Aboriginal culture – 'Who Loved a Sunburnt Country?' – and on immigration and multiculturalism – '"Whingeing Poms" and Others' – together with more on themes as diverse as education – 'We're All Going Back to School' – and radical youth culture – 'Revolt of the Long Hairs'. *Don Dunstan's Australia* was a celebration of the nation but Dunstan warned that there was still much to do to create a fair and inclusive society. 'Australians talk of this country as a democracy', he agreed: 'It is a nice word ... But Australia is not yet truly democratic.' For democracy or 'peoples' rule' to really flourish, he argued, there had to be much greater participation in decision-making at all levels – in business, in trade unions, in government – for Australia 'will not be an effective democracy – a *social* democracy – until the democratic principle pervades all aspects of our community life'.[61]

During his time in power, Dunstan tried to put this principle into practice. He remained electorally popular, and in the State election of March 1973 the ALP was returned to power with a comfortable majority over the LCL and a breakaway Country Party. Moreover, in the Legislative Council half-election, Labor gained seats outside its 'Central No. 1' heartland, taking both vacancies in Midland, the first electoral shift since 1944, leaving the ALP with six seats as opposed to the LCL's fourteen. Meanwhile, uncertainty in the Opposition ranks continued, with Hall and Millhouse resigning from the LCL, together with Martin Cameron in the Legislative Council, to form the independent Liberal Movement (LM). This turbulence assisted Dunstan in finally achieving the long-standing aim of all radical governments in South Australia since the days of 'Charlie' Kingston – reform of the Legislative Council. Fearing further ALP or even LM gains at future half-elections under the existing constitutional arrangements, the Legislative Council agreed to a compromise bill which not only incorporated the long sought-after full adult franchise but included a 'list' system of proportional representation.[62]

Difficult times

Yet it was not all plain sailing. In the early days of Gough Whitlam's Labor government, there appeared to be a remarkable Dunstan–Whitlam partnership, the ALP pursuing harmonious social democratic policies

275

dovetailed together at State and Federal levels. Whitlam had long acknowledged his regard for Dunstan, and recalled how together they had finally defeated the ALP's traditional commitment to the White Australia policy. 'My chief ally Don Dunstan and I removed White Australia from the [ALP] Platform', Whitlam recalled: 'It was the beginning of a genuine multicultural society, inclusive, outward-looking, forward-looking.'[63] However, by the middle of 1975 the Whitlam government had become deeply unpopular, and in the State election that year Dunstan was forced to distance himself from his Federal colleague, stressing that the contest was about the governance of South Australia and not a judgement on what was going on in Canberra. In the event, the Labor Party in South Australia held up remarkably. In the House of Assembly it lost two rural seats to the Liberals (as they now called themselves), together with the usually safe seat of Port Pirie to an Independent Labor candidate (who on election was promptly admitted into the party, becoming Speaker). Labor's share of first-preference votes had fallen to 46.3%, its twenty-four seats in the House of Assembly giving it the slimmest overall majority over the Liberals' twenty seats, the LM's two and the Country Party's one. In the half-election for the Legislative Council, the ALP took six of the available eleven seats, the Liberals and the LM winning two apiece.[64]

After 1975, the climate became tougher for the Dunstan government. The dismissal of the Whitlam government on 11 November 1975, and the subsequent election of Malcolm Fraser's Liberal-Country coalition government, left Labor at the nadir of its fortunes at Federal level.[65] Inevitably, some of this rubbed off on the ALP in South Australia. Moreover, the ALP government in South Australia appeared to have lost something of its earlier reformist zeal, possibly because it had already achieved so much. Nonetheless, significant legislation included the *Sex Discrimination Act* of 1975, described by Helen Mills as 'the show-piece of the Labor administration's response to the demands of the women's movement'.[66] A Women's Advisory Unit was set-up within the Premier's Department, as was an Equal Opportunity Unit in the State public service. Among other progressive legislation, was the government's support for a private member's bill decriminalising homosexual acts between consenting adults. There was also further electoral reform of the House of Assembly, achieving at last a full equality of apportionment between electorates, together with the creation of an independent Electoral Commission to oversee redistribution. In the early election of September 1977, the Dunstan government was returned once again. The trauma of the Whitlam period now past, and Fraser's austerity package drawing widespread criticism, the external pressures were now correspondingly fewer on the ALP in South Australia. Achieving 51.6% of the primary vote, Labor won twenty-seven seats to nineteen for the Liberals, together with one each for the Australian Democrats (as the LM had become) and the Country Party.[67]

However, economic difficulties were now increasingly apparent. The State began to slip into recession and unemployment grew, exacerbated by the removal of Federal subsidy for shipbuilding at Whyalla, which effectively ended the industry. Plans to establish a new city at Monarto faltered, again partly a result of the withdrawal of Federal funding, and moves to encourage industrial democracy made frustratingly slow progress. However, it was not so much the clouds of economic downturn that began to dent Dunstan's hitherto invincible image but rather a series of unfortunate incidents, some tragic. First of all, there was the dismissal in 1978 of Police Commissioner Harold Salisbury. As Salisbury eventually admitted, and as a Royal Commission confirmed, Harold Salisbury had calculatedly misled Dunstan about the activities of the South Australian Special Branch. As became apparent, the Special Branch had for many years maintained surveillance and dossiers on a large number of individuals (including Labor MPs, Dunstan among them) which it deemed subversive or radical, as well as those with alleged homosexual tendencies. Incredibly, Salisbury justified his action in deceiving Dunstan by arguing that his ultimate responsibility was not to the State government but to the higher authority of the Crown. Not surprisingly, he was sacked. Nonetheless, the damaging 'outcry from anti-Labor interests', as Ross McMullin has put it, 'was noisy and prolonged', although Dunstan's actions were later vindicated by the Royal Commission.[68]

The Salisbury affair proved personally disconcerting for Don Dunstan. So too did growing difficulty and trauma in his increasingly complex private life. His long, politically advantageous and hitherto close marriage to his wife

277

Don Dunstan and Adele Koh celebrate Labor's victory in 1977.
[Courtesy News Limited and Flinders University Library]

Gretel had begun to break up. They separated in April 1972, the final split precipitated by Dunstan's intense affair with Judith Pugh, partner of the artist Clifton Pugh who was then painting Dunstan's portrait. When Judith Pugh became pregnant, it was not clear whether Clifton Hugh or Don Dunstan was the father-to-be. The three came to an understanding that, when his divorce came through, Dunstan would marry Judith Pugh. However, she went into early labour and the baby was stillborn. The affair fizzled out thereafter, and Dunstan and the Pughs went their separate ways.[69] Subsequently, during 1973, Dunstan met Adele Koh, a Malaysian of Chinese ethnicity who had recently been expelled from Singapore for criticising the government in the paper *Singapore Herald*, which was closed down soon after by Lee Kwan Yew. She was appointed by Dunstan as a research assistant, and gradually she and Dunstan drew close. In December 1976 they were married. Shortly after the September 1977 election, Adele Koh suffered a miscarriage. But there was far worse to come. In March 1977, with the Salisbury Royal Commission in full swing, she was diagnosed with terminal cancer. Dunstan nursed her at home, and she died on 24 October 1978, aged only thirty-five. As Dino Hodge has observed, a 'moderating and stabilising influence had been removed from Dunstan's life ... [and he] visibly aged during Adele's illness'.[70] Dunstan threw himself into his work after her death but he was by now suffering from depression. Years later, he reflected on the 'great tragedy' that had overtaken him and his late wife, and admitted that it was a 'very punishing time'.[71]

Those pink shorts

Dunstan's marriage to Adele Koh had stilled for a moment the gossip and innuendo that had surfaced from time to time about his sexuality. Although the evidence suggested that his primary relationships were with women, Dunstan had also surrounded himself with athletic and attractive young men whose company he obviously enjoyed and found stimulating. The suggestion that he might be sexually ambivalent or possibly gay, had hung in the air for many years, a source of tittle-tattle and nod-and-wink in some conservative circles. His mischievously flamboyant style served sometimes to tease such prejudiced opinion, not least on the famous occasion when he had appeared in Parliament wearing pink shorts. Somewhat disingenuously, Dunstan framed the incident as an example of sartorial diversity and freedom. He noted that, earlier, he had turned up at the opening of the Festival of Arts in Adelaide, wearing a Nehru-style jacket. An affronted woman exclaimed: 'Mr Dunstan – I know that you like the people of Asia. But their ways are not our ways and you should at least dress like an Australian.' Suitably offended, Dunstan 'looked at her coldly, and replied, "Provincial old biddy, aren't you"'. As Dunstan observed: 'That incident did not upset the populace, a later one did.'[72]

As Dunstan explained it, under a new parliamentary rule, members were permitted to wear shorts in the House. His tailor, he continued, had made two pairs to a more convenient and comfortable design, shorter in the waist than the ones he had been used to. One of the new pairs was grey, the 'other a dull rose shade – very similar to a denim colour quite widely used in men's clothing of the day'. On 'one boiling hot day', as he put it, he appeared in Parliament in

279

Those pink shorts –
Don Dunstan posing on the steps of Parliament House in Adelaide.
[Courtesy News Limited and Flinders University Library]

the rose-coloured shorts, and the press – as he had no doubt anticipated – 'went wild'. It was a publicity coup, and yet it had its nastier side, as Dunstan later admitted. Here suddenly, according to his critics, was a 'public endorsement of effeminacy', the 'Flesh-pink hot pants' indicating some 'sexual connotation', which he found 'quite irrational and absurd' as well as distasteful. Perhaps the publicity stunt had backfired, the question of Dunstan's sexual orientations now acquiring political significance. As he reflected, 'I had clearly pushed innovation too far. I put those shorts away . . . and wore the blue-grey ones'.[73]

Public opinion had questioned the desirability of wearing pink shorts in Parliament. There were others, as Dino Hodge has explained, who in the early 1970s had also questioned the wisdom of his relationship with John Ceruto, a young man Dunstan had met at a gymnasium. He had been given a job in the Premier's office, and Dunstan later helped him set up a restaurant.[74] It was an issue that threatened to come back to haunt Dunstan, when in 1978 a forthcoming book entitled *It's Grossly Improper*, written by two Adelaide journalists (Des Ryan and Mike McEwin), was rumoured to include damaging details of the compulsory purchase by the government of the property later made available for use by John Ceruto, together with other salacious allegations. By now, Dunstan's physical health was beginning to fail and, as Hodge has observed, this together with 'his depression following the death of his wife, and his distressed state of mind about the media coverage her illness and the Salisbury Royal Commission had received could only have been worsened by a fearful anticipation of a book containing revelations that would injure him and his Government'.[75]

To add to Dunstan's difficulties, controversy had arisen in Labor ranks over the proposal to exploit the uranium deposits discovered at Roxby Downs in the north of the State. There were those opposed to uranium mining on principle but others saw it as the answer to the State's economic problems. Dunstan decided to go on an overseas fact-finding tour to assess the current state of nuclear safety technology. (In his absence, and much to his dismay, some ALP parliamentarians had convened anti-uranium meetings.) He arrived home ill and exhausted, suffering from what was thought to be a viral infection. In February 1979 he collapsed in the House of Assembly, and was taken to hospital. His doctor advised a lengthy break. On 15 February 1979, Dunstan dramatically announced his resignation as Premier and as a Member of Parliament. It was truly the end of an era and, although Dunstan would continue to write on political themes, his political career was suddenly over.

'Returning to the radical ... Chartist heritage'
In assessing the Dunstan period, what is at first most striking is the contrast with what had gone before, not only with the long Playford era but also the increasingly staid Labor Opposition before and after the war, led successively by Richards, O'Halloran and Walsh. Yet, for all his extraordinarily innovative style and theatrical, even provocative, persona, Dunstan saw himself first and

foremost as integral to South Australia's long-standing radical tradition, within which he placed himself unequivocally. As he had explained on assuming the Labor leadership in 1967, his first task was to rekindle that radical spirit. As he put it then, 'I see South Australia as returning to the radical era which is its Chartist heritage'.[76]

This was a theme to which Dunstan would return later in his memoir *Felicia* (see Chapter 1), where he stressed strands of continuity as well as change in South Australia's political history. Here, according to Dunstan, the 'Chartist heritage' was observable from the State's earliest days, voiced by the colony's 'puritans' and 'dissenters' – the Methodists and other Nonconformists – and given strength by the thousands of Cornish copper miners and their families who first began arriving in the late 1830s and 1840s. Conscious of his own Cornish background, Dunstan had encouraged the formation of the Kernewek Lowender Cornish festival (of which he became patron) on northern Yorke Peninsula in 1973, a device to promote heritage tourism in the locality but also, perhaps, a recognition of the venerable position of the Wallaroo constituency in the long narrative of the Labor Party in South Australia. Alive to South Australia's distinctive past, Dunstan was intent on re-inventing its radical tradition to suit the needs and mores of the second half of the twentieth century, as he saw them, a strategy designed to create a modern social democracy, re-establishing the State as Australia's foremost beacon of progress and enlightenment. After Labor's long stagnation, he was determined to reinvigorate the party, returning it firmly to its Chartist roots.

Inevitably, such a view attracted detractors. Among the most pungent was Sir Walter Crocker, who poured scorn on Dunstan's rhetoric. Lieutenant-Governor of South Australia from 1973 until 1982, Crocker saw Dunstan in action at firsthand. Far from perpetuating the State's traditions, Crocker insisted, Dunstan was responsible 'for dismantling the old social values of South Australia'.[77] It was a conservative critique – Crocker was writing in his almost hagiographic short biography of Tom Playford – but it was heartfelt. Aspects of Dunstan's behaviour were 'alien in traditional South Australia', Crocker complained, and, he asserted, 'Dunstan was certainly provocative, at times unpleasant'.[78] Dunstan's libertarian values were questionable, he continued, an extreme example being his apparent 'toleration of the vile traffic in pornography'. As Crocker explained:

> When Sir Mark Oliphant [the State Governor], after being shown by Police Commissioner Salisbury a hundred or so examples of the pornography available in delicatessen shops and around schools, and after bringing myself as Lieutenant-Governor into the matter, had a conference with Dunstan, the latter took the line that censorship would not be tolerated by the Government: people could see or hear whatever they wanted.[79]

Seen in this light, according to Crocker, the elevation of Revd Keith Seaman to the governorship in 1977 was a self-serving media-relations exercise, although, he added, the public, profoundly discomforted by the pornography issue, 'was not entirely reassured by the appointment, just before an election, of a Methodist social-worker clergyman as Governor'.[80] Crocker's perfunctory description of Sir Keith as 'a Methodist social-worker clergyman' had a pejorative ring. So too did his scathing criticism of Dunstan's 'one "first" after another' achievements, in which Crocker singled out both Keith Seaman and his predecessor, Pastor Doug Nicholls, 'the first Methodist clergyman Governor' and 'the first Aboriginal Governor'.[81] And just as Crocker was dismissive of Keith Seaman as an overtly political appointment, designed to ameliorate the damage done by the pornography controversy, so he was inclined to see the earlier appointment of Sir Douglas Nicholls as something of a gimmick, part of Dunstan's 'predilections' for Aboriginal affairs 'on a level that now seems more emotive than constructive'.[82]

However, in arguing that Dunstan's behaviour and policies were inimical to South Australia's traditions, and were by no means (as Dunstan averred) a continuation of the radical strand in the State's political history, Crocker had alighted unwittingly upon the paradox already made plain in Dunstan's *Felicia*. Although Dunstan's programs seemed at times startlingly novel and, as he himself had explained, were designed to shake South Australia from its apparent torpor, there *was* a radical tradition to which Dunstan could lay claim. This Crocker acknowledged, although, of course, he considered Dunstan's claim to be spurious. As he put it, rather quaintly, 'Dunstan's place was South Australia'. This, Crocker agreed, was at root 'a British colony of unusual origins resulting in unusual qualities ... most of them virtues, strong traditions, rather much self-satisfaction about them, and Puritan values of the Huguenot kind mixed with radicalism and public conscience'.[83] Significant here, Crocker added, was the 'substantial increment of Cornish miners and their Methodism', together with the State's early mix of small independent landowners and artisans, 'of literates ... and of evangelicals – a notable mixture of Puritanism, yeomanry, and radicalism'.[84] But if South Australia was Dunstan's place, then Dunstan's time was an entirely different era, far removed temporally and culturally from the distant colonial period. His was 'the epoch following on the second of ... the two world wars', Crocker explained, 'an era of high hopes, high promises, high illusions, typified by the founding of the welfare states ... of resolutions and conventions on human rights and equality. A heady time'.[85] Dunstan 'symbolized' this period, as 'the old standards were loosened', and by the 1960s South Australia was ready to embrace the new global mood.[86] Playford had been in power too long, Crocker conceded, and the public had had enough of thrift and restraint: 'people were getting tired of virtue and wanted fun'.[87]

As Crocker observed, Dunstan had sought to locate himself within the State's radical tradition but in doing so had offered a distinctly different post-Second World War brand of radical thought and action, one in tune with recent global trends that were now to be applied in South Australia. It was a paradox that puzzled Crocker, who saw that there was a radical-evangelical tradition in South Australia but considered Dunstan's new-fangled ideas and enthusiasms its complete antithesis. However, traditions are not static, and are subject to continuous renegotiation and re-invention, as they respond to changed conditions. Dunstan was instinctively aware of this but Crocker was not. Thus Dunstan was able to claim inheritance of the 'Chartist heritage', while Crocker saw only an affront to long-cherished values. In October 1981 a review of the Parkin and Patience book *The Dunstan Decade* appeared in the journal *Quadrant*. The reviewer found the cover image, 'depicting Dunstan as a psychedelic "Captain Adelaide" as stunningly appropriate'.[88] Walter Crocker added: 'And surely horrid too.'[89]

'Technocratic managerialism'

Criticism from the political right was to be expected. But Dunstan came increasingly under fire from the left. A social democrat, Dunstan was determinedly interventionist on economic issues and believed in public enterprise. As Neal Blewett has noted, Dunstan combined the boards of the two State-owned banks and created the State Government Insurance Office to compete with private firms on the open market. He allocated State government funding to wineries, canneries, dairy farmers and small businesses, and led the foundation of a number of public sector authorities, including the South Australian Film Corporation, the Development Corporation, the Adelaide Festival Centre Trust, and the Craft Authority. In the early 1970s, his government introduced what Blewett has described as 'the most ambitious consumer protection in Australia', covering such areas as land and house purchase, building contracts, second-hand cars, and hire-purchase agreements.[90] Yet Dunstan was also anxious to work with business. Again, as a social democrat, he advocated a mixed economy, arguing that a healthy private sector provided the economic conditions – not least through taxation – that enabled governments to fund and implement social welfare policies for the benefit of the community as a whole. Business groups responded warmly to Dunstan's overtures, the business magazine *Rydges* observing in July 1973:

> He [Dunstan] is ... a socialist. But whereas businessmen genetically distrust socialists, there is comfort in knowing that Dunstan needs them ... He wants business expansion and business diversification for South Australia ... If he does make South Australia a model socialist state with low housing and living costs, a stable and contented labour force is likely ... South Australia is a state where things tend to get done and, at that, done well.[91]

In other words, it was in the interests of business that there should be a healthy, well-fed, well-housed, well-educated, gainfully employed work force, and this was exactly what Dunstan's social democracy promised.

However, there were those on the left who looked askance at what they saw as far too intimate a relationship between Dunstan and the world of business.

Put simply, in their view, Labor in power had capitulated to the demands of capitalism and the ruling class. John Lonie, who had written so perceptively of the ALP in the inter-war period, concluded that 'Dunstan is a reformer whose policies and philosophy are much more in line with the needs of capitalism in Australia than are those of the Liberals'.[92] John Wanna thought Dunstan obsessed with 'technocratic managerialism', which 'ignored and preserved the roots of inequality within the nature of capitalism itself'.[93] Terry O'Shaughnessy (who saw South Australia as a 'peripheral state', comparable to Queensland) agreed, arguing that capitalism would always seek to align itself in new ways to promote its interests, and this was a 'role played by Dunstan and the Whizz kids in the Economic Intelligence Unit in the Premier's Department'.[94] Jim Moss conceded that 'Dunstan ... achieved many worthwhile reforms' but insisted that he had 'made no attempt to alter the real causes of workers' exploitation and alienation'. Instead, Dunstan had 'encouraged the multinational corporations, the private sector, and the profit system'.[95]

As Andrew Parkin has noted, this neo-Marxist critique can be challenged in terms of 'its own closed logic' and its narrow, simplistic view of the complex relationships between society, economic circumstances and the exercise of political power.[96] But Dunstan took the criticisms seriously enough to confront them in his 1976 Chifley Memorial Lecture, where he defended the practical, pragmatic ('technocratic') approach of social democracy against the unfeasible and undesirable doctrine of revolutionary change. For all Dunstan's modernity, it was an argument that would have been familiar to Tom Price and John Verran, who would have nodded in agreement. Again, Dunstan was locating himself firmly within the context and character of South Australia's radical tradition.

Although, according to his lights, Dunstan had worked closely and successfully with business, it would be wrong to see him as a precursor of the Hawke–Keating period of Labor in power at Federal level, or indeed of the 'New Labour' Blair project in Britain. By the late 1970s, as the Dunstan era drew to a close, social democracy was everywhere challenged by a newly emergent neo-liberal orthodoxy. Rapid oil-price rises had profoundly disturbed western economies, confidence in Keynesian economic management had collapsed (due to the seemingly intractable problem of 'stagflation'), and globalisation made it increasingly difficult for social democratic governments to plough their own furrows while trying to ignore world trends. Capitalism too had become more hard-nosed, less sympathetic to the aims of social democracy, and no longer seeing full employment and a socially content and well-provided workforce as prerequisites for optimum economic performance. Indeed, by the end of the decade the *Rydges* analysis of 1973 already appeared hopelessly outdated. According to historian Selina Todd, by the late 1970s, in western democracies, 'governments had accepted that profit-making and the people's welfare were ultimately irreconcilable – a conclusion made more stark by the oil crisis and its repercussions'.[97]

Be that as it may, neo-liberalism, with its call for lower taxes, de-regulation, privatisation, and the 'freeing up' of the global market, found a ready appeal in Australia. Significantly, it fell to Labor – in the Bob Hawke and Paul Keating administrations – to embrace the new orthodoxy. The result, according to Neal Blewett, was 'perhaps the most complete accommodation with neo-liberalism of any social democratic party in the world, apart perhaps from New Zealand'.[98] Remarkably, this was achieved with the full co-operation of the trade union movement. Whether Dunstan would have embraced this accommodation if he had stayed in power into the 1980s, is a moot point. He was not averse to privatisation in genuinely competitive situations but was implacably opposed to the privatisation of 'natural' monopolies, believing that these should be run in the public interest rather than for private profit, and that public rather than private ownership was actually more efficient. Moreover, Dunstan was afraid that social democracy was ceding its right to criticise capitalism, and that in doing so the Labor Party was in danger of losing its moral authority and commitment to principle.

'If it were not so tragic, it would be laughable'

Observing from the side lines, as it were, Don Dunstan contributed a series of frequently angry articles to the *Adelaide Review* in the 1990s, the last just weeks before he died on 6 February 1999. In these articles he attacked the so-called 'economic rationalism' of neo-liberalism, and defended the tenets of traditional social democracy, as well as reiterating his passion for social justice and his abhorrence of discrimination of all kinds. Typical was his essay 'The Uncaring Society', published in July 1996, where he attacked the now all-pervasive orthodoxy of neo-liberalism. Central to this orthodoxy, he argued, were the following notions:

> Governments should own less, tax less, spend less and do less; they should not be about redistribution of income, but should remove all social regulation which protects the poor against the rapacious, and as far as possible remove the responsibility for the disadvantaged, the sick and the destitute to private charity; state services, including education, health and public utilities such as water and electricity should be removed from community control to market control; the principle of user pays and reliance on private profit in the market place should obtain in all areas.[99]

Moreover, Dunstan added:

> The effect of this 'orthodoxy' is to propound these propositions: in order to increase employment and economic growth we must dispose of tens of thousands of jobs which provide services to the public, dispose of publicly owned assets wherever possible at fire-sale prices, reduce the money paid in support of the poor and underprivileged, open up opportunities for investors (who always seem to be foreign) to make money out of provision of services to the public previously provided at cost. This is somehow supposed to ensure increased local investment and saving.[100]

Dunstan's conclusion was that, 'If it were not so tragic it would be laughable'.[101] Neal Blewett, musing on such polemics, conceded that some might well regard Dunstan's analysis as prescient. Others, however, 'his critics', would 'tend to see all this as a nostalgic lament for a world that had gone'.[102] Writing in 1977, Dean Jaensch had marvelled at the complete transformation of the ALP in South Australia under Dunstan's leadership, to the extent of wondering whether Labor was now the natural party of government in the State. In the following year, Richard Yeeles published his *Don Dunstan: The First 25 Years in Parliament*, with its unspoken expectation in the title that there might be another quarter century ahead.[103] But, as we know, Don Dunstan's political career came abruptly to an end on 15 February 1979, when he announced his resignation. Nonetheless, he had won four successive election victories, unprecedented in Labor's history in South Australia. And if Labor did not become exactly the natural party of government, it has now (in 2016) governed the State for all but twelve years since 1967.

However, as Dean Jaensch recognised later, in 1989, a little over a decade since his prophetic pronouncements in 1977, the 'dynamism and charisma' of Don Dunstan had not had the lasting impact on the conduct of Labor Party politics – at State or Federal level – that he and other observers had once expected. As Neal Blewett has noted with wry insight, there was by 1989 no longer room for Dunstan in Jaensch's latest reassessment of the characteristics of modern Labor. Instead, Jaensch observed that the ALP 'under Whitlam and Hawke nationally and under Bannon, Cain, Burke and Wran in the states, has been involved in a transformation of organisation, style, tactics and appeals'.[104] Dunstan had already disappeared from view. 'Dunstanism' too was apparently dead and, as Andrew Parkin observed, it 'never rose from the grave'.[105] Thereafter, as Blewett has explained, Dunstan's successors in South Australia avoided following too overtly in his footsteps, in both style and substance, deliberately moving in other directions and adopting contrasting managerial techniques and public personas.[106]

This abrupt change in image, manners and conduct was best exemplified, perhaps, in the comment attributed to the Labor leader John Bannon, who was heard in shadow cabinet to express a preference for 'grey suits' over 'pink shorts'.[107] In retrospect, Don Dunstan had been a one off, despite his central place in the State's radical tradition. In many ways he had indeed transformed South Australia, as he had intended, ushering in a more tolerant and relaxed lifestyle, achieving lasting reform in key areas such as Aboriginal rights and equal opportunities for women, cultivating the arts, and dragging the South Australian constitution into the twentieth-century. But his dramatic exit from mainstream politics, together with the emergence of new-look Labor in the Hawke-Keating era, left him marginalised and out of step with the ALP as it changed directions in the 1980s and beyond. He was glad, no doubt, to turn away from 'the world that had gone', and to put his hand to other things.

Chapter Ten

Life After Dunstan –
To Bannon and Beyond

After the shock of Don Dunstan's resignation, the ALP parliamentary caucus elected Des 'The Colonel' Corcoran as Premier, with Hugh Hudson as his deputy. A former Army officer, Corcoran was seen as a safe pair of hands, a moderate and no-nonsense military man who would appeal to a range of opinion across the community, from the trade unions to the world of business. He was swift to quash the recommendations of a Royal Commission that the laws relating to marijuana use be liberalised, and moved quickly to address 'massive waste' that had become apparent in the State's hospital system. Public opinion appeared to welcome this change of style, and approved of Corcoran's cautious but confident manner. Hoping to capitalise on this honeymoon period, Corcoran went to the polls early in September 1979. It was a disaster. In a sudden about turn, public opinion moved decisively against Labor. Overall, there was a swing of 11% against Corcoran's government, with even higher percentages in some metropolitan areas. For the first time since the Second World War, the ALP lost metropolitan seats, including that of Hugh Hudson, the Deputy Premier. The Liberal leader (the affable David Tonkin, who liked to remind people that it was not only Labor politicians who were of Cornish descent[1]) became Premier, the Liberals having won twenty-five seats to Labor's nineteen, with one each for the Australian Democrats, the Country Party and an Independent Labor candidate. In the Legislative Council, Labor won only four of the eleven seats up for contestation, demolishing the fondly held hope that the party might actually achieve an unprecedented majority in the upper house.[2]

Dunstan and his successor as Labor Premier, Des 'The Colonel' Corcoran.
[Courtesy News Limited and Flinders University Library]

'Follow the Leader'?

Labor's collapse took most people by surprise. ALP strategists had been ill-prepared for the election that had been sprung upon them, and the inept campaign slogan 'Follow the Leader' seemed at best a demand for military-style obedience, at worst a silly children's game. Either way, the electorate was not impressed. Added to this was a surprisingly slick Liberal campaign, aided and abetted by a partisan news media and the strong mobilisation of business resources in support of Tonkin. Overall, as Andrew Parkin has concluded, the Liberals were able to paint 'a picture of malaise in South Australia'. They pointed to 'a deteriorating economy, lack of business confidence, crushing state taxes, an inefficient and bloated public sector, a stagnating mining industry, the traditional family under threat, interference by government in police administration, deteriorating standards in public schools'.[3] It was, perhaps, a reaction against the Dunstan era as much as it was a rejection of his less colourful successor. At any rate, the voting public had decided that it was time for a change of government.

The Labor Party was stunned. Something of the trauma in ALP ranks was caught in Don Hopgood's remembrance of the election's aftermath, penned a little over a decade later. Senior members of the party's parliamentary team had gathered to consider their options. 'There were five of us sitting around in John Bannon's backyard', Hopgood recalled, 'Bannon himself, Chris Sumner, Jack Wright, Chris Schacht and me'. As Hopgood explained, the 'question on everyone's lips was "Where on earth do we go from here?". We had just lost the 1979 election and all the Olympian figures who had dominated the party, and indeed the South Australian political scene for a decade, were gone'. As he mused: 'Dunstan, in ill health, had stepped down some months prior to the election. Hudson had lost his seat. [Geoff] Virgo had not sought re-election, and Corcoran, still in Parliament, was mortally politically wounded. The Dunstan–Corcoran decade had come to an abrupt and spectacular end.'[4] Who was to lead the party thereafter?

As Don Hopgood went on to elaborate, it became increasingly clear that the man for the job was John Bannon, who was subsequently elected leader unopposed by the parliamentary caucus. 'John Bannon accepted the leadership', Hopgood recalled, 'albeit with some reluctance.'[5] It proved to be an inspired choice. Bannon's style contrasted with those of both Corcoran and Dunstan. He was not the bluff ex-soldier but neither did he try to adopt Dunstan's flamboyant manner, which he considered 'less appropriate in difficult economic times and did not suit his personality anyway'.[6] Instead, in Opposition, Bannon developed a quiet professionalism which was able to capitalise on the Liberal government's failure to address economic decline, one of Tonkin's key election promises. He played his cards well in dealing with the Roxby Downs uranium issue, helping to persuade the ALP National Conference in July 1982 to support mining at the site, and was able to reassure the South Australian public that 'Roxby Downs can and will go ahead under a Labor government'.[7] The strong support from business that the Liberals had enjoyed in 1979 failed to materialise to the same extent in the State election of November 1982, and this time there were few surprises when

Labor was returned to government, with John Bannon as Premier. Yet Labor had scraped home with a slim majority of twenty-four seats (together with the support of an Independent Labor member), against twenty-one Liberals and one National Party. In the Legislative Council half-election, overall control still eluded the ALP.

John Bannon, Labor Premier in the age of 'restraint'.
[Courtesy Angela Bannon]

The Bannon Decade

The *Advertiser* newspaper detected that there would now be a very different type of Labor government – 'make way for the "new puritanism"' it warned – and indeed there was a new atmosphere of austerity and caution.[8] What was to become known as the Bannon Decade was characterised by 'the politics of restraint', as Andrew Parkin and Allan Patience described it.[9] As the *Australian* explained much later, John Bannon was, 'in the main, a no-frills, no fuss, no fireworks premier' who demonstrated a 'shrewd understanding of the electorate and led a largely competent and cautious, yet popular, administration'.[10] Although eschewing Dunstan's style, Bannon was aware of South Australia's distinctive radical tradition, and was keen to locate himself within it.[11] However, economic recovery, which had eluded the Liberals, was Bannon's first priority. He recognised that the State's industrial profile, inherited from the Playford era, was lopsided and unbalanced. Further job losses in the motor vehicles industry during 1983 convinced him that South Australia ought to be less reliant on the manufacture of cars and consumer durables, and that there should be greater efforts to embrace new technologies.[12] Here his greatest coup was winning for South Australia the contract for the new Collins class submarines. The first of these technologically advanced boats was laid down at Port Adelaide by the Australian Submarine Corporation on 14 February 1990; the sixth and final vessel was commissioned into the Royal Australian Navy in 2001.[13] Kim Beazley, then leader of the Federal Labor Opposition, opined in 2005 that the 'Collins class is the most complex industrial artefact Australia has ever built, and the effort transformed the quality of many Australian support industries'.[14] It was exactly as Bannon had planned, and the electorate was impressed.

Continuity in Labor's radical tradition –
John Bannon, Jim Toohey, Don Dunstan. [Courtesy Angela Bannon]

There were other prestige projects during the early Bannon period. The Adelaide Railway Station complex was comprehensively redeveloped to produce the Hyatt (now Intercontinental) hotel, a convention centre and a casino (the latter the subject of a free conscience vote in Parliament). Bannon also oversaw the introduction of 'pokies' – poker machines in pubs and clubs – which proved to be great money spinners and helped keep many country hostelries in business. But the associated gambling addiction was something that Bannon had not fully anticipated, and he later regretted his decision.[15] Near unanimous approval, however, greeted his second great coup, the staging of the Formula One Adelaide Grand Prix in early November 1985. It was a spectacular event that brought 'Adelaide Alive', and a week later Bannon announced an election for 7 December. Riding high now, Labor won a commanding parliamentary dominance of twenty-nine seats to eighteen.[16] Already the press was beginning to talk about the possibility, even likelihood, of a 'Bannon Decade'.[17]

In this second Bannon government, the broad consensus that had been maintained in the parliamentary party since 1982 was unbalanced to a degree by John Cornwall, the Minister for Health and Community Welfare, who appeared increasingly frustrated, not only by Bannon's personal low-key manner but also by the government's technocratic managerial style. As Dean Jaensch observed of the ALP in 1985: 'It doesn't look like a traditional Labor Party, it does not act like a socialist party, the trade union influence is muted ... and it is run by the new technocrats.'[18] Cornwall was behind the Social Justice Strategy, in which he hoped to temper the government's pre-occupation with sound economic management by introducing a renewed focus on issues of social welfare and equality. He managed to convince his Cabinet colleagues that his plan was a good one. However, he let it be known that this strategy to restore 'traditional Labor values' would be financed by a tax on property transactions. The press had a field day, and Bannon immediately quashed the levy proposal. Later, in August 1988, a court awarded a defamation award against Cornwall for remarks he had made at a press conference, and subsequently he was forced to resign from the Cabinet. He left politics soon after.[19]

For the most part, then, the 'steady approach to policy which had characterised the first Bannon Government continued during the second'.[20] In July 1989 came the welcome news that the facilities constructed at Port Adelaide by the Adelaide Submarine Corporation would now be used to help build a new generation of frigates for the Navy.[21] Yet in the campaign leading up to the State election of 25 November 1989, Bannon found himself under pressure to distance himself from the Hawke Federal Labor government in Canberra. Like Dunstan's predicament in the Whitlam era, Bannon had to remind the electorate that the forthcoming election was about the governance of South Australia and was not a judgement on the performance of Bob Hawke. In the event, the Liberals almost won in South Australia, gaining a majority of the two-party preferred vote but failing to secure a majority of Assembly seats. As it was, Bannon had now to rely on the support in Parliament of two Independent Labor members.

At the ALP State Convention in 1989, before the election, John Bannon had announced confidently that 'Labor is indeed the party of Government in South Australia'.[22] By the end of the year the assertion was looking less credible, with Bannon's hold on the reins of government far less secure than before. Indeed, the third Bannon government – from 1989 to 1992 – became something of a nightmare, as it was dominated by the financial collapse of the State Bank. Ironically, Bannon's administrations had won a reputation for careful financial management (not least when compared to Western Australia and Victoria, both of which had experienced budgetary crises), so when irregularities became apparent in the affairs of the State Bank, it came as a considerable shock to a trusting public. Put simply, the source of the difficulty was the overheated property market of the 1980s, coupled with some slack banking practices, a mix not unlike that underlying the later and much bigger world banking crisis in 2007. Bannon had been careful to emphasise the distance between his government and the State Bank's management – he did not presume to interfere – but early in 1991 it became apparent that all was not well. The Bank had accumulated debts of about two billion Australian dollars, together with a portfolio of 'non-performing' loans of around two billion dollars. Bannon, visibly alarmed, put in place two inquiries – one under the Auditor-General of South Australia to investigate the Bank's finances in depth, the other a Royal Commission to consider (among other things) the relationship between the Bank and the government.[23]

When the Auditor-General reported in 1993, he pointed especially to the non-performing loans, blaming extraneous factors associated with the housing market but also criticising the Bank itself for a lack of supervision and control, including lending to high-risk borrowers unable to obtain funds from commercial banks. When the Royal Commission reported, it cleared Bannon of any specific wrong-doing but was, however, highly critical of him and his government. Bannon felt – and assumed – a deep sense of personal responsibility, and between January 1991 and September 1992 developed a financial strategy to enable support for the ailing State Bank. There were tough decisions – including tax rises – but by September 1992 Bannon considered that he had done enough to put South Australia on a secure footing. That achieved, he tendered his resignation as Premier. He had been in office for nine years and tenth months. His decision to stand down was an almost old-fashioned acceptance of ministerial responsibility. John Bannon apologised to the people of South Australia, explaining that he had 'stuffed this up', and his resignation was seen widely as an act of great integrity.[24] It was a measure of Bannon's achievement that his long premiership was remembered not solely for the State Bank debacle but for a range of innovative measures, from the establishment of South Australia's first metropolitan Aboriginal school to legislation to protect native flora.

A 'caretaker Premier'?

Lynn Arnold was elected unopposed as Premier by the Labor caucus on 3 September 1992. His task was difficult, if not impossible, given the ongoing State Bank crisis and an increasingly restless electorate that was tiring of another decade of Labor rule, just as it had when Corcoran succeeded Dunstan in 1979. Leader of an insecure minority government, Arnold took the inspired initiative of allowing two Independent Labor members into his Cabinet, one of whom subsequently re-joined the ALP. This lent a measure of stability to his government, allowing it to escape an Opposition vote of no-confidence in

November 1992 over the State Bank issue. But Lynn Arnold's position was not unlike that of R.S. Richards back in 1933. 'With little real hope that the ALP could win the next election', Robert Martin has explained, 'Mr Arnold played the role of caretaker Premier of a beleaguered minority government'.[25] In 1985 the parliamentary term had been increased from three years to four, allowing Arnold to 'tough it out' for longer than would have been possible hitherto. But the reckoning, when it came, was terrible. In the State election on 11 December 1993, the Liberals were swept into power under Dean Brown. Achieving 52.8% of the primary vote, compared to the ALP's derisory 30.4%, the Liberals won thirty-seven seats in the House of Assembly, to Labor's ten. It was the biggest defeat for Labor since the demise of Richards' government in 1933. In the Legislative Council, ironically, Labor's fortunes were less parlous. Here the party held nine seats to the Liberals' eleven and the Democrats' two, the latter effectively holding the balance of power.[26]

'Symbolic of the end of the Bannon era', observed Robert Martin, 'was the loss to Victoria of the Formula One Grand Prix, announced within days of Mr Brown taking office as Premier in December 1993'.[27] It was a low point for Labor, and those still-recent prophesies that the ALP was somehow poised to become the natural party of government in South Australia seemed increasingly hollow. Yet, whatever the feelings of despondency in Labor ranks in the aftermath of the 1993 election, the party remained keenly alive to its tradition and distinctive heritage, together with the firm opinion that it had been destined from the first to play a leading role in the shaping of South Australia. It was a self-belief and sense of history that Labor was still anxious to articulate. In 1991, a year before assuming the premiership, Lynn Arnold had penned a chapter 'The Labor Party and its Radical Tradition', in which he had posed the fundamental question: 'does it have a radical tradition?'. Like Dunstan before him, Arnold saw that it did, and argued that from its earliest days the Labor movement had possessed 'both radical platforms and "radicals" in all areas of its membership'. It had been equipped with policies that were designed to achieve radical reforms, and possessed able individuals who set the agenda for change as well as providing vision, inspiration and leadership. Moreover, in South Australia, Labor had 'proved that radicalism and revolution did not need each other'. However, as Arnold was quick to add, Labor's 'parliamentary members may have been gradualists, but the party from which they drew their support spearheaded much that was radical'.[28] Idealism and pragmatism had always gone hand-in-hand.

Lynn Arnold, Labor Premier and champion of multiculturalism.
[Courtesy Don Dunstan Foundation]

As Arnold implied, this sense of radical continuity was as vibrant in the closing decade of the twentieth century as it had been at the end of the nineteenth, notwithstanding the trauma of recent defeat. In 1994, a year after losing office, Arnold was in print again, this time addressing issues of multiculturalism. He argued that South Australia had been multicultural from the beginning. In addition to the indigenous Aboriginal people, early ethnic groups such as the Germans, the Poles, the Sorbs (or Wends), and the Cornish had lent the State its multicultural flavour. Arnold recognised that the Cornish and their religion, Methodism, had made a distinctive contribution to the Labor movement (see pp. 16–17), and, as he explained, before journeying to Spain to deliver the academic paper that would later appear as the chapter in question, he and his family had enjoyed a week holidaying at Moonta. 'I spent some of my time thinking about the struggle for multiculturalism in Australia', he said: 'There was much about Moonta that reminded me of some of the themes of Australian cultural history.'[29] Alongside Methodism, there were echoes of a pagan past in the 'midsummer' bonfires held on 24 June, and there were faint echoes of the old Cornish language in the rich Cornu–English dialect once spoken on northern Yorke Peninsula. As he observed, John Verran, 'the first leader of a democratic socialist government anywhere in the world, would, so he could be clearly understood, speak differently when in Parliament in Adelaide than he did in his home town'. Cornish cuisine persisted, he added, and today the 'area is still called Australia's Little Cornwall, while the Cornish Pastie and the ... Kernewek Lowender Festival are recognised ikons of that significant cultural impact'.[30]

'Multicultural mode'

As Lynn Arnold emphasised, political support for multiculturalism had become integral to Labor Party policy in South Australia in the decades after the Second World War. To the initial waves of Continental European migrants was added, after the abandonment of the White Australia policy, large numbers of people from Asia and elsewhere, all of whom introduced their languages, religions, cultures, customs, costumes and cuisines. This diversity had brought a richness to South Australian life that by the 1990s was everywhere apparent. Arnold was aware of the dangers of 'polyculturalism', as he termed it, where people from different cultures lived side by side but failed to interact or share their heritage at any substantial level. Instead, he encouraged a genuine multiculturalism in which people learned from each other to mutual benefit, an early example of which was the explosion of 'ethnic' restaurants – Italian, Greek, Chinese, Vietnamese, Thai, Japanese, Kurdish, Turkish, and so on – which had transformed the eating habits of South Australians. As Arnold explained, in 'South Australia from the time of two predecessors of mine, Don Dunstan as Premier and Chris Sumner as Minister of Ethnic Affairs, both in the arenas of government and parliament, efforts were made to *pursue* that "multicultural mode"'.[31] Moreover, he added, 'I was continuing that tradition when I introduced legislation to our parliament that, *inter alia*, wrote into law a definition of "multiculturalism". The law defines it as follows':

'Multiculturalism' means policies and practices that recognise and respond to the ethnic diversity of the South Australian community and have as their primary objects the creation of conditions under which all groups and members of the community may

(a) live and work together harmoniously,

(b) fully and effectively participate in, and employ their skills and talents for the benefit of, the economic, social and cultural life of the community; and

(c) maintain and give expression to their distinctive cultural heritages.[32]

Arnold had deftly woven multiculturalism into Labor's radical tradition, recognising, like Dunstan, that traditions were not static but were subject to constant contestation and renewal. 'White Australia' had remained a pillar of Labor Party policy, in South Australia as elsewhere, until well after the Second World War. However, Dunstan (like Whitlam) had played a key role in reversing Labor's position, and now, in a considerable *volte face*, the ALP was seen pre-eminently as the party of multiculturalism. Although Lynn Arnold left Parliament in September 1994, he had bequeathed the State a legislative framework and attendant public awareness of the potential benefits of an active multiculturalism and, especially, of South Australia's own 'distinctive cultural heritages'.

Rann to Weatherill

Following Arnold's resignation, Mike Rann became leader of the Labor Opposition. Born in the UK and brought up in New Zealand, Rann had arrived in South Australia in the late 1970s to work for Don Dunstan as press officer and speechwriter, tasks at which he excelled, and he entered Parliament as a Labor member in 1985. Although Rann, like other senior Labor figures, had been associated in the public mind with the State Bank fiasco, he nonetheless worked swiftly to restore Labor's standing. By late 1995, having been in office for two years, Dean Brown's Liberal government was already unpopular. Despite the growth of Roxby Downs and a buoyant wine industry, South Australia's economy appeared to lag behind the rest of the country, with youth

Labor Premiers all – Don Dunstan, John Bannon and Mike Rann.
[Courtesy Steven Cheng and Flinders University Library]

unemployment the highest of any State. Brown was committed to privatisation and the out-sourcing of government contracts but the scope of his ambitions caused some concern in a populace not yet convinced that the private sector was more efficient than the public. Liberal backbenchers became uneasy about their prospects for re-election, and in November 1996 Brown was forced to step down as Premier in favour of John Olsen. The change at the top was enough to prevent defeat in the October 1997 State election, although many of those discomforted backbenchers did indeed lose their seats. Overall, the Liberals lost thirteen seats, ten of which went to Labor, one to the National Party, another to an Independent Liberal, and yet another to a different Independent. Now a minority government, the Liberals would need to rely on the support of one or more of these at any one time. Among other things, Olsen pressed ahead with privatisation of the State electricity industry (which did not lead to the lower energy prices he had promised) but increasing criticism led to his replacement in October 2001 as Premier by his deputy, Bob Kerin. In the ensuing election in February 2002, the Liberals gained 50.9% of the vote when preferences were distributed, against Labor's 49.1%. Yet Labor won twenty-three seats against the Liberals' twenty, and to form a government the ALP had to rely on support from one or more of the three Independents returned to Parliament. There was also one National Party member.[33]

On 5 March 2002, Mike Rann became Premier of South Australia, as Labor was returned to power for the first time since 1993. He devoted much time and energy to shoring up his minority administration, yet by September 2002 he was reckoned the most popular of all Australia's State Premiers. Echoing the Bannon era, Rann's premiership was characterised initially by cautious economic management designed to secure debt reduction and to avoid 'big government', high taxes and public sector intervention. Despite the closure of the Mitsubishi plant at Lonsdale and the Mobil Oil Refinery at Port Stanvac, economic indicators generally were good, not least the expansion of the Olympic Dam uranium mine at Roxby Downs. When the South Australian electorate went to the polls in March 2006, Labor was rewarded with twenty-eight seats in the House of Assembly, providing the party with a convincing overall majority, the Liberals gaining just fifteen.[34] In this his second period of government, Rann initiated a series of high-profile projects, injecting something of the feel of the Dunstan era. John Hill, a minister in Rann's government, reckoned that Mike Rann 'behaved in every was as the true inheritor of the Dunstan legacy'.[35] The rail route to Adelaide's southern suburbs was electrified, the city's tram system extended, a vast new hospital was announced, and the Adelaide Oval was comprehensively modernised to provide a multi-purpose stadium of international standard. Rann's personal approval ratings continued to soar, until severe cutbacks following the global financial crisis caused unease among trade unions and the public at large. As a result, Rann stood down in October 2011, to be replaced as Premier by Jay Weatherill. In the 2014 State election, Labor took twenty-three seats, as opposed to the Liberals' twenty-two, and Weatherill had to rely on the support of two Independents. In a by-election later in the year, however, Labor gained an additional seat, thus winning an overall majority.

'Distinctive cultural heritages'

Among earlier ministerial portfolios held by Jay Weatherill, was that of Environment and Conservation. In 2009 he lent his ministerial support to

Jay Weatherill, Labor Premier of South Australia

the proposal that the Cornish copper-mining landscapes of South Australia be added to the National List of Heritage Sites recognised by the Australian Government under the auspices of the Australian Heritage Council. Comprising Burra and the Copper Triangle (as Moonta, Wallaroo and Kadina were designated), the intention was that, if National Listing was achieved, then this would be the prelude to an application to UNESCO for World Heritage Site status. When the hard-rock (mainly copper and tin) mining sites of Cornwall and West Devon had been awarded World Heritage Site status in 2006, it was acknowledged that there was a number of other Cornish mining sites in disparate parts of the globe that also warranted recognition. The most complete, it was argued, were those of South Australia, where the tell-tale Cornish engine houses were complemented by Methodist chapels, miners' cottages, and stone-built buildings constructed in the Cornish style. These were compelling examples of South Australia's 'distinctive cultural heritages', as Lynn Arnold had termed them. Burra was a product of Australia's earliest mining era, while the Copper Triangle – Moonta, Wallaroo and Kadina – spanned the entire period from 1859 until mining was finally at an end in the 1920s.[36]

As Jay Weatherill acknowledged (he was himself of Cornish descent), a major element of the national and international significance of the social and cultural dimensions of these Cornish mining sites was their role in the foundation and growth of South Australia's Labor movement. From the Burra strike in 1848 through to the rise of trade unionism at Moonta and Wallaroo and the Premierships of John Verran and R.S. Richards and beyond, they had been at the heart of South Australia's radical tradition, accounting, as we have seen, for many of its distinctive characteristics and helping to explain its differences from the Labor movement elsewhere in Australia. The quest for National Listing was timely recognition of this fine heritage, as the Labor Party in early twenty-first century South Australia contemplated its illustrious past, exemplified in the Cornish motto 'One and All'.

Epilogue

Don Dunstan considered himself a latter-day Chartist. His task, as he saw it, was to rekindle the flame of South Australia's Chartist heritage and to reanimate the Radical–Nonconformist tradition established by the State's founding fathers in the 1830s – the Reforming Thirties. Dunstan entitled his memoirs, published in 1981, *Felicia*, a name that had been suggested by Jeremy Bentham for the then newly created Province of South Australia, proclaimed in 1836, which Bentham saw not merely as a means of transferring British society to the Antipodes but rather 'as an opportunity to create a better, freer and happier place'.[1]

That by the early post-Second World War years the Chartist flame had dimmed and the radical tradition atrophied was only in small part a judgement on South Australia's Labor Party. The grievous splits over conscription during the Great War, and then over the Premiers' Plan in the 1930s, had been damaging in the extreme, while Labor's apparent acquiescence during the long Playford era had seemingly dulled the thirst for change and the quest for reform. However, as Dunstan understood, despite possessing at the outset the most progressive constitution of all the Australian colonies, South Australia had fallen under the constraining yoke of a conservative Legislative Council and, later, the infamous Playmander, with its in-built bias in favour of the country districts at the expense of metropolitan areas. When, finally, these twin disabilities were addressed, Labor – and the State's radical tradition – was able to re-assert itself in spectacular style, so much so that politicians and political scientists alike claimed periodically that the ALP was perhaps now the natural party of government in South Australia. The way was open for the premierships of Don Dunstan, Des Corcoran, John Bannon, Lynn Arnold, Mike Rann and Jay Weatherill.

Yet the battle against the Legislative Council – which exhausted Tom Price and defeated John Verran – was but one part of Labor's story in South Australia. Tom Price, as Labor Premier in what was effectively a coalition administration, established the Labor Party as a credible and effective participant in government. John Verran went further, forming the first majority social democratic Labor government anywhere in the world, an extraordinary achievement that afforded South Australia its special and enduring place in the history of the Labor movement – in Australia and internationally. More than this, South Australia was the home of 'conscience politics' and Christian Socialism, testament to the State's Nonconformist radical tradition that distinguished it from the predominantly Catholic flavour of Labor in the eastern States. As we have seen in detail, the radical Chartist influence in early South Australia was moulded to a considerable degree by Cornish immigrants, who arrived initially in the 1830s and 1840s and who, in the Burra mine strike of 1848, laid the first foundations of an embryonic Labor movement. Later, in the 1860s and 1870s, these and other newly arrived Cornish migrants established a trade union organisation in the mines of northern Yorke Peninsula that bore all the hallmarks of the Methodist-radical tradition, transferred from Cornwall and modified now to suit the new Australian conditions. Methodist local preachers at Moonta and Wallaroo became trade unionists first and then politicians, producing the premierships of John Verran and R.S. Richards, and establishing a Cornish–Methodist influence in the parliamentary Labor Party that was discernible until the Second World War and beyond.

Richard 'Dicky' Hooper, born in Cornwall in 1846, one-time president of the Moonta branch of the Amalgamated Miners Association, became the very first Labor member of the House of Assembly in South Australia's Parliament in 1891. Sponsored by local trade unionists, Hooper's election reflected a growing clamour for the interests and aspirations of Labor to be represented at parliamentary level. It was an anxiety shared by the newly emergent trade union movement in Adelaide. Craft trade unions had appeared in the 1870s and 1880s, and in 1884 a United Trades & Labor Council (UTLC) was established in the capital. Like the trade unionists of northern Yorke Peninsula, the UTLC wished to endorse parliamentary candidates who would articulate its opinions and agendas if elected. Initially it supported 'liberal' candidates sympathetic to the cause of trade unionism. However, after the disastrous Maritime Strike of 1890, the UTLC decided that the election of Labor members was now its first priority. Accordingly, the United Labor Party (ULP) was formed in 1891 for the purpose. In an extraordinary performance in May 1891, the ULP's first three official candidates won seats on the Legislative Council, forming a Labour Wedge in the notoriously conservative upper house.

The ULP's relationship with independent Labor members (including Dicky Hooper) was not always easy. However, while the Labor movement on Yorke Peninsula remained formally separate from the ULP until 1904, when John Verran brought them together, the two parallel organisations saw eye to eye on most issues (Federation excepted). Both were moderate and pragmatic, Fabian in outlook, and strongly influenced by Methodism and the other Nonconformist churches. It was the conscription debate in the Great War that caused dissension in Labor ranks, not least as the Methodist church proved firmly in favour of conscription to the armed forces while the Labor grassroots was staunchly 'Anti'. The controversy destroyed the Premiership of Crawford Vaughan who, like John Verran and other prominent parliamentarians, left the Labor fold to form his own National Labor Party. It also prompted the Labor Party in South Australia to move (ostensibly) to the left, exemplified in Norman Makin's comprehensive manifesto for the new-look party, published in 1917, and marked by a formal change of name from ULP to Australian Labor Party (ALP), South Australian Branch. In practice, however, the party retained its moderate, pragmatic stance, enabling it to recover from the trauma of the conscription crisis in time to win the State election of 1924, when the extremely able John Gunn became Premier. Unfortunately for Labor, Gunn was enticed away to an apparently plum public service post in

1926, handing the premiership to the less gifted Lionel Hill. Hill proceeded to lose the 1927 election but, in an atmosphere of economic deterioration and industrial conflict (not least the 'Waterfront War' of 1928), the electorate was prepared to give him another chance in 1930. Hill's second premiership was a disaster, undermined as it was by the Premiers' Plan debacle, which saw him expelled from the ALP and bowing out of politics altogether. The premiership, a poisoned chalice, then fell to R.S. Richards, who was in office for only sixty-four days before the government's defeat at the polls in 1933.

Thereafter, R.S. Richards was leader of the Labor Opposition from 1938 until 1949, during which time (and for years after) the ALP was systematically kept out of power by the Playmander, the parliamentary Labor Party reduced to supporting what it imagined to be the socialist elements of Tom Playford's Liberal Country League program. Indeed, Labor did not regain office until March 1965, when Frank Walsh became Premier, prelude to the heady Dunstan Decade and the lengthy periods of Labor Party government in South Australia that were to follow in the late twentieth and early twenty-first centuries. Although the Labor Party would take a very different turn under John Bannon and his successors, Don Dunstan was essentially correct when he asserted that South Australia's radical tradition had been rekindled in the years after 1965, and that the 'experiment in government' he had initiated had 'worked, and worked to a degree to which we [the ALP] can proudly say stands the cause of social democracy everywhere as an example of proven achievement'.[2] It was, with hindsight, an accolade that might also be usefully applied to the broader historical canvas of Labor and the radical tradition in South Australia, not least those early pioneers from Cornwall and elsewhere who strove to plant Chartist principles under the southern cross for the benefit of 'One and All'.

Notes

Chapter 1 • Radical Traditions – South Australia

1   Don Dunstan, *Felicia: The Political Memoirs of Don Dunstan*, Melbourne, 1981, p. 1.
2   Ibid., p. viii.
3   Ibid.
4   Allan Patience, 'Social Democracy in South Australia in the 1970s', in Andrew Parkin and Allan Patience (eds), *The Dunstan Decade: Social Democracy at the State Level*, Melbourne, 1981, p. 288.
5   Dunstan, 1981, p. 1.
6   Ibid., p. 23.
7   Ibid., p. 24.
8   Ibid., p. 10.
9   Ibid.
10 David Hilliard and Arnold D. Hunt, 'Religion' in Eric Richards (ed.), *The Flinders History of South Australia: Social History*, Adelaide, 1986, p. 204.
11 Ibid., p. 231.
12 Arnold D. Hunt, *This Side of Heaven: A History of Methodism in South Australia*, Adelaide, 1985, p. 117.
13 P.A. Howell, *South Australia and Federation*, Adelaide, 2002, p. 67.
14 Ibid., pp. 67–8.
15 Dunstan, 1981, p. 24.
16 Ibid., p. 4.
17 Frank Bongiorno, *The People's Party: Victorian Labor and the Radical Tradition 1875–1914*, Melbourne, 1996, p. 26.
18 Ruth Hopkins, *Where Now Cousin Jack?*, Bendigo, 1988, pp. 36–8.
19 Bongiorno, 1996, p. 28.

20 Ibid., p. 15.

21 *Age* (Melbourne), 22 February 1904.

22 Geoffrey Blainey, *A History of Victoria*, Melbourne, 2006, pp. 191–201.

23 Philip Payton, 'Competing Celticities: Cornish and Irish Constructions of Australia' in Pamela O'Neill (ed.), *Celts in Legends and Reality: Papers from the Sixth Australian Conference of Celtic Studies, University of Sydney, July 2007*, Sydney, 2010, pp. 478–9.

24 Blainey, 2006, p. 213.

25 Bongiorno, 1996, p. 165.

26 Ibid., p. 187.

27 Dean Jaensch, *The Politics of Australia*, Melbourne, 2 ed., 1997, p. 255.

28 Don Dunstan, *Australia: A Personal View*, Kenthurst (NSW), 1981, p. 8.

29 Ibid.

30 Ibid., p. 8 and p. 69; see also Don Dunstan, *Don Dunstan's Australia*, Adelaide, 1977, p. 89.

31 Flinders University Special Collections, Dunstan Collection/DUN/Speeches/2640/Speech at Kernewek Lowender (Cornish Festival) launching, Adelaide, 23/4/74.

32 This was the caption, inscribed in gold leaf, on the cardboard frame of the historic photograph showing Verran and his newly elected Ministry in 1910 (author's collection).

33 C.C. James, *A History of the Parish of Gwennap*, Penzance, 1947, p. 90.

34 Dunstan, 1981, p. 10.

35 Ibid., pp. 10–11.

36 Ibid., p. 11.

37 *Advertiser*, 8 June 1932.

38 R. Hetherington and R.L. Reid, *The South Australian Election, 1959*, Adelaide, 1962, p. 11.

39 Malcolm Saunders, '"Jim" Toohey (1909–1992): The "Father" of the Labor Party in South Australia', *Labor History*, 85, November 2003, p. 177.

40 Ibid., p. 189.

41 Malcolm Saunders, 'The Labor Party and the Industrial Groups in South Australia 1946–55: Precluding the Split', *Journal of the Historical Society of South Australia*, 33, 2005, p. 74.

42 John Lonie, 'Conservatism and Class in South Australia during the Depression Years 1924–1934', unpublished MA thesis, University of Adelaide, 1973, p. 335; see also Philip Payton, '"Vote Labor, and Rid South Australia of a Danger to the Purity of Our Race": The Cornish Radical Tradition in South Australia, 1900–1939', in Philip Payton (ed.), *Cornish Studies: Nine*, Exeter, 2001, pp. 173–201.

43 Donald J. Hopgood, 'A Psephological Examination of the South Australian Labor Party from World War One to the Depression', unpublished PhD thesis, Flinders University, 1973, p. 445.

44 Dean Jaensch, *The Government of South Australia*, St Lucia (Qld.), 1977, pp. 7–8.

45 Michael Atkinson, 'S.A. Labor Between the Wars 1915–1944', in Clarrie Bell (ed.), *Making History: A History of the Australian Labor Party (S.A. Branch) 1891–1991*, Adelaide, 1991, p. 4.

46 John Bannon, 'South Australia's Labor Leaders', in Bell (ed.), 1991, p. 51.

47 Lynn F.M. Arnold, 'Breaking the Tyranny of Monoculturalism and Monolingulism: The Austrlian Experience', in Richard J. Watts and Jerzy J. Smolicz (eds), *Cultural Democracy and Ethnic Pluralism: Multicultural and Multilingual Policies in Education*, Bern, 1994.

48 David Hilliard, 'Methodism in South Australia, 1855–1902', in Glen O'Brien and Hilary M. Carey (eds), *Methodism in Australia: A History*, Farnham, 2015, p. 65; see also Julie-Ann Ellis, *South Australian Methodists and Working-Class Organisation*, Adelaide, 1992. p. 186.

49 Dunstan, 1981, pp. 9–10.

50 Howard Coxon, John Playford and Robert Reid, *Biographical Register of the South Australian Parliament 1857–1957*, Adelaide, 1985, p. 184.

51 Ibid., p. 10.

52 Stephanie McCarthy, *Tom Price: From Stonecutter to Premier*, Adelaide, 2015.

53 Dunstan, 1981, p. 10.

54 Bill Jones, 'Cousin Dai and Cousin Dilys? South Australia's Nineteenth-century Welsh Heritage', *Journal of the Historical Society of South Australia*, 27, 1999, p. 40.

55 I am indebted to the late Bob Reid, Department of Politics, University of Adelaide, for this insight.

56 Ibid., p. 28.

57 Philip Payton, 'Cousin Jacks and Ancient Britons: Cornish Immigrants and Ethnic Identity', *Journal of Australian Studies*, 68, 2001, pp. 54–64.

58 *Advertiser* (Adelaide), 11 April 1930.

59 Hunt, 1985, p. 181.

60 Ibid., p. 183.

61 Dunstan, 1981, p. 3.

62 Eric Richards, 'South Australia Observed, 1836–1986', in Richards (ed.), 1986, p. 3.

63 J.M. Main, 'The Foundation of South Australia', in Dean Jaensch (ed.), *The Flinders History of South Australia: Political History*, Adelaide, 1986, p. 1.

64 Edwin Hodder, *George Fife Angas: Father and Founder of South Australia*, London, 1891, p. 239.

65   Douglas Pike, *Paradise of Dissent: South Australia, 1829–1857*, Melbourne, 1957.

66   Reg Hamilton, *Colony: Strange Origins of One of the Earliest Modern Democracies*, Adelaide, 2010.

67   Ibid., pp. 1–2.

68   Geoffrey Blainey, *The Story of Australia's People: The Rise and Fall of Ancient Australia*, Melbourne, 2015, p. 313.

69   This was the opinion of Henry Cornish in his *Under the Southern Cross*, published in Madras in 1880 (see Henry Cornish, *Under the Southern Cross*, republished Ringwood [Vic], 1975, p. 50).

70   Richards, in Richards (ed.), 1986, p. 3.

71   Douglas Pike, 'The Utopian Dreams of Adelaide's Founders', *Proceedings of the Royal Geographical Society of South Australia*, 53, 1951–52, p. 516.

72   Dunstan, 1981, p. 4.

73   Ibid., p. 5.

74   Ibid., p. 7.

75   Dean Jaensch, 'Electoral Reform', in Parkin and Patience (eds), 1981, p. 237.

76   Dunstan, 1981, p. 4.

77   Ibid., 9.

78   Gordon D. Combe, *Responsible Government in South Australia: From the Foundations to Playford*, Adelaide, 1957, revised edn 2009, Vol. 1, p. 200.

79   Geoffrey Blainey, *A Land Half Won*, Melbourne, 1980, p. 278.

80   Ibid.

81   Dunstan, 1981, p. 24.

Chapter 2 • Radical Traditions – The Cornish at Home and Abroad

1   Edwin Jaggard, *Cornwall Politics in the Age of Reform 1790–1885*, Woodbridge (Suffolk), 1999, p. 4.

2   Ibid., p. 18 and p. 12.

3   William White, *A Londoner's Walk to the Land's End, and a Trip to the Scilly Isles*, London, 1851, p. 17.

4   Jaggard, 1999, p. 21.

5   Philip Payton, 'Labour Failure and Liberal Tenacity: Radical Politics and Cornish Political Culture, 1880–1939', in Philip Payton (ed.), *Cornish Studies: Two*, Exeter, 1994, pp. 83–95; Garry Tregidga, 'The Politics of the Celto-Cornish Revival, 1886–1939', in Philip Payton (ed.), *Cornish Studies: Five*, Exeter, 1997, 125–50; Garry Tregidga, 'Socialism and the Old Left: The Labour Party in Cornwall during the inter-war Period', in Philip Payton (ed.), *Cornish Studies: Seven*, Exeter, 1999, pp. 74–93; Garry Tregidga, *The Liberal Party in South-West Britain Since 1918: Political Decline, Dormancy and Rebirth*, Exeter, 2000, pp. 18–20; Garry Tregidga, 'Party, Personality and Place: Researching the

Politics of Modern Cornwall', in Philip Payton (ed.), *Cornish Studies: Ten*, Exeter, 2002, pp. 190–204.

6   Cornwall Record Office (CRO) FS/3/1127 'Memoirs of Sir J.C. Rashleigh'.

7   R.L. Brett (ed.), *Barclay Fox's Journal*, London, 1979, p. 35.

8   Alan Bennett, *Cornwall Through the Mid Nineteenth Century*, Southampton, 1987, p. 4.

9   Brian Elvins, 'Cornwall's Unsung Political Hero: Sir John Colman Rashleigh (1772–1847)', in Philip Payton (ed.), *Cornish Studies: Six*, Exeter, 1998, p. 93.

10 Ibid., p. 81.

11 Edwin Jaggard (ed.), *Liberalism in West Cornwall: The 1868 Election Papers of A. Pendarves Vivian M.P.*, Exeter, 2000, p. xx.

12 Brian Elvins, 'Cornwall's Newspaper War: The Political Rivalry between the *Royal Cornwall Gazette* and the *West Briton*, 1810–1831', in Philip Payton (ed.), *Cornish Studies: Nine*, Exeter, 2001, p. 166.

13 *West Briton*, 20 July 1810.

14 *Royal Cornwall Gazette*, 7 April 1809, 15 September 1810, 27 October 1810; 12 October 1811.

15 *West Briton*, 9 November 1821, 23 November 1821, 7 December 1821, 14 December 1841.

16 *West Briton*, 15 June 1832.

17 Brian Elvins, 'Cornwall's Newspaper War: The Political Rivalry between the *Royal Cornwall Gazette* and the *West Briton*, Part Two, 1832–1855', in Philip Payton (ed.), *Cornish Studies: Eleven*, Exeter, 2003, pp. 57–84.

18 *Royal Cornwall Gazette*, 16 July 1841.

19 Elvins, 2003, p. 73.

20 Ibid., p. 78.

21 Claire Tomalin, *Charles Dickens: A Life*, London, 2011, p. 48 and p. 53.

22 A.C. Todd and David James, *Ever Westward the Land: Samuel James and his Cornish Family on the trail to Oregon and the Pacific North-West 1842–52*, Exeter, 1986, p. 9

23 *West Briton*, 27 April 1838.

24 *Royal Cornwall Gazette*, 29 September 1838.

25 *West Briton*, 1 March 1839.

26 Ibid.

27 Emigration Advertisement, c.1839, reproduced in D. Bradford Barton, *Essays in Cornish Mining History: Volume 1*, Truro, 1968, p. 72.

28 *West Briton*, 13 September 1839.

29 *West Briton*, 1 March 1839.

30 *West Briton*, 30 August 1839.

31 John Stephens, *The Land of Promise: Being an Authentic and Impartial History of the Rise and Progress of the New British Province of South Australia*, London, 1839, p. 1.

32 Ibid., p. 85.

33 *South Australian Record*, 2 December 1839, 11 December 1839, 30 May 1840; *South Australian News*, September 1847.

34 Philip Payton, '"Reforming Thirties" and "Hungry Forties": The Genesis of Cornwall's Emigration Trade', in Philip Payton (ed.), *Cornish Studies: Four*, Exeter, 1996, pp. 107–27.

35 *South Australian News*, January 1846.

36 John Stevenson, *Popular Disturbances in England 1700–1832*, London, 1979 republished 1992, p. 130.

37 *Royal Cornwall Gazette*, 4 June 1847.

38 Ibid, pp. 119–122. *See* also Philip Payton, *Cornwall: A History*, Fowey, 2004, pp. 170–5.

39 A. Rowe, 'The food riots of the Forties in Cornwall', *Report of the Royal Cornwall Polytechnic Society*, 10, 1942, pp. 51–67.

40 *West Briton*, 21 May 1847.

41 Ibid.

42 Thomas Oliver, *Autobiography of a Cornish Miner*, Camborne, 1914, pp. 12–13.

43 *Old Cornwall*, Vol. 1, 1925.

44 Rowe, 1842, pp. 51–67.

45 *Northern Star and Leeds General Advertiser*, 20 April 1839.

46 *The Chartist*, 31 March 1839.

47 John Rule, *Cornish Cases: Essays in Eighteenth and Nineteenth Century Social History*, Southampton, 2006; Eric Hobsbawm, *Labouring Men*, London, 1964, p. 9.

48 Bernard Deacon, '*Cornish Cases* and Cornish Social History', in Philip Payton (ed.), *Cornish Studies: Sixteen*, Exeter, 2008, p. 237.

49 Rule, 2006, pp. 190–200.

50 Deacon, 2008, p. 237.

51 Bernard Deacon, 'From Chartists in Cornwall to Cornish Chartists', unpublished paper, Redruth, 2014, p. 4. I am greatly indebted to Bernard Deacon for sharing this paper and discussing with me the history of Chartism in Cornwall.

52 Ibid., p. 5.

53 Joel Weiner, *William Lovett*, Manchester, 1989.

54 *The Charter*, 9 February 1840.

55 *The Charter*, 23 February 1840.

56 *Southern Star*, 15 March 1840; *Northern Star*, 25 April 1840.

57 *Northern Star*, 20 May 1848.

58 *The Chartist*, 14 April 1839.

59 *Northern Star*, 23 July 1842, 30 July 1842; Deacon, 2014, p. 15.

60 *West Briton*, 22 February 1839; *Northern Star*, 22 February 1841, 16 October 1841.

61 Daniel Simpson, 'Chartist Failure and Methodist Madness in Nineteenth-century Cornwall: A Reanalysis', in Garry Tregidga (ed.), *Cornish Studies: 1* (Third Series), Penryn, 2015, p. 138.

62 Geoffrey Blainey, *The Story of Australia's People: The Rise and Fall of Ancient Australia*, Melbourne, 2015, p. 240.

63 Simpson, 2015, p. 139.

64 John Rule, 'The Perfect Wage System? Tributing in the Cornish Mines', in John Rule and Roger Wells (eds), *Crime, Protest and Popular Politics in Southern England, 1740–1850*, London, 1997, pp. 53–66.

65 John Rule, 'The Misfortunes of the Mine: Coping with Life and Death in Nineteenth-century Cornwall', in Philip Payton (ed.), *Cornish Studies: Nine*, Exeter, 2001, pp. 127–44.

66 A.K. Hamilton Jenkin, *The Cornish Miner*, London, 1927, republished in Newton Abbot, 1972, p. 199.

67 L.L. Price, *'West Barbary' or Notes on the System of Work and Wages in the Cornish Mines*, London, 1891, republished in Roger Burt (ed.), *Cornish Mining: Essays on the Organisation of Cornish Mines and the Cornish Mining Economy*, Newton Abbot, 1969, pp. 154–6.

68 Jenkin, p. 198.

69 D. Bradford Barton, *A History of Tin Mining and Smelting in Cornwall*, Truro, 1967, republished Exeter, 1989, p. 148.

70 John Rowe, *Cornwall in the Age of the Industrial Revolution*, Liverpool, 1953, new edn, St Austell, 1993, p. 143.

71 *Mining Journal*, 26 March 1842.

72 *West Briton*, 15 April 1853.

73 *Royal Cornwall Gazette*, 4 March 1859.

74 Bernard Deacon, 'Attempts at Unionism by Cornish Metal Miners in 1866', *Cornish Studies* (first series), 10, 1982, pp. 27–36.

75 See Catherine Mills, *Regulating Health and Safety in the British Mining Industries, 1800–1914*, Farnham, 2010, Chapter 5, pp. 127–49.

76 Deacon, 1982, pp. 27–36.

77 See, for example, Philip Payton (ed.) and Cyril Noall, *Cornish Mine Disasters*, Redruth, 1989, p. 16.

78 John Rowe, 'The Declining Years of Cornish Tin Mining', in Jeffrey Porter (ed.), *Education and Labour in the South West: Exeter Papers in Economic History No. 10*, Exeter, 1975, p. 59.

79 Philip Payton, 'Cornish Emigration in Response to Changes in the International Copper Market in the 1860s', in Philip Payton (ed.), *Cornish Studies: Three*, Exeter, 1995, pp. 60–82.

80 *West Briton*, 4 January 1867.

81 *West Briton*, 7 May 1868.

82 *Kapunda Herald*, 13 May 1879.

83 *Kapunda Herald*, 24 June 1879, 11 July 1879.

84 *Yorke's Peninsula Advertiser*, 20 February 1877.

85 *Mining Journal*, 1 August 1874.

86 Bernard Deacon, 'Heroic Individualists? The Cornish Miners and the Five-week Month, 1872–74', *Cornish Studies* (first series), 14, 1986, pp. 39–52.

87 Gillian Burke, 'The Cornish Miner and the Cornish Mining Industry, 1870–1921', unpublished PhD thesis, University of London, 1981, p. 383.

88 Deacon, 1982, p. 34.

89 Henry Pelling, *Social Geography of British Elections 1885–1910*, London, 1962, p. 165.

90 *West Briton*, 24 September 1885; see also Bernard Deacon, 'Conybeare For Ever! Redruth and the 1885 Election', in Terry Knight (ed.), *Old Redruth: Original Studies of the Town's History*, Redruth, 1993, pp. 37–43.

91 Cited in J.P. Gabbedy, *Group Settlement, Part 1: Its Origins, Politics and Administration*, Perth (WA), 1988, pp. 202–3. I am grateful to Tony Nugent for this information.

92 John Rowe, *The Hard-Rock Men: Cornish Immigrants and the North American Mining Frontier*, Liverpool, 1974, p. 292.

93 Pelling, 1962, p. 165.

94 *Cornish Post*, 27 September 1900.

95 Tregidga, 1999, pp. 74–93.

96 Mills, 2010, p. 214.

97 Richard E. Lingenfelter, *The Hardrock Miners: A History of the Mining Labor Movement in the American West 1863–1893*, Berkeley (CA), 1974, p. 6.

98 Frederick Wolf, Bruce Finnie and Linda Gibson, 'Cornish Miners in California: 150 Years of a unique Socio-technical System', *Journal of Management History*, 14, 2, 2008, pp. 144–60; Philip Payton, *The Cornish Overseas: A History of Cornwall's 'Great Emigration'*, Fowey, 2005, pp. 219–20. For the survival of Cornish influence in the trade union movement in California's gold mines into the inter-war period, see Gage McKinney, *The 1930s: No Depression Here*, Grass Valley (Ca), 2009, pp. 449–451.

99 Lingenfelter, 1974, p. 103.

100 Ibid., p. 89.

101 Horst Rossler, 'Constantine Stonemasons in Search of Work Abroad, 1870–1900', in Payton (ed.), 2004, p. 77.

102 Richard D. Dawe, *Cornish Pioneers in South Africa: 'Gold and Diamonds, Copper and Blood'*, St Austell, 1998, p. 137, pp. 242–8.

103 The phrase 'the Cornish radical tradition' was coined in Philip Payton, 'The Cornish in South Australia: Their Influence and Experience from Immigration to Assimilation, 1836–1936', unpublished PhD thesis, University of Adelaide, 1978, p. 538; see also Philip Payton, *The Cornish Miner in Australia: Cousin Jack Down Under*, Redruth, 1984, p. 89, where it is argued that 'This tradition emerged in Cornwall in the nineteenth century and its principal elements were transferred to South Australia, where they developed in a manner reflecting the Cornish background but at the same time changing in response to new, Australian conditions'.

Chapter 3 • 1848 and All That – Antipodean Chartists?

1 An earlier version of this chapter appeared as Philip Payton, '1848 and All That: Early South Australia and the Cornish Radical Tradition', *Journal of The Historical Society of South Australia*, No. 42, 2014, pp. 17–28.

2 See Gillian Burke, 'The Cornish Diaspora in the Nineteenth Century', in Shula Marks and Peter Richardson (eds), *International Labour Migrations: Historical Perspectives*, London, 1984, pp. 57–75.

3 Robert Stephenson papers, Lily Library, Indiana University, USA; Robert Stephenson to Richard Illingworth at Bogota, 8 December 1826. Robert Stephenson was the son of the celebrated steam and railway engineer, George Stephenson.

4 D. Bradford Barton, *The Cornish Beam Engine*, Truro, 1965, republished, Vol. ll Books, Exeter, 1989, p. 252.

5 Roger Burt (ed.), George Henwood, *Cornwall's Mines and Miners*, Truro, 1972, p. 232.

6 See Philip Payton, *The Cornish Overseas: A History of Cornwall's 'Great Emigration'*, Fowey, 2005, and Philip Payton, Alston Kennerley and Helen Doe (eds), *The Maritime History of Cornwall*, Exeter, 2014, p. 240.

7 A.C. Todd, *The Search For Silver: Cornish Miners in Mexico 1824–1948*, Padstow, 1977, p. 36 and p. 42.

8 Ibid., p. 54.

9 State Library of South Australia [SLSA] 313 Passenger lists.

10 *[South Australian] Register*, 17 November 1846.

11 SLSA 94, Letters, Chiefly Commercial, to James and Robert Frew; George Fife Angas to Frew, 7 May 1846.

12 *South Australian News*, February 1847, citing *Devonport Telegraph*, 20 February 1847.

13 SLSA 313 Passenger Lists.

14 *South Australian News*, February 1847, citing *Plymouth, Devonport and Stonehouse Herald*, 23 January 1847.

15 La Trobe Library, Melbourne: Despatch: Cornwall and Devon Society to Governor Young, *Memorial as to Emigration of Cornish Miners*, Despatch No. 19, 31 January 1851.

16 SLSA BRG 22/960 *South Australian Mining Association, Directors's Letter Books*, Ayers to Von Sommer, 3 February 1846; Ayers to Burr, 20 November 1847.

17 Cited in Ian Auhl, *The Story of the 'Monster Mine': the Burra Burra Mine and its Townships 1845–1877*, Burra, 1986, p. 116.

18 *Burra Record*, 18 September 1901.

19 *Wesleyan Methodist Magazine*, combined volume, 1848, p. 1043.

20 *Register*, 3 October 1846.

21 SLSA 842m Diary of Johnson Frederick Hayward.

22 *Register*, 20 March 1847.

23 *Royal Cornwall Gazette*, 4 June 1847.

24 *West Briton*, 24 March 1848.

25 D. Bradford Barton, *A History of Tin Mining and Smelting in Cornwall*, Truro, 1965, republished Exeter, 1989, p. 86.

26 For a concise account of the Burra strike, see Mel Davies, 'Collective Action and the Cornish Miner in Australia: An Early Repudiation of the "Individualistic" Thesis', in Philip Payton (ed.), *Cornish Studies: Three*, Exeter, 1995, pp. 7–32.

27 South Australian Archives (SAA), GRG 24, series 6, *Colonial Office Correspondence*, A (1848) 1432, 15/9/1848.

28 *South Australian*, 19 September 1848.

29 *Register*, 20 September 1848.

30 Jason Shute, *Henry Ayers: The Man who became a Rock*, London, 2011, p. 23.

31 *Register*, 20 September 1848.

32 *Register*, 23 September 1848.

33 *Register*, 20 September 1848

34 *Register*, 20 September 1848.

35 E.J. Hobsbawn and George Rudé, *Captain Swing*, London, 1969, p. 130.

36 Ibid., pp. 105–6.

37 SLSA BRG 22/960, Ayers to Von Sommer, 9 January 1846.

38 *Register*, 4 October 1848.

39 Ibid.

40 *Register*, 21 October, 1848.

41 Thomas Gill, *The History and Topography of Glen Osmond*, Adelaide, 1904, republished 1974, p. 132; W. Frederick Morrison, *The Aldine History of South Australia*, Sydney and Adelaide, 1890, pp. 584–585; *Burra Record*, 22 February

1899; H.T. Burgess, *The Cyclopedia of South Australia*, 2 Vols, Adelaide, 1907, p. 556.

42   *Register*, 28 October 1848.

43   *Register*, 8 November 1848.

44   *Register*, 15 November 1848.

45   *Register*, 25 November 1848.

46   *Register*, 15 November 1848.

47   Ibid.

48   Payton, 2005, p. 199.

49   SLSA BR 22/961, *South Australian Mining Association, Letters to Burra Mines Officials (Superintendent's Letter Books)*, Ayers to Challoner, 23 December 1848.

50   Davies, 1995, p. 22.

51   *Register*, 6 June 1849.

52   *Register*, 24 January 1849.

53   *Register*, 13 December 1848.

54   *Register*, 4 November 1848.

55   *Register*, 8 November 1848.

56   *Register*, 4 October 1848.

57   W.L. Blamires and John B. Smith, *The Early Story of the Wesleyan Methodist Church in Victoria*, Melbourne, 1886, p. 211.

58   *Miscellaneous Annual Report of the Bible Christian Missionary Society Under the Direction of the Bible Christian Conference*, 1853, p. 24.

59   *Miscellaneous Annual Report of the Bible Christian Missionary Society Under the Direction of the Bible Christian Conference*, 1854, p. 24.

60   SLSA BRG 22/960, Ayers to Wilcocks, 3 November 1852.

61   Ibid., Ayers to Wilcocks, 24 December 1852.

62   Ibid., Ayers to Wilcocks, 25 January 1854; SLSA 313 Shipping Passenger Lists.

63   John Cashen, 'The Social Foundations of the South Australia: "Owners of Labour", in Eric Richards (ed.), *The Flinders History of South Australia: Social History*, Adelaide, 1986, p. 110.

64   H.R. Taylor, *The History of the Churches of Christ in South Australia, 1846–1959*, Adelaide, 1959, p. 163. George Pearce later joined the Church of Christ (Scotch Baptists).

65   According to Jim Moss in his 'South Australia's Colonial Labour Movement', *Journal of the Historical Society of South Australia*, No. 6, 1979, pp. 12–26.

66   *Register*, 2 November 1859, 5 November 1859, 30 December 1859; *People's Weekly*, 24 June 1899.

67   [*South Australian*] *Weekly Chronicle*, 22 February 1860.

68   Edwin Hodder, *The History of South Australia from its Foundation to the Year of it Jubilee*, Vol. 1, London, 1893, p. 319.

69   Moss, 1979, p. 19.

70   For a full account of this extraordinary event, see Stephanie James, 'Becoming South Australians? The Impact of the Irish on the County of Stanley, 1841–1871', unpublished MA thesis, Flinders University, 2010, pp. 182–8. I am indebted to Stephanie James for drawing my attention to this episode.

71   For a sketch of Boucaut's early political career, see P.L. Edgar, 'Sir James Penn Boucaut: His Political Life, 1861–75', unpublished BA Honours thesis, University of Adelaide, 1961.

72   *Northern Star*, 3 May 1862, 10 May 1862.

73   Philip Payton, *Making Moonta: The Invention of Australia's Little Cornwall*, Exeter, 2007, pp. 97–129.

Chapter 4 • Moonta, Wallaroo and the Rise of Trade Unionism

1   Peter Bell, 'The Power of Respectful Remonstrance: The Wallaroo and Moonta Miners' Strike of 1864', *Journal of the Historical Society of South Australia*, 1998, p. 68.

2   Ibid.

3   H.Y.L. Brown, *Records of the Mines of South Australia*, Adelaide, 1908, p. 150.

4   Oswald Pryor, *Australia's Little Cornwall*, Adelaide, 1962; Philip Payton, *Making Moonta: The Invention of 'Australia's Little Cornwall'*, Exeter, 2007.

5   Philip Payton, 'The Cornish in South Australia: Their Influence and Experience from Immigration to Assimilation, 1839–1936', unpublished PhD thesis, University of Adelaide, 1978, pp. 115–16.

6   Payton, 2007, pp. 7–9.

7   Bell, 1998, p. 56.

8   J.B. Austin, *The Mines of South Australia*, Adelaide, 1863, pp. 88–9.

9   *Yorke's Peninsula Advertiser*, 16 May 1873.

10   Bell, 1998, p. 57.

11   SLSA BRG 40/543 Moonta Mines Proprietors, Minute Books, 1861–91, 16 April 1862.

12   SLSA BRG 40/543, 16 June 1862.

13   SLSA BRG 40/543, 14 July 1862.

14   SLSA BRG 40/543, 6 October 1862.

15   SLSA BRG 40/542 Wallaroo Mines Proprietors, Minute Books, 1860–91, 1 February 1864.

16   Austin, 1863, p. 92.

17   [*South Australian*] *Advertiser*, 24 May 1862.

18   [*South Australian*] *Register*, 17 May 1862.

19   *Register*, 1 December 1862.

20   *Register*, 8 April 1862.

21 Bell, 1998, p. 59.

22 *Register*, 18 April 1864, 29 April 1864.

23 SLSA 4959 (L) Notes on Moonta and Wallaroo, by E. Major senior.

24 Ibid.

25 SLSA Dr Charles Davies, Biographies and Obituaries (27 Vols), unidentified newspaper cutting obituary dated January 1884.

26 G.E. Loyau, *Notable South Australians and Colonists – Past and Present*, Adelaide, 1885, pp. 61–2.

27 SLSA BRG 40/542, 31 March 1864.

28 *Adelaide Express*, 2 April 1864.

29 SLSA 4959 (L)

30 *Register*, 11 April 1864.

31 *West Briton*, 9 March 1866; *Cornish Times*, 10 March 1866.

32 *Register*, 8 April 1864.

33 *[Adelaide] Observer*, 2 April 1864.

34 Bell, 1998, p. 61.

35 *Wallaroo Times*, 29 June 1867; *Register*, 25 June 1880.

36 *Yorke's Peninsula Advertiser*, 21 July 1876.

37 *Register*, 15 April 1864.

38 *Register*, 29 April 1864.

39 *Register*, 7 May 1864.

40 Ibid.

41 *Bible Christian Magazine*, combined volume, 1876, p. 525.

42 James Penn Boucaut, *Letters to My Boys*, London, 1906, p. v; J.J. Pascoe, *History of Adelaide and Vicinity, with a General Sketch of the Province of South Australia and Biographies of Representative Men*, Adelaide, 1901, p. 264.

43 *Register*, 8 April 1864.

44 SLSA BRG 40/538 Moonta Mines Proprietors, Out-Letter Books, 1863–69, McCoull to A.L. Elder, 26 April 1864; McCoull to Young, 26 April 1864. See also SLSA BRG 40/543, Moonta Mines Proprietors, Minute Books 1861–91, 24 April 1864.

45 SLSA BRG 40/537 Wallaroo Mines Proprietors, Out-Letter Books 1860–70, Mair to Elder, 25 May 1868

46 SLSA 4959(L) Notes on Moonta and Wallaroo.

47 *Wallaroo Times*, 2 October 1869; Liz Coole and Jim Harbison, *Mine Captains of the Copper Triangle, Yorke Peninsula, South Australia*, Moonta, 2006; Richard D. Dawe, *Cornish Pioneers in South Africa: 'Gold and Diamonds, Copper and Blood'*, St Austell, 1998, pp. 59, 78, 234, 236, 284 and 285.

48 *Cornishman*, 28 February 1907.

49 Dawe, 1998, p. 285; see also *Cornubian*, 4 February 1909; *Cornishman*, 4 February 1909.

50 SLSA BRG 40/538, McCoull to Warmington, 27 July 1864.

51 SLSA BRG 40/538, McCoull to Young, 28 June 1864.

52 *Observer*, 18 June 1864.

53 *Register*, 1 July 1864.

54 SLSA BRG 40/543, 4 June 1864; SLSA BRG 40/538, McCoull to Young, 31 May 1864, McCoull to Trestrail, 4 June 1864, McCoull to Prisk, 8 June 1864.

55 SLSA BRG 40/537, Muir to A.L. Elder, 27 December 1866; Muir to A.L. Elder, 29 May 1867.

56 SLSA BRG 40/538, McCoull to Hancock, 4 October 1864.

57 SLSA BRG 40/538, McCoull to Hancock, 13 September 1865.

58 *Observer*, 12 May 1867.

59 SLSA BRG 40/538, McCoull to Hancock, 26 August 1867.

60 SLSA BRG 40/538, McCoull to Hancock, 26 August 1867.

61 SLSA BRG 40/538, McCoull to Hancock, 2 September 1867.

62 *Yorke's Peninsula Advertiser*, 14 April 1874.

63 *Yorke's Peninsula Advertiser*, 30 May 1873.

64 *Yorke's Peninsula Advertiser*, 8 November 1872.

65 *Australian Christian Commonwealth*, 9 May 1902.

66 John Rowe, *Cornish Methodists and Emigrants*, Camborne, 1967, p. 24.

67 *Yorke's Peninsula Advertiser*, 4 April 1876.

68 *Yorke's Peninsula Advertiser*, 2 June 1874.

69 *Northern Argus*, July 1873, cited in Nic Klaassen, *The Northern Flinders Ranges: Mountains, Minerals and Mines 1850–1920*, Adelaide, 1991, p. 147. I am indebted to Susan Pearl, manager of the Blinman Mine, for drawing my attention to this book.

70 *Yorke's Peninsula Advertiser*, 13 May 1873.

71 *Yorke's Peninsula Advertiser*, 10 October 1873.

72 *Yorke's Peninsula Advertiser*, 27 December 1872.

73 *Yorke's Peninsula Advertiser*, 26 December 1873, 30 December 1873.

74 For an important insight into health and gender issues, see Ella Stewart-Peters, 'Managing Crisis in Moonta Mines: Governance and Opposition to Biopolitical Interventions in a Cornish-South Australian Context, 1874–1875', unpublished Honours thesis, Flinders University, 2014; see also Ella Stewart-Peters, '"To Brave a Thousand Cornishmen": The Role of Cornish Identity in Opposition to Government Intervention at Moonta Mines', *Journal of the Historical Society of South Australia*, No. 43, 2015, pp. 81–91.

75 *Yorke's Peninsula Advertiser*, 10 April 1874.

76 SLSA D4876 (Misc.), The Great Strike, by W. Shelley, c.1874.

77 Payton, 2007, pp. 136–142; see also Charlotte White, 'Cousins Jack and Jenny in Phyllis Somerville's *Not Only in Stone*', in Philip Payton (ed.), *Cornish Studies: Nineteen*, Exeter, 2011, pp. 225–34.

78 Pryor, p. 37.

79 *Yorke's Peninsula Advertiser*, 10 April 1874.

80 *Yorke's Peninsula Advertiser*, 10 April 1874; see also *South Australian Register*, 8 April 1874.

81 Keith Bailey, *James Boor's Bonanza: A History of Wallaroo Mines, South Australia*, Kadina, 2002, p. 31.

82 SLSA D4876 (Misc).

83 W.G. Spence, *Australia's Awakening: Thirty Years in the Life of an Australian Agitator*, Sydney, 1909, p. 29.

84 *Barrier Miner*, 12 November 1889; see also *Pictorial Australian*, November–Christmas 1889.

85 *Pictorial Australian*, August 1892.

86 SLSA BRG40/543, 10 April 1874.

87 *Register*, 7 April 1874.

88 *Yorke's Peninsula Advertiser*, 14 April 1874.

89 SLSA BRG 40/543, 15 April 1874.

90 *Yorke's Peninsula Advertiser*, 14 April 1879.

91 *Yorke's Peninsula Advertiser*, 3 August 1877.

92 *Register*, 4 August 1874; *Yorke's Peninsula Advertiser*, 28 April 1874.

93 *Yorke's Peninsula Advertiser*, 14 August 1874, 31 March 1876, 9 September 1879.

94 *Yorke's Peninsula Advertiser*, 5 July 1878.

95 *Yorke's Peninsula Advertiser*, 25 February 1876.

96 *Yorke's Peninsula Advertiser*, 25 February 1876.

97 *Yorke's Peninsula Advertiser*, 20 February 1877.

98 *Yorke's Peninsula Advertiser*, 28 April 1874.

99 *Yorke's Peninsula Advertiser*, 21 April 1874.

100 *Yorke's Peninsula Advertiser*, 17 April 1874, 19 May 1874.

101 SLSA 98u, Boucaut Papers (Miscellaneous).

102 Arnold Caldicott, *The Verco Story: Hopes We Live By*, Adelaide, 1970, p. 165. For further details of Boucaut's early political career, see P.L. Edgar, 'Sir James Penn Boucaut: His Political Life, 1861–75', unpublished Honours thesis, University of Adelaide, 1961.

103 SLSA 97/379 Boucaut Papers (Political), Boucaut to McArthur, 18 September 1874.

104 SLSA 93/379, Boucaut to McArthur, 28 August 1874.

105 SLSA 93/379, Boucaut to McArthur, 28 August 1874.

106 SLSA 93/379, Boucaut to McArthur, 28 August 1874.

107 *Yorke's Peninsula Advertiser*, 12 May 1874, 5 May 1874.

108 *Register*, 5 August 1874.

109 SLSA BRG 40/543, 3 May 1875, 7 February 1876.

110 SLSA BRG 40/543, 8 June 1874, 15 June 1874, 13 July 1874, 7 August 1874; SLSA BRG 40.452, 14 July 1874.

111 SLSA D3627 (L), An Autobiography, by Stanley R. Whitford, p. 400.

112 SLSA BRG 40/543, 18 August 1874, 25 August 1874, 2 November 1874.

113 SLSA BRG 40/543, 21 September 1874.

114 *Yorke's Peninsula Advertiser*, 10 November 1874.

115 *Yorke's Peninsula Advertiser*, 31 March 1876.

116 *Yorke's Peninsula Advertiser*, 9 September 1879.

117 *Yorke's Peninsula Advertiser*, 20 February 1877, 6 June 1882; SLSA BRG 40/543, 27 February 1865, 5 March 1866, 12 August 1889.

118 *Yorke's Peninsula Advertiser*, 24 April 1880.

119 *Yorke's Peninsula Advertiser*, 8 January 1878.

120 *Yorke's Peninsula Advertiser*, 25 January 1878, 22 February 1889.

121 *Yorke's Peninsula Advertiser*, 1 June 1877; SLSA BRG 40/543, 7 December 1885, 29 February 1888, 1 March 1888, 2 March 1888, 5 March 1888.

122 *Advertiser* (Adelaide), 3 March 1888.

123 Pryor, 1962, p. 120.

124 SLSA BRG 40/543, 11 March 1889.

125 Spence, 1903, p. 27.

126 *Argus* (Melbourne), 15 May 1889.

127 Spence, 1903, p. 30.

128 Ibid., p. 31.

129 Ibid., pp. 30–1.

130 Ibid., p. 29.

131 *Argus* (Melbourne), 30 May 1889, 4 June 1889.

132 Spence, 1903, p. 30.

133 Ibid.

134 Pryor, 1962, p. 116, p. 120.

135 SAA BRG 40/543, 29 July 1889, 12 August 1889, 9 December 1889, 16 December 1889; *Register*, 30 July 1891, 20 August 1891, 18 September 1891, 23 September 1891, 28 September 1891, 29 September 1891, 30 September 1891.

136 *Register*, 28 October 1891, 14 January 1892; *People's Weekly* (Moonta), 10 October 1891, 21 October 1891, 14 November 1891, 28 November 1891, 12 December 1891, 28 December 1891, 30 January 1892.

137 SLSA D3627 (L), p. 118.

138 *South Australian Department of Mines Mining Review*, half-year ended December 1919, p. 12.

139 *People's Weekly*, 20 March 1895.

Chapter 5 • Towards Parliamentary Representation

1   Richard Cox, 'Social Democracy: A Study of the Dunstan Government', Flinders University unpublished PhD thesis, 1979, p. 154.

2   John B. Hirst, *Adelaide and the Country, 1870–1917: Their Social and Political Relationship*, Melbourne, 1973, p. 155.

3   R.J. Holton, 'Twentieth Century South Australia: From a Patrician to a Plebeian View', in Eric Richards (ed.), *The Flinders History of South Australia: Social History*, Adelaide, 1986, pp. 553–4.

4   See Geoffrey Blainey, *The Rush That Never Ended: A History of Australian Mining*, Melbourne, 1963, especially Chapters 10 and 11.

5   Brian Dickey, 'South Australia', in *Labor in Politics: The State Labor Parties in Australia 1880–1920*, St Lucia, 1975, p. 232.

6   Oswald Pryor, *Australia's Little Cornwall*, Adelaide, 1962.

7   Holton, 1986, p. 551.

8   Hirst, 1973, p. 155.

9   Dickey, 1975, p. 231.

10 *Yorke's Peninsula Advertiser*, 27 November 1885.

11 Anon, *The Barrier Silver and Tin Fields in 1888*, Adelaide, 1888, p. 5.

12 *People's Weekly*, 16 December 1893.

13 *People's Weekly*, 23 December 1893.

14 SLSA BRG 40/1034, Wallaroo and Moonta Mining and Smelting Company, Minute Books 1895–1923, 22 October 1895.

15 Brian Kennedy, *Silver, Sin and Sixpenny Ale: A Social History of Broken Hill, 1883–1921*, Melbourne, 1978, p. 48.

16 Anon, 1885, p. 9.

17 Kennedy, 1978, p. 20.

18 Ibid., p. 53.

19 Ibid., p. 57.

20 Ibid., p. 56.

21 Ibid.

22 Ibid.

23 *Barrier Truth*, 6 April 1900, 1 June 1900.

24 *Barrier Truth*, 20 December 1901.

25 *Socialist*, 18 January 1908.

26 *Observer*, 28 March 1908.

27 Kennedy, 1978, p. 143.

28 Cox, 1979, p. 154.

29 Roy Hattersley, 'Foreword', in Elizabeth Durbin, *New Jerusalems: The Labour Party and the Economics of Democratic Socialism*, London, 1985, p. xi.

30 *Yorke's Peninsula Advertiser*, 6 May 1887.

31 *Burra Record*, 2 March 1892.

32 *Yorke's Peninsula Advertiser*, 19 March 1889, 29 November 1889.

33 *People's Weekly*, 9 October 1890.

34 Kennedy, 1978, p. 53.

35 *People's Weekly*, 16 July 1892.

36 Kennedy, 1978, p. 66.

37 Ibid., p. 70.

38 Charles Rasp Library (Broken Hill), Amalgamated Society of Engineers, Broken Hill Branch, Minute Books 1891–1896, 1 November 1892; *Burra Record*, 21 September 1892.

39 *Yorke's Peninsula Advertiser*, 13 March 1876.

40 *Yorke's Peninsula Advertiser*, 12 February 1875, 16 February 1875.

41 *Yorke's Peninsula Advertiser*, 28 October 1881; Howard Coxon, John Playford and Robert Reid (eds), *Biographical Register of the South Australian Parliament 1857–1957*, Adelaide, 1985, p. 189.

42 Coxon et al. (eds), 1985, p. 15; *Advertiser* (Adelaide), 2 June 1917.

43 *People's Weekly*, 21 March 1891, 16 May 1891, 30 May 1891; Coxon et al. (eds), 1985, pp. 111–12.

44 Pryor, 1962, p. 125.

45 Hirst, 1973, p. 154; see also L.E. Kiek, 'The History of the South Australian Labour Unions', unpublished MA thesis, University of Adelaide, 1948.

46 *Register*, 1 September 1886.

47 *Advertiser*, 11 May 1890; for a full discussion of the ensuing strike see K.R. Bowes, 'The 1890 Maritime Strike in South Australia', unpublished MA thesis, University of Adelaide, 1957.

48 *Advertiser*, 12 June 1890.

49 *Advertiser*, 25 July 1890.

50 Bruce Scates, 'Gender, Household and Community Politics: The 1890 Maritime Strike in Australia and New Zealand', *Labour History*, No. 61, November 1991.

51 *Advertiser*, 25 July 1890.

52 Ibid.

53 Ibid.

54 *Advertiser*, 6 September 1890.

55 *Advertiser*, 1 October 1890.

56 Ibid.

57 Robin Walker, 'The Maritime Strikes in South Australia, 1887–1890', *Labor History*, No. 14, May 1968.

58 Nick Dyrenfurth, *Heroes and Villains: The Rise and Fall of the Early Australian Labor Party*, Melbourne, 2011, p. 53; see also SLSA 1347 m, History of the S.A. Labor Party 1882–1900, by F.S. Wallis; and J. Ian Craig, 'A History of the South Australian Labour Party to 1917', unpublished MA thesis, University of Adelaide, 1940.

59 Dean Jaensch, 'Party, Party System and Federation: 1890–1912', in Dean Jaensch (ed.), *The Flinders History of South Australia: Political History*, Adelaide, 1986, p. 180.

60 Jim Moss, *The Sound of Trumpets: History of the Labour Movement in South Australia*, Adelaide, 1985, citing United Trades & Labor Council, Minutes, 12 December 1890, 9 January 1891, 20 February 1891. UTLC Minutes are on Microfilm M15, Australian National University Archives.

61 Moss, 1985, pp. 164–5.

62 Dickey, 1975, p. 238.

63 Ibid., p. 240.

64 Dean H. Jaensch, 'Political Representation in Colonial South Australia', unpublished PhD thesis, University of Adelaide, 1973, p. 597.

65 Ibid., p. 593.

66 Michael Davitt, *Life and Progress in Australasia*, London, 1898, p. 53.

67 Janet Scarfe, 'The Labour Wedge: The First Six Labour Members of the South Australian Legislative Council', unpublished Honours thesis, University of Adelaide, 1968.

68 Ross McMullin, *The Light on The Hill: The Australian Labor Party 1891–1991*, Melbourne, 1991, p. 8.

69 Unidentified edition of the *Cornishman* in 1919, republished in pamphlet form by the Cornish Association of South Australia, Adelaide, c. 1920.

70 *Observer*, 16 May 1891; *Christian Weekly and Methodist Journal*, 5 September 1890.

71 *Register*, 10 April 1890.

72 *Cornishman*, 1919.

73 D.M. Charleston, *Universal Depression: Its Cause and Cure*, Adelaide, 1895, p. 1; D.M. Charleston, *New Unionism*, Adelaide, 1890, p. 1.

74 Charleston, 1890, p. 5.; see also D.M. Charleston, *What is Sociology?*, Adelaide, n.d..

75 D.M. Charleston, *Address to the Electors of Port Adelaide*, Adelaide, 1906.

76 *Observer*, 21 August 1897.

77 Dickey, 1975, p. 232.

78 *Age* (Melbourne), 21 January 1921; *Westralian Worker*, 4 February 1921; Peter Cook, 'Guthrie, Robert Storrie (1857–1921)', *Australian Dictionary of Biography*,

National Centre of Biography, Australian National University, http://adb.anu. edu.au/biography/guthrie-robert-storrie-6510/text11173, published first in hard copy (Melbourne, 1983), accessed 25 February 2015.

79   E.J. Prest, *Sir John Langdon Bonython: Newspaper Proprietor, Politician and Philanthropist*, Melbourne, 2011, p. 10.

80   Dean Jaensch, 'Kirkpatrick, Andrew Alexander (1848–1928)', *Australian Dictionary of Biography*, National Centre for Biography, Australian National University, http://adb.anu.edu.au/biography/kirkpatrick-andrew-alexander-6973/text12115, published first in hard copy (Melbourne, 1983), accessed 25 February 2015.

81   *Observer*, 28 January 1893.

82   For a concise explanation of the development of party politics in South Australia, see Jaensch, 1986.

83   Dickey, 1975, p. 245.

84   *Observer*, 10 February 1894.

85   John Hirst, *Sense and Nonsense in Australian History*, Melbourne, 2006, p. 2.

86   Ian Craig, 'A History of the South Australian Labour Party to 1917', unpublished MA thesis, University of Adelaide, 1940, p. 53.

87   R. Norris, 'Economic Influences on the 1898 South Australian Federation Referendum', in A.W. Martin (ed.), *Essays in Australian Federation*, Melbourne, 1969, p. 150.

88   Don Dunstan, *Felicia: The Political Memoirs of Don Dunstan*, Melbourne, 1981, p. 9

89   Dickey, 1975, p. 234

90   Eric Glenie Bonython, *History of the Families of Bonython of Bonython and Bonython of Carclew in the Duchy of Cornwall*, Adelaide, 1966, p. 108.

91   *Advertiser*, 17 February 1893.

92   *Register*, 7 March 1887 and 11 March 1887; see also Prest, 2011, p. 87.

93   John McConnell Black, *Memoirs*, Adelaide, 1971, p. 70.

94   Prest, 2011, p. 31.

95   *Commercial, Shipping and General Advertiser for West Cornwall*, 5 April 1890.

96   SLSA 552, Draft of First Hustings Speech, By John George Bice, March 1894.

97   *South Australian Parliamentary Debates (Hansard) (SAPD)*, September 1893.

98   *Register*, 8 June 1926.

99   *Southern Cross*, 21 April 1899.

100 Dickey, 1975, p. 250.

Chapter 6 • Labor in Power – Tom Price and John Verran

1   T.H. Smeaton, *From Stone Cutter to Premier and Minister of Education: The Story of the Life of Tom Price, a Welsh Boy Who Became an Australian Statesman*, Adelaide, 1926, p. 222.

2   *Herald*, 1 March 1902. See also Stephanie McCarthy, *Tom Price: From Stonecutter to Premier*, Adelaide, 2015, p. 25. I am deeply indebted to Stephanie McCarthy for her generous permission to draw from her book and to use newspaper and other original sources that she has discovered during her extensive research for Tom Price's biography.

3   *Advertiser*, I June 1909.

4   McCarthy, 2015, p. 27.

5   Smeaton, 1926, p. 31 and pp. 144–5.

6   McCarthy, 2015, p. 59.

7   Smeaton, 1926, p. 61.

8   Nick Dyrenfurth, *Heroes and Villains: The Rise and Fall of the Early Australian Labor Party*, Melbourne, 2011, p. 61.

9   Fabian Society of South Australia, *Tracts No. 1: What Socialism Is – The Effects of Unsocialism*, Adelaide, c.1891, p. 3; see also Dyrenfurth, 2011, p. 61.

10 *South Australian Parliamentary Debates (Hansard) (SAPD)*, 1893, p. 1514; see also McCarthy, 2015, p. 70 and pp. 76–81 for Price's support of the Murray scheme.

11 Michael Davitt, *Life and Progress in Australasia*, London, 1898, p. 95.

12 McCarthy, 2015, p. 81.

13 McCarthy, 2015, pp. 96–98.

14 *Weekly Herald*, 18 March 1895.

15 McCarthy, 2015, pp. 91–106.

16 Smeaton, 1926, p. 82.

17 McCarthy, p. 129.

18 *Weekly Herald*, 12 March 1898.

19 *Herald*, 18 March 1898.

20 Smeaton, 1926, pp. 78–9.

21 *Herald*, 23 March 1901; see also McCarthy, 2015, p. 186.

22 State Library of South Australia (SLSA) PRG 979/3, Miscellaneous Correspondence from Sir John Langdon Bonython, 1897–1932, Bonython to Cockburn, 14 March 1901; see also E.J. Prest, *Sir John Langdon Bonython: Newspaper Proprietor, Politician and Philanthropist*, Melbourne, 2011, p. 113.

23 *Herald*, 18 May 1901.

24 *SAPD*, 1903, p. 758.

25 Quoted in Jim Moss, *Sound of Trumpets: History of the Labour Movement in South Australia*, Adelaide, 1985, p. 210.

26 *SAPD*, 1901, p. 59.

27 *Herald*, 17 May 1902.

28 Cited in Dean Jaensch, 'Party, Party System and Federation: 1890–1912', in Dean Jaensch (ed.), *The Flinders History of South Australia: Political History*, Adelaide, 1986, p. 197.

29 *Herald*, 26 April 1902.

30 McCarthy, 2015, p. 213,

31 ULP Minutes, 24 September 1903; see Brian Dickey, 'South Australia', in D.J. Murphy (ed.), *Labor in Politics: The State Labor Parties in Australia: 1880–1920*, St Lucia, 1975, p. 253.

32 *Herald*, 26 March 1904.

33 *Herald*, 14 June 1902.

34 Dickey, 1975, p. 253–5.

35 *Advertiser*, 2 May 1904.

36 Jaensch, 1986, p. 201.

37 *Advertiser*, 5 July 1904.

38 *Herald*, 17 May 1902.

39 Jaensch, 1985, p. 203.

40 Dickey, 1975, pp. 255–6.

41 R. Daunton Fear, 'Sir Richard Butler: A Study in Political Stance 1890–1921', unpublished BA Hons thesis, Flinders University, 1970.

42 *Herald*, 26 April 1905.

43 *Herald*, 28 May 1904.

44 McCarthy, 2015, p. 253.

45 *Herald*, 8 April 1905.

46 *Weekly Herald*, 29 July 1905.

47 Moss, 1985, p. 211.

48 Dickey, 1975, p. 258.

49 Ibid.

50 *Herald*, 2 December 1905.

51 Jaensch, 1986, p. 203.

52 Ibid., p. 204.

53 Dickey, 1975, p. 259.

54 Moss, 1985, p. 214.

55 Dickey, 1975, p. 259.

56 J. B. Hirst, *Adelaide and the Country 1870–1917: Their Social and Political Relationship*, Melbourne, 1973, p. 198.

57 Elizabeth Kwan, 'Williams, Alfred (1863–1913)', Australian Dictionary of Biography, National Centre for Biography, Australian National University, http://adb.anu.edu.au.biography/Williams-alfred-9107/text16059, published

first in hard copy 1990, accessed online 24 September 2015; see also Hedley Beare, 'The Influence of Alfred Williams, and the Price Ministry, on Public Education in South Australia', unpublished MEd thesis, University of Melbourne, 1964; and Colin Thiele and Ron Gibbs, *Grains of Mustard Seed*, Adelaide, 1975, p. 77.

58   Hirst, 1973, p. 198.

59   McCarthy, 2015, p. 355.

60   *Advertiser*, 1 June 1909; cited in Dickey, 1975, p. 261.

61   John McConnell Black, *Memoirs*, Adelaide, 1971, p. 66.

62   *Advertiser*, 21 June 1910.

63   *Kadina and Wallaroo Times*, 6 April 1889.

64   *People's Weekly*, 8 April 1899.

65   Oswald Pryor, *Australia's Little Cornwall*, Adelaide, 1962, p. 128.

66   Ella Stewart-Peters, ' "To Brave a Thousand Cornishmen": The Role of Cornish identity in Opposition to Government Intervention at Moonta Mines', *Journal of the Historical Society of South Australia*, No. 43, 2015, pp. 81–91.

67   *People's Weekly*, 3 April 1897.

68   *People's Weekly*, 16 September 1922.

69   *Westralian Worker*, 9 June 1911.

70   *Methodist*, 18 June 1910.

71   *Plain Dealer*, 11 March 1911.

72   *People's Weekly*, 17 May 1910; see also, for example, *Observer*, 14 May 1910; *Methodist*, 11 June 1910.

73   Ibid.

74   *People's Weekly*, 18 May 1917.

75   *People's Weekly*, 21 May 1904.

76   *Barrier Miner*, 3 June 1910.

77   *Methodist*, 11 June 1910.

78   R.J. Miller, 'The Fall of the Verran Government, 1911–12: The most determined attempt to abolish the Legislative Council of Australia, and its Failure', unpublished BA Hons thesis, University of Adelaide, 1975.

79   *Weekly Herald*, 12 June 1909.

80   *Critic*, 23 March 1910.

81   *Daily Herald*, 7 March 1910.

82   *Advertiser*, 31 October 1919.

83   *Methodist*, 22 October 1910.

84   Ross McMullin, *The Light on the Hill: The Australian Labor Party 1891–1991*, Oxford, 1991, new edn 1992, p. 69.

85   *Methodist*, 18 June 1910; *Register*, 3 June 1910.

86   *Register*, 3 June 1910.

87 *Methodist*, 22 October 1910.

88 Cited in *Observer*, 14 May 1910.

89 *Register*, 3 June 1910.

90 *Observer*, 14 May 1910.

91 *Register*, 21 June 1910.

92 SLSA PRG96, Oswald Pryor Papers, Scrapbook: Electorate of Wallaroo, John Verran etc, unidentified cutting from *Kadina and Wallaroo Times* (c. June 1910).

93 *People's Weekly*, 25 June 1910.

94 Pryor, 1960, pp. 129–30.

95 T.H. Smeaton, *The People in Politics: A Short History of the Labor Movement in South Australia, 1891–1914*, Adelaide, 1914, p. 17.

96 Jaensch, 1986, pp. 210–11.

97 J.J. Craig, 'History of the South Australian Labor Party to 1917', unpublished BA Hons thesis, University of Adelaide, 1940, pp. 101–2.

98 *Register*, 2 September 1910.

99 *Daily Herald*, 6 October 1910.

100 *International Socialist*, 10 September 1910.

101 Dickey, 1975, p. 265.

102 *Kadina and Wallaroo Times*, 15 October 1910.

103 Ibid.; *Advertiser*, 11 October 1910.

104 *Advertiser*, 24 October 1910.

105 *International Socialist*, 22 October 1910.

106 *Daily Herald*, 12 December 1910.

107 McConnell Black, 1971, p. 66.

108 *Advertiser*, 2 March 1910; see also Bernard O'Neil, *In Search of Mineral Wealth: The South Australian Geological Survey and Department of Mines to 1944*, Adelaide, 1982, p. 162.

109 *People's Weekly*, 3 August 1910.

110 *Kadina and Wallaroo Times*, 1 November 1911.

111 *Daily Herald*, 26 April 1911, 18 My 1912; *Register*, 6 May 1911.

112 *Kadina and Wallaroo Times*, 13 May 1911.

113 *Daily Herald*, 20 February 1912.

114 Miller, 1965, p. 24.

115 Cited in G.D. Combe, *Responsible Government in South Australia, Volume One, From the Foundations to Playford*, Adelaide, 1957, new edn 2009, p. 145.

116 Ibid., p. 146.

117 SLSA PRG22 Coneybeer Papers, Ser. 24, Vol. 13, p. 9; see also *A Letter from Ramsay MacDonald to the Premier of South Australia The Hon John Verran*, Mosman (NSW), 1970.

118   Combe, 2009, p. 146.

119   *People's Weekly*, 20 January 1912.

120   *Liberal Union*, 1 February 1912.

121   *People's Weekly*, 17 February 1912.

122   *Australian Christian Commonwealth*, 16 February 1912.

123   *Australian Christian Commonwealth*, 1 November 1911.

124   *People's Weekly*, 20 January 1912.

125   *People's Weekly*, 26 July 1913.

126   *People's Weekly*, 23 May 1914.

127   *People's Weekly*, 30 May 1914.

128   Unidentified cutting from the *Advertiser* newspaper, c. 1985–6, courtesy of Liz Coole.

129   *People's Weekly*, 9 September 1916, 27 October 1917, 5 October 1918.

130   *People's Weekly*, 11 November 1922.

Chapter 7 • Labor and the Conscription Crisis

1   Dean Jaensch, 'Stability and Change, 1910–1939', in Dean Jaensch (ed.), *The Flinders History of South Australia: Political History*, Adelaide, 1986, p. 229.

2   *Daily Herald*, 14 October 1913.

3   Brian Dickey, 'South Australia', in D.J. Murphy (ed.), *Labor in Politics: The State Labor Parties in Australia 1880–1920*, St Lucia, 1975, p. 269.

4   Ibid., pp. 269–70.

5   Marnie Haig-Muir, 'The Economy at War', in Joan Beaumont (ed.), *Australia at War, 1914–18*, St Leonards (NSW), 1995, p. 107.

6   *People's Weekly*, 8 August 1914.

7   Keith Bailey, *James Boor's Bonanza: A History of Wallaroo Mines, South Australia*, Kadina, 2002, pp. 134–7.

8   *Yorke's Peninsula Advertiser*, 27 November 1914.

9   Haig-Muir, 1995, p. 103.

10   *Register*, 4 August 1914.

11   Philip Payton, *Making Moonta: The Invention of Australia's Little Cornwall*, Exeter, 2007, p. 181.

12   This chapter draws extensively on Chapter 6 'Conscription' in Philip Payton, *Regional Australia and the Great War: 'The Boys from Old Kio'*, Exeter, 2012; and Chapter 7 'Trouble at Home: The Conscription Crisis', in Philip Payton, *Australia in the Great War*, London, 2015.

13   Bailey, 2002, p. 136.

14   *Yorke's Peninsula Advertiser*, 16 April 1915.

15   Geoffrey Blainey, *The Rush That Never Ended: A History of Australian Mining*,
      Melbourne, 1963, republished 1969, pp. 278–80; Geoffrey Blainey, *The Rise of
      Broken Hill*, Melbourne, 1968, p. 79–80.

16   ULP Minutes, 1914–19; cited in Dickey, 1975, p. 272.

17   *Australian Worker*, 3 August 1916.

18   J.M. Stock, 'The 1916 Conscription Referendum in the Rural Areas of South
      Australia', unpublished PhD thesis, Flinders University, 1978, p. 111.

19   Jim Moss, *Sound of Trumpets: History of the Labour Movement in South Australia*,
      Adelaide, 1985, p. 242.

20   John McQuilton, *Rural Australia and the Great War: From Tarrawingee to
      Tangambalanga*, Melbourne, 2001, pp. 54–60, discusses the regional dimension
      of the conscription debate in north-eastern Victoria.

21   Ibid., pp. 23–4; for a general survey of the conscription crisis see P.M. Gibson,
      'The Conscription Issue in South Australia', unpublished BA Hons thesis,
      University of Adelaide, 1965.

22   UTLC Minutes, 30 June 1916; cited in Dickey, 1975, p. 273.

23   Cited in Joan Beaumont, 'The Politics of a Divided Society', in Beaumont (ed.),
      1995, p. 44.

24   L.L. Robson, *Australia and the Great War*, Melbourne, 1969, p. 15.

25   Stock, 1978, p. 25. For examples of acrimonious meetings on northern Yorke
      Peninsula, see *Advertiser*, 12 October 1916, 17 October 1917; *Plain Dealer*,
      27 October 1917.

26   Bailey, 2002, pp. 140–1.

27   Ibid., p. 141.

28   Ibid.

29   Payton, 2012, pp. 36–7.

30   *Advertiser*, 17 October 1916; see also Stock, 1978, p. 27.

31   H. Lipson Hancock, 'Welfare Work in the Mining Industry', *Australian Chemical
      Engineering and Mining Review*, October 1918; *South Australian Department of
      Mines Mining Review*, Half Year Ended June 1919.

32   *South Australian Department of Mines Mining Review*, Half Year Ended June 1919,
      pp. 53–4.

33   H. Lipson Hancock and William Shaw, *A Sunday School of Today*, Adelaide, 1912.

34   H. Lipson Hancock and William Penhall, *The Missionary Spirit in Sunday School
      Work*, Adelaide, 1918.

35   H. Lipson Hancock, *Modern Methods in Sunday School Work*, Adelaide, 1916,
      p. 20.

36   H. Lipson Hancock, *A Digest of Reports: Read at the Half-Yearly Meeting of Officers
      and Teachers of the Above School, August 18th 1913, with other Recent Records*,
      Moonta Mines, 1914.

37 H. Lipson Hancock, *The Rainbow Course of Bible Study*, Adelaide, 1919, p. 7.

38 Hancock, 1914, p. 98.

39 Hancock, 1916, pp. 20–1.

40 *Yorke's Peninsula Advertiser*, 18 May 1877.

41 A.D. Hunt, *Methodism Militant: Attitudes to the Great War*, Adelaide, 1975, p. 11; *Australian Christian Commonwealth*, 3 December 1915.

42 *Australian Christian Commonwealth*, 7 April 1916.

43 *Australian Christian Commonwealth*, 27 October 1916.

44 *Australian Christian Commonwealth*, 1 November 1911; see Ross McMullin, *The Light on the Hill: The Australian Labor Party 1891–1991*, Oxford, 1991, republished 1992, p. 31 and p. 78.

45 *Australian Christian Commonwealth*, 5 May 1916.

46 *Australian Christian Commonwealth*, 26 May 1916.

47 See *Daily Herald*, 6 November 1916, 7 November 1918, 8 November 1918, 11 November 1918, 13 November 1918.

48 *Daily Herald*, 4 September 1916.

49 Cited in Gibson, 1965, p. 9.

50 Cited in Dickey, 1975, p. 274.

51 *People's Weekly*, 29 April 1916.

52 SLSA D3627(L) Stanley R. Whitford, 'An Autobiography', unpublished MS, 1956, p. 352.

53 Ibid., pp. 478, 401, 399.

54 A.D. Hunt, *This Side of Heaven: A History of Methodism in South Australia*, 1985, p. 290.

55 Ibid., p. 291.

56 Ibid.

57 J.R. Robertson, 'The Scaddan Government and the Conscription Crisis 1911–1917', unpublished MA thesis, University of Western Australia, 1958.

58 J.R. Robertson, 'Scaddan, John (1876–1934', *Australian Dictionary of Biography*, Australian National University, http://adb.anu.edu.au/biography/scadden-john-8348/text14651, first published in hard-copy 1988, accessed on-line 25 October 2015.

59 *Kadina and Wallaroo Times*, 2 April 1913.

60 Cited in Bobbie Oliver, *War and Peace in Western Australia: The Social and Political Impact of the Great War 1914–1926*, Nedlands, 1995, p. 111.

61 Retrospective article in *People's Weekly*, 19 May 1917.

62 *Yorke's Peninsula Advertiser*, 18 May 1917.

63 Ibid.; *People's Weekly*, 19 May 1917.

64 Richard Williams, *These Are Facts: The Autobiography of Air Marshal Sir Richard Williams, KBE, CB, DSO*, Canberra, 1977, p. 4.

65 *People's Weekly*, 10 June 1933.

66 *Australian Christian Commonwealth*, 14 November 1902.

67 *Royal Cornwall Gazette*, 29 December 1892.

68 Gordon Rowe, 'The Moonta Story', 1961, unpublished MS in the author's collection – my thanks to Liz Coole for the donation of her copy.

69 Howard Coxon, John Playford and Robert Reid, *Biographical Register of the South Australian Parliament 1857–1957*, Adelaide, 1985, p. 101.

70 National Trust of South Australia, Moonta Branch Archives (NTSAMBA), '" In the Best of Spirits": The Letters and Diaries of Signaller Lance Corporal Leonard John Harvey No. 1029 of the 43rd Battalion A.I.F. to his Parents and Family in South Australia during the First World War when he served Overseas in England and France between 1916 and 1919', unpublished MS compiled by Rob and Carol Howard, Elizabeth M. Scott, Diana Kay Arula, and John Campbell Harvey, n.d.; Letter, 27 August 1916.

71 Ibid., Letter, 10 September 1916.

72 Ibid., Letter, 1 October 1916.

73 Ibid., Letter, 4 December 1916.

74 Ibid., Letter, 5 January 1917.

75 Dickey, 1975, p. 275; see also *Daily Herald*, 12 February 1917.

76 Dickey, 1975, p. 275.

77 *People's Weekly*, 21 October 1916, 21 April 1917.

78 *Australian Christian Commonwealth*, 7 December 1917.

79 *Australian Christian Commonwealth*, 19 July 1918.

80 *Australian Christian Commonwealth*, 23 November 1917.

81 Bailey, 2002, p. 141.

82 *People's Weekly*, 15 September 1917.

83 Donald J. Hopgood, 'Richards, Robert Stanley (1885–1967)', *Australian Dictionary of Biography*, National Centre for Biography, Australian National University, http://adb.edu.au/biography/richards-obert-stanley-8195/text14335, first published in hard-copy 1988, accessed online 30 September 2015.

84 I am grateful for the insights into this period provided by the late Jan Thomas of Moonta Mines.

85 *People's Weekly*, 5 April 1918.

86 *People's Weekly*, 18 June 1921.

87 Rowe, 1961, p. 94.

88 Bailey, 2002, p. 146.

89 *Yorke's Peninsula Advertiser*, 27 April 1917.

90 *Yorke's Peninsula Advertiser*, 11 May 1917.

91 *Yorke's Peninsula Advertiser*, 14 December 1917.

92   Ibid.

93   Ibid.

94   NTSAMBA, 'In the Best of Health and Spirits'; Letter, 11 April 1917.

95   Ibid., Letter, 25 April 1917.

96   Ibid., Letter, 1 October 1917.

97   Ibid., Letter, 21 January 1918.

98   Rowe, 1961, p. 98.

99   Dickey, 1975, p. 278

100 *People's Weekly*, 27 April 1918. Curiously, Verran did not mention his *Advances for Homes Act* (1910), a truly pioneering piece of legislation. See D. Kilner, 'The Evolution of South Australian Urban Housing Policy 1836–1937', unpublished PhD thesis, University of Adelaide, 1988.

101 Ibid.

102 *People's Weekly*, 18 August 1914.

103 *People's Weekly*, 8 April 1916.

104 *Register*, 21 February 1916.

105 *South Australian Parliamentary Debates (Hansard) (SAPD)*, 1916, p. 1095.

106 Ibid., p. 1094.

107 Cited in Stock, 1978, p. 266.

108 *People's Weekly*, 18 August 1917.

109 *People's Weekly*, 16 August 1919.

110 *People's Weekly*, 29 March 1919.

111 *People's Weekly*, 14 June 1919.

112 *People's Weekly*, 29 March 1919.

113 *People's Weekly*, 15 March 1924.

114 *People's Weekly*, 29 April 1922.

115 *People's Weekly*, 29 April 1922.

116 *People's Weekly*, 11 November 1922.

117 *People's Weekly*, 2 July 1927.

118 *People's Weekly*, 11 November 1922.

119 An amusing example of John Verran's propensity to fall out with others appears in Keith Bailey, *Copper City Chronicle: A History of Kadina*, Kadina, 1990, p. 189. As Bailey explains, the *Kadina and Wallaroo Times* was edited between 1908 and 1913 by Reuben Rose. An ordained Congregationalist minister, Rose had decided he could best serve the community as a layman. In an editorial in June 1910 he criticised aspects of John Verran's triumphant return to the Wallaroo constituency as newly appointed Premier. Verran retorted that 'the paper is a rag – it is edited by a broken down parson'. Suitably enraged, Rose replied in a further editorial:

Mr Verran was of the opinion that he could discount the force of the article by belittling the writer. For about 15 years the present occupant of the editorial chair of this newspaper was what the Premier terms a 'parson' in active service. We, however, deny the statement that he is a 'broken down parson', either in health, mind, pocket or ministerial status. His name still appears in the official records of the body of which he is a recognised minister, and he holds credentials and testimonials as to his character and ability, of which he has no reason to be ashamed.

We are of the opinion that, had he through misfortune, mental or moral weakness drifted into that state which would give grounds for saying that he was 'broken down', it would have been more in keeping with the Premier's claim to be an uplifter of humanity, to have come to his assistance rather than refer to him in a sneering manner.

We are, however, thankful that we do not need Mr Verran's sympathy, and the fact that we have his ill will does not trouble us at all.

Chapter 8 • Between the Wars

1   ULP Minutes, 13 September 1917, cited in Brian Dickey, 'South Australia', in D.J. Murphy (ed.), *Labor in Politics: The State Labor Parties in Australia 1880–1920*, St Lucia, 1975, p. 277.

2   Norman J.O. Makin, *A Progressive Democracy: A Record of Reference concerning the South Australian Branch of the Australian Labor Party in Politics*, Adelaide, 1918, p. iv.

3   Jim Moss, *Sound of Trumpets: History of the Labor Movement of South Australia*, Adelaide, 1985, p. 251.

4   Makin, 1918, p. 4 and p. 5.

5   Ibid., pp. 7–8.

6   Ibid., p. 79.

7   Ibid., p. 73.

8   Ibid., p. 74.

9   Ibid., p. 69.

10   Ibid.

11   Ibid., p. 9.

12   Ibid., pp. 33–4.

13   Ibid., p. 82.

14   *Register*, 18 September 1919; see also Dickey, 1975, p. 279.

15   John Lonie, 'Conservatism and Class in South Australia during the Depression Years, 1924–1934', unpublished MA thesis, University of Adelaide, 1973, p. 335.

16   Keith Bailey, *James Boor's Bonanza: A History of Wallaroo Mines, South Australia*, Kadina, 2002, p. 157.

17   Ibid., p. 155.

18   Ibid.

19   *People's Weekly*, 29 April 1922.

20   Bailey, 2002, p. 162.

21   Ibid., p. 170

22   State Library of South Australia (SLSA) D5341(T), Peter Thomas, Scrapbook Relating to Kapunda, Burra, Wallaroo, and Moonta Mines, Pamphlet issued by R.S. Richards MP.

23   Bailey, 2002, p. 172.

24   Oswald Pryor, *Australia's Little Cornwall*, Adelaide, 1960,

25   Melville Pethick, *Reminiscences Told My Way*, Renmark, 1974, p. 8.

26   Gordon Rowe, 'The Moonta Story', unpublished MS, 1961, p. 95.

27   Cited in Bailey, 2002, p. 175.

28   Graham Jenkin, *Calling Me Home: The Romance of South Australia in Story and Song*, Adelaide, 1989, p. 147.

29   G.J. Drew and J.E. Connell, *Cornish Beam Engines in South Australian Mines*, Adelaide, 1992.

30   Michael Atkinson, 'S.A. Labor Between the Wars 1915–1944', in Clarrie Bell (ed.), *Making History: A History of the Australian Labor Party (S.A. Branch) 1891–1991*, Adelaide, 1991, p. 5.

31   *Advertiser*, 5 April 1924; see also *Advertiser*, 7 July 1924.

32   Dean Jaensch, 'Stability and Change, 1910–1938', in Dean Jaensch (ed.), *The Flinders History of South Australia: Political History*, Adelaide, 1986, p. 232.

33   Neal Blewett, 'Gunn, John' (1884–1959), *Australian Dictionary of Biography*, National Centre for Biography, Australian National University, http://abd.anu.edu.au/biography/gunn-john-6507/text11165, published originally in hard copy 1983, accessed online 7 November 2015.

34   Ross McMullin, *The Light on The Hill: The Australian Labor Party 1891–1991*, Melbourne, 1991, republished 1992, p. 174.

35   Moss, 1985, p. 270.

36   Ibid., p. 271.

37   *Advertiser*, 22 November 1926.

38   *Advertiser*, 27 March 1927.

39   Jaensch, 1986, pp. 234–5.

40   Moss, 1985, pp. 275–6.

41   *Advertiser*, 20 September 1928.

42   Cited in Andrew Faulkner, *Albert Blackburn VC: An Australian Hero, His Men, and Their Two World Wars*, Adelaide, 2010, p. 151.

43   *Advertiser*, 21 September 1928.

44   Cited in Faulkner, 2010, p. 152.

45   Moss, 1985, p. 279.

46 Ibid., pp. 281–2.

47 *Advertiser*, 4 October 1928.

48 Moss, 1985, p. 283.

49 *Advertiser*, 1 October 1928; *South Australian Worker*, 5 October 1928.

50 Jaensch, 1986, p. 235.

51 Jim Moss, *Representative of Discontent: History of the Communist Party in South Australia, 1921–1981*, Melbourne, 1983, p. 13.

52 Moss, 1985, p. 299.

53 Cited in Ibid., p. 230.

54 Moss, 1985, pp. 300–1.

55 *South Australian Worker*, 5 September 1930.

56 McMullin, 1992, p. 174.

57 Cited in ibid.

58 Ibid., pp. 174–6.

59 Donald Hopgood, 'Lang Labor in South Australia', unpublished BA Hons thesis, University of Adelaide, 1967.

60 SLSA D3627(L) Stanley R. Whitford, 'Autobiography', p. 857.

61 Don Hopgood, 'Lang Labor in South Australia', *Labour History*, Vol. 17, 1969, p. 161.

62 Ibid.

63 Ibid., p. 163.

64 *South Australian Worker*, 13 September 1929.

65 Hopgood, 1969, p. 163.

66 *South Australian Worker*, 6 March 1931.

67 *South Australian Worker*, 17 April 1931; *Advertiser*, 17 April 1931.

68 J. Playford, 'History of the Left-Wing of the South Australian Labor Movement, 1908–1936', unpublished BA Hons thesis, University of Adelaide, 1958, p. 99.

69 McMullin, 1992, p. 174.

70 Hopgood, 1969, p. 169.

71 Pryor, 1960, p. 136.

72 Jaensch, 1986, p. 238.

73 *Advertiser*, 13 April 1933.

74 Nick Dyrenfurth and Frank Bongiorno, *A Little History of the Australian Labor Party*, Sydney, 2011, p. 83.

75 *Advertiser*, 11 October 1933.

76 Hopgood, 1969, p. 172.

77 Ibid.

78 Ibid., p. 173.

79   Donald J. Hopgood, 'Richards, Robert Stanley (1885–1967), *Australian Dictionary of Biography*, National Centre of Biography, Australian National University, http://adb.anu.edu.au/biography/richards-robert-stanley-8195/text14335, first published in hard copy in 1988, accessed 30 September 2015.

80   Don Dunstan, *Felicia: The Political Memoirs of Don Dunstan*, Melbourne, 1981, p. 17.

81   *People's Weekly*, 15 September 1927.

82   *People's Weekly*, 11 June 1932.

83   Cited in Bernard O'Neil, *In Search of Mineral Wealth: The South Australian Geological Survey and Department of Mines to 1944*, Adelaide, 1982, p. 242.

84   *South Australian Department of Mines Mining Review*, half-year ended June 1929; half-year ended December 1931.

85   SLSA D3627(L), p. 70.

86   A.R.G. Griffiths, 'Whitford, Stanley R. (1879–1959), *Australian Dictionary of Biography*, National Centre of Biography, Australian National University, http://adb.anu.edu.au/biography/whitford-stanley-r-9083/text16013, first published in hard copy 1990, accessed 30 September 2015.

87   Joan Tiver, *Harry Kneebone: Son of Little Cornwall*, Adelaide, n.d., p. 74.

88   Ibid., p. 73.

89   'Kneebone, Henry (1876–1933) Senator for South Australia, 1931 (Australian Labor Party)', *The Biographical Dictionary of the Australian Senate*, http://biography.senate.gov.au/index.php/knebone-henry/9/30/2015

90   Vide the title of her book; *Tiver*, n.d.

91   H. Kneebone, 'The "Blacks" of Australia and Papua', in Harry Golding (ed.), *The Wonder Book of Empire for Girls and Boys*, London (and Melbourne and Toronto), n.d., pp. 137–42.

92   *Advertiser*, 23 December 1933.

93   *Recorder*, 23 December 1933.

94   *Peoples' Weekly*, 7 June 1930, 6 September 1952.

95   *People's Weekly*, 27 November 1920.

96   Ibid.

97   *People's Weekly*, 9 November 1935.

98   *Advertiser*, 4 September 1931.

99   Rob Charlton, *The History of Kapunda*, Melbourne, 1971, p. 92.

100   *Advertiser*, 28 September 1951.

101   Carol Fort, 'Hunkin, Leslie Claude (1884–1984)', *Australian Dictionary of Biography*, National Centre of Biography, Australian National University, http://abd.anu.edu.au/biography/hunkin-leslie-claude-12669/text22833, published first in hard copy, Melbourne, 2007, accessed online 30 September 2015.

102   SLSA PRG 30/21, Leslie Claude Hunkin Papers, Material relating to the ALP.

103 Atkinson, 1991, p. 9.

104 Jaensch, 1986, p. 239.

105 Dean Jaensch, 'The Playford Era', in Dean Jaensch (ed.), *The Flinders History of South Australia: Political History*, Adelaide, 1986, p. 250.

106 *Workers' Weekly Herald*, 5 August 1959.

107 *Workers' Weekly Herald*, 12 October 1945.

108 Cited in Jaensch, 1986, p. 252.

109 Dunstan, 1981, p. 41.

Chapter 9 • The Dunstan Era

1   Dean Jaensch, *The Government of South Australia*, St Lucia, 1977, p. i.

2   *Nation*, 12 September 1959; see also Dean Jaensch, 'The Playford Era', in Dean Jaensch (ed.), *The Flinders History of South Australia: Political History*, Adelaide, 1986, p. 258.

3   Jaensch, 1986, p. 258–9.

4   Andrew Parkin, 'Transition, Innovation, Readjustment: The Political History of South Australia since 1965', in Jaensch (ed.), 1986, p. 293.

5   Malcolm Saunders, '"Jim" Toohey (1909–1992): The "Father" of the Labor Party in South Australia', *Labour History*, No. 85, November 2003, p. 177.

6   Nick Dyrenfurth and Frank Bongiorno, *A Little History of the Australian Labor Party*, Sydney, 2011, pp. 104–5

7   Ibid., p. 105.

8   Don Dunstan, *Felicia: The Political Memoirs of Don Dunstan*, Melbourne, 1981, p. 29.

9   Ibid., p. 30.

10   Dyrenfurth and Bongiorno, 2011, p. 115.

11   Robert Murray, *The Split: Australian Labor in the Fifties*, Melbourne, 1970.

12   Dyrenfurth and Bongiorno, 2011, p. 116.

13   Saunders, 2003, pp. 177–8; Bill Guy, *A Life on The Left: A Biography of Clyde Cameron*, Adelaide, 1999, p. 133.

14   Malcolm Saunders, 'The Labor Party and the Industrial Movement in South Australia, 1946–1955: Precluding the Split', *Journal of the Historical Society of South Australia*, Vol. 23, 2005, p. 74.

15   Josephine Laffin, *Matthew Beovich: A Biography*, Adelaide, 2008, pp. 176–204.

16   Cited in ibid., p. 172.

17   Ibid., pp. 172–3.

18   Saunders, 2005, pp. 77–9.

19   Laffin, 2008, p. 173.

20   Cited in ibid, p. 174.

21 Clyde Cameron, *The Confessions of Clyde Cameron, 1913–1990*, Sydney, 1990, p. 104; see also Laffin, 2008, p. 185.

22 *Southern Cross*, 20 March 1955; see also Laffin, 2008, p. 187.

23 *Advertiser*, 12 November 1955.

24 Laffin, 2008, p. 190.

25 See Geraldine Little, 'The Democratic Labor Party in South Australia', unpublished BA Hons thesis, University of Adelaide, 1968.

26 Malcolm Saunders and Neil Lloyd, 'Remembering the Past and Hoping for the Future: Why there was no Labor Split in South Australia', in Brian Costar, Peter Love and Paul Strangio (eds), *The Great Labor Schism: A Retrospective*, Melbourne, 2005, p. 88.

27 Laffin, 2008, p. 192.

28 *Advertiser*, 13 April 1956.

29 Saunders, 2003, p. 179.

30 *Advertiser*, 8 March 1950; see also Saunders, 2003, p. 180.

31 Jim Moss, *The Sound of Trumpets: History of the Labour Movement in South Australia*, Adelaide, 1985, p. 378.

32 Neal Blewett and Dean Jaensch, *Playford to Dunstan: The Politics of Transition*, Melbourne, 1971, p. 28.

33 Dunstan, 1981, p. 65.

34 Blewett and Jaensch, 1971, p. 28.

35 Ibid., p. 30.

36 Ibid., p. 35.

37 Ibid.

38 Ibid., p. 35–6.

39 Ibid., p. 38.

40 *Bulletin*, 28 June 1975.

41 Dunstan, 1981, p. 27.

42 Blewett and Jaensch, 1971, p. 36.

43 Parkin, 1986, p. 296.

44 John Summers, 'Aboriginal Policy', in Andrew Parkin and Allan Patience, *The Dunstan Decade: Social Democracy at the State Level*, Melbourne, 1981, p. 127.

45 Ibid.

46 Parkin, 1986, p. 295.

47 Cited in ibid., p. 295.

48 Dunstan, 1981, p. 132.

49 Geoff Stokes, 'South Australia: Consensus Politics', in Andrew Parkin and John Warhurst (eds), *Machine Politics in the Australian Labor Party*, Sydney, 1983, p. 140.

50 Parkin, 1986, p. 296.

51   Richard Cox, 'Social Democracy: A Study of the Dunstan Labor Government',
      unpublished PhD thesis, Flinders University, 1979, p. 326.

52   Ibid., pp. 329–30.

53   Parkin, 1986, pp. 297–8.

54   Blewett and Jaensch, 1971, p. 208.

55   Ibid., p. 269.

56   Parkin and Patience (eds), 1981.

57   Parkin, 1986, p. 302.

58   Dino Hodge, *Don Dunstan: Intimacy and Liberty – A Political Biography*, Adelaide,
      2014.

59   Parkin, 1986, pp. 304–5.

60   Don Dunstan, *Don Dunstan's Australia*, Adelaide, 1978; Don Dunstan, *Australia:
      A Personal View*, Kenthurst, 1981.

61   Dunstan, 1978, pp. 95–6.

62   Parkin, 1986, p. 309.

63   Cited in Jenny Hocking, *Gough Whitlam: His Time – The Biography, Volume II*,
      Melbourne, 2012, p. 477.

64   Parkin, 1986, pp. 310–11.

65   Paul Kelly and Troy Bramston, *The Dismissal in the Queen's Name*, Melbourne,
      2015.

66   Helen Mills, 'Equal Opportunities', in Parkin and Patience (eds), 1981, p. 118.

67   Parkin, 1986, p. 313.

68   Ross McMullin, *The Light on the Hill: The Australian Labor Party 1891–1991*,
      Melbourne, 1991, republished 1992, p. 392.

69   Judith Pugh, *Unstill Life: Art, Politics, and Living with Clifton Hugh*, Crows Nest,
      2008, pp. 154–64; Hodge, 2014, p. 218.

70   Hodge, 2014, p. 231.

71   *Age*, 9 January 1994; see Hodge, 2014, p. 232.

72   Dunstan, 1981, p. 194.

73   Ibid., pp. 194–5; see also Kerryn Goldsworthy, *Adelaide*, Sydney, 2011,
      Chapter 8.

74   Hodge, 2014, pp. 181–5.

75   Ibid., p. 258.

76   *Advertiser*, 31 May 1967.

77   Walter Crocker, *Sir Thomas Playford: A Portrait*, Melbourne, 1983, p. 121.

78   Ibid., p. 127 and p. 120.

79   Ibid., p. 136.

80   Ibid.

81   Ibid., p. 130.

82   Ibid., p. 126.

83   Ibid., p. 124.

84   Ibid., p. 4.

85   Ibid., p. 124.

86   Ibid., pp. 124–5.

87   Ibid., p. 121.

88   John Playford, Review of Parkin and Patience, 1981, in *Quadrant*, October 1981.

89   Crocker, 1983, p. 136.

90   Neal Blewett, 'Don Dunstan and the Social Democratic Moment in Australian History', in Robert Foster and Paul Sendzuik (eds), *Turning Points: Chapters in South Australian History*, Adelaide, 2012, p. 114.

91   *Rydges*, July 1973; see also Jaensch, 1977, p. 186.

92   John Lonie, 'The Dunstan Government', *Arena*, No. 25, 1975, p. 58.

93   John Wanna, *Defence not Defiance: The Development of Organized Labour in South Australia*, Adelaide, 1981, p. 88.

94   Terry O'Shaughnessy, 'Joh and Don: Capital and Politics in Two Peripheral States', *Intervention*, No. 12, 1979, p. 25. For a flavour of left-wing criticisms of the ALP current in this period, see John Playford and Douglas Kirsner (eds), *Australian Capitalism: Towards a Socialist Critique*, Ringwood, 1972.

95   Moss, 1986, pp. 388–9.

96   Parkin, 1986, p. 319.

97   Selina Todd, *The People: The Rise and Fall of the Working Class 1910–2010*, London, 2014, p. 314.

98   Blewett, 2012, p. 116.

99   Don Dunstan, 'The Uncaring Society', in John Spoehr (ed.), *Politics and Passion: Selected Essays from the Adelaide Review*, Adelaide, 2000, p. 119.

100 Ibid., pp. 119–20.

101 Ibid., p. 121.

102 Blewett, 2012, p. 117.

103 Richard Yeeles (ed.), *Don Dunstan: The First 25 Years in Parliament*, Melbourne, 1978.

104 Dean Jaensch, *The Hawke-Keating Hijack: The ALP in Transition*, Sydney, 1989, p. 155.

105 Andrew Parkin, 'Looking Back on the Bannon Decade', in Andrew Parkin and Allan Patience (eds), *The Bannon Decade: The Politics of Restraint in South Australia*, Sydney, 1992, p. 6.

106 Blewett, 2012, p. 104.

107 Brian Chatterton, *Roosters and Featherdusters*, Castel di Fiori [Italy], 2003, pp. 260–1.

Chapter 10 • Life After Dunstan – To Bannon and Beyond

1   As David Tonkin, then Leader of the Opposition, remarked to the present author at a Cornish Association seminar c. 1977–8.

2   Andrew Parkin, 'Transition, Innovation, Consolidation, Readjustment: The Political History of South Australia Since 1965', in Dean Jaensch (ed.), *The Flinders History of South Australia: Political History*, Adelaide, 1986, p. 321.

3   Andrew Parkin, 'Embracing the Dunstan Decade: A Tale of Two Elections', in Jaensch (ed.), 1986, p. 483.

4   Don Hopgood, 'The Bannon Years', in Clarrie Bell (ed.), *Making History: A History of the South Australian Labor Party (S.A. Branch) 1891–1991*, Adelaide, 1991, p. 43.

5   Ibid.

6   Ross McMullin, *The Light on the Hill: The Australian Labor Party 1891–1991*, Melbourne, 1991, republished 1992, p. 402.

7   Parkin, 'Transition, Innovation . . .', 1986, p. 329.

8   *Advertiser*, 8 November 1982.

9   Andrew Parkin and Allan Patience (eds), *The Bannon Decade: The Politics of Restraint in South Australia*, St Leonards (NSW), 1992.

10 *Australian*, 14 December 2015.

11 John Bannon, 'South Australia's Labor Leaders', in Clarrie Bell (ed.), *Making History: A History of the Australian Labor Party (S.A Branch) 1891–1991*, Adelaide, 1991, p. 51.

12 Hopgood, 1991, p. 44.

13 Jon Davison and Tom Allibone, *Beneath Southern Seas: The Silent Service*, Perth [WA], 2005, p. 230.

14 Ibid., p. 5.

15 *Australian*, 14 December 2015.

16 Andrew Parkin, 'Looking Back on the Bannon Decade', in Parkin and Patience (eds), 1992, pp. 10–13.

17 *Advertiser*, 9 December 1985.

18 *Advertiser*, 21 December 1985.

19 Parkin, 1992, p. 14,

20 Ibid., pp. 14–15.

21 Hopgood, 1991, p. 44.

22 Cited in Andrew Parkin, 'The Bannon Decade: Restraint with Integrity', in Parkin and Patience (eds), 1992, p. 339.

23 Parkin, 'Looking Back . . .', 1992, pp. 17–21.

24 *Australian*, 14 December 2015.

25 Robert Martin, *Responsible Government in South Australia, Volume Two, Playford to Rann 1957–2007*, Adelaide, 2009, p. 136.

26 Ibid., pp. 136–7.

27 Ibid., p. 141.

28 Lynn Arnold, 'The Labor Party and Its Radical Tradition', in Bell (ed.), 1991, p. 21.

29 Lynn M.F. Arnold, 'Breaking the Tyranny of Monoculturalism and Monolingualism: The Australian Experience', in Richard J. Watts and Jerzy J. Smolicz (eds), *Cultural Democracy and Ethnic Pluralism: Multicultural and Multilingual Policies in Education*, Bern, 1994, p. 185.

30 Ibid., p. 186.

31 Ibid., p. 202.

32 Ibid.

33 Martin, 2009, pp. 141–59.

34 Ibid., pp. 163–73

35 John Hill, *On Being a Minister: Behind the Mask*. Adelaide, 2016, p. xiii.

36 See Philip Payton, *Making Moonta: The Invention of Australia's Little Cornwall*, Exeter, 2007, especially pp. 206–7.

Epilogue

1 Don Dunstan, *Felicia: The Political Memoirs of Don Dunstan*, Melbourne, 1981, dustcover notes.

2 Ibid., p. 320.

Index

ON BEING A MINISTER
Behind the mask

John Hill

'*On Being a Minister is a welcome how-to book for those truly interested in politics and public service. Always a passionate thinker, John Hill's wise book is flecked with the same urbanity that characterised his time in public life. What a relief to have a book about politics written with charm and true insight, instead of melodrama and vengeance.*' – Nicola Roxon

'It's hard to imagine a job that requires less education than that of government minister,' says John Hill. 'It's also hard to imagine a job where the occupant is less likely to seek help than that of government minister.'

John Hill knew when he quit as a government minister that what he had learnt – often painfully – over 11 years was likely to disappear with him. So he wrote it down ...

Praise for *On Being a Minister*:
'On Being a Minister is a delightful political memoir and an ideal primer for anyone seeking representative office at either state or federal level. It is also an absorbing guide for the reader interested in the nuances of the political process, all the way from grass-roots action to the polished benches of Parliament.' –Bernard Whimpress, *Newton Review of Books*

'A rollicking good read and rates up there with Barry Cohen's *How To Become Prime Minister* as a manual for the aspiring politician. Along the way John Hill's intelligence, wisdom and urbanity shines and it is even self-deprecatory in places. The ending is as heart-warming as Bert Facey's in *A Fortunate Life*.' – Michael Atkinson, *InDaily*

ISBN 978 1 74305 397 3

For more information visit www.wakefieldpress.com.au

DON DUNSTAN, INTIMACY AND LIBERTY
A political biography

Dino Hodge

Don Dunstan, Premier of South Australia in the late 1960s and throughout the 1970s, is acknowledged as one of Australia's foremost civil rights advocates of the twentieth century. He actively promoted the rights of Indigenous Australians and women, and he passionately pursued multiculturalism. More than any other political leader in the country's history, Dunstan championed the rights of homosexual citizens at a time when they were treated as criminals, classified as insane, and regarded as outcasts. He was also bisexual.

This book records the change in public discourse over issues of homosexuality – from morality to state security and then civil liberties. Dunstan worked as a member of parliament for more than twenty-five years, and then throughout the remainder of his life, to realise his vision of full equality for same-sex attracted citizens. He focused on both legislative and cultural reforms, and introduced changes to the Police Force that were unprecedented and strongly resisted. His efforts and the backlash he suffered are fully documented here for the first time, finally giving due recognition to one of the country's most remarkable champions of human rights.

Praise for *Don Dunstan, Intimacy and Liberty*:
'This book will inform teaching and research across a broad canvas of Australian history. I commend it as both intellectually compelling and thoroughly enjoyable.' – Barbara Baird, *Australian Historical Studies*

'The biography has been much needed to reveal more clearly the outstanding achievements of the Dunstan era and the special humanity of the man himself.' - Maggie Tate, *Global Media Post*

ISBN 978 1 74305 296 9

For more information visit www.wakefieldpress.com.au

Wakefield Press is an independent publishing and
distribution company based in Adelaide, South Australia.
We love good stories and publish beautiful books.
To see our full range of books, please visit our website at
www.wakefieldpress.com.au
where all titles are available for purchase.

Find us!

Twitter: www.twitter.com/wakefieldpress
Facebook: www.facebook.com/wakefield.press
Instagram: instagram.com/wakefieldpress